Contents

24

29

32

39

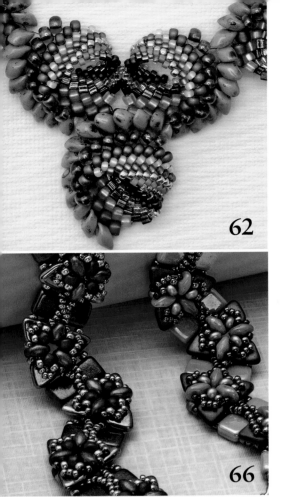

62

66

75

78

MULTIPLE-STITCH PROJECTS

94

110

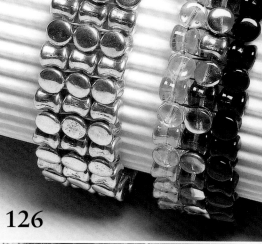

126

147

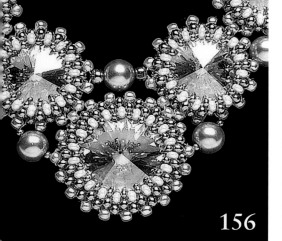

156

166

173

178

218

220

224

245

Introduction

Welcome to *Creative Beading, Volume 11*, our annual collection of projects from a year of *Bead&Button* magazine. Our talented contributors continue to work with the latest materials and techniques to create gorgeous necklaces, earrings, bracelets, and rings—and all of that creativity can be found within these pages.

This compendium includes a wide range of styles, stitches, and beads. Some projects offer a new twist on standard techniques, such as peyote stitch, herringbone, right-angle weave, and bead crochet. Other designs explore new methods for working with multi-hole seed beads in many different shapes and sizes. Each project is fully illustrated with the complete step-by-step instructions that *Bead&Button* is known for.

As in previous volumes, projects are organized into three categories: single-stitch projects, multi-stitch projects, and other techniques. There are more than 75 lovely designs, each with color options and helpful tips, and you can flip to the Basics section for a review of stitching techniques. Whether you are a beginner or an advanced beader, you'll find projects to suit your taste and skill level.

So, pick a project, gather your beading supplies, and dive into *Creative Beading Vol. 11.*

Happy beading!

Julia Gerlach

Julia Gerlach
Editor, *Bead&Button*

Tools & Materials

Excellent tools and materials for making jewelry are available in bead and craft stores, through catalogs, and on the Internet. Here are the essential supplies you'll need for the projects in this book.

TOOLS

Chainnose pliers have smooth, flat inner jaws, and the tips taper to a point. Use them for gripping, bending wire, and for opening and closing loops and jump rings.

Roundnose pliers have smooth, tapered, conical jaws used to make loops. The closer to the tip you work, the smaller the loop will be.

Use the front of a **wire cutters'** blades to make a pointed cut and the back of the blades to make a flat cut. Do not use your jewelry-grade wire cutters on memory wire, which is extremely hard; use heavy-duty wire cutters, or bend the memory wire back and forth until it breaks.

Crimping pliers have two grooves in their jaws that are used to fold and roll a crimp tube into a compact shape.

Make it easier to open split rings by inserting the curved jaw of **split-ring pliers** between the wires.

Beading needles are coded by size. The higher the number, the finer the beading needle. Unlike sewing needles, the eye of a beading needle is almost as narrow as its shaft. In addition to the size of the bead, the number of times you will pass through the bead also affects the needle size that you will use; if you will pass through a bead multiple times, you need to use a thinner needle.

A **hammer** is used to harden wire or texture metal. Any hammer with a flat head will work, as long as the head is free of nicks that could mar your metal. The light ball-peen hammer shown here is one of the most commonly used hammers for jewelry making.

A **bench block** provides a hard, smooth surface on which to hammer wire and metal pieces. An anvil is similarly hard but has different surfaces, such as a tapered horn, to help form different shapes.

bench block

chainnose pliers

roundnose pliers

wire cutters

crimping pliers

hammer

split-ring pliers

beading needles

Tools & Materials

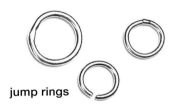

head pin

eye pin

jump rings

split ring

crimp beads and tubes

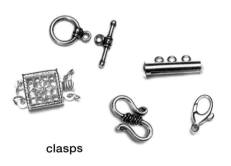

clasps

earring findings

FINDINGS

A **head pin** looks like a long, blunt, thick sewing pin. It has a flat or decorative head on one end to keep beads on. Head pins come in different diameters (gauges) and lengths.

Eye pins are just like head pins except they have a round loop on one end instead of a head. You can make your own eye pins from wire.

A **jump ring** is used to connect components. It is a small wire circle or oval that is either soldered closed or comes with a cut so it can be opened and closed.

Split rings are used like jump rings but are much more secure. They look like tiny key rings and are made of springy wire.

Crimp beads and tubes are small, large-holed, thin-walled metal beads designed to be flattened or crimped into a tight roll. Use them when stringing jewelry on flexible beading wire.

Clasps come in many sizes and shapes. Some of the most common (clockwise from the top left) are the toggle, consisting of a ring and a bar; slide, consisting of one tube that slides inside another; lobster claw, which opens when you pull on a tiny lever; S-hook, which links two soldered jump rings or split rings; and box, with a tab and a slot.

Earring findings come in a huge variety of metals and styles, including (from left to right) lever back, post, hoop, and French hook. You will almost always want a loop (or loops) on earring findings so you can attach beads.

WIRE

Wire is available in a number of materials and finishes, including brass, gold, gold-filled, gold-plated, fine silver, sterling silver, anodized niobium (chemically colored wire), and copper. Brass, copper, and craft wire are packaged in 10- to 40-yd. (9.1–37 m) spools, while gold, silver, and niobium are sold by the foot or ounce. Wire thickness is measured by gauge—the higher the gauge number, the thinner the wire. It is available in varying hardnesses (dead-soft, half-hard, and hard) and shapes (round, half-round, square, and others).

STITCHING & STRINGING MATERIALS

Selecting beading thread and cord is one of the most important decisions you'll make when planning a project. Review the descriptions below to evaluate which material is best for your design.

Threads come in many sizes and strengths. Size (diameter or thickness) is designated by a letter or number. OO and A/O are the thinnest; B, D, E, F, and FF are subsequently thicker. **Cord** is measured on a number scale; 0 corresponds in thickness to D-size thread, 1 equals E, 2 equals F, and 3 equals FF.

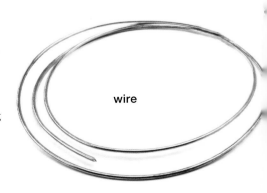

wire

Parallel filament nylon, such as Nymo or C-Lon, is made from many thin nylon fibers that are extruded and heat-set to form a single-ply thread. Parallel filament nylon is durable and easy to thread, but it can be prone to fraying and stretching. It is best used in beadweaving and bead embroidery.

Plied nylon thread, such as Silamide, is made from two or more nylon threads that are extruded, twisted together, and coated or bonded for further strength, making them strong and durable. It is more resistant to fraying than parallel filament nylon, and some brands do not stretch. It's a good material to use for twisted fringe, bead crochet, and beadwork that needs a lot of body.

Plied gel-spun polyethylene (GSP), such as Power Pro or DandyLine, is made from polyethylene fibers that have been spun into two or more threads that are braided together. It is almost unbreakable, it doesn't stretch, and it resists fraying. The thickness can make it difficult to make multiple passes through a bead. It is ideal for stitching with larger beads, such as pressed glass and crystals.

Parallel filament GSP, such as Fireline, is a single-ply thread made from spun and bonded polyethylene fibers. It's extremely strong, it doesn't stretch, and it resists fraying. However, crystals may cut through parallel filament GSP, and smoke-colored varieties can leave a black residue on hands and beads. It's most appropriate for bead stitching.

Polyester thread, such as Gutermann, is made from polyester fibers that are spun into single yarns and then twisted into plied thread. It doesn't stretch and comes in many colors, but it can become fuzzy with use. It is best for bead crochet or bead embroidery when the thread must match the fabric.

Flexible beading wire is composed of wires twisted together and covered with nylon. This wire is stronger than thread and does not stretch. The higher the number of inner strands (between 3 and 49), the more flexible and kink-resistant the wire. It is available in a variety of sizes. Use .014 and .015 for stringing most gemstones, crystals, and glass beads. Use thicker varieties, .018, .019, and .024, for heavy beads or nuggets. Use thinner wire, .010 and .012, for lightweight pieces and beads with very small holes, such as pearls. The thinnest wires can also be used for some bead-stitching projects.

flexible beading wire

nylon threads

parallel filament GSP

Tools & Materials

SEED BEADS

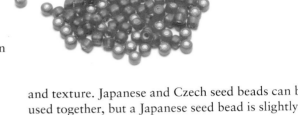
seed beads

A huge variety of beads is available, but the beads most commonly used in the projects in this book are **seed beads**. Seed beads come in packages, tubes, and hanks. A standard hank (a looped bundle of beads strung on thread) contains 12 20-in. (51 cm) strands, but vintage hanks are often much smaller. Tubes and packages are usually measured in grams and vary in size.

Seed beads have been manufactured in many sizes ranging from the largest, 5° (also called "E beads"), which are about 5 mm wide, to tiny size 20° or 22°, which aren't much larger than grains of sand. (The symbol $^{\circ}$ stands for "aught" or "zero." The greater the number of aughts, e.g., 22°, the smaller the bead.) Beads smaller than Japanese 15°s have not been produced for the past 100 years, but vintage beads can be found in limited sizes and colors. The most commonly available size in the widest range of colors is 11°.

Most round seed beads are made in Japan and the Czech Republic. **Czech seed beads** are slightly irregular and rounder than **Japanese seed beads**, which are uniform in size and a bit squared off. Czech beads give a bumpier surface when woven, but they reflect light at a wider range of angles. Japanese seed beads produce a uniform surface and texture. Japanese and Czech seed beads can be used together, but a Japanese seed bead is slightly larger than the same size Czech seed bead.

Seed beads also come in sparkly cut versions. Japanese **hex-cut** or hex beads are formed with six sides. **2-** or **3-cut** Czech beads are less regular. **Charlottes** have an irregular facet cut on one side of the bead.

Japanese **cylinder beads**, otherwise known as Delicas (the Miyuki brand name), Toho Treasures (the brand name of Toho), and Toho Aikos, are extremely popular for peyote stitch projects. These beads are very regular and have large holes, which are useful for stitches requiring multiple thread passes. The beads fit together almost seamlessly, producing a smooth, fabric-like surface.

Bugle beads are thin glass tubes. They can be sized by number or length, depending on where they are made. Japanese size 1 bugles are about 2 mm long, but bugles can be made even longer than 30 mm. They can be hex-cut, straight, or twisted, but the selection of colors, sizes, shapes, and finishes is limited. Seed beads also come in a variety of other shapes, including **triangles, cubes,** and **drops**.

In stitches where the beads meet each other end to end or side by side — peyote stitch, brick stitch, and square stitch — try using Japanese cylinder beads to achieve a smooth, flat surface. For a more textured surface, use Czech or round Japanese seed beads. For right-angle weave, in which groups of four or more beads form circular stitches, the rounder the seed bead, the better; otherwise you risk having gaps. Round seed beads also are better for netting and strung jewelry.

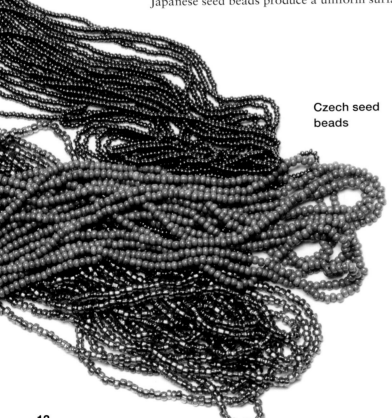
Czech seed beads

cube beads

triangle beads

drop beads

twisted bugle beads

hex-cut beads

Basics

THREAD AND KNOTS

Adding thread

To add a thread, sew into the beadwork several rows or rounds prior to the point where the last bead was added, leaving a short tail. Follow the thread path of the stitch, tying a few half-hitch knots (see "Half-hitch knot") between beads as you go, and exit where the last stitch ended. Trim the short tail.

Conditioning thread

Use beeswax or microcrystalline wax (not candle wax or paraffin) or Thread Heaven to condition nylon beading thread and Fireline. Wax smooths nylon fibers and adds tackiness that will stiffen your beadwork slightly. Thread Heaven adds a static charge that causes the thread to repel itself, so don't use it with doubled thread. Both conditioners help thread resist wear. To condition, stretch nylon thread to remove the curl (Fireline doesn't stretch). Lay the thread or Fireline on top of the conditioner, hold it in place with your thumb or finger, and pull the thread through the conditioner.

Ending thread

To end a thread, sew back through the last few rows or rounds of beadwork, following the thread path of the stitch and tying two or three half-hitch knots (see "Half-hitch knot") between beads as you go. Sew through a few beads after the last knot, and trim the thread.

Half-hitch knot

Pass the needle under the thread bridge between two beads, and pull gently until a loop forms. Cross back over the thread between the beads, sew through the loop, and pull gently to draw the knot into the beadwork.

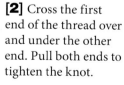

Overhand knot

Make a loop with the thread. Pull the tail through the loop, and tighten.

Square knot

[1] Cross one end of the thread over and under the other end. Pull both ends to tighten the first half of the knot.
[2] Cross the first end of the thread over and under the other end. Pull both ends to tighten the knot.

Stop bead

Use a stop bead to secure beads temporarily when you begin stitching.

Choose a bead that is different from the beads in your project. Pick up the stop bead, leaving the desired length tail. Sew through the stop bead again in the same direction, making sure you don't split the thread. If desired, sew through it one more time for added security.

Surgeon's knot

[1] Cross one end of the thread over and under the other twice. Pull both ends to tighten the first half of the knot.
[2] Cross the first end of the thread over and under the other end. Pull both ends to tighten the knot.

Crochet
Slip knot and chain stitch

[1] Make a slip knot: Leaving the desired length tail, make a loop in the cord, crossing the spool end over the tail. Insert the hook in the loop, yarn over, and pull the cord through the loop.
[2] Yarn over the hook, and draw through the loop. Repeat this step for the desired number of chain stitches.

Beaded backstitch

To stitch a line of beads, come up through the fabric from the wrong side, and pick up three beads. Place the thread where the beads will go, and sew through the fabric right after the third bead. Come up between the second and third beads, and go through the third bead again. Pick up three more beads, and repeat. For a tighter stitch, pick up only one or two beads at a time.

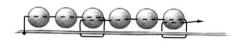

Basics

STITCHES

Brick stitch

[1] To work the typical method, which results in progressively decreasing rows, work the first row in ladder stitch (see "Ladder stitch") to the desired length, exiting the top of the last bead added.

[2] Pick up two beads, sew under the thread bridge between the second and third beads in the previous row, and sew back up through the second bead added. To secure this first stitch, sew down through the first bead and back up through the second bead.

[3] For the remaining stitches in the row, pick up one bead per stitch, sew under the thread bridge between the next two beads in the previous row, and sew back up through the new bead. The last stitch in the new row will be centered above the last two beads in the previous row, and the new row will be one bead shorter than the previous row.

Increasing

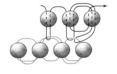

To increase at the start of the row, repeat step 1 above, then repeat step 2, but sew under the thread bridge between the first and second beads in the previous row. To increase at the end of the row, work two stitches off of the thread bridge between the last two beads in the previous row.

Tubular

[1] Begin with a ladder of beads, and join the ends to form a ring (see "Ladder stitch: Forming a ring"). Position the thread to exit the top of a bead.

[2] Following the instructions for flat brick stitch, pick up two beads to begin the row. Stitch around the ring in brick stitch.

[3] Join the first and last beads of the round by sewing down through the first bead and up through the last bead.

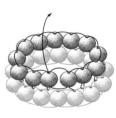

Herringbone stitch
Flat

[1] Work the first row in ladder stitch (see "Ladder stitch") to the desired length, exiting the top of an end bead in the ladder.

[2] Pick up two beads, and sew down through the next bead in the previous row (a–b). Sew up through the following bead in the previous row, pick up two beads, and sew down through the next bead (b–c). Repeat across the first row.

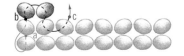

[3] To turn to start the next row, sew down through the end bead in the previous row and back through the last bead of the pair just added (a–b). Pick up two beads, sew down through the next bead in the previous row, and sew up through the following bead (b–c). Continue adding pairs of beads across the row.

Tubular

[1] Work a row of ladder stitch (see "Ladder stitch") to the desired length using an even number of beads. Form it into a ring to create the first round (see "Ladder stitch: Forming a ring"). Your thread should exit the top of a bead.

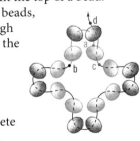

[2] Pick up two beads, sew down through the next bead in the previous round (a–b), and sew up through the following bead. Repeat to complete the round (b–c).

[3] You will need to step up to start the next round. Sew up through two beads — the next bead in the previous round and the first bead added in the new round (c–d).

[4] Continue adding two beads per stitch. As you work, snug up the beads to form a tube, and step up at the end of each round until your rope is the desired length.

Twisted tubular
[1] Work a ladder and two rounds of tubular herringbone as explained above.

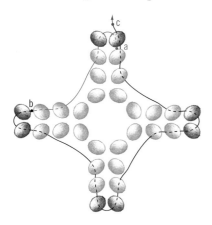

[2] To create a twist in the tube, pick up two beads, sew down through one bead in the next stack, then sew up through two beads in the following stack (a–b). Repeat around, adding two beads per stitch. Step up to the next round through three beads (b–c). Snug up the beads. The twist will begin to appear after the sixth round. Continue until your rope is the desired length.

Ladder stitch
Making a ladder
[1] Pick up two beads, and sew through them both again, positioning the beads side by side so that their holes are parallel (a–b).

[2] Add subsequent beads by picking up one bead, sewing through the previous bead, then sewing through the new bead (b–c). Continue for the desired length.

This technique produces uneven tension, which you can correct by zigzagging back through the beads in the opposite direction or by choosing the "Crossweave method" or "Alternative method."

Crossweave technique
[1] Thread a needle on each end of a length of thread, and center a bead.
[2] Working in crossweave technique, pick up a bead with one needle, and cross the other needle through it (a–b and c–d). Add all subsequent beads in the same manner.

Alternative method

[1] Pick up all the beads you need to reach the length your project requires. Fold the last two beads so they are parallel, and sew through the second-to-last bead again in the same direction (a–b).

[2] Fold the next loose bead so it sits parallel to the previous bead in the ladder, and sew through the loose bead in the same direction (a–b). Continue sewing back through each bead until you exit the last bead of the ladder.

Forming a ring
With your thread exiting the last bead in the ladder, sew through the first bead and then through the last bead again. If using the "Crossweave method" or "Alternative method" of ladder stitch, cross the threads from the last bead in the ladder through the first bead in the ladder.

Basics

Peyote stitch

Flat even-count

[1] Pick up an even number of beads, leaving the desired length tail **(a–b)**. These beads will shift to form the first two rows as the third row is added.

[2] To begin row 3, pick up a bead, skip the last bead  added in the previous step, and sew back through the next bead, working toward the tail **(b–c)**. For each stitch, pick up a bead, skip a bead in the previous row, and sew through the next bead until you reach the first bead picked up in step 1 **(c–d)**. The beads added in this row are higher than the previous rows and are referred to as "up-beads."

[3] For each stitch in subsequent rows, pick up a bead, and sew through the next up-bead in the previous row **(d–e)**. To count peyote stitch rows, count the total number of beads along both straight edges.

Flat odd-count

Odd-count peyote is the same as even-count peyote, except for the turn on odd-numbered rows, where the last bead of the row can't be attached in the usual way because there is no up-bead to sew through.

Work the traditional odd-row turn as follows:

[1] Begin as for flat even-count peyote, but pick up an odd number of beads. Work row 3 as in even-count, stopping before adding the last bead.

[2] Work a figure-8 turn at the end of row 3: Pick up the next-to-last bead (#7), and sew through #2, then #1 **(a–b)**. Pick up the last bead of the row (#8), and sew through #2, #3, #7, #2, #1, and #8 **(b–c)**.

[3] In subsequent odd-numbered rows, pick up the last bead of the row, sew under the thread bridge between the last two edge beads, and sew back through the last bead added to begin the next row.

Tubular even-count

Tubular peyote stitch follows the same stitching pattern as flat peyote, but instead of sewing back and forth, you work in rounds.

[1] Start with an even number of beads tied into a ring (see "Square knot").

[2] Sew through the first bead in the ring. Pick up a bead, skip a bead in the ring, and sew through the next bead. Repeat to complete the round.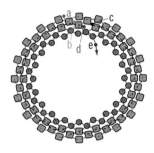

[3] To step up to start the next round, sew through the first bead added in round 3 **(a–b)**. Pick up a bead, and sew through the next bead in round 3 **(b–c)**. Repeat to complete the round.

[4] Repeat step 3 to achieve the desired length, stepping up after each round.

Tubular odd-count

[1] Start with an odd number of bead tied into a ring (see "Square knot").

[2] Sew through the first bead into the ring. Pick up a bead, skip a bead in the ring, and sew though the next bead. Repeat to complete the round. At the end of the round, you will sew through the last bead in the original ring. Do not step up. Pick up a bead, and sew through the first bead in the previous round. You will be stitching in a continuous spiral.

Two-drop

[1] Work two-drop peyote stitch the same as basic peyote, but treat pairs of beads as if they were single beads.

[2] Start with an even number of beads divisible by four. Pick up two beads (stitch 1 of row 3), skip two beads, and go through the next two beads. Repeat across the row.

Bezels

[1] Pick up enough seed beads to fit around the circumference of a rivoli or stone, and sew through the first bead again to form a ring **(a–b)**.

[2] Pick up a bead, skip the next bead in the ring, and sew through the following bead **(b–c)**. Continue working in tubular peyote stitch to complete the round, and step up through the first bead added **(c–d)**.

[3] Work the next two rounds in tubular peyote using beads one size smaller than those used in the previous rounds **(d–e)**. Keep the tension tight to decrease the size of the ring.

[4] Position the rivoli or stone in the bezel cup. Using the tail thread, repeat steps 2 and 3 to work three more rounds on the other side of the stone.

Increasing

[1] At the point of increase, pick up two beads instead of one, and sew through the next bead.

[2] When you reach the pair of beads in the next row, sew through the first bead, pick up a bead, and sew through the second bead.

Decreasing

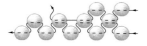

[1] At the point of decrease, sew through two up-beads in the previous row.

[2] In the next row, when you reach the two-bead space, pick up one bead.

Zipping up or joining

To join two sections of a flat peyote piece invisibly, match up the two pieces so the end rows fit together. "Zip up" the pieces by zigzagging through the up-beads on both ends.

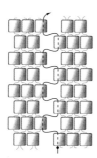

Right-angle weave
Flat strip

[1] To start the first row of right-angle weave, pick up four beads, and tie them into a ring (see "Square knot"). Sew through the first three beads again.

[2] Pick up three beads. Sew through the last bead in the previous stitch (a–b), and continue through the first two beads picked up in this stitch (b–c).

[3] Continue adding three beads per stitch until the first row is the desired length. You are stitching in a figure-8 pattern, alternating the direction of the thread path for each stitch.

Adding rows

[1] To add a row, sew through the last stitch of row 1, exiting an edge bead along one side.

[2] Pick up three beads, and sew through the edge bead your thread exited in the previous step (a–b). Continue through the first new bead (b–c).

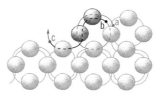

[3] Pick up two beads, and sew back through the next edge bead in the previous row and the bead your thread exited at the start of this step (a–b). Continue through the two new beads and the following edge bead in the previous row (b–c).

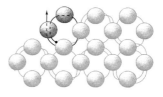

[4] Pick up two beads, and sew through the last two beads your thread exited in the previous stitch and the first new bead. Continue working a figure-8 thread path, picking up two beads per stitch for the rest of the row.

Square stitch

[1] String all the beads needed for the first row, then pick up the first bead of the second row. Sew through the last bead of the first row and the first bead of the second row again. Position the two beads side by side so that their holes are parallel.

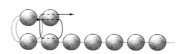

[2] Pick up the next bead of row 2, and sew through the corresponding bead in row 1 and the new bead in row 2. Repeat across the row.

Basics

STRINGING & WIREWORK

Crimping

Use crimp beads to secure flexible beading wire. Slide the crimp bead into place over two strands of wire, and squeeze it firmly with chainnose pliers to flatten it. For a more finished look, use crimping pliers:

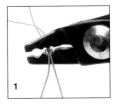

[1] Position the crimp bead in the hole that is closest to the handle of the crimping pliers.

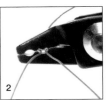

[2] Holding the wires apart, squeeze the pliers to compress the crimp bead, making sure one wire is on each side of the dent.

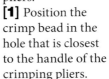

[3] Place the crimp bead in the front hole of the pliers, and position it so the dent is facing the tips of the pliers. Squeeze the pliers to fold the crimp in half.

Opening and closing loops and jump rings

[1] Hold a loop or a jump ring with two pairs of pliers, such as chainnose, flatnose, or bentnose pliers.

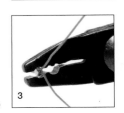

[2] To open the loop or jump ring, bring the tips of one pair of pliers toward you, and push the tips of the other pair away from you.

[3] The open jump ring. Reverse the steps to close.

Plain loop

[1] Using chainnose pliers, make a right-angle bend in the wire directly above a bead or other component or at least ¼ in. (6 mm) from the end of a naked piece of wire. For a larger loop, bend the wire further in.

[2] Grip the end of the wire with roundnose pliers so that the wire is flush with the jaws of the pliers where they meet. The closer to the tip of the pliers that you work, the smaller the loop will be. Press downward slightly, and rotate

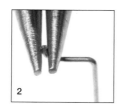

the wire toward the bend made in step 1.

[3] Reposition the pliers in the loop to continue rotating the wire until the end of the wire touches the bend.

[4] The plain loop.

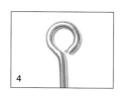

Wrapped loop

[1] Using chainnose pliers, make a right-angle bend in the wire about 2 mm above a bead or other component or at least 1¼ in. (3.2 cm) from the end of a naked piece of wire.

[2] Position the jaws of the roundnose pliers in the bend. The closer to the tip of the pliers that you work, the smaller the loop will be.

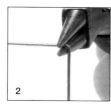

[3] Curve the short end of the wire over the top jaw of the roundnose pliers.

[4] Reposition the pliers so the lower jaw fits snugly in the loop. Curve the wire downward around the bottom jaw of the pliers. This is the first half of a wrapped loop.

[5] To complete the wraps, grasp the top of the loop with one pair of pliers.

[6] With another pair of pliers, wrap the wire around the stem two or three times. Trim the excess wire, and gently press the cut end close to the wraps with chainnose pliers.

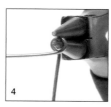

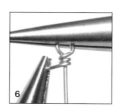

Loops, wrapped above a top-drilled bead

[1] Center a top-drilled bead on a 3-in. (7.6 cm) piece of wire. Bend each wire end upward, crossing them into an X above the bead.

[2] Using chainnose pliers, make a small bend in each wire end so they form a right angle.

[3] Wrap the horizontal wire around the vertical wire as in a wrapped loop. Trim the excess wrapping wire.

Single-Stitch Projects

NETTING

Hex-a-lot
bracelet

Create an eye-catching bracelet with a zigzagging pattern of hex-cut seed beads.

designed by **Alice Kharon**

Base

1 On a comfortable length of thread, string a stop bead, leaving a 12-in. (30 cm) tail, and pick up three color A 11º seed beads. Pick up a repeating pattern of an 8º hex-cut seed bead and three color B 11º seed beads three times. Pick up a hex and three As **(figure 1, a–b)**.
2 Pick up a 3 mm round bead and two As, and sew back through the first A in the previous set of As to form a loop **(b–c)**.
3 Keeping a tight tension, pick up a hex and two Bs,

skip the next hex and two Bs in the previous row, and sew through the following B **(c–d)**. Repeat this stitch twice **(d–e)**. Pick up a hex and two As, skip the next hex and two As in the previous row, and sew through the following A **(e–f)**.
4 Pick up a 3 mm and two As, and sew through the first A added in the previous stitch to form a loop **(figure 2, a–b)**.
5 Pick up a hex and two Bs, and sew through the center bead of the next loop in the previous row **(b–c)**.

tip Always sew through the 11º that is just before the next hex or 3 mm.

Repeat this stitch twice **(c–d)**. Pick up a hex and two As, skip the next hex and A in the previous row, and sew through the following A **(d–e)**.
6 Repeat steps 4–5 **(e–f)** for the desired length of the bracelet, leaving ¾ in. (1.9 cm) for the clasp, and ending and adding thread as needed. After the sixth row, the zigzag pattern will

become evident. End the final row with the thread exiting the same side as the tail **(as in figure 2, point f)**.

Clasp

1 With the working thread, sew through the beadwork as shown to exit the second-

●	11º seed bead, color A
●	11º seed bead, color B
▭	8º hex-cut seed bead
●	3 mm round bead

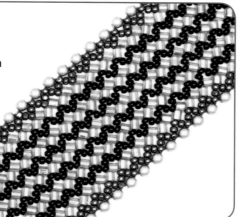

design option

Form a wider base (right) by picking up a hex and three color Bs in a repeating pattern four times instead of three in the first row. Continue with steps 2–6 of "Base," but in step 5, pick up a hex and two Bs three times instead of twice. Replace the clasp with a 5-strand tube clasp following steps 1–5 of "Clasp" but work one more connection to accomodate the extra loop on the clasp.

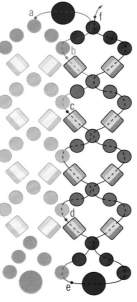

FIGURE 1

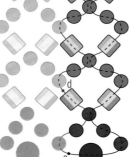

FIGURE 2

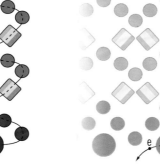

FIGURE 3

to-last A just added in the last row **(figure 3, a–b)**.

2 Pick up two Bs, sew through the first loop of the clasp, and sew back through the last B just added. Pick up two Bs, and sew through the center bead in the next loop **(b–c)**.

3 Repeat step 2 for the second and third loop of the clasp **(c–d)**.

4 Pick up two Bs, sew through the last loop of the clasp, and sew back through the last B just added. Pick up a B and an A, and sew through the end A and 3 mm **(d–e)**.

Sew through the bead-work, and retrace the clasp connection. End the working thread.

5 Remove the stop bead from the tail, and flip the beadwork to position the tail in the same place as the working thread before adding the clasp. Repeat steps 1–4, and end the tail. ●

add a pop of color

For an added design element, work a wide base as in "design option," but replace the two outer hex beads in row 1 with 3 mm round beads. Skip three rows, and in row 4, replace the center hex with a 3 mm round bead. Continue in a repeating pattern for the length of the bracelet.

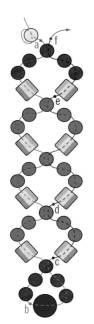

Floral garland bracelet

A unique flower toggle makes a statement alongside a floral garland adorning a peyote-stitched base.

designed by **Katie Dean**

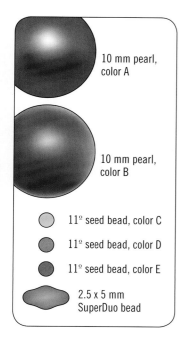

10 mm pearl, color A

10 mm pearl, color B

11º seed bead, color C

11º seed bead, color D

11º seed bead, color E

2.5 x 5 mm SuperDuo bead

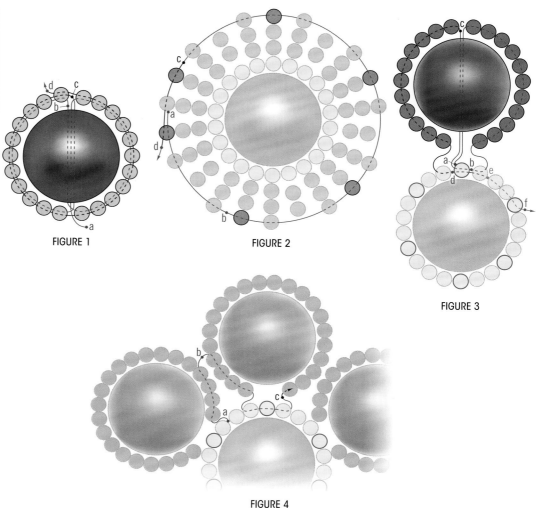

FIGURE 1

FIGURE 2

FIGURE 3

FIGURE 4

Toggle center

1 On 2 yd. (1.8 m) of thread, pick up a color A 10 mm pearl and 11 color C 11º seed beads. Sew through the A again in the same direction, leaving a 6-in. (15 cm) tail **(figure 1, a–b)**. This forms a loop of Cs around one side of the pearl. Pick up 11 Cs, and sew through the A once more, forming a loop around the other side of the pearl **(b–c)**. Retrace the thread path through all the Cs again **(c–d)**.

2 Work rounds of peyote off the ring of 11ºs, stepping up at the end of each round:

Rounds 1–5: Working in tubular peyote stitch, work five rounds using color D 11º seed beads, adding a total of 11 beads in each round.

Round 6: Pick up a D, and sew through the next two Ds in the previous round **(figure 2, a–b)**. Repeat this stitch four times **(b–c)**. Pick up a D, sew through the next D in the previous round, and step up **(c–d)**, adding a total of six beads in this round.

Rounds 7–8: Working in tubular peyote stitch, work two rounds using Ds, adding

six beads for each round.

Round 9: Pick up a D, and sew through the next two Ds in the previous round. Repeat this stitch twice, adding three beads in this round.

Rounds 10–13: Working in tubular peyote stitch, work three rounds using Ds, adding three beads for each round. This forms a stem on the underside of the toggle center.

Toggle petals

1 Sew through the beadwork to exit a C in the ring surrounding the toggle center. This bead will be referred to as an anchor bead to which you will attach a petal. The anchor and the C on each side of it will be referred

as an anchor set. The six Cs highlighted in red in **figure 3** will be the anchors for the six petals.

2 Pick up a color B 10 mm pearl and 11 color E 11º seed beads, and sew through the C to the right of the anchor **(a–b)**. Continue through the anchor and the B **(b–c)**.

3 Pick up 11 Es, sew through the C to the left of the anchor **(c–d)**. Retrace the thread path through all the beads added (not shown for clarity), and continue through the anchor set **(d–e)** and the next three Cs in the ring **(e–f)**. The bead your thread is exiting will be your new anchor for the next petal.

4 Repeat steps 2–3 twice to add two more petals, but end by sewing through only two Cs instead of three.

5 Repeat steps 2–3 three more times to add three more petals, but don't sew through any Cs after sewing through the last anchor set.

6 Sew up through the next four Es in the last petal **(figure 4, a–b)**, down through the corresponding four Es in the adjacent petal, and through the following anchor set **(b–c)**. Repeat these stitches for the remaining petals, making sure you are sewing through the correct beads for each anchor set. End the working thread and tail, and set aside.

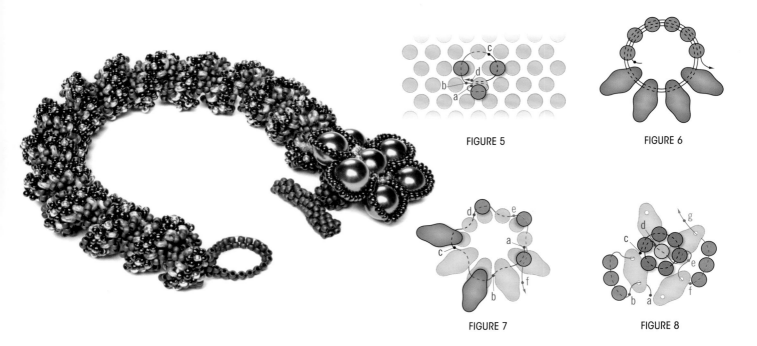

FIGURE 5

FIGURE 6

FIGURE 7

FIGURE 8

Toggle bar

1 On 1 yd. (.9 m) of thread, pick up 14 Ds, leaving a 6-in. (15 cm) tail. Using Ds, work a strip of flat even-count peyote that is 14 beads wide and 12 rows long. Align the ends, and zip them up to form a tube.

2 Sew through the beadwork to exit a bead in the center of the tube **(figure 5, point a)**. Pick up a D, and sew through the same bead in the tube your thread is exiting **(a-b)**. Pick up a D, and sew through the adjacent D in the tube **(b-c)**. Pick up a D and sew through the D in the tube your thread exited at the start of this step **(c-d)**. Reinforce the connection and the surrounding beads in the toggle bar, and step up through the first D added.

3 Working in tubular peyote stitch, work three rounds off the three beads added in the previous step to form a stem, stepping up at the end of each round.

4 With your thread exiting an up-bead, sew through

an up-bead in the stem on the toggle center and the next up-bead in the stem of the toggle bar. Continue zipping up the two ends of the stem. Retrace the thread path several times to reinforce the join. Sew through the entire stem to reinforce it, and end the working thread and tail.

Bracelet base

1 On a comfortable length of thread, pick up six Ds and four SuperDuo beads, sewing through the beads again to form a ring, and leaving a 14-in. (36 cm) tail. Continue through the six Ds **(figure 6)**.

2 Working in tubular peyote stitch, pick up a D, skip the next SuperDuo, and sew through the inner hole of the following SuperDuo **(figure 7, a-b)**. Pick up a SuperDuo, skip the next SuperDuo, and sew through the inner hole of the following SuperDuo **(b-c)**. Pick up a SuperDuo, skip the next D, and sew through the following D **(c-d)**. Pick up a D, skip the next D, and

sew through the following D **(d-e)**. Pick up a D, skip the next D, and sew through the D your thread exited at the start of this step. Step up by sewing through the first D added in this round **(e-f)**.

3 Continue working in tubular peyote stitch for the desired length of the base, minus 1½ in. (3.8 cm) for the clasp. For each round you will be working a stitch using a D, two stitches using SuperDuos, and two stitches using Ds, and stepping up through the first D added in the round. When adding the SuperDuos, make sure you are always sewing through the inner hole, and all new beads added sit on top of the beads in the previous round. End and add thread as needed, and do not end the working thread and tail when the base is complete.

Flower embellishment

1 Position the base horizontally on your bead mat. The SuperDuos spiral

around the base in pairs. The SuperDuo pairs will not be side by side. The SuperDuo on the right sits slightly lower than the one on the left as they spiral. Sewing away from you through the SuperDuos will be referred to as front to back, and sewing toward you through the SuperDuos will be back to front. Be sure not to skip any SuperDuos when embellishing.

2 Add a comfortable length of thread to the base, exiting the inner hole of the left SuperDuo in the first pair from back to front **(figure 8, a-b)**.

3 Pick up three Ds, and sew through the outer hole of the same SuperDuo from front to back **(b-c)**. For the remainder of the base you will be sewing through just the outer holes of the SuperDuos.

4 Pick up six color E 11º seed beads, and sew through the first E added to form a ring **(c-d)**. Gently snug up the beads close to the SuperDuo. Pick up a C, skip the next two Es, and sew through the following E going in the same

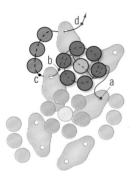

FIGURE 9

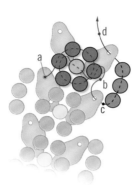

FIGURE 10

FIGURE 11

FIGURE 12

direction **(d-e)**.

5 Sew through the right SuperDuo in the same pair from front to back **(e-f)**. Pick up three Ds, and sew through the right SuperDuo in the next pair from back to front **(f-g)**.

6 Repeat step 4 **(figure 9, a-b)**. Sew through the left SuperDuo in the same pair from front to back **(b-c)**. Pick up three Ds, and sew through the left SuperDuo in the next pair from back to front **(c-d)**.

7 Repeat step 4 **(figure 10, a-b)**. Sew through the right SuperDuo in the same pair from front to back **(b-c)**. Pick up three Ds, and sew through the right SuperDuo in the next pair from back to front **(c-d)**.

8 Repeat steps 6–7 for the remainder of the base. End and add thread as needed. After adding the last flower, sew through the beadwork to exit the last SuperDuo on the left side going front to back. Pick up three Ds, and sew through the inner hole of the same SuperDuo.

Toggle loops

1 On each end of the base, there will be three D up-beads and one pair of SuperDuos showing (outlined in red in **figure 11**; other beads are not shown for clarity).

2 With your thread exiting the D up-bead at **figure 11, point a**, work two tubular peyote stitches using Ds **(a-b)**. Pick up a D, and sew through the next two SuperDuos **(b-c)**. Work one more stitch using a D, and step up through the first D added in this step **(c-d)**.

3 Working in tubular peyote stitch, work three rounds using Ds, adding four Ds in each round, and stepping up after each round.

4 Pick up a D, and sew through the next D in the previous round **(figure 12, a-b)**. Pick up a D, and sew back through the D just added, going in the opposite direction **(b-c)**. Working in flat even-count peyote stitch, repeat this stitch **(c-d)**, using a tight tension, to make a

strip of peyote with one bead in each row for a total of approximately 30 rows. The strip should end with a row that can be zipped up to the remaining two Ds from the last tubular peyote round added in step 3. Add or remove a row if needed. Zip up the strip to the base, and test the fit of the toggle bar before securing. Add or remove two rows at a time if needed for the toggle bar to work properly. Reinforce the connection, and sew back through the strip to tighten it up if your tension is a little loose. End the threads.

5 Repeat steps 1–4 at the other end of the base.

6 To clasp the bracelet, slide the toggle bar through the two toggle loops. ●

Difficulty rating

Materials
bracelet 8 in. (20 cm)
- 10 mm pearls (Swarovski)
  - **1** color A (iridescent purple)
  - **6** color B (deep brown)
- 15 g 2.5 x 5 mm SuperDuo beads (opaque green luster)
- 11º seed beads
  - **2 g** color C (Toho PF557, permanent finish galvanized starlight)
  - **15 g** color D (Toho 221F, frosted bronze)
  - **11 g** color E (Miyuki 455D, metallic dark variegated iris)
- Fireline, 6 lb. test
- beading needles, #11 or #12

change it up
The flower toggle is removeable, so have a little fun and make several interchangeable toggles for a single base.

BRICK STITCH

Wheels of fun earrings

These whimsical earrings are a dangling sensation.

designed by **Cassie Donlen**

Difficulty rating

Materials
earrings 1½ in. (3.8 cm)
- 11º seed beads
  - **1 g** color A (yellow green)
  - **1 g** color B (matte transparent purple velvet)
  - **1 g** color C (matte sky blue)
- **1 g** 15º seed beads (pink-lined transparent amethyst)
- **6** 9 mm pewter hammered ring components (TierraCast)
- **6** 10 mm jump rings
- **2** 4 mm jump rings
- **1** pair of earring findings
- Fireline, 8 lb. test
- beading needles, #12
- **2** pairs of chainnose, flatnose, and/or bentnose pliers

Components

1 On 1 yd. (.9 m) of thread, tie a square knot around a 9 mm ring component, leaving a 6-in. (15 cm) tail.

2 Work rounds of brick stitch as follows:

Round 1: Pick up two color A 11º seed beads, sew through the ring, and continue back through the second bead added **(figure 1, a–b)**. Pick up an A, sew through the ring, and continue back through the bead just added **(b–c)**. Repeat this stitch around the perimeter of the ring. After adding the final bead, sew down through the first A added, through the ring, and back through the same A **(figure 2, a–b)**.

Round 2: Pick up two 15º seed beads. Working clockwise, sew under the thread bridge of the 11ºs in round 1 about one bead's width away from

where the thread is exiting. Sew back through the second 15º **(b–c)**, and pull the thread tight. Pick up a 15º, sew under the thread bridge next to the bead just added, sew back through the same 15º **(figure 3)**, and pull the thread tight. Repeat this stitch around the perimeter to complete the round. You will need to add a second 15º to some of the thread bridges in order to prevent gaps between the 15ºs. After adding the final 15º, sew down through the first 15º added in this round, under the nearest thread bridge, and back up through the last 15º just added **(figure 4)**. End the working thread and tail.

3 Make a matching component for the other earring.

4 Work as in steps 1–3, replacing color A with color B 11º seed beads, and repeat

again replacing color A with color C 11º seed beads. Make two in each color combination.

Assembly

1 Open a 10 mm jump ring, and attach a color A and a color C component. Repeat this step using a color B component and the color A component.

2 Open a 10 mm jump ring, and attach it to the color B component.

3 Open a 4 mm jump ring, and attach it to the 10 mm jump ring you just added to the color B component. Before closing the jump ring, attach it to the loop of an earring finding.

4 Make a second earring. ●

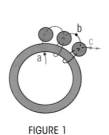

9 mm pewter ring

11º seed bead, color A

15º seed bead

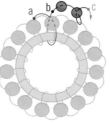

FIGURE 1

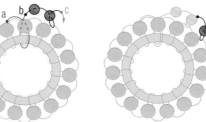

FIGURE 2

FIGURE 3

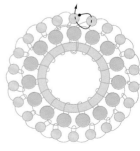

FIGURE 4

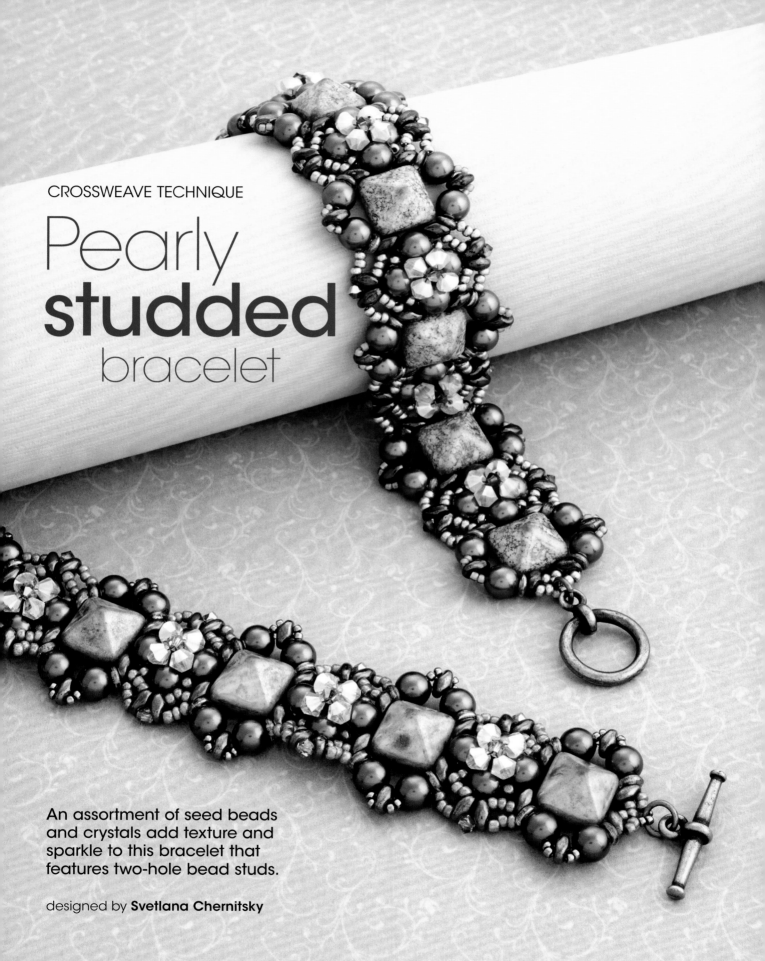

CROSSWEAVE TECHNIQUE

Pearly
studded
bracelet

An assortment of seed beads
and crystals add texture and
sparkle to this bracelet that
features two-hole bead studs.

designed by **Svetlana Chernitsky**

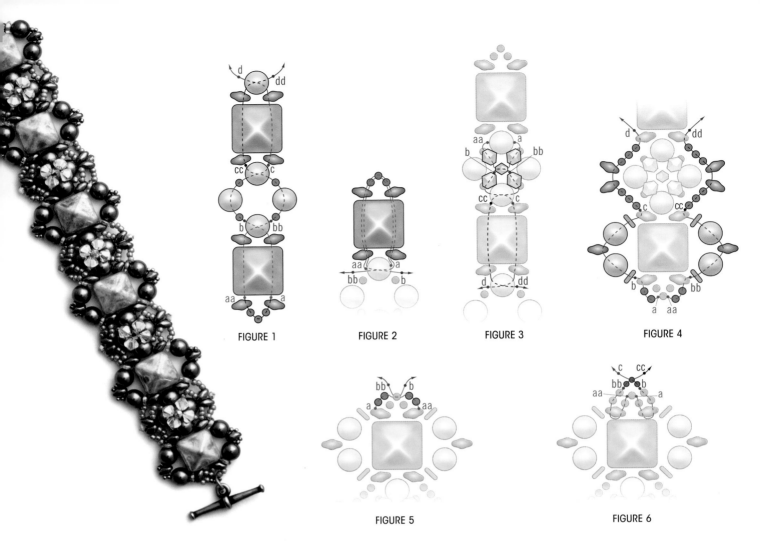

FIGURE 1

FIGURE 2

FIGURE 3

FIGURE 4

FIGURE 5

FIGURE 6

Base

For the purposes of these instructions, the bead studs will have a right side hole (RH) and a left side hole (LH), and we will refer to the needle as being on the right or left side of the base when needed.

1 Thread a needle on each end of a comfortable length of thread. With one needle, pick up a SuperDuo bead, three 11º seed beads, and a SuperDuo, and center the beads on the thread **(figure 1, a and aa)**.

2 With the right needle, pick up a bead stud (RH), a SuperDuo, and a 6 mm pearl. With the left needle, sew through the bead stud (LH), pick up a SuperDuo, and cross the needle through the pearl **(a-b and aa-bb)**.

3 With each needle, pick up an 11º, a pearl, and an 11º. With one needle, pick up a pearl, and cross the other needle through it **(b-c and bb-cc)** to make one pearl unit.

4 With the right needle, pick up a SuperDuo, a bead stud (RH), a SuperDuo,

and a pearl. With the left needle, pick up a SuperDuo, sew through the bead stud (LH), pick up a SuperDuo, and cross the needle through the pearl **(c-d and cc-dd)** to make one bead stud unit.

5 Repeat steps 3–4 for a total of five pearl units and five bead stud units for a 7-in. (18 cm) bracelet (end with a pearl unit). End and add thread as needed.

6 To make one more bead stud unit: With the right needle, pick up a SuperDuo, a bead stud (RH), a SuperDuo, three 11ºs, and a SuperDuo. Sew through the bead stud (LH), pick up a SuperDuo, and sew through the pearl your thread exited at the start of this step **(figure 2, a-b)**. With the left needle, sew through all the beads just added, and cross the needle through the pearl your thread exited at the start of the step **(aa-bb)**. Tighten the beadwork.

7 With each needle, pick up a 4 mm bicone crystal. With one needle, pick up a 3 mm bicone crystal, and cross

the other needle through it **(figure 3, a-b and aa-bb)**. With each needle, pick up a 4 mm, and cross the needle through the next pearl **(b-c and bb-cc)**.

8 With the right needle, sew through the SuperDuo, bead stud (RH), SuperDuo, and the next pearl **(c-d)**. With the left needle, sew through the SuperDuo, bead stud (LH), and SuperDuo, and cross the needle through the same pearl **(cc-dd)**.

9 Repeat steps 7–8 for the length of the base. At the end of the base, sew through an 11º with each thread, and cross through the center 11º.

Edge embellishments

1 With each needle, pick up two 11ºs, and sew through the open hole of the next SuperDuo **(figure 4, a-b and aa-bb)**.

2 With each needle, pick up an O-bead, a pearl, a SuperDuo, a pearl, and an O-bead. Skip the adjacent bead stud, and sew through the open hole of the

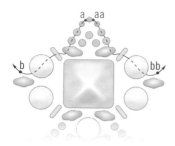

FIGURE 7

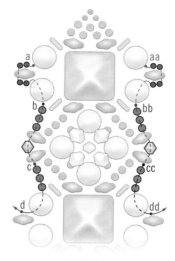

FIGURE 8

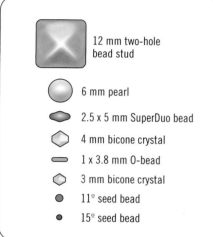

	12 mm two-hole bead stud
	6 mm pearl
	2.5 x 5 mm SuperDuo bead
	4 mm bicone crystal
	1 x 3.8 mm O-bead
	3 mm bicone crystal
	11º seed bead
	15º seed bead

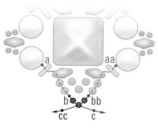

FIGURE 9

next SuperDuo **(b–c and bb–cc)**.

3 With each needle, pick up three 11ºs, two SuperDuos, and three 11ºs, and sew through the open hole of the next SuperDuo **(c–d and cc–dd)**.

4 Repeat steps 2–3 for the length of the base, ending with step 2. End and add thread as needed.

5 With the each needle, pick up two 11ºs, and sew through the center 11º at this end of the base **(figure 5, a–b and aa–bb)**.

6 With each needle, sew through the next 11º and inside hole of the adjacent SuperDuo. Continue through the outside hole of the same SuperDuo and the following two 11ºs **(figure 6, a–b and aa–bb)**.

7 With each needle, pick up a 15º seed bead. With one needle, pick up a 15º, and cross the other needle through it **(b–c and bb–cc)**.

8 With each needle, sew through the following: 15º, two 11ºs, SuperDuo (outside hole), O-bead, and pearl **(figure 7, a–b and aa–bb)**.

9 With each needle, pick up two 15ºs, and sew through the open hole of the next SuperDuo. Pick up two 15ºs, and sew through the following pearl **(figure 8, a–b and aa–bb)**.

10 With each needle, pick up three 11ºs, and sew through the open hole of the next SuperDuo. Pick up a 3 mm crystal, and sew through the open hole of the following SuperDuo **(b–c and bb–cc)**. With each needle, pick up three 11ºs, and sew through the next pearl **(c–d and cc–dd)**.

11 Repeat steps 9–10 for the length of the bracelet, ending with step 9.

12 With each needle, sew through the following O-bead, SuperDuo (outside hole), and two 11ºs **(figure 9, a–b and aa–bb)**. With each needle, pick up a 15º. With one needle, pick up a 15º, and cross the other needle through it **(b–c and bb–cc)**. End the threads.

13 Open a 6 mm jump ring. Attach it to the small loop created in the previous step and half of the clasp. Repeat for the other end. ●

Difficulty rating

◆ ◆ ◆ ◇ ◇

Materials

blue bracelet 7 in. (18 cm)
- **6** 12 mm two-hole bead studs (chalk green lumi)
- **44** 6 mm pearls (Swarovski, Tahitian)
- **20** 4 mm bicone crystals (Swarovski, crystal AB2X)
- **15** 3 mm bicone crystals (Preciosa, Venus)
- **4 g** 2.5 x 5 mm SuperDuo beads (chocolate bronze)
- **24** 1 x 3.8 mm O-beads (crystal blue rainbow)
- **2 g** 11º seed beads (Toho 1208, marbled opaque turquoise blue)
- **1 g** 15º seed beads (Toho 460G, steel blue metallic)
- **2** 6 mm jump rings (antique brass)
- toggle clasp
- Fireline 6 lb. test
- beading needles, #11 or #12
- **2** pairs of chainnose, flatnose, and/or bentnose pliers

purple bracelet colors
- 12 mm two-hole bead studs (chalk bronze lumi)
- 6 mm pearls (Swarovski, burgundy)
- 4 mm bicone crystals (Swarovski, chrysolite opal AB2X)
- 3 mm bicone crystals (Swarovski, amethyst AB)
- 2.5 x 5 mm SuperDuo beads (purple iris)
- 1 x 3.8 mm O-beads (magic purple)
- 11º seed beads (Miyuki 94204-TB, Duracoat galvanized champagne)
- 15º seed beads (Japanese 329B, green/celadon lined)

ST. PETERSBURG CHAIN

4part harmony bracelet

St. Petersburg stitch takes on a tubular shape when worked in four sections making a fun bracelet in bright, whimsical colors.

designed by **Beth Kraft**

PATTERN

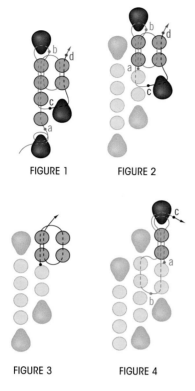

FIGURE 1 FIGURE 2

FIGURE 3 FIGURE 4

2.8 mm drop bead

11º seed bead, color A

11º seed bead, color B

11º seed bead, color C

11º seed bead, color D

12 mm glass bead

7 mm Czech rondelle bead

4 mm Czech rondelle bead

Section 1

1 On a comfortable length of thread, attach a 2.8 mm drop as a stop bead, leaving a 10-in. (25 cm) tail. This stop bead will become part of the design. Pick up six color A 11º seed beads, and sew through the third and fourth As in the same direction so the fifth and sixth As form a new column **(figure 1, a–b)**. Pick up a drop, and sew back through the next three As in the first column **(b–c)**.
2 Pick up a drop, and sew through the two As in the next column **(c–d)**.
3 Pick up four As, sew through the first and second As just added in the same direction, and snug them up to the previous beads **(figure 2, a–b)**. Pick up a drop, and sew back through the next three As in the same column **(b–c)**.
4 Pick up a drop, and sew through the two As in the next column **(c–d)**.

5 Repeat steps 3–4 for the desired length of the bracelet minus 1½ in. (3.8 cm) for the clasp. Follow the **pattern** to change colors, and end and add thread as needed.

changing colors
To make a color change:
Pick up two 11ºs in the current color and two 11ºs in the new color **(figure 3)**, and continue as directed in steps 3–4.

6 To make the final row, pick up two As and a drop. Sew back through the two As just added and the following two As in the same column **(figure 4, a–b)**. Sew through the beadwork as shown to exit the last drop just added **(b–c)**.

Difficulty rating

Materials
green bracelet 8½ in. (21.6 cm)
- 11º seed beads
  - **5 g** color A (Miyuki 416, opaque chartreuse)
  - **1 g** color B (Miyuki 406, opaque orange)
  - **1 g** color C (Miyuki 352, fuchsia-lined aqua luster)
  - **1 g** color D (Miyuki 2029, matte opaque turquoise)
- **8 g** 2.8 mm drops (Miyuki DP401, black)
- **1** 12 mm glass bead for clasp (green)
- **1** 7 x 3 mm rondelle bead (Czech, turquoise)
- **1** 4 x 3 mm rondelle bead (orange)
- Fireline, 6 lb. test
- beading needles, #12

red bracelet
- 11º seed beads
  - color A (Miyuki 401, black)
  - color B (Miyuki 406, opaque orange)
  - color C (Miyuki 416, opaque chartreuse)
  - color D (Miyuki F412D, matte opaque turquoise)
- 3 mm magatama drops (Toho, opaque pepper red)
- 12 mm glass bead for clasp (red)
- 7 x 3 mm rondelle bead (Czech, turquoise)
- 4 x 3 mm Czech rondelle bead (orange)

turquoise bracelet
- 11º seed beads
  - color A (Miyuki 492, opaque cream)
  - color B (Miyuki 406, opaque orange)
  - color C (Miyuki 416, opaque matte soft brown)
  - color D (Toho 45, opaque pepper red)
- 3 mm magatama drops (Toho, opaque turquoise)
- 12 mm glass bead for clasp (blue)
- 7 x 3 mm rondelle bead (Czech, turquoise)
- 4 x 3 mm Czech rondelle bead (orange)

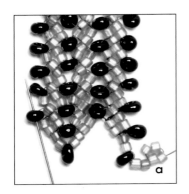

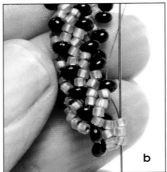

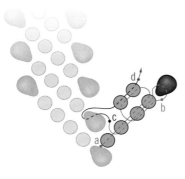

FIGURE 5

FIGURE 6

Sections 2 and 3

1 With the working thread, pick up six As, and sew through the third and fourth As in the same direction so the fifth and sixth As form a new column **(figure 5, a–b)**. Pick up a drop, and sew back through the next three As in the first column **(b–c)**.

2 Instead of picking up a drop, sew through the following drop in section 1, and continue through the two As in the next column **(c–d)**. Pull the thread tight to make the shared drop pop out.

3 Pick up four As, sew through the first and second As just added in the same direction, and snug them up to the previous beads **(figure 6, a–b)**. Pick up a drop, and sew back through the next three As in the same column **(b–c)**. Sew through the following drop in section 1, and continue through the two As in the new column **(c–d)**. Pull the thread tight.

4 Repeat step 3 for the length of the

bracelet, following the established color changes.

5 Work the last row as in step 6 of "Section 1."

6 Repeat steps 1–5 to complete section 3.

Section 4

The fourth section joins the beadwork into a tube by adding only seed beads and sewing through the existing drops on the first and third sections. When forming the tube, make sure the rounded area of the drop beads are facing outward.

1 With the working thread, pick up six As, and sew through the third and fourth As in the same direction so the fifth and sixth As form a new column. Sew through the corresponding drop in section 1 **(photo a)**. Pull the thread tight to form the sections into a tube, and continue back through

the corresponding three As in the first column of section 4 **(photo b)**.

2 Sew through the adjacent drop in section 3, and continue through the two As in the new column of section 4 **(photo c)**.

3 Pick up four As. Sew through the first and second A just added in the same direction, and snug them up to the previous beads. Sew through the adjacent drop in section 1 **(photo d)**, and sew back through the next three As in the same column of section 4 **(photo e)**.

4 Sew through the corresponding drop in section 3, and continue through the following two As in the new column. Pull the thread tight.

5 Repeat steps 3–4 for the length of the bracelet following the established color changes.

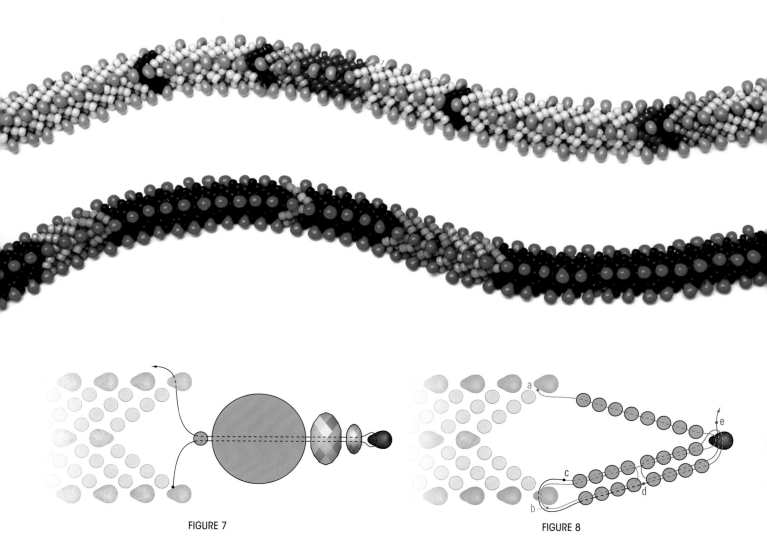

FIGURE 7

FIGURE 8

Clasp

1 With the tail thread, pick up an A, a 12 mm glass bead, a 7 mm rondelle bead, a 4 mm rondelle bead, and a drop. Skip the drop, and sew back through all the beads just added. Continue through the adjacent drop bead on the end of the beadwork **(figure 7)**. Sew through the beadwork to retrace the thread path and reinforce the join. End the tail thread.

2 With the working thread, pick up eight As, a drop, and eight As, and sew through the opposite drop at this end of the bracelet **(figure 8, a–b)**. Make sure the loop fits around the glass bead, and add or omit beads if needed.

3 Pick up four As, and sew through the last four As added in step 2 with the needle facing toward the bracelet **(b–c)**. Continue through the drop bead and the four As just added **(c–d)**.

4 Pick up four As, and sew through the following drop and the corresponding four beads added in step 2. Continue through the four As just added, and the following drop **(d–e)**.

5 Work as in steps 3–4 to add two sets of four As on the other side of the loop, and end the thread. ⬤

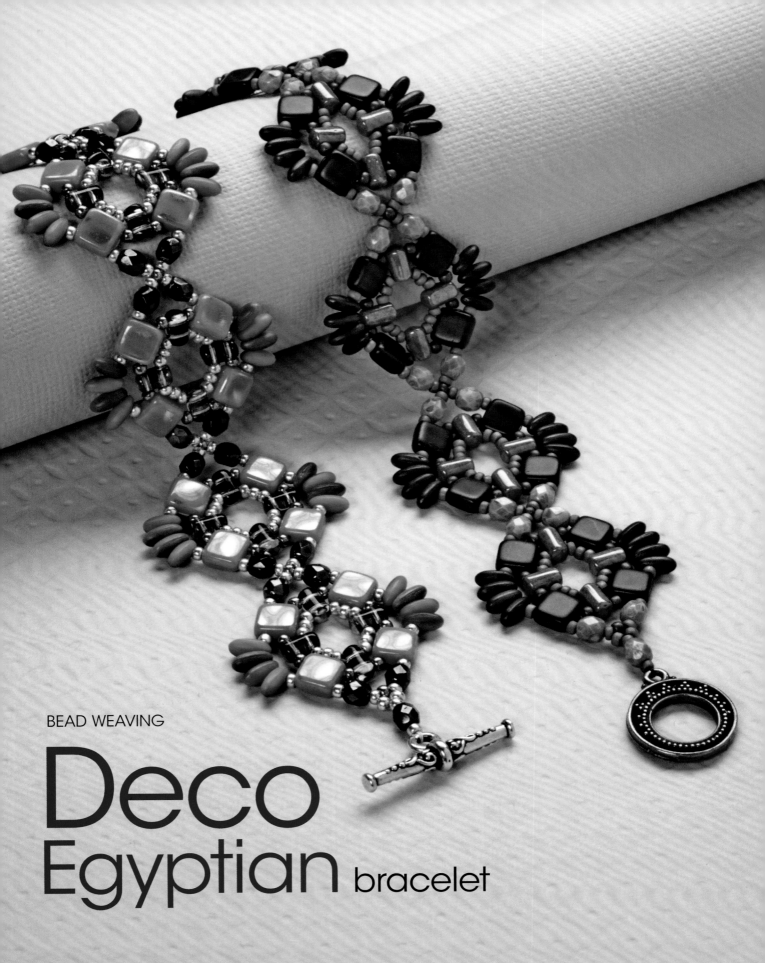

BEAD WEAVING

Deco
Egyptian bracelet

Rich colors and bold geometric shapes come together for a stunning yet simple bracelet.

designed by **Colleen Ewart**

Difficulty rating

Materials
turquoise bracelet 7½ in. (19.1 cm)
- **20** 6 x 6 mm CzechMates two-hole tile beads (opaque green turquoise peacock)
- **20** 3 x 5 mm Rulla beads (silver blue crystal)
- **40** 2.5 x 6 mm Rizo beads (matte jade celsian)
- **22** 4 mm fire-polished beads (iris blue metallic)
- 11º seed beads
  - **1 g** color A (Miyuki 4201, Duracoat galvanized silver)
  - **1 g** color B (Miyuki 4217, Duracoat galvanized seafoam)
- **1** toggle clasp
- Fireline, 6 lb. test
- beading needles, #10 or #11

purple bracelet colors
- 6 x 6 mm CzechMates two-hole tile beads (chocolate brown matte)
- 3 x 5 mm Rulla beads (opaque luster amethyst)
- 2.5 x 6 mm Rizo beads (matte iris blue)
- 4 mm fire-polished beads (opaque turquoise Picasso)
- 11º seed beads
  - color A (Toho F463R, olive metal matte)
  - color B (Toho F460T, dessert sun)

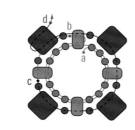

FIGURE 1

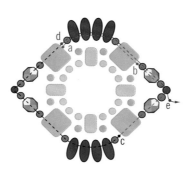

FIGURE 2

●	11º seed bead, color A
•	11º seed bead, color B
▭	3 x 5 mm Rulla bead
■	6 mm two-hole tile bead
⬬	2.5 x 6 mm Rizo bead
⬡	4 mm fire-polished bead

First component

1 On a comfortable length of thread, pick up a repeating pattern of three color A 11º seed beads and a Rulla bead four times, leaving a 6-in. (15 cm) tail. Sew through the beads again, and continue through the open hole of the last Rulla **(figure 1, a–b)**.

2 Pick up a color B 11º seed bead, a two-hole tile bead, and a B, and sew through the open hole of the next Rulla **(b–c)**. Repeat this stitch three times, and sew through the beads again (not shown in illustration for clarity). Continue through the next B and tile, and sew back through the open hole of the same tile **(c–d)**.

3 Pick up an A, four Rizo beads, and an A, and sew through the open hole of the next tile **(figure 2, a–b)**.

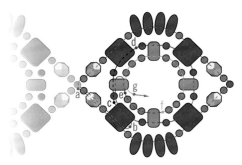

FIGURE 3

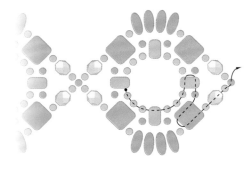

FIGURE 4

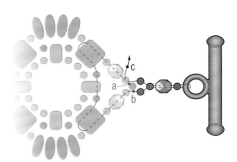

FIGURE 5

4 Pick up an A, a 4 mm fire-polished bead, an A, a B, an A, a 4 mm, and an A, and sew through the open hole of the next tile **(b-c)**.

5 Repeat steps 3–4 **(c-d)**, and sew through the beads again (not shown in the illustration for clarity). Sew through the beadwork to exit the next B **(d-e)**.

Remaining components

1 Pick up an A, a 4 mm, an A, a tile, an A, four Rizos, an A, a tile, an A, a 4 mm, an A, a B, an A, a 4 mm, an A, a tile, an A, four Rizos, an A, a tile, an A, a 4 mm, and an A. Sew through the B your thread exited at the start of this step, and sew through the beads again (not shown in illustration for clarity). Continue through the following A, 4 mm, A, and tile **(figure 3, a-b)**. Sew through the open hole of the same tile **(b-c)**.

2 Pick up a B, a Rulla, and a B, and sew through the open hole of the next tile **(c-d)**. Repeat this stitch three times, and sew through the beads again

(not shown in illustration for clarity). Sew through the following B and Rulla, and sew back through the open hole of the same Rulla **(d-e)**.

3 Pick up three As, and sew through the open hole of the next Rulla **(e-f)**. Repeat this stitch three times **(f-g)**.

4 Sew through the beadwork as shown to exit the end B **(figure 4)**.

5 With the working thread, repeat steps 1–4 to make an additional three components. End and add thread as needed.

Clasp

1 Sew through the beadwork as shown **(figure 5, a-b)**. Pick up two As, a 4 mm, and an A, and the loop of the clasp. Sew back through the last A, 4 mm, and A. Pick up an A, skip the end B, and sew through the following A on the last component **(b-c)**. Retrace the thread path through the clasp connection.

2 Repeat step 1 for the other half of the clasp, and end the thread. ●

RIGHT-ANGLE WEAVE

Flower-path
bracelet

Embellish a right-angle weave base
with an assortment of crystals and
seed beads for a luxurious bracelet.

designed by **Ora Shai**

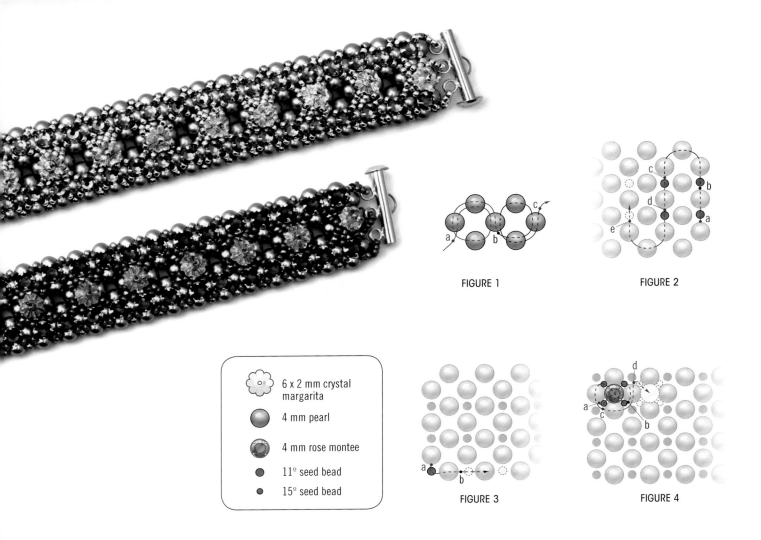

6 x 2 mm crystal margarita

4 mm pearl

4 mm rose montee

11º seed bead

15º seed bead

FIGURE 1

FIGURE 2

FIGURE 3

FIGURE 4

Base

1 On a comfortable length of thread, pick up four 4 mm pearls. Sew through the beads again to form a ring, leaving a 10-in. (25 cm) tail. Continue through the first three pearls so your working thread is exiting opposite the tail, and snug up the beads **(figure 1, a–b)**.

2 Working in right-angle weave, pick up three pearls, and sew through the pearl your thread exited at the start of this step. Retrace the thread path (not shown in the figure), and continue through the first two pearls added in this step **(b–c)**.

3 Repeat step 2 for the desired length bracelet, leaving ½ in. (1.3 cm) for the clasp. End with an odd number of pearls along each edge. For the last stitch, sew through the last three pearls added to exit an edge pearl. End and add thread as needed.

4 Work in right-angle weave using pearls to add two more rows, retracing the thread path as you go. Exit the end pearl in the last row added **(figure 2, point a)**. If your thread is exiting in the opposite direction, sew under the next thread bridge, and continue back through the end pearl.

5 Pick up an 11º seed bead, and sew through the next end pearl **(a–b)**. Repeat this stitch once more. Sew through the next edge pearl, and continue through the adjacent pearl with the needle pointing toward the other edge of the base **(b–c)**.

6 Pick up an 11º, and sew through the next pearl **(c–d)**. Repeat this stitch once more, and sew through the next two pearls so your needle is pointing toward the other edge of the base **(d–e)**.

7 Work as in step 6 for the remainder of the base. For the last row, add two 11ºs as before, and exit a corner pearl **(figure 3, point a)**.

8 Pick up an 11º, and sew through the next edge pearl **(a–b)**. Repeat this stitch for both edges of the base, making sure to add an 11º at each corner and keeping an even tension. Exit an end pearl **(figure 4, point a)**.

Crystal embellishment

1 Pick up a 15º seed bead, a 4 mm rose montee, and a 15º. Cross the stitch diagonally, and sew through the opposite pearl **(a–b)**. Pick up a 15º, sew back through the other channel of the rose montee, pick up a 15º, and sew through the pearl your thread exited at the start of this step **(b–c)**. Continue through the next two pearls **(c–d)**. Repeat these stitches for the length of the base, exiting the adjacent end 11º **(figure 5, point a)**.

2 Pick up five 15ºs, skip the next pearl, and sew through the following 11º to form a loop **(a–b)**. Repeat this stitch three more times, working around the RAW stitch, and

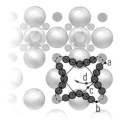

FIGURE 5

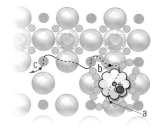

FIGURE 6

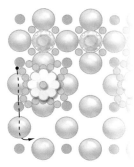

FIGURE 7

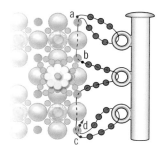

FIGURE 8

Difficulty rating

Materials
**purple bracelet
6¾ in. (17.1 cm)**
- **14** 6 x 2 mm crystal margaritas (Swarovski, crystal transmission V)
- **54** 4 mm rose montees (Swarovski, amethyst)
- **192** 4 mm crystal pearls (Swarovski, mauve)
- **1 g** 11º seed beads (Miyuki T11-D4218, Duracoat mauve)
- **2 g** 15º seed beads (Japanese 430K, mallard blue opaque luster)
- 3-strand tube clasp (silver)
- Fireline 6 lb. test
- beading needles, #11 or #12

gray bracelet colors:
- 6 x 2 mm crystal margaritas (Swarovski, crystal transmission V)
- 4 mm rose montees (Swarovski, black diamond)
- 4 mm crystal pearls (Swarovski, platinum)
- 11º seed beads (Japanese SB2580, gray sage permanent galvanized)
- 15º seed beads (Toho P470 silver permanent galvanized)

sew through the first three 15ºs added at the start of this step **(b–c)**.
3 Sew through the center 15º of each of the loops added in step 2 to form a ring **(c–d)**. Pull snug, retrace the thread path, and continue through the next 15º **(figure 6, point a)**.
4 Pick up a 6 x 2 mm margarita crystal and a 15º, sew back through the margarita, and sew through the 15º on the opposite side of the center ring with your needle pointing toward the other end of the base **(a–b)**. Continue through the next two 15ºs, 11º, pearl, and 11º as shown **(b–c)**.
5 Repeat steps 2–4 to add a total of 14 margarita embellishments, noticing that

there will be an open right-angle weave stitch between each margarita embellishment. Take care when adding the margaritas, as they can cut your thread if you pull too tight. End and add thread as needed. After adding the last embellishment, sew through the end pearl, 11º, and pearl as shown in **figure 7**.
6 Repeat step 1 to embellish this side of the bracelet with rose montees.

Clasp
1 Sew through the beadwork to exit a corner 11º **(figure 8, point a)**. Pick up three 15ºs, sew through the end loop of the clasp, pick up three 15ºs, and sew back through the corner 11º, the next pearl, and the following 11º **(a–b)**.

2 Pick up three 11ºs, sew through the center loop of the clasp, and pick up three 11ºs. Skip the next pearl, and sew through the following 11º, pearl, and corner 11º **(b–c)**.
3 Pick up three 15ºs, sew through the last loop of the clasp, pick up three 15ºs, and sew back through the corner 11º **(c–d)**.
4 Retrace the thread path of the clasp connections, and end the working thread.
5 With the tail, repeat steps 1–4 at the other end of the base. ●

Half Tilas all the fun

This easy-to-make multistrand bracelet boosts the hues with three color schemes.

designed by **Kenji Katsuoka, Miyuki Bead**

Outer strands

1 Open a 4 mm jump ring, and attach it to the toggle bar loop. Open another 4 mm jump ring and attach it to the previous ring and the soldered jump ring.

2 On 28 in. (71 cm) of thread, pick up a color A Half Tila bead ("Tila" from now on) and two color A 15º seed beads, leaving a 6-in. (15 cm) tail. Sew through the soldered jump ring twice, and back through the last 15º just added **(figure 1, a–b)**. Pick up an A 15º, and sew through the open hole of the Tila **(b–c)**.

3 Pick up a repeating pattern of an A 15º, an 11º seed bead, an A 15º, and two A Tilas 20 times. Pick up the pattern once more, ending with a single Tila. This will make a 7½ in. (19.1 cm) bracelet. Snug up the beads so that no thread shows.

4 Pick up two A 15ºs, sew through the loop of the toggle ring twice, and sew back through the last 15º just added **(figure 2, a–b)**. Pick up an A 15º, and sew through the open hole of the next two Tilas **(b–c)**.

5 Pick up an A 15º, an 11º, and an A 15º, and sew through the open hole of the next two A Tilas **(c–d)**. Repeat this stitch for the length of the bracelet. For the final stitch, sew through the remaining Tila. Snug up the beads.

6 Sew through the following two A 15ºs, the soldered jump ring, and back through the end A 15º. End the working thread and tail.

7 Repeat steps 2–6 for the second outer strand.

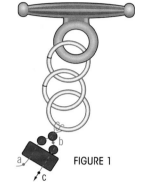

- ● 15º seed bead, color A
- ○ 15º seed bead, color B
- ● 11º seed bead
- ▢ 10º cylinder bead
- ▪ 11º cylinder bead
- ▬ Half Tila, color A
- ▭ Half Tila, color B
- ▬ Half Tila, color C

FIGURE 1

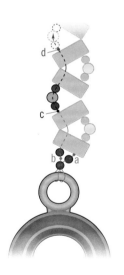

FIGURE 2

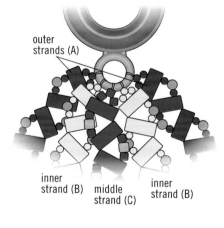

outer
strands (A)

inner
strand (B)   middle
strand (C)   inner
strand (B)

FIGURE 3

Materials

bracelet 7½ in. (19.1 cm)

- 5 x 2.3 x 1.9 mm Half Tila beads
  - **6 g** color A (Miyuki 301, transparent rose gold luster)
  - **6 g** color B (Miyuki 593, light caramel Ceylon)
  - **3 g** color C (Miyuki 2035, antique bronze metallic matte rainbow)
- **2 g** 11º seed beads (Miyuki 003, silver-lined gold)
- 15º seed beads
  - **2 g** color A (Miyuki 313, gold luster burgundy)
  - **2 g** color B (Miyuki 593, light caramel Ceylon)
- **1 g** 10º cylinder beads (Miyuki Delicas, DBM331, 24k matte metallic bright gold)
- **1 g** 11º cylinder beads (Miyuki Delicas, DB380, matte metallic khaki iris)
- jump rings
  - **1** 4 mm soldered
  - **2** 4 mm open
- toggle clasp
- Fireline, 6 lb. test, or size D nylon beading thread
- beading needles, #11 or #12
- **2** pairs of chainnose, flatnose, and/or bentnose pliers

Inner strands

Using color B Tilas, color B 15ºs, and 11º seed beads, repeat steps 2–6 of "Outer strands" to make two inner strands.

Middle strand

With color C Tilas, 11º cylinders in place of 15ºs, and 10º cylinders in place of 11ºs, repeat steps 2–6 of "Outer strands" to make the middle strand. ●

strand plan

Order the Tila strand colors like this, left to right: A, B, C, B, A (figure 3). Push the threads from each strand up to the top of the jump ring or loop of the toggle ring to leave enough space for the middle strand, which will be added last.

Two-hole rickrack bracelet

Both texture and bling take center stage in this uniquely designed Half Tila bracelet.

designed by **Karen Bruns**

There are two sides to the Half Tila bead (referred to as "Tila" in the instructions). The top has a small bump in the center and the bottom is flat. When picking up a Tila, make sure the top is facing up, and sew through either the left hole (LH) or the right hole (RH) as directed. The Tilas will flip over as they are added to the beadwork. With your beadwork positioned horizontally from left to right, the holes in the Tilas will again be referred to as LH or RH as they are positioned.

Center row

1 On a comfortable length of thread, pick up two Tila beads (RH), and sew through the RH of the first Tila again, leaving an 8-in. (20 cm) tail. Tighten the beads so the end of the second Tila is positioned under the RH of the first Tila **(photo a)**.

2 Sew through the same hole of the second Tila, and continue through the open hole of the same Tila **(photo b)**.

3 Pick up a Tila (RH), sew through the RH of the Tila

a

b

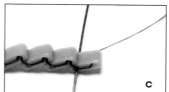

c

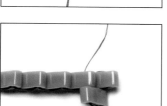

d

e

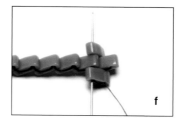

f

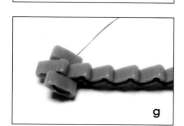

g

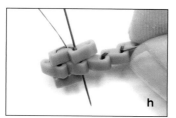

h

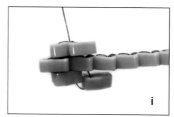

i

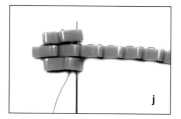

j

k

your thread exited at the start of the step, and tighten to position the end of the new Tila under the RH of the existing Tila. Sew through the LH of the Tila just added, and continue through the open hole of the same Tila. Repeat this stitch for the desired bracelet length, minus ¾ in. (1.9 cm) for the clasp. This becomes the center row as the other rows are added.
4 Sew through the LH of last Tila **(photo c)**.

Adjacent rows

1 To begin the row below the center row, pick up a Tila (LH). Sew through the open hole of the same Tila, and continue through the RH of the next Tila in the center row **(photo d)**.
2 To begin the row above the center row, pick up a Tila (RH), and sew through the open hole of the same Tila. Continue through the LH of the end Tila in the center row, and the RH of the new Tila in the row below **(photo e)**.
3 Sew through the LH of the same Tila, the RH of the Tila in the center row, and the

LH of the Tila in the top row **(photo f)**.
4 Flip the beadwork as shown **(photo g)** to work from left to right.
5 Pick up a Tila (RH), sew through the RH of the Tila your thread is exiting, and tighten. Sew through the same hole of the Tila just added and the RH of the center Tila **(photo h)**.
6 Pick up a Tila (RH), and sew through the RH of the previous Tila in the bottom row, the LH of the Tila in the center row, and the RH of the Tila in the top row **(photo i)**.
7 Sew through the LH of the Tila just added in the top row, and continue straight through the beadwork to exit the LH of the Tila in the bottom row. Continue through the open hole of the same Tila, and continue straight through the beadwork to exit the corre-

sponding open hole of the Tila in the top row **(photo j)**.
8 Repeat steps 5–7 for the length of the beadwork, ending and adding thread as needed. After the last stitch, sew through the LH of the Tila your thread is exiting in the top row, and continue straight through the beadwork to exit the LH of the last Tila in the bottom row.
9 Flip the beadwork as shown so your thread is exiting the RH of the Tila in the top row **(photo k)**.

Outer rows

1 To begin the top outer row, pick up a Tila (LH), sew through the open RH of the same Tila, and the LH of the Tila directly below the one your thread is exiting. Continue straight through the beadwork to exit the LH

Difficulty rating

    ⬡

Materials
orange bracelet 7¼ in. (18.4 cm)
- **9 g** 5 x 2.3 x 1.9 mm Half Tila beads (Miyuki 462, metallic gold iris)
- **146** 3 mm bicone crystals (Swarovski, astral pink)
- **2 g** 15º seed beads in each of 2 colors:
  - color A (Japanese P486, permanent metallic burnt orange)
  - color B (Miyuki 460A, raspberry bronze iris)
- toggle clasp
- Fireline 4 lb. test
- beading needles, #11 or #12

fuchsia bracelet colors
- 5 x 2.3 x 1.9 mm Half Tila beads (Miyuki 4571, crystal magic orchid)
- 3 mm bicone crystals (Swarovski, fuchsia)
- 15º seed beads
  - color A (Japanese SB3249, silver-lined transparent amethyst)
  - color B (Japanese 329B, celadon-lined green)

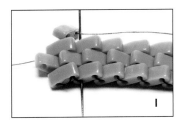

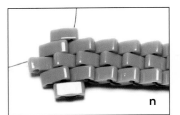

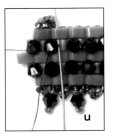

of the corresponding Tila in the bottom row **(photo l)**.

2 To begin the bottom outer row, pick up a Tila (LH), sew through the open RH of the same Tila, and the RH of the previous Tila in the next row. Continue straight through the following two Tilas **(photo m)**. Skip the LH of the Tila in the top outer row, and sew though the RH of the same Tila **(photo n)**.

3 Pick up a Tila (RH), and sew through the RH of the Tila your thread is exiting and the same hole of the Tila just added, and continue straight through the next three Tilas.

4 Pick up a Tila (RH), and sew through the RH of the previous Tila in the same row. Continue straight through the beadwork to exit the RH of

the Tila in the top outer row.

5 Sew through the LH of the Tlia just added in the top row, and continue straight through the beadwork to exit the LH of the Tila in the bottom row. Sew through the open hole of the same Tila, and continue straight through the beadwork to exit the open hole of the Tila in the top row.

6 Repeat steps 3–5 for the length of the beadwork, ending and adding thread as needed. Sew through the LH of the Tila in the top outer row.

Crystal embellishment

1 Pick up a 3 mm bicone crystal, and sew through the LH of the second-to-last Tila in the center row **(photo o)**. Pick up a crystal, and sew

through the LH of the end Tila in the bottom row **(photo p)**.

2 Sew through the RH of the next Tila in the bottom row, and continue through the beadwork to exit the corresponding RH of the Tila in the top row. Sew through the LH of the same Tila **(photo q)**.

3 Repeat steps 1–2 for the remainder of the beadwork, ending and adding thread as needed. When finished, your thread should exit the LH of the last Tila in the bottom row.

4 Pick up a color A 15º seed bead, a color B 15º seed bead, a crystal, and a B, and sew back through the crystal. Pick up a B and an A, and sew through the RH of the same Tila. Continue through the LH of the next Tila in the same row **(photo r)**.

5 Pick up an A, a B, an A, a B, and an A, and sew through the RH of the same Tila. Continue through the LH of the next Tila in the same row **(photo s)**.

6 Repeat steps 4–5 for this

side of the beadwork, exiting the RH of the last Tila in the bottom row.

7 Pick up a crystal, and sew through the LH of the corresponding Tila in the center row. Pick up a crystal, and sew through the RH of the corresponding Tila in the top row **(photo t)**. End the thread.

8 Add 4 ft. (1.2 m) of thread to the beadwork, and exit the LH of the end Tila in the top row on the left end of the band. Repeat step 5 and then step 4 so that the embellishment alternates with the embellishment in the bottom row **(photo u)** for the remainder of the beadwork.

9 Sew through the beadwork to exit the open hole of the end Tila in the center row. Pick up five As, the clasp, and five As, and sew through the same hole of the Tila to form a loop **(photo v)**. Retrace the thread path several times, and end the working thread. Repeat this step at the tail end of the beadwork, and end the tail. ●

plain and simple

This bracelet also looks great without the top embellishment. If desired, skip steps 1–4 of "Crystal embellishment," and just embellish the edges.

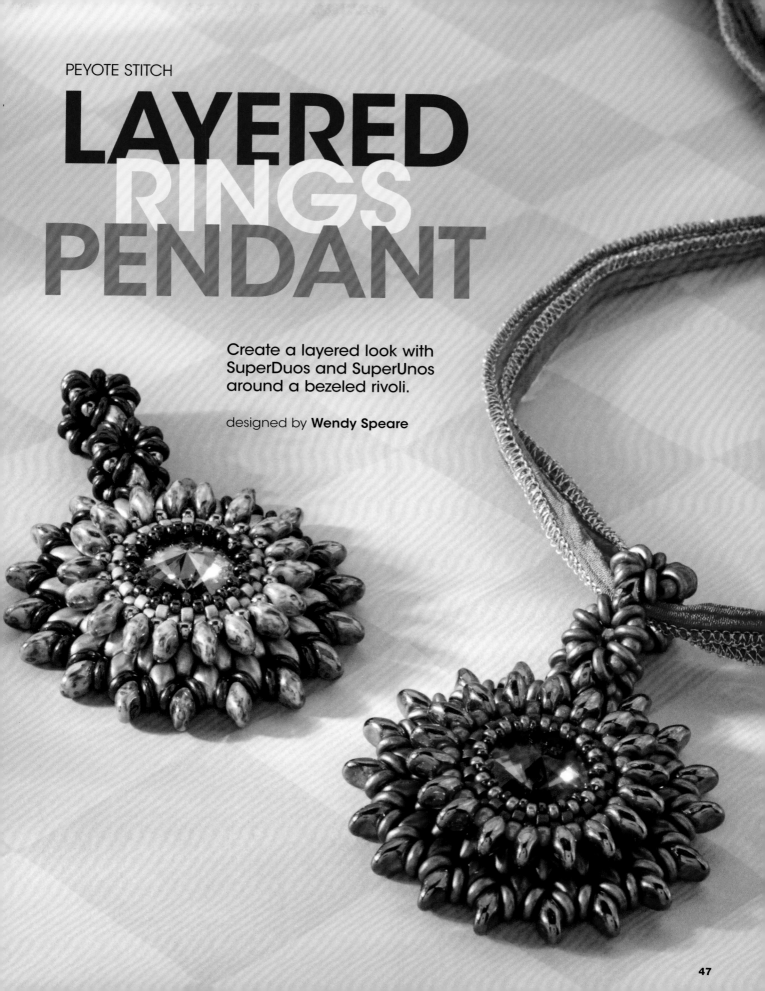

PEYOTE STITCH

LAYERED RINGS PENDANT

Create a layered look with SuperDuos and SuperUnos around a bezeled rivoli.

designed by **Wendy Speare**

Difficulty rating

Materials

purple/gold pendant 1⅝ in.
(4.1 cm)
- **1** 14 mm rivoli (Swarovski, volcano)
- **3 g** 2.5 x 5 mm SuperUno beads
  (gold luster)
- 2.5 x 5 mm SuperDuo beads
  - **3 g** color A (pastel Bordeaux)
  - **4** color B (a color similar to the
  SuperUnos; gold luster)
- **3 g** 1 x 3.8 mm O-beads (metallic mix)
- **1 g** 11º seed beads (Toho PF485, rose
  copper matte permanent galvanized)
- **1 g** 11º cylinder beads (Miyuki DB323,
  matte metallic purple iris)
- **1 g** 15º seed beads (Miyuki 4208,
  Duracoat galvanized berry)
- **1 g** 15º Charlotte beads (purple iris)
- Fireline, 6 lb. test
- beading needles, #11 or #12
- thread bobbin or piece of cardboard

green/brown pendant
- 14 mm rivoli (Swarovski, verde)
- 2.5 x 5 mm SuperUno beads (chalk
  lazure blue)
- 2.5 x 5 mm SuperDuo beads
  - color A (matte metallic flax)
  - color B (a color to match SuperUnos;
  luster opaque green)
- 1 x 3.8 mm O-beads (jet bronze)
- 11º seed beads (Toho 512, galvanized
  blue haze)
- 11º cylinder beads (Miyuki DB1834F,
  Duracoat galvanized matte champagne)
- 15º seed beads (Toho 222, dark bronze)
- 15º Charlotte beads (84, green iris/brown)

FIGURE 1

FIGURE 2

Bezel

1 On 5 ft. (1.5 m) of thread, pick up 36
11º cylinder beads, and sew though the
first three beads again to form a ring,
leaving a 3 ft. (.9 m) tail. These beads
will shift to form rounds 1 and 2 as the
next round is added. Wrap the tail on
a thread bobbin or piece of cardboard.
2 Work rounds of tubular peyote stitch
for the back of the bezel as follows, and
step up at the end of each round:
Round 3: Work a round using cylinders.
Rounds 4–5: Work both rounds using
15º seed beads.
Round 6: Work a round using 15º
Charlotte beads, using a tight tension,
and sew through the beadwork to exit
a cylinder in round 1.
3 Flip the beadwork over, and place
the rivoli face up into the beadwork.
Stitching off the cylinders in round 1,
work a round of 15º seed beads and
a round of 15º Charlottes for the front
of the bezel, using a tight tension.
4 Sew through the beadwork to exit
a cylinder in round 2. This is the center
round of cylinders in the bezel.

Upper layer of embellishment

Work rounds of circular peyote stitch
as follows:
Round 1: Working off the center round
of the bezel, stitch a round using 11º
seed beads, and step up at the end of
the round **(figure 1, a–b)**. Only round 2
of the cylinders in the bezel is shown for
clarity in the illustration.
Round 2: Working off the 11ºs just
added, stitch a round using SuperUnos
(b–c), and retrace the thread path.
End the thread.

Lower layer of embellishment

1 Unwind the tail from the thread
bobbin, and attach a needle. With
the back of the bezel facing up, sew
through the beadwork to exit a round
1 cylinder in the bezel.
2 Work rounds of circular peyote stitch
as follows:
Round 1: Working off the round 1
cylinders, stitch a round using 15º seed
beads, and step up at the end of the
round **(figure 2, a–b)**. Only round 1 of
the cylinders in the bezel is shown for
clarity in the illustration.

FIGURE 3

FIGURE 4

FIGURE 5

Round 2: Working off the 15ºs just added, stitch a round using color A SuperDuos **(b–c)**, and retrace the thread path (not shown in the illustration). Sew through the first A added, and continue through the open hole of the same A **(c–d)**.
Round 3: Sewing through the open holes of the As, work another round using As **(d–e)**, and retrace the thread path (not shown in the illustration). Sew through the first A added in this round, and continue through the open hole of the same A **(e–f)**.
Round 4: Pick up an O-bead, a SuperUno, and an O-bead, and sew

through the next A. Repeat this stitch 16 times, leaving one space open **(figure 3, a–b)**. Pick up an O-bead, a color B SuperDuo, and an O-bead, and sew through the next A **(b–c)**. Retrace the thread path, and end the thread.

Bail

1 On 2 ft. (61 cm) of thread, attach a stop bead leaving a 6-in. (15 cm) tail. With the front of the pendant facing up, sew through the open hole of the SuperDuo added in the last round **(figure 4, point a)**.
2 Pick up an O-bead and an 11º seed bead three times, and then pick up an O-bead and a B. Continue by picking up an O-bead and an 11º seed bead three times, and then pick up an O-bead. Sew though the hole in the B your thread exited at the start of the step to form a ring **(a–b)**. Retrace the thread path (not shown in the illustration), and sew through the first eight beads added **(b–c)**. Continue through the open hole of the B your thread is exiting **(c–d)**.

■	11º cylinder bead
●	11º seed bead
◗	2.5 x 5 mm SuperUno bead
●	15º seed bead
◗	2.5 x 5 mm SuperDuo bead, color A
▬	1 x 3.8 mm O-bead
◗	2.5 x 5 mm SuperDuo bead, color B

3 Repeat step 2 two more times.
4 Turn the beadwork over so the back of the pendant is facing up, and remove the stop bead. Pick up an O-bead and an 11º seed bead three times, and then pick up an O-bead. Sew through the bottom hole of the B in the outer round of the pendant **(figure 5, a–b)**. Pick up an O-bead and an 11º seed bead three times, and then pick up an O-bead. Sew through the hole in the B your thread exited at the start of the step **(b–c)**. Retrace the thread path, and end the working thread and tail. ●

Artfully
adorned
bracelet

Stitch two-hole lentils, tiles, and fire-polished beads into an arching statement bracelet.

designed by **Nichole Starman**

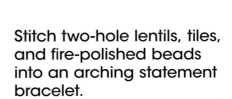

know as you go
Double-check that both holes of all two-hole beads are open.

Difficulty rating

Materials
teal bracelet 7½ in. (19.1 cm)
- **19** 6 mm CzechMates two-hole tile beads (ash halo)
- 6 mm CzechMates two-hole lentil beads
  - **40** color A (steel blue)
  - **84** color B (chartreuse bronze Picasso)
- **18** 6 mm pearls (Swarovski, iridescent green)
- **38** 4 mm fire-polished beads (azurite halo)
- **19** 3 mm fire-polished beads (azurite halo)
- **3 g** 11º seed beads (Toho 1703, gilded marble turquoise)
- **1 g** 15º seed beads (Toho 284, aqua gold-lined)
- Fireline, 8 lb. test
- beading needles, #12
- double-strand slide lock clasp

purple bracelet
- 6 mm CzechMates two-hole tile beads (luster opaque green)
- 6 mm CzechMates two-hole lentil beads
  - color A (iris purple)
  - color B (ashen gray moon dust)
- 6 mm pearls (iridescent purple)
- 4 mm fire-polished beads (luster opaque amethyst)
- 3 mm fire-polished beads (opaque green luster)
- 11º seed beads (Czech, silver-lined deep amethyst)
- 15º seed beads (Toho 999, gold-lined black diamond AB)

Base
For the purposes of these instructions, the two-hole tile beads will have a right side hole (RH) and a left side hole (LH).
1 On 2 yd. (1.8 m) of thread and leaving a 6-in. (15 cm) tail, pick up a two-hole tile bead. Sew through the open hole of the same tile (RH), and continue through both holes again, exiting the RH **(figure 1)**.
2 Pick up an 11º seed bead, a color A two-hole lentil, an 11º, and a tile, sewing through both holes **(figure 2, a–b)**. Repeat this stitch **(b–c)** until you've used all of the tiles. If you need to adjust the length of the bracelet, do so now but be sure to finish with an odd number of tiles. Each tile adds about ⅜ in. (1 cm) to the finished length. Sew back through the last tile (LH) added **(figure 3, a–b)**. It is important to leave a little wiggle room between the beads in the base. The beadwork will naturally cinch up as you add layers.
3 Pick up an 11º, an A lentil, and an 11º, and sew through the next tile (RH), and continue through the LH of the same tile **(b–c)**. Repeat this stitch **(c–d)** for the length of the base.
4 At the end of the base, pick up two 11ºs, a 4 mm fire-polished bead, and an 11º, and sew through the inner hole of the following A lentil **(figure 4, a–b)**.
5 Pick up an 11º, a 4 mm, and an 11º, and sew through the inner hole of the following A lentil **(b–c)**. Repeat this stitch for the length of the base. The slack in the bracelet will start to cinch up as this layer is added.

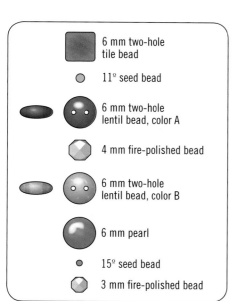

■	6 mm two-hole tile bead
●	11º seed bead
⬭ ●	6 mm two-hole lentil bead, color A
⬡	4 mm fire-polished bead
⬭ ●	6 mm two-hole lentil bead, color B
●	6 mm pearl
•	15º seed bead
⬡	3 mm fire-polished bead

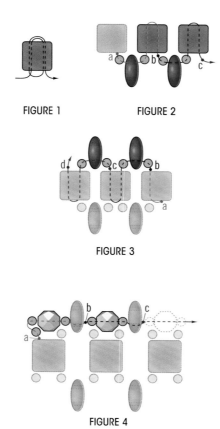

FIGURE 1   FIGURE 2

FIGURE 3

FIGURE 4

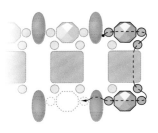

FIGURE 5

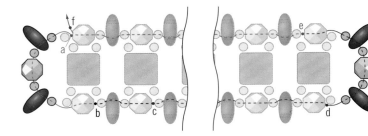

FIGURE 6

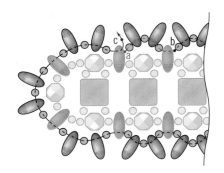

FIGURE 7

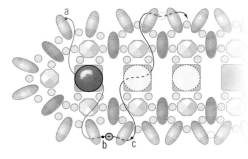

FIGURE 8

6 At the end of the bracelet pick up an 11º, a 4 mm, and two 11ºs, and sew through the RH of the last tile. Pick up two 11ºs, a 4 mm, and an 11º, and sew through the inner hole of the following A lentil **(figure 5)**.

7 Keeping the tension the same as the first side, repeat step 5 for the length of the bracelet. After sewing through the last lentil, pick up an 11º, a 4 mm, and two 11ºs, and sew through the LH of the last tile. Massage the base between your fingers to ease any stiff points, and end the threads.

8 Place the base horizontally on your work surface, and attach a comfortable length of thread, exiting the end 4 mm on the top left edge of the base with the needle facing away from the beadwork **(figure 6, point a)**.

9 Pick up an 11º, an A lentil, an 11º, a 4 mm, an 11º, an A lentil, and an 11º, and sew through the corresponding 4 mm on the bottom edge of the base **(a–b)**.

10 Sew through the following 11º, A lentil (inner hole), 11º, and 4 mm **(b–c)**. Repeat to sew through the entire edge, exiting the last 4 mm **(c–d)**.

11 Repeat step 9 for this end of the base except sew through the corresponding 4 mm on the top edge of the base **(d–e)**. Repeat step 10 **(e–f)**, and end the working thread and tail.

12 With the base horizontally on your work surface, attach a stop bead to 1 yd. (.9 m) of thread and sew through the open hole of the end A lentil on the top left edge of the base with the needle pointing away from the end

of the base **(figure 7, point a)**. Pick up an 11º, a color B lentil, an 11º, a B lentil, and an 11º, and sew through the open hole of the following A lentil **(a–b)**. Repeat this stitch around the perimeter, exiting the A lentil your thread exited at the beginning of this step **(b–c)**. Remove the stop bead, and end the working thread and tail.

Top layer

1 With the base placed horizontally on your work surface, attach a stop bead to 1 yd. (.9 m) of thread, and sew through the open hole of the second to last B lentil added in step 12 of "Base" with the needle pointing toward the beadwork **(figure 8, point a)**.

2 Pick up a 6 mm pearl, cross over to the bottom edge of the base, and sew

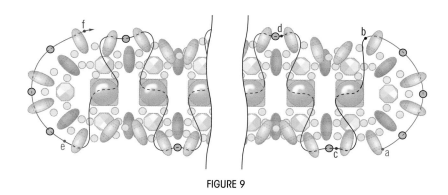

FIGURE 9

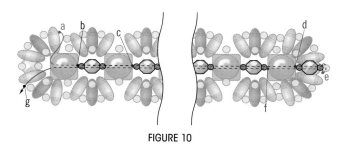

FIGURE 10

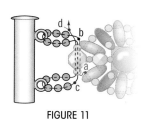

FIGURE 11

through the open hole of the second B lentil in the opposite set **(a–b)**. Pick up an 11º, and sew through the open hole of the next B lentil **(b–c)**. Repeat these stitches in an alternating zigzag pattern for the length of the base, pulling the pearls to the center of the base. End after adding a pearl.

3 Pick up an 11º, and sew through the open hole of the next B lentil. Repeat this stitch twice **(figure 9, a–b)**. Sew back through the next pearl and the open hole of the following B lentil on the other edge of the base **(b–c)**.

4 Pick up an 11º, and sew through the open hole of the next B lentil, the following pearl, and the open hole of the next B lentil on the top edge **(c–d)**. Repeat this stitch in an alternating zigzag pattern for the remainder of the base **(d–e)**.

5 Pick up an 11º and sew through the open hole of the next B lentil. Repeat this stitch twice **(e–f)**. Note after picking up the last 11º, you will be back at the start. Remove the stop bead, and tie the working thread and tail together. With the working thread, sew through the next lentil. End the tail.

6 Sew through the end pearl **(figure 10, a–b)**. Pick up a 15º seed bead, a 3 mm fire-polished bead, and a 15º, and sew through the next pearl **(b–c)**. Repeat this stitch for the length of the band **(c–d)**.

7 Pick up a 15º, a 3 mm, and a 15º, and sew through the 11º at the end of the band **(d–e)**. Sew back through the 15º, 3 mm, and 15º just added, and continue through the following pearl **(e–f)**.

8 Continue through the remaining sets of a 15º, a 3 mm, a 15º and a pearl on the center of the band exiting the first pearl added **(f–g)**.

9 For the final stitch, work as in step 7. End the working thread.

Clasp

1 Add 12 in. (30 cm) of thread to the base, and exit the 11º, 4 mm, and 11º on the end of the base **(figure 11, a–b)**.

2 Pick up three 11ºs, sew through a loop of the clasp, pick up three 11ºs, and sew back through the 11º, 4 mm, and 11º **(b–c)**. Repeat for the other clasp loop **(c–d)**, retrace the thread path twice, and end the thread.

3 Repeat steps 1 and 2 on the other end of the base. ◐

THREE-DROP PEYOTE STITCH

Christmas sweater
bracelet

Stitch up a Christmas sweater motif (and not the ugly kind!) for some holly-jolly holiday wear.

designed by **Josie Fabre**

Bracelet band

1 On a comfortable length of thread, attach a stop bead, leaving a 6-in. (15 cm) tail. Starting at the lower-left corner of the **pattern**, pick up 11º cylinder beads for rows 1 and 2: one green, one cream, one red, one green, 16 cream, one green, one cream, one green, and one cream.

2 Following the **pattern**, work in three-drop peyote stitch using the appropriate color cylinders. End and add thread as needed while you stitch, and end the working thread and tail when you complete the band.

Toggle button

Add 12 in. (30 cm) of thread to the starting end of the bracelet, and exit a trio of up-beads in the end row so that your thread is exiting closest to the center of the row. Pick up seven red cylinders, the shank of the button, and seven red cylinders, and sew back through the same trio of up-beads **(figure 1)**. Sew through the beadwork to exit the same trio of up-beads with your thread once again exiting closest to the center of the row, and retrace the thread path of the button connection. End the thread.

Toggle ring

1 Add 12 in. (30 cm) of thread to the other end of the bracelet. Notice that one corner on this end begins with a trio of up-beads. Sew through the beadwork to exit these three up-beads, and then continue through the next three down-beads and three up-beads.

2 Pick up 37 cream cylinders, and sew through the next trio of up-beads with your needle pointing toward the beads your thread exited at the start of this step **(figure 2, a–b)**.

3 Sew through the beadwork to exit the first cream cylinder added in step 2. Work in peyote stitch around the loop, using one cream cylinder per stitch **(b–c)**. Sew into the bracelet and end the thread. ●

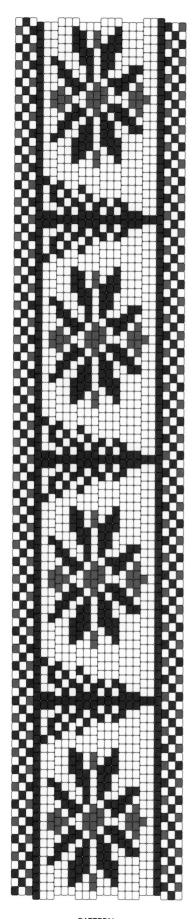

PATTERN

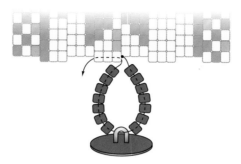

- ☐ 11º cylinder bead, cream
- ☐ 11º cylinder bead, green
- ☐ 11º cylinder bead, red

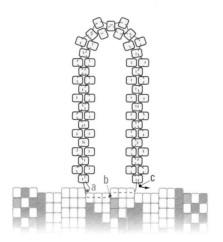

FIGURE 1

FIGURE 2

Difficulty rating

Materials
bracelet 8 in. (20 cm)

- $^{13}/_{16}$-in. (2.1 cm) shank button
- 11º Miyuki Delica cylinder beads
  - **7 g** cream (DB0732, opaque dark cream)
  - **5 g** green (DB0663, dyed opaque olive)
  - **1 g** red (DB0723, opaque red)
- nylon beading thread, or Fireline 6 lb. test
- beading needles, #12

BEAD WEAVING

QUADRA WEAVE BRACELET

Add QuadraTiles to seed beads and fire-polished beads for a casual bracelet and pair of earrings.

designed by **Olga Haserodt**

Base

With the QuadraTile in the position shown **(figure 1)**, the holes will be referred to as top hole (TH), bottom hole (BH), left hole (LH), and right hole (RH). Make sure all the holes of the QuadraTiles are open.

1 On 7 ft. (2.1 m) of thread, pick up a QuadraTile (LH) leaving a 12-in. (30 cm) tail.

2 Pick up a color A 15º seed bead, an 11º seed bead, and an A, and sew through the QuadraTile (RH) from top to bottom **(figure 2, a–b)**. Pick up an A, an 11º, and an A, and sew through the QuadraTile (LH) from bottom to top **(b–c)**. Continue through the next A, 11º, A, and the QuadraTile (RH) from top to bottom **(c–d)**, and pull the thread tight.

3 Pick up an A, an 11º, an A, a QuadraTile (LH), an A, an 11º, and an A, and sew through the RH in the previous QuadraTile again, from top to bottom **(figure 3, a–b)**. Continue through the next A, 11º, A, and QuadraTile (LH) from bottom to top **(b–c)**.

4 Repeat steps 2–3 for the desired length minus ½ in. (1.3 cm) for the clasp, and then repeat step 2 once more to embellish the last QuadraTile.

5 Pick up two As, and sew through the QuadraTile (BH) from bottom to top **(figure 4, a–b)**. Pick up two As, and sew through the QuadraTile (RH) from top to bottom **(b–c)**.

6 Pick up two As, and sew through the QuadraTile (TH) from bottom to top **(figure 5, a–b)**. Pick up two As, and sew through the QuadraTile (RH) from top to bottom **(b–c)**. Continue through the first two As added in this step, and the QuadraTile (TH)

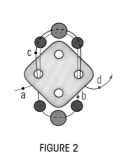

top hole

left hole ___ right hole

bottom hole

FIGURE 1

FIGURE 2

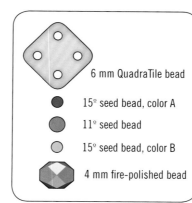

6 mm QuadraTile bead

● 15º seed bead, color A

● 11º seed bead

○ 15º seed bead, color B

⬡ 4 mm fire-polished bead

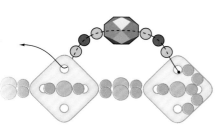

FIGURE 3

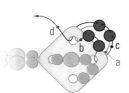

FIGURE 4

FIGURE 5

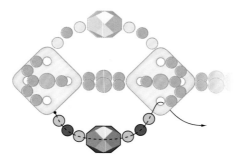

FIGURE 6

FIGURE 7

Difficulty rating

Materials

bracelet 6¾ in. (17.1 cm)
- **18** 6 mm CzechMates four-hole QuadraTile beads (opaque luster Picasso)
- **34** 4 mm fire-polished beads metallic suede-light green
- **1 g** 11º seed beads (Toho 421, gold lustered transparent pink)
- **1 g** 15º seed beads
  - color A (Toho 706, matte iris teal)
  - color B (Toho 221, bronze)
- **1** lobster claw clasp
- **1** 5 mm split or jump ring
- **1**¾ in. (4.4 cm) extension chain (optional)
- Fireline, 6 lb. test
- beading needles, #11 or #12
- **2** pairs of chainnose, flatnose, and/or bentnose pliers

pair of earrings 1⅛ in. (2.9 cm)
- same beads and colors used in the bracelet
- **1** pair of earring findings

from bottom to top **(c–d)**.

7 Pick up a color B 15º seed bead, an A, a B, a 4 mm fire-polished bead, a B, an A, and a B, and sew through the next QuadraTile (TH) from bottom to top **(figure 6)**. Repeat this stitch for the length of the base.

8 Pick up two As, and sew through the QuadraTile (LH) from top to bottom. Pick up two As, and sew through the QuadraTile (TH) from bottom

to top. Continue through the first two As added in this step, and the QuadraTile (LH) from top to bottom.

9 Pick up two As, and sew through the QuadraTile (BH) from bottom to top. Pick up two As, and sew through the QuadraTile (LH) from top to bottom. Continue through the first two As added in this step, but do not sew through the QuadraTile.

10 With the thread exiting

the two 15ºs on the bottom of the end QuadraTile, pick up a B, an A, a B, a 4 mm, a B, an A, and a B, and sew through the next QuadraTile (BH) from top to bottom **(figure 7)**. Repeat this stitch for the length of the base, making sure the base is not twisted and is a mirror image of the first side.

11 Sew through the next two As and the QuadraTile (RH) bottom to top.

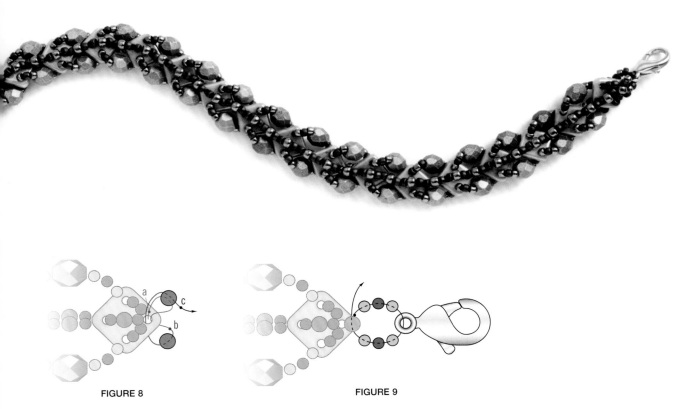

FIGURE 8

FIGURE 9

12 Pick up an 11º, and sew back down through the same hole in the QuadraTile **(figure 8, a–b)**. Pick up an 11º, and continue back up through the same hole of the QuadraTile, and the 11º added at the beginning of the step **(b–c)**.

Clasp

1 Pick up a B, an A, a B, the loop of the lobster claw, a B, an A, and a B, and sew through the 11º your thread exited at the start of the step, going in the same direction to form a loop **(figure 9)**. Retrace the

thread path, and sew down through the QuadraTile (RH) and the nearest 11º. Pick up a B, an A, and a B, and sew through the loop of the lobster claw just added. Pick up a B, an A, and a B, and sew through the 11º your thread is exiting to form another loop. Retrace the thread path, and end the thread.

2 If desired, attach the extension chain to a 5 mm split ring. Repeat step 1 with the tail thread, sewing through the split ring instead of the lobster claw, and end the tail.

Earrings

1 On 1 yd. (.9 m) of thread, repeat the steps for "Base" using three QuadraTiles for each earring.

2 For each earring, repeat step 1 of "Clasp," sewing through the loop of an earring wire instead of the lobster claw. ●

Mouchette
bangle

The term mouchette refers to the dagger-like pattern in the Gothic windows and vaulted ceilings that inspired this elegant, edgy design.

designed by **Nichole Starman**

Difficulty rating

Materials

silver/khaki bangle 7¾ in. (19.7 cm) circumference
- 5 x 16 mm CzechMates two-hole daggers
  - **21** color A (silver)
  - **40** color B (opaque ultra luster green)
- **40** 5 mm melon beads (milky caramel)
- **12 g** 8º hex-cut beads (Toho 512F, higher-metallic frosted blue haze)
- **3 g** 11º seed beads in each of **2** colors:
  - color C (Toho 999, gold-lined rainbow black diamond)
  - color D (Toho 459, gold-lustered dark topaz)
- Fireline 6 lb. test
- beading needles, #10
- bobbin or piece of cardboard

blue bangle colors:
- 5 x 16 mm CzechMates two-hole daggers
  - color A (matte iris purple)
  - color B (Persian turquoise)
- 5 mm melon beads (satin lavender)
- 8º hex-cut beads (Toho 705, matte raku blue/plum)
- 11º seed beads in each of **2** colors:
  - color C (Toho 87DF, frosted transparent cobalt AB)
  - color D (Toho 132, opaque lustered turquoise)

salmon bangle colors:
- 5 x 16 mm CzechMates two-hole daggers
  - color A (opaque luster Picasso)
  - color B (milky pink Celsian)
- 5 x 6 mm rondelles (white opal, in place of 5 mm melon beads)
- 8º hex-cut beads (Miyuki 275, dark peach lined crystal AB)
- 11º seed beads in each of **2** colors:
  - color C (Miyuki F471, galvanized gold matte)
  - color D (Miyuki 372, semi-frosted berry)

FIGURE 1

FIGURE 2

FIGURE 3

FIGURE 4

FIGURE 5

FIGURE 6

Bangle base

The two-hole daggers will be referred to as having a lower hole (near the end of the bead) and an upper hole (closer to the middle of the bead).

1 Attach a stop bead at the center of a comfortable length of thread. Wind half of the thread onto a bobbin or piece of cardboard to keep it out of the way temporarily; this will be called the tail thread. With the remaining thread, pick up a repeating pattern of a color A 5 x 16 mm two-hole dagger bead (lower hole) and three 8º hex-cut beads 21 times. To adjust the size of the bangle, pick up more or fewer repeats. Each repeat equals about ⅜ in. (1 cm). Sew through the first dagger to form a ring. These beads will form the first two rounds as the next round is added.

2 Work in rounds of tubular peyote stitch as follows, stepping up through the first bead added in each round to get into position to begin the next round. To keep the tension even, you will alternate the threads you stitch with.

Rounds 3 and 4: Work each round using hex beads **(figures 1 and 2)**.

Round 5: Unwind the tail thread, and remove the stop bead. With the tail, sew through the adjacent hex bead to exit the edge opposite round 4. Work a round with hex beads **(figure 3)**.

Round 6: With the first thread, work a round using hex beads **(figure 4, a–b)**.

Round 7: With the tail, work a round using hex beads **(c–d)**.

Round 8: With the first thread, work a round by alternating a hex bead and a color B dagger bead (lower hole). Note that the daggers added in this round should be spaced halfway between the daggers in the initial round **(figure 5)**.

Round 9: With the first thread, work the entire round with hex beads **(figure 6)**. End this thread.

Rounds 10 and 11: With the tail, repeat rounds 8 and 9 on the other edge **(figures 7 and 8)**. End the tail.

Embellishments

1 On a comfortable length of thread, attach a stop bead, leaving a 6-in. (15 cm) tail, and sew through the upper hole of a B dagger in an outer round.

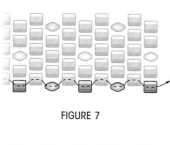

FIGURE 7

FIGURE 8

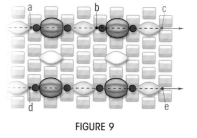

FIGURE 9

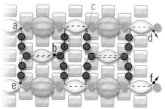

FIGURE 10

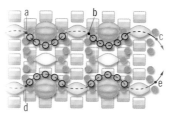

FIGURE 11

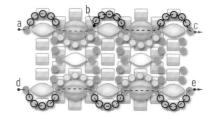

FIGURE 12

FIGURE 13

Pick up a color C 11º seed bead, a 5 mm melon bead, and a C, and sew through the upper hole of the next B dagger in the round **(figure 9, a–b)**. Repeat this stitch **(b–c)** to complete the round, and tie the working thread and tail together with a square knot. End the tail but not the working thread.

2 Repeat step 1 to add another thread with a stop bead and embellish the other outer round of B daggers **(d–e)**.

3 With one thread, exit the upper hole of a B dagger in an outer round. Pick up three color C 11º seed beads, and sew through the upper hole of the next A dagger in the middle round **(figure 10, a–b)**. Pick up three Cs, and sew through the next B dagger in the same outer round **(b–c)**. Repeat these two stitches **(c–d)** to complete the round.

4 With the other thread, work as in step 3, but for each stitch pick up only two Cs instead of three, and sew through a C both before and after each center dagger instead of sewing through only the dagger **(e–f)**.

5 With one thread, exit the upper hole of a B dagger in an outer round. Pick up five D 11ºs, and sew through the next dagger, forming a loop around the inner edge of the adjacent melon bead **(figure 11, a–b)**. Repeat this stitch **(b–c)** to complete the round. Repeat this step with the other thread **(d–e)**.

6 With one thread, sew through the beadwork to exit a C 11º, melon, and C 11º. Pick up five D 11ºs, and sew through the next C 11º, melon, and C 11º **(figure 12, a–b)**. Repeat this stitch **(b–c)** to complete the round. Repeat this step with the other thread to embellish the other edge **(d–e)**.

7 With one thread, exit a hex bead in an outer round, next to a melon bead. Pick up four C 11ºs, and sew through the first C again, forming a small loop. Sew through the next hex bead in the outer round **(figure 13, a–b)**. Pick up a D 11º, sew through the third D 11º added in step 6, pick up a D 11º, and sew through the next hex bead **(b–c)**. Repeat these stitches to complete the round **(c–d)**, and end the thread. Repeat this step with the other thread. **o**

bottom	side	top	
⬭	▬▬	⬭	5 x 16 mm two-hole dagger bead, color A
⬭	▬▬	⬭	5 x 16 mm two-hole dagger bead, color B
	🔴		5 mm melon bead
	▭		8º hex-cut bead
	●		11º seed bead, color C
	○		11º seed bead, color D

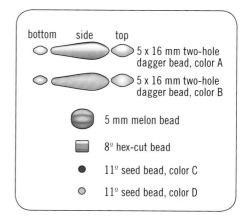

TUBULAR PEYOTE

Swirls. & twirls

necklace and earrings

Create stunning jewelry using
a wide assortment of colorful seed beads
to form curved shell-shaped components.

designed by **Annette Mackrel**

know before you go

- With so many colors to keep track of, label your beads and arrange them in alphabetical order (below, showing the beads we used for testing).

- Magatama holes are angled. On one side, the hole is near the center of the bead; on the other side, the hole is closer to the end of the bead. Always pick up the bead with the needle exiting near the center.

- For rounds 3–9 on each component, always sew through the furthest bead of the next color.

- To properly form each component, it is important to pull the tension tight after each stitch.

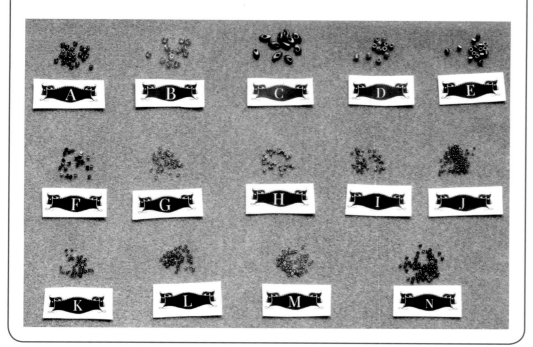

Difficulty rating

◆ ◆ ◆ ◆ ◇

Materials
necklace 19 in. (48 cm)
- **13 g** 4 mm magatama drop beads, color C (opaque turquoise Picasso)
- 6º seed beads
  - **18 g** color B (Toho 162C, transparent rainbow topaz)
  - **18 g** color D (Miyuki 2425F, silver-lined matte teal)
- 8º seed beads
  - **5 g** color A (Miyuki 2035, khaki iris matte)
  - **5 g** color E (Miyuki 93F, silver-lined matte gold)
- **3 g** 11º triangle beads, color F (Toho 223, bronze metallic)
- 11º seed beads
  - **2 g** color G (Toho 2120, silver-lined light pink opal)
  - **2 g** color H (F460C, matte metallic copper rainbow)
  - **2 g** color L (Toho PF551, peach gold metallic)
  - **2 g** color M (Toho 997, gold-lined rainbow light sapphire)
  - **2 g** color N (Toho 2104, silver-lined turquoise opal)
- 11º cylinder beads
  - **2 g** color I (Miyuki DB0608, silver-lined blue zircon)
  - **2 g** color K (Miyuki DB0855, matte orange AB)
- **1 g** 15º seed beads, color J (Toho 994, gold-lined rainbow crystal)
- **1** 10 mm strong magnetic clasp
- Fireline 8 lb. test
- beading needles, #12

pair of earrings 2 in. (5 cm)
(same colors used in necklace)
- **2** 5 mm pearls (olive green)
- **1** pair of earring findings

Neck straps

1 On a comfortable length of thread, pick up two of each bead as follows: Color A 8º seed bead, color B 6º seed bead, color C magatama bead, color D 6º seed bead, color E 8º seed bead, color F 11º triangle bead, color G 11º seed bead, color H 11º seed bead, color I 11º seed bead, color J 15º seed bead, color K 11º seed bead, color L 11º seed bead, color M 11º seed bead, and color N 11º seed bead. Sew through the beads again, and continue through the first two As to form a ring leaving an 18-in. (46 cm) tail

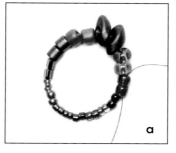

a

(photo a). These beads will shift to form rounds 1 and 2 as the next round is added.
2 Work round 3 in tubular peyote as follows (picking up the same type of bead as the one your thread is exiting for each stitch): Pick up an A, skip the first B, and sew through the following B.

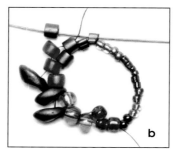

b

Pick up a B, skip the first C, and sew through the next C. Pick up a C, skip the first D, and sew through the following D. Pick up a D, skip the first E, and sew through the next E. Pick up an E, skip the first F, and sew through the following F **(photo b).** Continue picking up beads

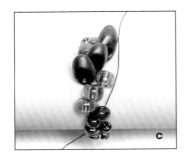
c

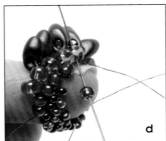
d

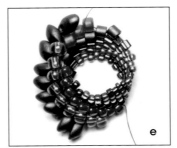
e

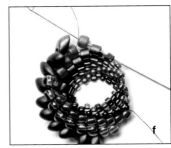
f

g

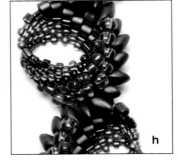

h

i

j

k

in alphabetical order. Step up through the A added in this round **(photo c)**. As you work this component, be sure to position the previous rounds on the left and add new rounds on the right. Also, angle the magatamas to the left. This will determine the direction the beads will swirl or counter swirl.

3 Rounds 4–9: Work as in round 3 **(photos d and e)**, being sure to step up through the A added in each round before starting the next round.

4 Sew through the next two Bs and two Cs. Pick up a C, and sew through the following D. Pick up a D, and sew through the next E **(photo f)**. Sew through the outer edge for reinforcement, and exit the last C added.

5 Pick up a C, and sew through the following D. Pick up a D and two each

of the following colors: E, F, G, H, I, J, K, L, M, N, A, B. Form a ring by sewing through the last two Cs **(photo g)** to form rounds 1 and 2 for the next component. Retrace the thread path to reinforce the connection.

6 To form the next component with a counter swirl, continue working in tubular peyote, following the established color pattern but position the existing rounds on the right, and add new rounds on the left. Angle the magatamas to the right. Work a total of nine rounds **(photo h)**, stepping up through color C at the end of each round.

7 Repeating steps 2–6, continue adding components in a swirl and counter swirl pattern until you have a total of nine components. End and add thread as needed. Do not end the

working thread or tail. Set the strand aside for later.

8 For the second neck strap, follow steps 1–3, but work in the opposite direction (counter swirl) by positioning existing rounds on the right and adding new rounds on the left **(photo i)**. Work in tubular peyote stitch for a total of nine rounds, making sure to step up through a color A at the end of each round **(photo j)** for the first component.

9 Repeat steps 4–7 following the alternating swirl pattern for the second neck strap, but on the ninth round of the ninth component, end after picking up a D and sewing through the following E.

Connection

1 Place the first neck strap on the left of your work surface and the second

neck strap on the right with the working thread ends next to each other and closest to you. Flip the pieces over, if needed, to position the color D 6º beads face up on each strap.

2 With the working thread from the second neck strap, zip the straps together: Sew through the F in round 9 of neck strap one, and then sew through the adjacent G in round 9 on neck strap two and the G in round 9 on neck strap one. Continue through the H on neck strap two **(photo k)**. Retrace the thread path several times to reinforce the join.

Centerpiece

1 Using the working thread from neck strap one, pick up a C, and sew through the following D. Pick up a D, and sew through the following E.

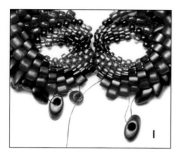

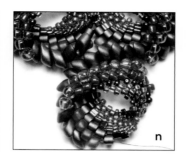

Sew through the beadwork to exit the outer C on the adjacent component of neck strap two with your needle exiting toward the center. Pick up a C, and sew through the following D. Pick up a D, and sew through the following E **(photo l)**.

2 Sew through the beadwork, and exit the C bead just added with the needle exiting toward the center. Pick up a C, and sew through the following D. Pick up a D and two each of the following colors: E, F, G, H, I, J, K, L, M, N, A, B. Form a ring by sewing through the last two Cs on the adjacent component from neck strap one to form rounds 1 and 2 for the centerpiece component **(photo m)**. Pick up a C and sew through the following D added in the new ring. Pick up a D, and sew through the next E.

3 Flip the necklace over so the B 8°s on each component are face up. Continue in tubular peyote stitch for a total of nine rounds stepping up through the C at the end of each round. After the ninth round, pick up a C, and sew through the following D. Pick up a D, and sew through the following E **(photo n)**.

4 Flip the necklace over so that the color B 8°s on each component are face down. With a new 18-in. (46 cm) thread, join the centerpiece component to the second neck strap by sewing through the last color D 8° added in the centerpiece

component, and the last color D 8° in each adjacent component **(photo o)**. Retrace the thread path for reinforce the connection, and end the thread.

Clasp

1 Using the tail thread from the first neck strap, retrace the thread path through the first two rounds and exit the A in round 1. Pick up an N, half the clasp, and an N, and sew through the following B **(photo p)**. Retrace the thread path several times, and end the thread.

2 Repeat step 1 for the second neck strap. End the working thread and tails for the entire necklace.

Earrings

1 Repeat steps 1–3 of "Neck straps" to make two separate components, but complete a total of 10 rounds for each component. Be sure to make the second component swirl in the opposite direction of the first.

2 Sew through the outer edge to add extra strength, and then sew diagonally through the beadwork to exit the first B added in round 1 with the needle exiting toward the color C magatama beads.

3 Pick up a J, an N, an L, a 6 mm pearl, an M, an L, the loop from an earring finding, a K, and an L, and sew back through the pearl **(photo q)**.

4 Pick up an H and an M, and sew through the adjacent B with the needle facing away from the magatamas **(photo r)**. Retrace the thread path several times. End the working thread and tail.

5 Repeat steps 2–4 with the second earring finding. ●

Winding trios bracelet

Make intricate components using two-hole triangles and SuperDuos, and connect them using two-hole tiles in a stylish zigzag pattern.

designed by **Akiko Nomura**

Triangle components

How to pick up triangle beads: With the point of the triangle with no hole facing away from you, pick up the bead through the left hole (LH) or the right hole (RH), per the instructions.

1 On 2 ft. (61 cm) of thread, pick up a repeating pattern of an 8º seed bead and a SuperDuo bead three times, leaving a 6-in. (15 cm) tail. Sew through the beads again, and tie a square knot with the working thread and tail. Sew through the following 8º **(figure 1)**.

2 Pick up an 11º seed bead, three color A 15º seed beads, and an 11º, and sew through the 8º your thread exited at the start of this step **(figure 2, a–b)**. Sew through the next SuperDuo and 8º **(b–c)**. Repeat this stitch twice to complete the round, and continue through the next 11º **(c–d)**.

3 Pick up a two-hole triangle (RH) from front to back and three 11ºs, and sew

through the open hole of the triangle from back to front, positioning the triangle behind the loop of beads added in the previous step **(figure 3, a–b)**. Continue through the adjacent 11º, 8º, and 11º **(b–c)**.

4 Pick up a color B 15º seed bead, and sew through the open hole of the next SuperDuo. Pick up a B, and sew through the next 11º, 8º, and 11º **(c–d)**.

5 Repeat steps 3–4 twice to complete the round, and then sew through the

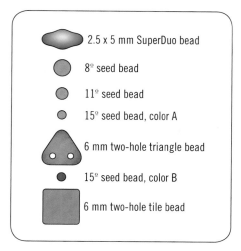

2.5 x 5 mm SuperDuo bead

8º seed bead

11º seed bead

15º seed bead, color A

6 mm two-hole triangle bead

15º seed bead, color B

6 mm two-hole tile bead

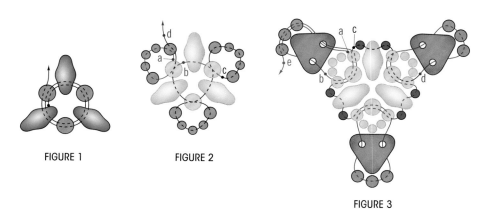

FIGURE 1

FIGURE 2

FIGURE 3

FIGURE 4

FIGURE 5

Difficulty rating

   ◯ ◯

Materials

teal bracelet 7¼ in. (18.4 cm)
- **30** 6 mm CzechMates two-hole triangle beads (matte iris brown)
- **20** 6 x 6 mm CzechMates two-hole tile beads (brown iris French beige)
- **30** 2.5 x 5 mm SuperDuo beads (BT6313, turquoise bronze Picasso)
- **3 g** 8º seed beads (Czech, matte gold)
- **4 g** 11º seed beads (Toho 221, bronze)
- 15º seed beads
  - **1 g** color A (Toho 221, bronze)
  - **1 g** color B (Toho 84, metallic green iris)
- **1** toggle clasp
- Fireline 6 lb. test
- beading needles, #11 or #12

purple bracelet colors
- 6 mm CzechMates two-hole triangle beads (bronze)
- 6 x 6 mm CzechMates two-hole tile beads (polychrome black currant)
- 2.5 x 5 mm SuperDuo beads (metallic suede pink)
- 8º seed beads (Toho 706, matte iris teal)
- 11º seed beads (Miyuki 4218, Duracoat dusty orchid)
- 15º seed beads
  - color A (Miyuki 4217, Duracoat sea foam)
  - color B (Toho 221, bronze)

first triangle added (RH), and the next set of three 11ºs **(d-e)**. This completes the front of the triangle component. Flip the beadwork so the back of the component faces up.
6 Pick up an 11º and an A, and sew through the inner hole of the next SuperDuo **(figure 4, a-b)**. Pick up an A and an 11º, and sew through the next set of three 11ºs **(b-c)**. Repeat these stitches twice to complete the round **(c-d)**.

7 Pick up an 11º, an 8º, and an 11º, and sew through the next set of three 11ºs **(figure 5, a-b)**. Repeat this stitch twice to complete the round **(b-c)**, and retrace the thread path. End the threads. Make nine more components for a 7¼-in. (18.4 cm) bracelet.

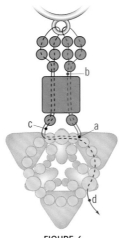

FIGURE 6

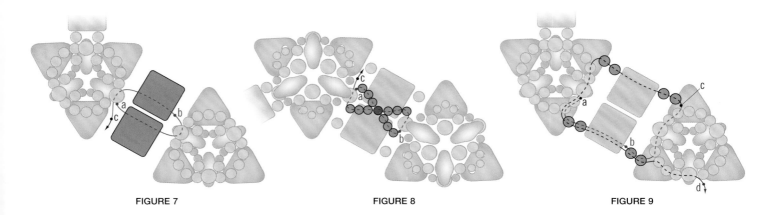

FIGURE 7   FIGURE 8   FIGURE 9

Connections

1 On a comfortable length of thread, add a stop bead, leaving a 6-in. (15 cm) tail, and sew through an 11º, 8º, and 11º on the back of a component.

2 Pick up an 11º, a two-hole tile bead, three 11ºs, the loop of a toggle ring, and two 11ºs. Sew back through the first 11º of the three just added **(figure 6, a–b)**. Continue through the same hole of the tile bead, and the next two 11ºs, 8º, and 11º **(b–c)**. Repeat these stitches, sewing through the other side of the tile bead, and retrace the thread path. Sew through the beadwork on the back of the component to exit the 8º on the adjacent side **(c–d)**.

3 Pick up a tile bead, and sew through an 8º on the back of a new component **(figure 7, a–b)**. Pick up a tile bead, and sew through the 8º your thread exited at the start of the step **(b–c)**. Flip the beadwork to work on the front.

4 Pick up three As, a B, and three As, and sew through the corresponding 8º on the new component, positioning the beads on top of the tile beads **(figure 8, a–b)**. Pick up three As, sew through the B just added, pick up three As, and sew through the 8º your thread exited at the start of the step **(b–c)**. Flip the beadwork to work on the back.

5 Sew through the next two 11ºs, pick up two 11ºs, and sew through the open hole of the nearest tile bead **(figure 9, a–b)**. Pick up two

11ºs, and sew through the next five beads as shown **(b–c)**. Pick up two 11ºs, sew through the open hole of the adjacent tile bead, pick up two 11ºs, and sew through the next 14 beads as shown to exit an 8º **(c–d)**.

6 Repeat steps 3–5 to add the remaining components making sure the components form a zigzag pattern. End and add thread as needed.

7 Work as in step 1–2 to add the toggle bar to the other end of the bracelet. Adjust the amount of 11ºs if needed for the toggle bar to work properly. Remove the stop bead, and end the remaining threads. ●

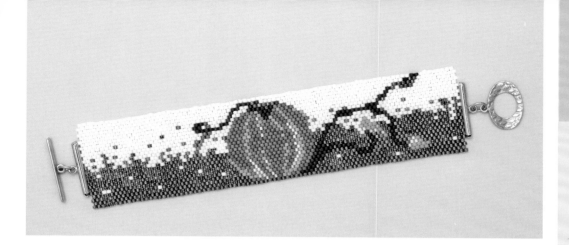

Materials

bracelet 7 in. (18 cm)

- 11º Miyuki Delica cylinder beads
  - 5 g white (DB0200, opaque white)
  - 3 g purple (DB0906, sparkling purple-lined crystal)
  - 3 g amethyst (DB0108, gold luster amethyst)
  - 1 g olive (DB0133, olive AB)
  - 1 g dark green (DB0797, matte opaque olive)
  - 2 g dark orange (DB0653, opaque pumpkin)
  - 1 g light orange (DB0651, opaque squash)
  - 1 g pale yellow (DB0233, lined crystal/yellow luster)
- toggle clasp
- **2** 20 mm Toob findings
- **2** 4 mm jump rings
- nylon beading thread, size D, or Fireline 6 lb. test
- beading needles, #11
- **2** pairs of chainnose, flatnose, and/or bentnose pliers

PEYOTE STITCH

Pumpkin patch bracelet

Get ready for fall with a peyote band featuring a favorite seasonal icon.

designed by **Julia Gerlach**

stepbystep

[1] On a comfortable length of thread, attach a stop bead (Basics), leaving a 10-in. (25 cm) tail. Reading the **pattern** starting at the bottom left-hand corner, pick up 26 11º cylinder beads for rows 1 and 2: one olive, nine purple, four amethyst, one white, one amethyst, and 10 white. Complete the band in flat even-count peyote stitch (Basics). End and add thread as needed (Basics), but do not end the working thread or tail when you complete the band.

[2] With the working thread, sew through the last row to exit the third up-bead from one edge with your needle pointing toward the other edge.

[3] Pick up a cylinder in the same color as the one your thread is exiting, and sew through the up-bead again. Continue through the last row to exit the next up-bead. Attach a cylinder to each of the next eight up-beads. End the thread.

[4] Slide a Toob finding over the beads added in the previous step, and use chainnose pliers to bend each end flap down to secure the finding.

[5] Open a 4 mm jump ring (Basics), and attach the Toob finding to half of the clasp.

[6] Remove the stop bead from the tail, and work as in steps 2–5 to finish the other end of the bracelet. ●

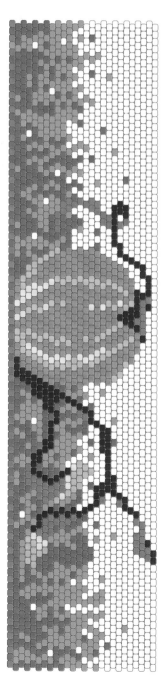

11º cylinder beads

- ⬜ white
- ⬛ purple
- ◩ amethyst
- ◩ olive
- ⬛ dark green
- ◩ dark orange
- ◩ light orange
- ⬜ pale yellow

PATTERN

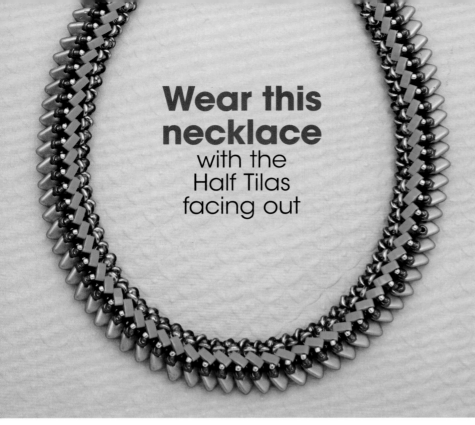

Wear this necklace with the Half Tilas facing out

Twist it for a spiral look

BEAD WEAVING

3 IN 1 NECKLACE

This unique necklace looks great with either side facing out or twisted.

designed by **Isabella Lam**

Necklace

When picking up the triangles, the point with no hole should be facing out and an open hole should be pointing up.

1 On a comfortable length of thread, pick up a 15º seed bead, an 11º seed bead, an 8º seed bead, a SuperDuo bead, a 15º, an 11º, an O-bead, a 3 mm bicone crystal, an O-bead, a Half Tila, a 15º, an 11º, an 8º, and a two-hole triangle. Sew through the beads again, and tie a square knot with the working thread and tail. Continue through the next 15º, 11º, 8º,

and SuperDuo, and exit the open hole of the same SuperDuo **(figure 1)**.

2 Pick up a SuperDuo, an 8º, an 11º, and a 15º, and sew through the open hole of the next triangle **(figure 2, a–b)**, making sure the new beads sit on top of the existing beads and the triangle still has the point with no hole pointing to the outside, and the hole your thread is exiting is pointing up.

3 Pick up a triangle, an 8º, an 11º, and a 15º, and sew through the open hole of the next Half Tila **(b–c)**.

4 Pick up a Half Tila, an O-bead, a crystal, an O-bead, an 11º, and a 15º, and sew through the open hole of the next SuperDuo **(c–d)**.

5 Repeat steps 2–4 for the desired length of the necklace, keeping a tight tension.

6 To work the last round, pick up an 8º, an 11º, and a 15º, and sew through the open hole of the next triangle **(figure 3, a–b)**. Pick up an 8º, an 11º, and a 15º, and sew through the open hole of the following Half Tila **(b–c)**. Sew through the next O-bead, crystal, O-bead, 11º, 15º, and the hole in the SuperDuo your

thread exited at the start of this step **(c–d)**. Retrace the thread path to tighten, exiting the same SuperDuo.

Clasp

1 Open a 6 mm jump ring, and attach the lobster claw clasp.

2 With the working thread, pick up six 11ºs and the jump ring with the clasp attached. Skip the next 8º, 11º, 15º, triangle, and 8º, and sew through the following 11º and 15º in the last round of the base **(figure 4, a–b)**. Pick up six 11ºs, and sew through the jump ring just added

Flip it so
the Super Duos
are facing
out

Difficulty rating

Materials
necklace 19 in. (48 cm)
plus extender chain
- **110** 6 mm CzechMates two-hole triangle beads (matte metallic copper)
- **110** 2.5 x 5 mm SuperDuo beads (pearl coat teal)
- **110** 5 x 2.3 x 1.9 mm Half Tila beads (412, opaque turquoise green)
- **7 g** 1 x 3.8 mm O-beads (crystal copper)
- **110** 3 mm bicone crystals (Swarovski, blue Zircon)
- **7 g** 8º seed beads (Toho 222, dark bronze)
- **4 g** 11º seed beads (Toho 2223, Takumi large-hole silver-lined dragonfruit)
- **2 g** 15º seed beads (Toho PF557, permanent-finish galvanized starlight)
- **1–2** 6 mm jump rings
- **1** lobster claw clasp
- **1** 3½ in. (8.9 cm) chain extender (optional)
- Fireline, 6 lb. test
- beading needles, #11 or #12
- **2** pairs of chainnose, flatnose, and/or bentnose pliers

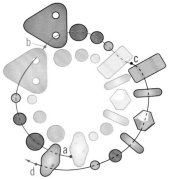

FIGURE 1

FIGURE 2

FIGURE 3

and the SuperDuo your thread exited at the start of this step **(b-c)**. Retrace the thread path of the clasp connection, and sew through the last couple of rounds of the base. If your tension is loose, sew back through the length of the base to tighten. End the working thread.

3 With the tail thread, sew through the beadwork to exit the SuperDuo in the first round. Repeat step 2, but pick up the end link of the extender chain instead of a jump ring. If needed, attach a jump ring to the chain first. End the tail. ◕

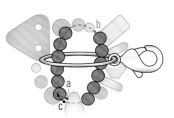

FIGURE 4

	15º seed bead
	11º seed bead
	8º seed bead
	2.5 x 5 mm SuperDuo bead
	1 x 3.8 mm O-bead
	3 mm bicone crystal
	5 x 2.3 x 1.9 mm Half Tila
	6 mm two-hole triangle bead

Fan
favorite
bracelet

Make an impressive bracelet with SuperDuos formed into an intricate yet simple pattern.

designed by **Svetlana Chernitsky**

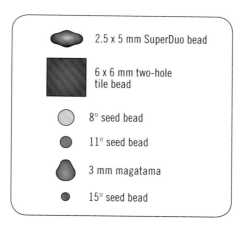

2.5 x 5 mm SuperDuo bead

6 x 6 mm two-hole tile bead

8º seed bead

11º seed bead

3 mm magatama

15º seed bead

Difficulty rating

  ◯ ◯ ◯

Materials

purple bracelet 8 in. (20 cm)

- **23** 6 mm CzechMates two-hole tile beads (polychrome orchid aqua)
- **9 g** 2.5 x 5 mm SuperDuo beads (metallic suede pink)
- **2 g** 3 mm magatama drop beads (Toho 505, metallic dragonfly)
- **1 g** 8º seed beads (Toho 741, copper-lined alabaster)
- **1 g** 11º seed beads (Toho 1204, opaque light amethyst marbled)
- **1 g** 15º seed beads (Miyuki 360, aqua-lined amethyst AB)
- toggle clasp
- **2** 6 mm jump rings
- Fireline, 6 lb. test
- beading needles, #11 or #12
- **2** pairs of chainnose, flatnose, and/or bentnose pliers

green bracelet 7½ in. (19.1 cm)

- 5 mm Tila beads (Miyuki 2002, metallic matte silver gray)
- 2.5 x 5 mm SuperDuo beads (turquoise Picasso)
- 3 mm magatama drop beads (Toho Y151, hybrid topaz gold)
- 8º seed beads (Toho 221F, frosted bronze)
- 11º seed beads (Miyuki 1074, galvanized sea green)

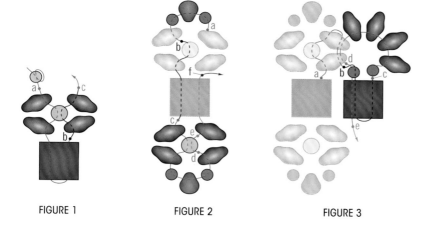

FIGURE 1   FIGURE 2   FIGURE 3

Base

1 On a comfortable length of thread, attach a stop bead, leaving a 12-in. (30 cm) tail. Pick up a SuperDuo bead, an 8º seed bead, a SuperDuo, and a two-hole tile bead, and sew through the open hole of the same tile bead **(figure 1, a–b)**. Pick up a SuperDuo, sew through the following 8º, and pick up a SuperDuo **(b–c)**.

2 Pick up an 11º seed bead, a 3 mm magatama drop bead, and an 11º, and sew through the inner hole of the adjacent SuperDuo to form a loop **(figure 2, a–b)**. Continue through the following 8º, the inner hole of the next SuperDuo, and the tile bead **(b–c)**.

3 Pick up a SuperDuo, an 8º, a SuperDuo, an 11º, a magatama, an 11º, and a SuperDuo **(c–d)**. Sew back through the 8º just added to form a loop **(d–e)**. Pick up a SuperDuo, and sew through the next tile bead **(e–f)**.

4 Sew through the inner hole of the next SuperDuo, 8º, and SuperDuo. Continue through the open holes of the next two SuperDuos **(figure 3, a–b)**.

5 Pick up an 11º and a tile bead, and sew through the open hole of the same tile bead **(b–c)**. Pick up an 11º and four SuperDuos, and sew through the outer holes of the adjacent two SuperDuos to form a loop **(c–d)**. Keeping a tight tension, continue through the following 11º and tile bead **(d–e)**.

6 Pick up an 11º, and sew through the open holes of the next two SuperDuos

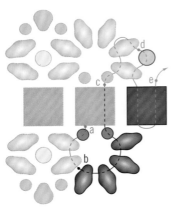

FIGURE 4

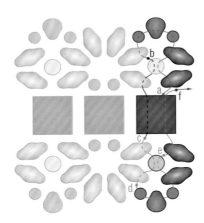

FIGURE 5

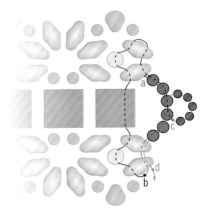

FIGURE 6

(figure 4, a–b). Pick up four SuperDuos and an 11º, and sew through the following tile bead **(b–c)**. Continue through the next 11º and the inner holes of the next two SuperDuos. Pull the thread tight, and sew through the open hole of the same SuperDuo your thread is exiting **(c–d)**.

7 Pick up an 8º, and sew through the open hole of the next SuperDuo. Pick up a tile bead, and sew through the open hole of the same tile bead **(d–e)**.

8 Pick up a SuperDuo, and sew through the following 8º. Pick up a SuperDuo, an 11º, a magatama, and an 11º, and sew through the outer hole of the adjacent SuperDuo to form a loop **(figure 5, a–b)**. Continue through the next 8º, SuperDuo, and tile bead **(b–c)**.

9 Sew through the open hole of the next SuperDuo, pick up an 8º, and continue through the open hole of the following SuperDuo **(c–d)**. Pick up an 11º, a magatama, an 11º, and a SuperDuo, and sew back through the 8º just added to form a loop **(d–e)**. Pick up a SuperDuo, and sew through the following tile bead **(e–f)**.

10 Repeat steps 4–9, ending and adding thread as needed, for the desired length of the bracelet minus 1¼ in. (3.2 cm) for the clasp. End the final row after completing step 4.

Clasp

1 With the working thread, pick up six 11ºs, and sew through the open hole of the following two SuperDuos

(figure 6, a–b). Sew through the beadwork as shown to exit the fourth 11º just added **(b–c)**.

2 Pick up five 15º seed beads, and sew through the middle two 11ºs added in step 1 to form a loop. Continue through the following two 11ºs and the outer holes of the next two Super Duos **(c–d)**. Sew through the beadwork, and retrace the thread path to reinforce the loop. End the thread.

3 Open a jump ring, and attach half the toggle clasp to the loop of 15ºs.

4 Remove the stop bead from the tail, and sew through the open holes of the next two SuperDuos. Repeat steps 1–3 to attach the other half of the toggle clasp. ●

design options
• In the loops of SuperDuos added in steps 5 and 6 of "Base," the center two SuperDuos have exposed outer holes. To prevent this, use SuperUnos in a coordinating color instead of the second two SuperDuos picked up in step 5 and the first two SuperDuos picked up in step 6.
• As shown in the green bracelet, you can substitute Tila beads in place of tile beads with a few simple adjustments to the clasp connections. In step 1 of "Clasp," pick up four 11ºs instead of six, and then sew through the beadwork to exit the third 11º added.
• If desired, use 11º seed beads in place of 15ºs for the loop.

BEAD CROCHET

Loopy for
LENTILS

Learn bead crochet the easy way
with a reusable starter stump to
create lively, textural bracelets
using lentil beads.

designed by **Barbara Zaner**

Difficulty rating

Materials
turquoise bangle with 2¼-in. (5.7 cm) inner diameter
- **1** 6 x 8 mm rondelle or other focal bead (aqua Picasso)
- **2** 6–8 mm bead caps
- **250–300** 6 mm lentil beads (teal luster)
- **10–12 g** 10º cylinder beads (Miyuki DBM0084, light seafoam)
- **30** 8º seed beads (for starter stump)
- YLI Jean Stitch or Gutermann topstitch thread
- Fireline, 6 lb. test, or size D nylon beading thread (to make starter stump)
- Big Eye beading needle (to string beads)
- beading needles, #11 (to make starter stump)
- tapestry needle, #28 (for finishing)
- steel crochet hook, 0.75–1.0 mm

red bangle colors
- 6 x 8 mm rondelle (Siam ruby)
- 6 mm lentil beads (light garnet)
- 10º cylinder beads (Miyuki DBM0683, silver-lined ruby red)

black bangle colors
- 6 x 8 mm rondelle (jet)
- 6 mm lentil beads (jet)
- 10º cylinder beads (Miyuki DBM0010, black)

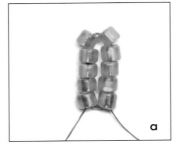
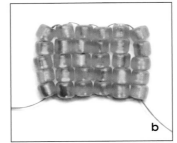
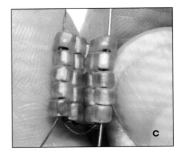
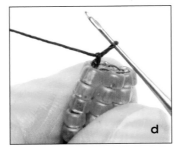
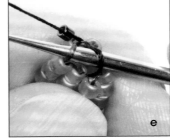
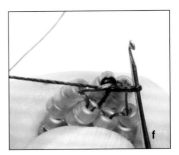

Starter stump
Many people find it difficult to start bead crochet, mainly because there is little to hold onto at first and the order of stitches is hard to make out. A reusable starter stump eliminates the frustration and confusion inherent in starting bead crochet.
1 To make a starter stump: On 2 ft. (61 cm) of beading thread, pick up 10 8º seed beads, and sew through all the beads again to make two stacks of five beads each **(photo a)**.
2 Work in ladder stitch with five beads per stitch until you have a total of six rows **(photo b)**. Join the ladder ends into a ring **(photo c)**, and end the threads.

Bead crochet rope
1 Attach the Big Eye needle to the end of the YLI Jean Stitch or Gutermann thread (don't cut it from the spool).
2 String 12 10º cylinder beads followed by approximately 36 in. (.9 m) in a repeating pattern of a lentil and a cylinder. String another 3 in. (7.6 cm) of cylinders.
3 Leaving a 6-in. (15 cm) tail, use your crochet hook to pull a small loop of the cord under a thread bridge at one end of the starter stump. Catch the working thread with the hook (also called a yarn over), and pull it through the loop **(photo d)**. Pull to tighten.
4 Slide the hook under the adjacent thread bridge on

the stump, and slide a cylinder up to the hook **(photo e)**. Yarn over just beyond the bead, and pull through the thread bridge and the loop on the hook **(photo f)**. Repeat this stitch all around the stub, attaching a cylinder to each of the six thread bridges **(photo g)**. Note that these beads sit perpendicular to the beads below.

size wise
To size your bangle correctly, first measure the widest part of your hand, and then subtract the total length of the bead caps and focal bead. This is about how long your bead crochet rope needs to be. The rule of thumb for a 6-around bead crochet project is that every 6 in. (15 cm) of strung beads yields 1 in. (2.5 cm) of bead crochet rope. So, if your finished bracelet requires a 6-in. (15 cm) rope, for example, you will need to string a total of 37½ in. (95 cm) of beads as described above (include 12 cylinders at each end in this measurement—don't forget that the rest of the cylinders in the end section will be removed).

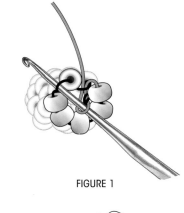

FIGURE 1

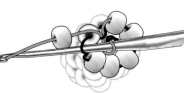

FIGURE 2

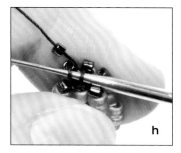

h

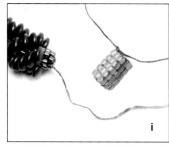

i

j

5 Work in bead slip stitch: Insert the hook to the left of the next bead in the previous round, and flip that bead to the right **(figure 1)**. Slide the next bead down to the hook **(photo h)**, yarn over **(figure 2)**, and pull through both the stitch and the loop on the hook.

6 Working counterclockwise, continue in bead slip stitch until all the beads have been used. Your rope will begin

with about ½ in. (1.3 cm) of cylinders, and then it will switch to an alternating pattern of a lentil and a cylinder, with three pairs per round. Starting in the second round of the lentil section, note that each new bead that gets crocheted in place will be stitched to a bead of the same type—the cylinders will always be attached to other cylinders, and lentils will always be attached to other lentils. The rope will finish with two rounds of cylinders.

7 Bind off the rope by working a slip stitch in each end bead without adding beads. Leaving a 10-in. (25 cm) tail,

trim the cord, and pull it through the last loop.

8 Carefully cut the cord that attaches the rope to the starter stump. Do not cut the thread of the starter stump itself so you can use it again.

9 Carefully remove enough rounds of cylinders from this end of the rope so only two round remain **(photo i)**.

10 Attach a tapestry needle to one end of the cord, and string a bead cap (wide end first), the focal bead, and a bead cap (narrow end first). Sew into the center of the rope at the other end and exit the beadwork at least ½ in. (1.2 cm) from the end.

Using the other end of the cord, sew through the bead caps and focal and into the other end of the rope **(photo j)**. Pull tight. With each cord end, retrace the thread path back through the focal bead and end caps. Working with one cord end at a time, sew back and forth through the rope widthwise a few times, sewing through the beadwork and catching the internal cords with each pass. Be careful that the cords don't loop around any of the beads. After you've passed the cord through the rope several times, trim the cord as close to the work as possible. ●

change it up

Try shapes other than lentils, such as 10 x 4 mm daggers (bronze bracelet) or 7 mm pressed petals (purple bracelet). To make an 18-in. (46 cm) necklace, string about 3 ft. (.9 m) of cylinders before and after a 3-ft. (.9 m) section of alternating lentils and cylinders.

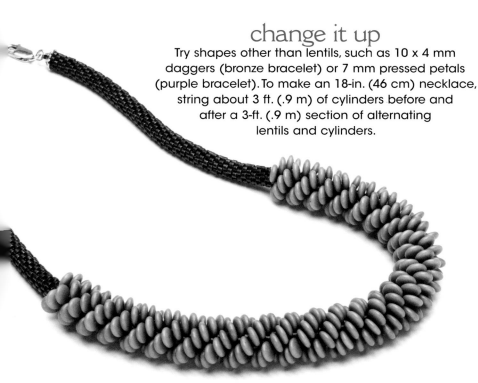

Wings of flight

BANGLE BRACELET

Make this stunning bangle, inspired by the popular
"flying geese" quilt block pattern, using a modified
form of peyote stitch referred to as quilted peyote.

designed by **Diane Hertzler**

edge turn

Pick up an A, and sew through the corresponding A on the other layer.

sew-through edge turn

Pick up an A, and sew through the next edge A. Pick up an A, and sew through the following quilt bead.

Materials

bangle 2³⁄₈ in. (6 cm) inside diameter

- **120** 2.5 mm bicone crystals (Swarovski, jet)
- 11º Miyuki Delica cylinder beads
  - **13 g** color A (DB1458, silver-lined honey opal)
  - **1 g** color B (DB0010, black)
  - **1 g** color C (DB0047, silver-lined cobalt)
  - **1 g** color D (DB0693, semi-frosted silver-lined dusk blue)
  - **1 g** color E (DB0921, sparkle blue-lined topaz)
  - **1 g** color F (DB0149, silver-lined capri blue)
  - **1 g** color G (DB1847, Dura-coat galvanized sea foam)
  - **1 g** color H (DB0027, dark green iris)
  - **1 g** color I (DB0011, metallic olive)
  - **1 g** color J (DB0182, silver-lined jade green)
  - **1 g** color K (DB0105, garnet gold luster)
  - **1 g** color L (DB0296, lined ruby AB)
  - **1 g** color M (DB0103, dark topaz rainbow gold luster)
  - **1 g** color N (DB0281, fuchsia-lined crystal luster)
  - **1 g** color O (DB1743, hot pink-lined crystal AB)
  - **1 g** color P (DB0609, dyed silver-lined dark purple
  - **1 g** color Q (DB0610, dyed silver-lined dark violet)
- beading needles, #12
- Fireline 6 lb. test

* Kits are available at www.dianehertzler.com.

Base

1 On a comfortable length of thread, attach a stop bead, leaving a 6-in (15 cm) tail. Pick up 36 color A 11º cylinder beads, and sew through the first A again. These beads will shift to form rounds 1 and 2 as the next round is added.
2 Work three rounds of tubular peyote in a clockwise direction, stepping up at the end of each round. These five rounds will form the bangle's base, and will be removed once the final length is reached.
3 Flatten the tube to create a front and back with the working thread exiting the far right front column and pointing toward the other edge. There should be 17 columns on both the front and back, and a single column on each outer edge.
4 Work rounds of quilted tubular peyote as follows:
Round 6: Pick up a color B 11º cylinder bead, and sew through the next A **(figure 1, a–b)**. This will be referred to as a "B quilt" bead. Work six stitches using As **(b–c)**. Pick up a B quilt, and sew through the next A **(c–d)**. Work an edge turn: Pick up an A, and sew through the corresponding A on the other layer **(d–e)**. Sew through the B quilt just added and the next A on the back layer **(e–f)**. Work six stitches using As **(f–g)**. Sew through the next B quilt and the following A on the back

*back of beadwork

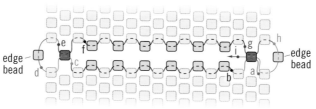

*front of beadwork

FIGURE 1

* *FIGURES 2–9 HAVE THE SAME FRONT AND BACK POSITIONING.*

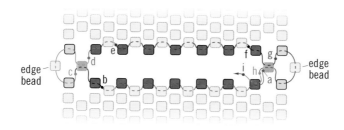

FIGURE 2

(g–h), and pull the thread tight. Work an edge turn, and step up through the following B quilt **(h–i)**.
Round 7: Work six stitches using color C 11º cylinder beads **(figure 2, a–b)**. Pick up a C, and sew through the next quilt bead **(b–c)**. Work a sew-through edge turn: Pick up an A, and sew through the next edge A. Pick up an A, and sew through the following quilt bead **(c–d)**. Pick up a C, and sew through the following A **(d–e)**. Work five stitches using Cs **(e–f)**. Pick up a C, and sew through the next quilt bead **(f–g)**. Work a sew-through edge turn **(g–h),** and step up through

quilted peyote

Diane has created a unique modified form of tubular peyote referred to as quilted peyote where the front and back layers in columns 2 and 16 share a single bead. These shared beads will be referred to as a "quilt" bead in the project.

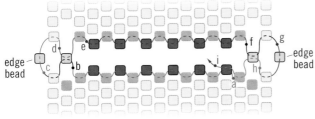

FIGURE 3

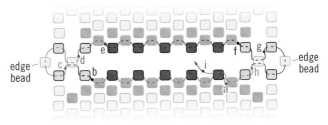

FIGURE 4

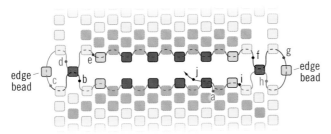

FIGURE 5

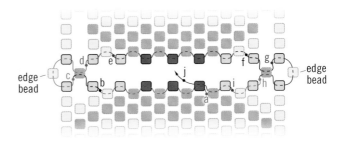

FIGURE 6

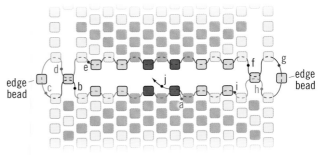

FIGURE 7

the following C on the front **(h–i)**.

Round 8: Work six stitches using Cs **(figure 3, a–b)**. Pick up a color A 11º cylinder bead (an "A quilt"), and sew through the following A **(b–c)**. Work an edge turn **(c–d)**. Sew through the following A quilt and the next C on the back **(d–e)**. Work six stitches using Cs **(e–f)**. Pick up an A quilt, and sew through the following A **(f–g)**. Work an edge turn **(g–h)**. Sew through the following quilt bead and the next C on the front, and step up through the following C **(h–i)**.

Round 9: Work five stitches using Cs **(figure 4, a–b)**. Pick up an A, and sew through the next quilt bead **(b–c)**. Work a sew-through edge turn **(c–d)**. Pick up an A, and sew through the next C on the back **(d–e)**. Work five stitches using Cs **(e–f)**. Pick up an A, and sew through the next quilt bead **(f–g)**. Work a sew-through edge turn **(g–h)**. Pick up an A, sew through the next C, and step up through the following C **(h–i)**.

Round 10: Work four stitches using Cs and one using an A **(figure 5, a–b)**. Pick up a B quilt, and sew through the following A on the front **(b–c)**. Work an edge turn **(c–d)**. Sew through the next B quilt and the following A on the back **(d–e)**. Work one stitch using an A, four using Cs, and one using an A **(e–f)**. Pick up a B quilt, and sew through the next A on the back **(f–g)**. Work an edge turn, and sew through the following quilt bead and an A on the front **(h–i)**. Work one stitch using an A, and step up through the following C **(i–j)**.

Round 11: Work three stitches with Cs and one with an A **(figure 6, a–b)**. Pick up an A, and sew through the following quilt bead **(b–c)**. Work a sew-through edge turn **(c–d)**. Pick up an A, and sew through the next A on the back **(d–e)**. Work one stitch using an A, three using Cs, and one using an A **(e–f)**. Pick up an A, and sew through the following quilt bead **(f–g)**. Work a

sew-through edge turn **(g–h)**. Pick up an A, and sew through the next A **(h–i)**. Work one stitch using an A, and step up through the next C **(i–j)**.

Round 12: Work two stitches using Cs, and two using As **(figure 7, a–b)**. Pick up an A quilt, and sew through the next A on the front **(b–c)**. Work an edge turn **(c–d)**. Sew through the following A quilt, and continue through the next C on the back **(d–e)**. Work two stitches using As, two using Cs, and two using As **(e–f)**. Pick up an A quilt, and sew through the following A on the back **(f–g)**. Work an edge turn **(g–h)**. Sew through the following A quilt, and continue through the next A on the front **(h–i)**. Work

two stitches using As, and step up through the next C **(i–j)**.

Round 13: Work one stitch using a C, and two using As **(figure 8, a–b)**. Pick up an A, and sew through the next quilt bead **(b–c)**. Work a sew-through edge turn, and sew through the following quilt **(c–d)**. Pick up an A, and sew through the next A **(d–e)**. Work two stitches using As, one using a C, and two using As **(e–f)**. Pick up an A, and sew through the next quilt bead **(f–g)**. Work a sew-through edge turn **(g–h)**. Pick up an A, and sew through the next A **(h–i)**. Work two stitches using As, and step up through the following C **(i–j)**.

Round 14: Work three stitches using As **(figure 9, a–b)**. Pick

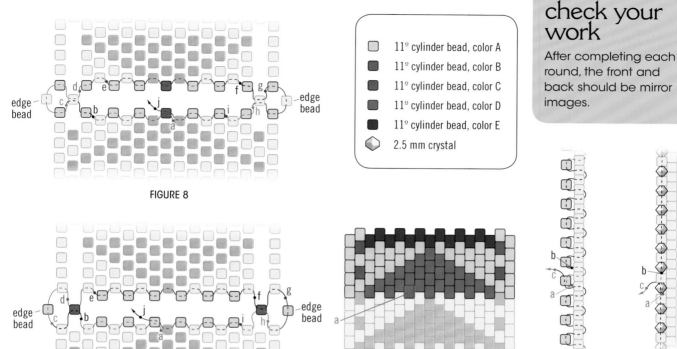

FIGURE 8

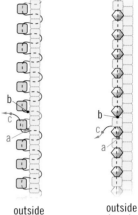

check your work

After completing each round, the front and back should be mirror images.

FIGURE 9

PATTERN

FIGURE 10

FIGURE 11

outside edge view

outside edge view

up a B quilt, and sew through the following A on the front **(b–c).** Work an edge turn **(c–d).** Sew through the following B quilt, and continue through the following A on the back **(d–e).** Work six stitches using As **(e–f).** Pick up a B quilt, and sew through the following A **(f–g).** Work an edge turn **(g–h).** Sew through the following B quilt and the next A on the front **(h–i).** Work three stitches using As, and step up through the following A **(i–j).**

Rounds 15–21: Starting at **point A** on the **pattern**, continue working in quilted tubular peyote, using color D cylinder beads in place of the Cs and stepping up at the end of each round. End and add thread as needed.

Rounds 22+: The pattern starts repeating itself on the back in round 22. Repeat rounds 6–21, cycling through colors C–Q in alphabetical order until each triangle

color has been repeated twice, or you reach the desired length.

Join the ends

1 Sew through the beadwork to exit an A in the last round's outer column with the needle pointing toward the beadwork. Remove the stop bead, and pull out rounds 1–5 that were stitched in steps 1 and 2 of the "Base."

2 Zip the ends together by starting on the inside area of the bangle and working around the edge to zip the opposite side. Tie a half-hitch knot, but do not end the thread.

Edge embellishment

1 With the working thread, sew through the beadwork to exit an edge A with the needle facing the front of the bangle. Pick up an A, sew through the next edge A, and continue through the following edge A **(figure 10,**

a–b). Repeat this stitch to complete the round, and step up through the first A added **(b–c).**

2 Pick up a 2.5mm bicone crystal, and sew through the following A added in step 1 **(figure 11, a–b).** Repeat this stitch to complete the round, and step up through first crystal added **(b–c).**

3 Repeat steps 1 and 2 on the opposite side of the bangle and end the working thread and tail. ●

For added flair, flip the color pattern on the inside of the bangle (right). Change all the triangles to the base color A, and the background to the same color used on the outside.

Framed latticework earrings

Create a dimensional look with these prismatic double-layered earrings.

designed by **Ora Shai**

Base

1 On a comfortable length of thread, pick up a repeating pattern of an 11º seed bead and a 4mm bicone crystal four times. Sew through the beads again to form a ring, leaving a 6-in. (15cm) tail. Tie a square knot with the working thread and tail, and sew through the next 11º and crystal **(figure 1, a–b)**.

2 Work in modified right-angle weave: Pick up an 11º, a 3mm bugle bead, an 11º, a crystal, an 11º, a bugle, and an 11º, and sew through the crystal your thread exited at the beginning of this step **(b–c)**.

3 Sew through the next 11º, bugle, 11º, and crystal **(c–d)**.

4 Pick up an 11º and a crystal three times and then another 11º, and sew through the crystal your thread exited at the start of this step **(d–e)**.

5 Sew through the following 11º, crystal, 11º, and crystal **(e–f)**.

6 Repeat steps 2–5 twice, and sew through the next 11º and following crystal **(f–g)**.

7 Pick up an 11º, a bugle, an 11º, a crystal, an 11º, a bugle, and an 11º, and sew through the crystal your thread exited at the start of this step. Continue through the first 11º and bugle just added **(figure 2, a–b)**.

8 Pick up an 11º, a bugle, an 11º, a bugle, and an 11º, and sew through the next bugle in the adjacent column **(b–c)**.

9 Pick up an 11º, sew through the adjacent bugle in the previous unit, and the following 11º, bugle, 11º, and bugle added in this unit **(c–d)**.

10 Pick up an 11º, and sew through the next crystal in the adjacent column **(d–e)**.

11 Pick up an 11º, a bugle, an 11º, a crystal, and an 11º, and sew through the adjacent bugle in the previous unit. Continue through the following 11º, crystal, 11º, and bugle **(e–f)**.

12 Repeat steps 8–11 twice, and sew through the next 11º and crystal.

13 Repeat step 4, and sew through the next 11º and crystal just added **(figure 3, a–b)**.

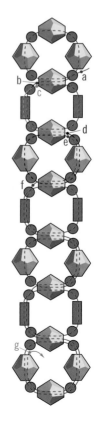

FIGURE 1

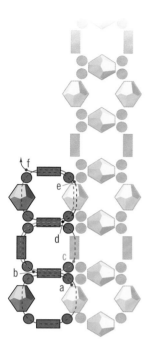

FIGURE 2

14 Pick up an 11º, a bugle, an 11º, a crystal, and an 11º, and sew through the next bugle in the adjacent column **(b–c)**. Pick up an 11º, and sew through the next crystal, 11º, bugle, 11º, and crystal **(c–d)**.

15 Pick up an 11º, and sew through the next crystal in the adjacent column **(d–e)**. Pick up an 11º, a crystal, an 11º, a crystal, and an 11º, and sew through the adjacent crystal in the previous unit **(e–f)**. Sew through the next 11º, crystal, 11º, and crystal **(f–g)**.

16 Repeat steps 14–15 twice. Sew through the beadwork to exit the middle bugle on one long side **(point h)**.

Side A

1 Fold the base in half to create a double layer square with three open sides **(figure 4)**. Your thread should be exiting an edge bugle on the fold.

2 Pick up an 11º, and sew through the next crystal on the adjacent layer **(figure 5, a–b)**. Pick up an 11º, a bugle, and an 11º, and sew through the adja-

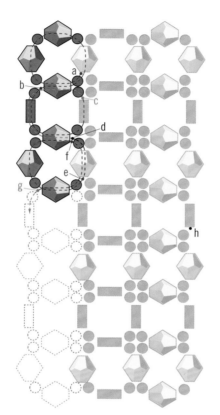

FIGURE 3

cent edge crystal on the opposite layer **(b–c)**. Pick up an 11º, and sew through the center bugle your thread exited at the beginning of this step **(c–d)**.

3 Sew through the next 11º, crystal, 11º, and bugle **(d–e)**. Pick up an 11º, and sew through the next edge bugle **(e–f)**.

4 Pick up an 11º, a bugle, and an 11º, and sew through the next edge bugle on the opposite layer **(f–g)**.

5 Pick up an 11º, and sew through the adjacent center bugle, 11º, bugle, 11º, and center bugle **(g–h)**.

6 Repeat step 2 **(h–i)**. Sew through the next 11º, crystal, 11º, and bugle **(i–j)**.

Difficulty rating

Materials
pair of earrings 1 in. (2.5cm)
- **68** 4mm bicone crystals (Swarovski, erinite AB)
- **2 g** 3mm bugle beads (Miyuki 457, metallic dark bronze)
- **2 g** 11º seed beads (Toho 221, bronze)
- **1 g** 15º seed beads (Toho 221, bronze)
- **1** pair of earring findings
- **2** 4mm jump rings
- Fireline 8 lb. test
- beading needles, #11 or #12
- **2** pairs of chainnose, flatnose, and/or bentnose pliers

side A

folding edge

side B

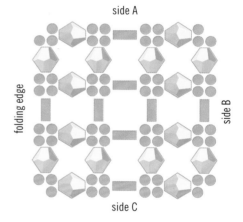

side C

FIGURE 4

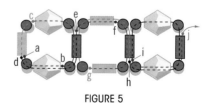

FIGURE 5

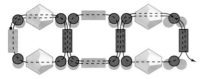

FIGURE 6

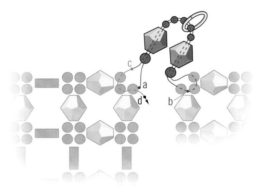

FIGURE 7

FIGURE 8

Side B

Repeat steps 2–6 of "Side A" **(figure 6)**.

Side C

1 Repeat steps 2–5 of "Side A" **(figure 7, a–b)**.
2 Pick up an 11º, and sew through the next crystal. Pick up an 11º, and sew through the following bugle. Pick up an 11º, and sew through the adjacent edge crystal. Pick up an 11º, and sew through the center bugle your thread exited at the beginning of this step **(b–c)**.
3 Sew through the following 11º, crystal, and 11º **(c–d)**.

Earring wires

1 Pick up an 11º, a crystal, five 15º seed beads, a 4 mm jump ring, a crystal, and an 11º, and sew through the adjacent 11º on the opposite side of the beadwork **(figure 8, a–b)**. Continue through the next two 11ºs, and sew back through the beads just added **(b–c)**. Sew through the next three 11ºs on the first side to exit the bead your thread exited at the start of this step **(c–d)**. Retrace the thread path to reinforce the join, and end the working thread and tail.
2 Open the loop of an earring wire and attach it to the 4mm jump ring.
3 Make a second earring. ●

take notice

The beadwork corners contain groups of three 11ºs, and the inner connections contain groups of four 11ºs.

CIRCULAR PEYOTE STITCH

Kaleidoscope
contours

Make a colorful and dimensional
bracelet with a hint of sparkle
around the edges.

designed by **Michelle Heim**

Difficulty rating

Materials

gold bracelet 6½ x 1 in. (16.5 x 2.5 cm)

- 2.5 x 5 mm SuperDuo beads
  - **6 g** color A (orange luster on chalk)
  - **10 g** color B (crystal bronze pale gold)
- **6** 3 mm round beads (garnet)
- **84** 3 x 2 mm crystal rondelles (Thunder Polish, red velvet)
- **1 g** 11º seed beads (Toho 332, gold-lustered cranberry)
- 3-strand clasp
- Fireline 6 lb. test
- beading needles, #11

turquoise bracelet colors:

- 2.5 x 5 mm SuperDuo beads
  - color A (opaque turquoise Picasso)
  - color B (jet Picasso)
- 3 mm round beads (dark brown)
- 3 x 2 mm crystal rondelles (Thunder Polish, aqua)
- 11º seed beads (Miyuki 2006, matte metallic dark bronze)

First component

1 On 1 yd. (.9 m) of thread, pick up a repeating pattern of an 11º seed bead and a color A 2.5 x 5 mm SuperDuo bead six times. Sew through all the beads again to form a ring, exiting the next A and leaving an 8-in. (20cm) tail. Continue through the open hole of the same A **(figure 1)**. Set the working thread aside for the next step.

2 With the tail, sew through the next A, pick up a 3mm round bead, and continue through the A on the opposite side of the ring **(figure 2, a–b)**. Sew back through the 3mm, and continue through the A your thread exited at the start of this step, going in the same direction **(b–c)**. End the tail.

3 With the working thread, pick up two color B 2.5 x 5mm SuperDuo beads, and sew through the open hole of the next A **(figure 3, a–b)**. Repeat this stitch to complete the round, and continue through the first two Bs added in this round **(b–c)**. Sew through the open hole of the second B **(c–d)**.

4 Pick up two Bs, and sew through the next B **(d–e)**. Pick up one A, and sew through the next B **(e–f)**. Repeat these stitches to complete the round, and continue through the first two Bs added in this round **(f–g)**. Sew through the open hole of the same B **(g–h)**.

5 Pick up an A, and sew through the next B **(figure 4, a–b)**.

6 Pick up a 3 x 2 mm crystal rondelle, and sew through the next SuperDuo **(b–c)**. Work another stitch with a rondelle and another one with a B **(c–d)**.

7 Work five more stitches using the rondelles **(d–e)**.

8 Repeat steps 5–7 to complete the round **(e–f)**, retrace the thread path of the round to tighten, and exit the first A added **(f–g)**. Sew through the open hole of the same A **(g–h)**. Set the component aside, and do not end the working thread.

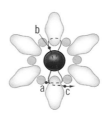

FIGURE 1

FIGURE 2

FIGURE 3

 2.5 x 5 mm SuperDuo bead, color A

 2.5 x 5 mm SuperDuo bead, color B

 3 mm pearl

 1.5 x 2.5 mm crystal rondelle

 11º seed bead

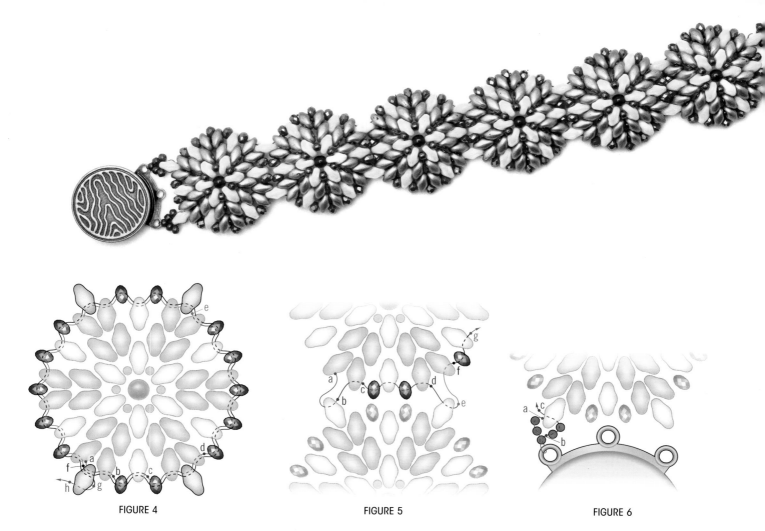

FIGURE 4

FIGURE 5

FIGURE 6

Remaining components

1 Repeat steps 1–4 of "First component."

2 Position the first component next to the new component so two adjacent As added in the last round are nearest the new component (these As should have two rondelles between them). The working thread from the new component should be pointing toward the first component, and the working thread from the first component should be on the opposite side.

3 With the working thread from the new component, sew through the open hole of the nearest A in the first component with the needle pointing

toward the two rondelles **(figure 5, a–b)**. Continue through the next B in the new component **(b–c)**.

4 Work two stitches with rondelles **(c–d)**.

5 Sew through the open hole of the nearest A in the first component **(d–e)**, and continue through the next B in the new component **(e–f)**.

6 Work a stitch with a rondelle **(f–g)**. Repeat this stitch four more times.

7 Work a stitch with an A, two stitches with rondelles, and a stitch with an A.

8 Work five stitches with rondelles, and retrace the thread path of the entire round. Make sure to not over-tighten the beadwork, or the two components will not bend at the connection properly. End the working thread of the new component.

9 Repeat steps 1–8 to make and attach four more components.

Clasp

1 With the working thread from the first component, pick up three 11ºs, sew through the first loop of the clasp, and sew back through the last 11º added **(figure 6, a–b)**. Pick up two 11ºs, and sew through the A your thread exited at the start of this step **(b–c)**. Retrace the thread path twice, and sew through the other hole of the same A.

2 Sew through the beadwork to exit the open hole of the next A in the last round.

3 Repeat step 1 to attach the third loop of the clasp, and end the working thread. The center loop of the clasp will not be attached to the beadwork.

4 Add 14 in. (36 cm) of thread to the other end of the bracelet, and exit the open hole of an A with the needle pointing away from the beadwork.

5 Repeat steps 1–3 to attach the other half of the clasp. ●

note:

The thickness of the coating on your SuperDuos affects how much your components will dome. The thicker the coating, the less doming.

Beaded S-hook clasp

Make your own clasps with just a handful of seed beads.

designed by **Julia Gerlach**

Difficulty rating

Materials

S-hook clasp 1 in. (2.5 cm)
- 1 g 8º seed beads
- 1 g 11º seed beads
- 1 g 15º seed beads
- Fireline, 6 lb. test
- beading needles, #12

1 On 1 yd. (.9 m) of thread, pick up two 11º seed beads, 13 15º seed beads, seven 11º seed beads, 13 8º seed beads, and three 11ºs. Sew back through the last 8º **(figure 1)**, leaving a 6-in. (15 cm) tail.

2 Work back across the strand of beads in peyote: six stitches with 8ºs, four stitches with 11ºs, and six stitches with 15ºs. Work one more stitch with an 11º, sewing through the end 11º in the same direction as when you picked it up in step 1 **(figure 2)**. The working thread and tail should be exiting opposite sides of the end 11º. Pull snug so the end 11º sits perpendicular to the adjacent beads.

3 Sew through the adjacent 11º, and then work around the piece in peyote as follows:

Bottom edge: Work a total of 17 stitches in peyote using one 11º per stitch along the entire edge **(figure 3, a–b)**, and then sew through the following two 11ºs at the end **(b–c)**.

Top edge: Work 17 stitches using 11ºs **(c–d)**. Sew through the end 11º **(d–e)**.

4 Pick up an 11º, and sew through the next 11º on the bottom edge **(figure 4, a–b)**. Work six stitches with 8ºs, four stitches with 11ºs, and six stitches with 15ºs **(b–c)**. Pick up an 11º, and sew through the end 11º **(c–d)**. Pick up an 11º, and sew through the next 11º on the top edge **(d–e)**. Work across the beadwork, working the pattern in reverse: six stitches with 15ºs, four stitches with 11ºs, and six stitches with 8ºs **(e–f)**. Pick up an 11º, and sew through the end 11º **(f–g)**. The beadwork will be kind of wonky but don't worry about the shape at this point; it will look like an S at the end of the final row.

5 Once again, work across the beadwork in peyote: Sew through the next 11º, and then work seven stitches with 8ºs, three stitches with 11ºs, and seven stitches with 15ºs **(figure 5, a–b)**. Skip the end 11º, and sew through the next 11º **(b–c)**.

6 Sew back through the last 15º added **(figure 6, a–b)**. To complete the clasp, zigzag through the up-beads on the two edges: first sew through the 15ºs to close up this end of the tube, then sew through the 11ºs to close up the center section of the tube, and finally sew through the 8ºs to close the other end, sewing through the end 11º on the top edge for the last stitch **(b–c)**. Retrace the thread path of the join, and end the working thread and tail. ●

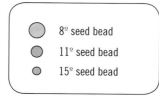

8º seed bead
11º seed bead
15º seed bead

FIGURE 1

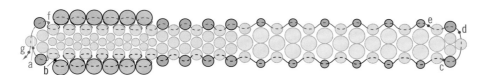

FIGURE 2

FIGURE 3

FIGURE 4

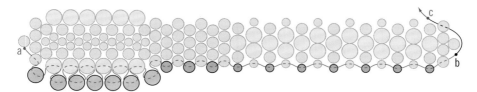

FIGURE 5

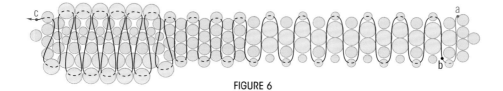

FIGURE 6

BEAD EMBROIDERY

Bead STUD collar

Clean lines and a tight color palette
combine to create this dramatic collar.

designed by **Maggie Roschyk**

Bead embroidery

1 Cut out the **template**, p. 93 (or download it from www.BeadAndButton. com/resources), and trace it onto the beading foundation with a silver marker. Do not cut out the shape.

2 If using a button as the focal, cut off the shank. File any burrs or sharp edges.

3 Apply E6000 to the back of the button or focal cabochon, and press it in place at the center of the foundation. Allow the glue to dry.

4 Tie an overhand knot at one end of 2 yd. (1.8 m) of thread, and sew up through the foundation next to the focal piece. Using color A 11º seed beads, work in beaded backstitch around the focal: For each stitch, pick up two beads, line them up next to the focal piece, and sew back through the foundation. Sew up between the two beads, and sew through the second bead just added **(photo a)**.

5 After completing the round, sew up

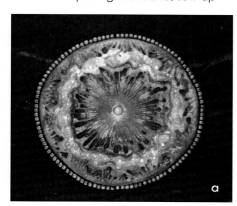

through the foundation right next to the round of As. Using color B 11º seed beads, work a round of brick stitch edging as follows: Pick up two Bs, and sew down through the foundation one bead's width from where your thread is exiting. Angle your needle so it slides under the round of backstitch. This should cause the Bs to sit perpendicular to the previous round. Sew up through the foundation and back through the second bead just added **(photo b)**. For each subsequent stitch, pick up a B, sew down and up through the foundation, and continue back through the bead just added. Repeat this stitch to complete the round. After adding the final bead, sew down through the first bead in the round, through the foundation, and back up through the foundation and the first bead. End the thread.

6 Use white glue to temporarily place a row of six 12 mm bead studs separated by 5 mm Tila beads on each side of the focal piece, with the holes positioned perpendicular to the focal piece. Leave enough room for a bugle bead between the brick stitch edging and the first bead stud. Be sure to keep the beads centered on the foundation, following the curve of the template. After the last bead stud, continue to glue Tila beads to the foundation **(photo c)**, leaving about ½ in. (1.3 cm) of open foundation at each end.

7 With a new thread, sew up through the foundation at the point where you

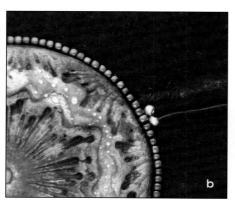

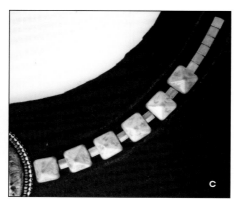

Materials

collar 15 in. (38 cm) plus extender chain

- Nicole's Beadbacking beading foundation (black)
- 1 1⅝-in. (4.1cm) button or cabochon
- 12 12 mm two-hole bead studs (black)
- 2 g 9 mm bugle beads (black)
- 10 6 mm pearls (gray)
- 32 5 mm Tila beads (Miyuki TL-401, black)
- 2 g 11º seed beads in each of 2 colors: color A (black), color B (silver)
- 1–2 g 15º seed beads (optional)
- lobster claw clasp
- chain (gunmetal) in 3 styles:
  - 16 in. (41 cm) small link
  - 16 in. (41 cm) medium link
  - 6 in. (15 cm) large link
- 2 10–12 mm oval jump rings
- 1 4 mm jump ring
- beading thread
- beading needles, #12
- ½-in. (1.3cm) brass collar blank
- thin kidskin leather or Ultrasuede
- E6000 adhesive
- white glue
- beading awl
- file (optional)
- silver marker
- 2 pairs of chainnose, flatnose, and/or bentnose pliers
- wire cutters

d

e

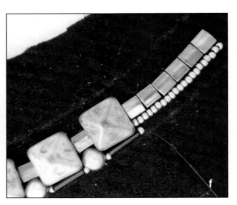

f

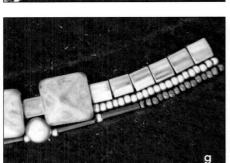

g

h

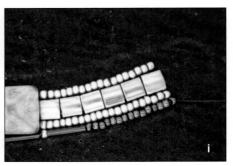

i

j

k

l

will attach the first bead stud on one side. Sew through one hole of the bead stud and the foundation on the other side. Repeat to attach the other hole of the bead stud. Retrace the thread paths of both connections. Attach the remaining Tilas and bead studs in the same manner.

8 Sew up through the foundation between the focal piece and the first bead stud, and stitch a 9mm bugle bead parallel to the edge of the stud. Sew up through the foundation just to one side and below the stud, and work a stitch with a B, a bugle, and a B **(photo d)**. Work a stitch to add a 6 mm pearl below the following Tila **(photo e)**. Repeat these two stitches along the entire bead stud section, and then work a row of beaded backstitch with Bs below the Tila-only section **(photo f)**. Work a row of backstitch below the Bs

using bugles and/or As **(photo g)**. End the thread.

9 With a new thread, exit between the first two bead studs, above the first Tila. Work a row of beaded backstitch using three or four Bs above the Tila **(photo h)**. Repeat between all the pairs of bead studs, and then work a row of backstitch above the Tila-only section using Bs **(photo i)**.

10 Using bugles, work a row of beaded backstitch along the entire upper edge **(photo j)**. If needed, add As or Bs to space your bugles as desired.

11 Repeat steps 7–10 on the other side of the focal piece.

12 Temporarily center your beadwork on the brass blank, and make sure the Tilas go up to each end of it. Leaving a small opening after the last Tila on each end, extend the rows of backstitch so they make a nice curve and connect at

the end **(photo k)**. The small opening in the beadwork should extend beyond the end of the brass blank; this is where you will add a jump ring and extender chain later.

13 There will be a bit of exposed foundation both above and below the bead stud portions and the outline of the collar shape at this point. Using A 11ºs and/or 15º seed beads, fill in with additional rows of beaded backstitch **(photo l)**. End the thread.

14 Cut out the collar shape close to the beadwork, being careful to avoid cutting any threads.

Chains

1 Cut the medium-link chain into two 8-in. (20 cm) chains. Repeat with the small-link chain.

2 Tie an overhand knot at the end of 1 yd. (.9 m) of thread, and anchor it to

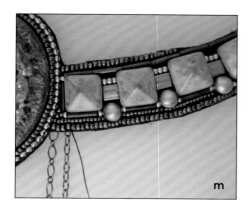
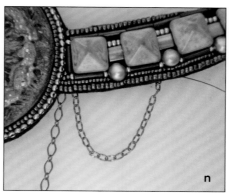
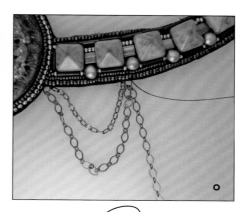

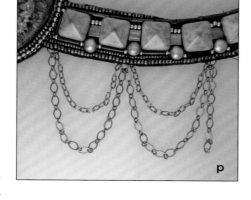

the foundation on the lower edge near the focal with a couple of tiny stitches. Exit at the lower edge of the foundation where the beadwork meets the focal piece, with your needle exiting the back of the foundation. Pick up one end of a medium-link chain, and tack it in place with a few small stitches near the edge. Pick up one end of a small-link chain, and tack it in place 2–3 mm away from the medium-link chain **(photo m)**.

3 Make small running stitches along the back of the piece for about 1 in. (2.5 cm). Drape the small-link chain below the collar, and tack it to the foundation as before **(photo n)**. Trim the small-link chain. Drape the medium-link chain so it hangs below the small-link chain, and tack it in place **(photo o)**. Don't trim the medium-link chain.

4 Add another swag of small-link chain as before, and trim any extra. Drape the medium-link chain below it, and tack it in place. Trim the medium-link chain if needed so approximately 1¾ in. (4.4 cm) hangs down after the second swag attachment **(photo p)**. End the thread.

5 Repeat steps 2–4 on the other side of the focal piece.

Finishing

1 Trace the collar foundation onto a piece of kidskin or Ultrasuede, and cut it out. Apply adhesive to the front of the brass blank, and press the beaded foundation in place. Allow the glue to

dry. Apply adhesive to the back of the blank, press the backing in place, and allow the glue to dry.

2 Tie an overhand knot at the end of a new thread, and sew up through the foundation anywhere along the perimeter of the collar. Using A 11ºs, work a brick stitch edging all around the collar as in step 5 of "Bead embroidery," sewing through both the backing and the foundation for each stitch. End and add thread as needed.

3 Locate the small opening in the beadwork at one end of the necklace. Using a beading awl, pierce the layers of backing and foundation. Open a 10–12 mm jump ring, thread it through the hole you just made, and attach a 4-in. (10 cm) piece of large-link chain. Repeat at the other end of the necklace, attaching a 1½-in. (1.3 cm) piece of chain.

4 Open a 4 mm jump ring, and attach a lobster claw clasp to the end of the 1½-in. (1.3 cm) chain.

TEMPLATE

"O" darlings bracelet

This sparkly stunner drips with crystals offset by O-beads.

designed by **Marcia Balonis**

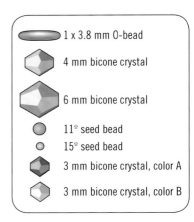

1 x 3.8 mm O-bead
4 mm bicone crystal
6 mm bicone crystal
11º seed bead
15º seed bead
3 mm bicone crystal, color A
3 mm bicone crystal, color B

Base

1 Thread a needle on each end of 7 ft. (2.1 m) of thread. With one needle, pick up an O-bead, a 4 mm bicone crystal, an O-bead, a 6 mm bicone crystal, an O-bead, a 4 mm, and an O-bead, and center the beads on the thread **(figure 1, a and aa)**.

2 With one needle, pick up a 6 mm, and cross the other needle through it **(a–b and aa–bb)**.

3 With each needle, pick up an O-bead, a 4 mm, and an O-bead. With one needle, pick up a 6 mm, and cross the other needle through it **(b–c and bb–cc)**.

4 Repeat step 3 for the desired length, leaving about ¾ in. (1.9 cm) for the clasp. Wrap the thread exiting the right side of the end 6 mm on a thread bobbin or piece of cardboard.

5 With the other working thread, pick up four 11º seed beads and half of the clasp. Sew back through the last 11º, pick up three 11ºs, and sew through the 6 mm your thread exited at the start of this step, going in the same direction **(figure 2)**. Retrace the thread path through the clasp connection.

Edge embellishment

1 Sew through the beadwork to exit an edge 4 mm. Pick up a 15º seed bead, an 11º, an O-bead, an 11º, and a 15º, and sew through the next 4 mm on the same edge **(figure 3)**. Repeat this stitch for the length of the

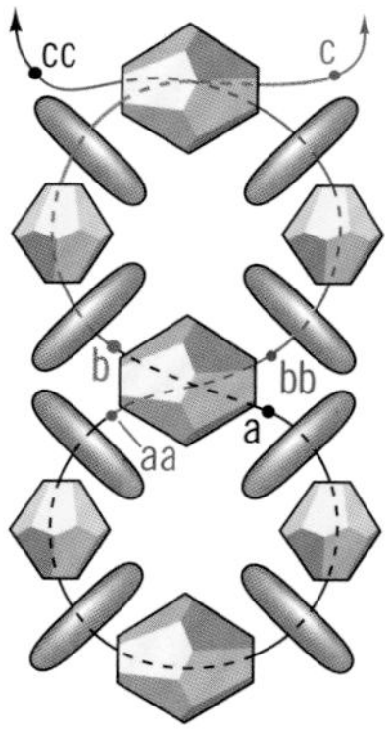

FIGURE 1

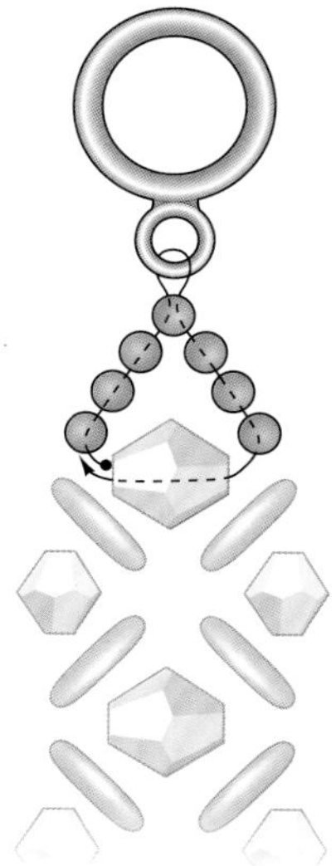

FIGURE 2

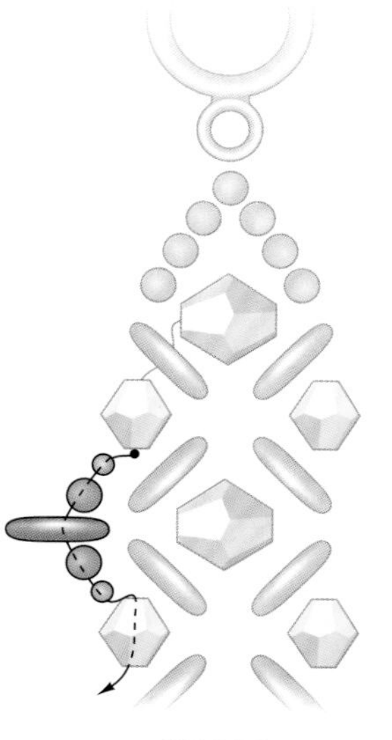

FIGURE 3

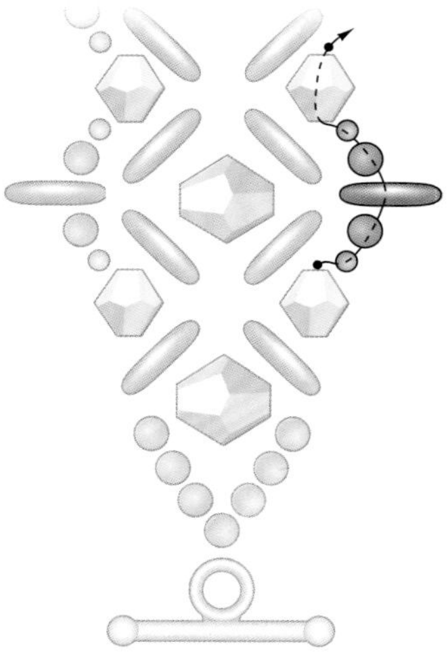

FIGURE 4

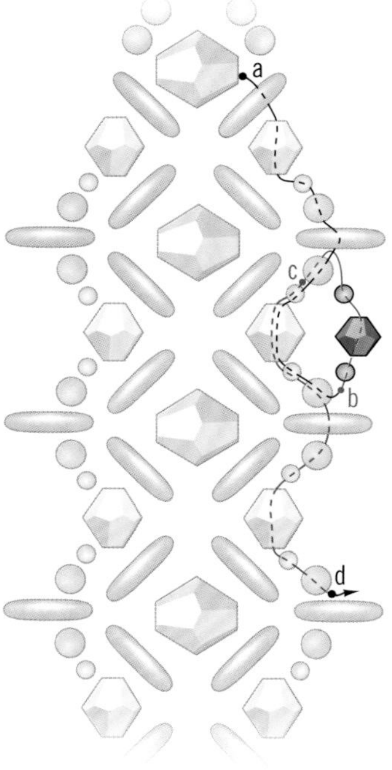

FIGURE 5

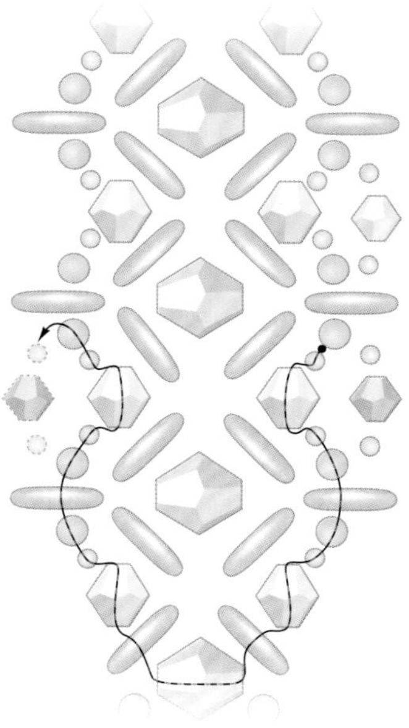

FIGURE 6

Difficulty rating

Materials
blue bracelet 7¼ in. (18.4 cm)
- **22** 6 mm bicone crystals (Swarovski, capri blue)
- **42** 4 mm bicone crystals (Swarovski, light emerald)
- 3 mm bicone crystals
  - **20** color A (Swarovski, crystal CAL)
  - **18** color B (Swarovski, metallic blue 2X)
- **124** O-beads (crystal full labrador)
- **1 g** 11º seed beads (Miyuki 2008, matte metallic patina iris)
- **1 g** 15º seed beads (Toho 558, galvanized aluminum)
- clasp
- Fireline 8 lb. test
- beading needles, #11 or #12

pink bracelet colors
- 6 mm bicone crystals (Swarovski, fuchsia)
- 4 mm bicone crystals (Swarovski, Indian pink)
- 3 mm bicone crystals
  - color A (Swarovski, light rose AB)
  - color B (Swarovski, light smoked topaz)
- O-beads (crystal blue rainbow)
- 11º seed beads (Toho PF558, galvanized aluminum)
- 15º seed beads (Toho 332, gold lustered raspberry)

Taut thought

As you're working, tape the loose thread and clasp to the bobbin to keep the tension tight on the other side.

base, and continue through the end 6 mm.

2 Work as in step 5 of "Base" to add the other half of the clasp.

3 Sew through the beadwork to exit the next 4 mm on the other edge. Repeat step 1 for this edge of the bracelet **(figure 4)**. End this thread.

4 Unwind the other thread, and sew through the next 10 edge beads **(figure 5 a–b)**.

5 Pick up a 15º, a color A 3 mm bicone crystal, and a 15º, and sew through the 11º after the previous O-bead **(b–c)** to form a loop. Continue through the next 10 edge beads **(c–d)**.

6 Repeat step 5 for the remainder of the edge, alternating color A and color B 3 mms. After adding

the final embellishment on this edge, sew through the next 20 beads as shown to exit the other edge **(figure 6)**.

7 Repeat step 5 for this edge, and end the thread. Begin with the same color 3 mm bicone that was used last on the previous edge. **○**

DIAGONAL TUBULAR PEYOTE STITCH

Celtic knot earrings

Twist and weave a flat peyote tube into a traditional Celtic knot that's lightweight and easy to wear.

designed by **Susan Harle**

stepbystep

Leg 1
[1] On a comfortable length of thread, pick up four color A 11º cylinder beads, four color B 11º cylinder beads, four As, and four Bs. Tie the beads into a ring with a square knot (Basics), leaving a 6-in. (15cm) tail, and sew through the first two As.

[2] Work a round as follows:
• Pick up two As, and sew through the next A **(photo a)** to begin an increase spine.
• Work two peyote stitches (Basics) using Bs and one stitch using an A **(photo b)**.
• Skip the next two As to begin a decrease spine, and sew through the following A **(photo c)**.
• Work one stitch using an A and two stitches using Bs. Step up through the next A in the spine **(photo d)**.

[3] Work a round as follows:
• Pick up two As, and sew through the next A in this spine.
• Work two stitches using Bs and one stitch using an A.
• Sew through the adjacent A on the opposite side of this spine to work a decrease **(photo e)**.
• Work one stitch using an A and two stitches using Bs. Step up through the next A in this spine **(photo f)**. The beadwork will begin to fold **(photo g)**.

[4] Repeat step 3 until you have seven pairs of As along both spines **(photo h)**.

Leg 2
[1] To change direction, sew through the next A in this spine without picking up any beads.

[2] Work a round as follows:
• Work one stitch using an A and two stitches using Bs.
• Pick up two As, and sew through the next A to work an increase in this spine.
• Work two stitches using Bs and one stitch using an A.
• Sew through the adjacent A on the opposite side of this spine to work a decrease, and step up through the next A **(photo i)**.

[3] Repeat step 2 until you have 38 pairs of As along both spines of the new leg **(photo j)**. End and add thread (Basics) as needed.

[4] Work two stitches using Bs and one stitch using an A.

Leg 3
[1] To change direction,

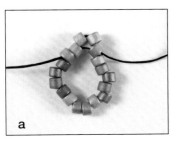

a

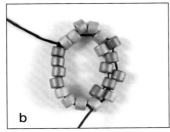

b

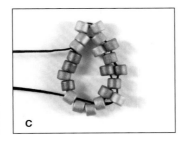

c

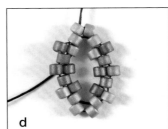

d

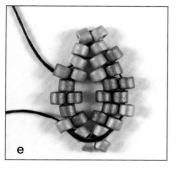

e

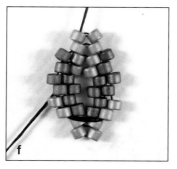

f

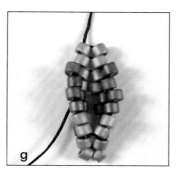

g

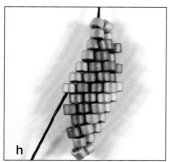

h

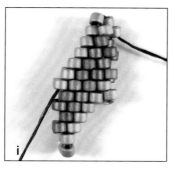

i

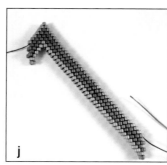

j

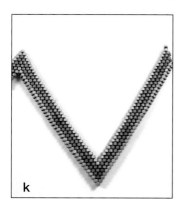

k

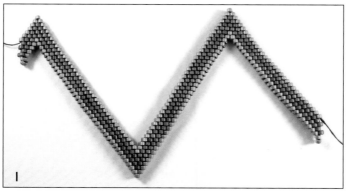

l

Difficulty rating

Materials

purple earrings 2 in. (5 cm)
- 4 g 11° cylinder beads in each of **2** colors: A (Miyuki DB1851, Duracoat light pewter), B (Miyuki DB0611, dyed silver-lined wine)
- 2 4–5 mm jump rings
- pair of earring findings (silver)
- Fireline 6 lb. test or Nymo D
- beading needles, #11 or #12
- 2 pairs of chainnose, flat-nose, and/or bentnose pliers

gunmetal earrings (p. 48) colors:
- 11° cylinder beads: A (Miyuki DB1843, Duracoat dark mauve), B (Miyuki DB0301, matte gunmetal)

sew through the next A in this spine without picking up any beads.

[2] Work one stitch using an A and two stitches using Bs. Pick up two As, and sew through the next A to work an increase in this spine. Step up through the next B.

[3] Work one stitch using a B and one stitch using an A. Sew through the adjacent A on the opposite side of this spine to work a decrease.

[4] Work one stitch using an A and two stitches using Bs. Pick up two As, and sew through the next A to work an increase in this spine.

[5] Work one stitch using a B, and step up through the next B, noticing the change

in position of the step up.

[6] Work one stitch using an A, and sew through the adjacent A on the opposite side of this spine to work a decrease.

[7] Work one stitch using an A and two stitches using Bs. Pick up two As, and sew through the next A to work an increase in this spine.

[8] Work two stitches using Bs, and step up through the next A in this spine. Sew through the adjacent A on the opposite side of this spine to work a decrease.

[9] Work a round as follows:
- Work one stitch using an A and two stitches using Bs.
- Pick up two As, and sew through the next A to work an increase in this spine.

- Work two stitches using Bs and one stitch using an A.
- Sew through the adjacent A on the opposite side of this spine to work a decrease, and step up through the next A.

[10] Repeat step 9 until you have 38 pairs of As along both spines of the new leg (photo k).

Completion of Leg 1

Note that Leg 1 is incomplete (with just seven pairs of As along each spine). You will now work the remainder of Leg 1, even though the two will not come together to form the complete Leg 1 until "Assembly."

[1] Work two stitches using Bs and one stitch using an A.

[2] Work steps 1–9 of "Leg 3," and then repeat step 9 until you have 31 pairs of As along both spines of the new leg **(photo l)**.

Assembly

[1] Position the beadwork on your work surface so that the short end of Leg 1 is at the top right-hand corner. Holding that part of the beadwork down, bring the other end of the bead-work over to the right side so that there is a twist in Leg 2 **(photo m)**. Twist Leg 3 toward the front, and bring it behind Leg 2 **(photo n)**. Bring the longer end of Leg 1 over Leg 2, through the opening, and under Leg 3 **(photo o)**.

[2] Zip up (Basics) the two ends of Leg 1, and end the working thread and tail.

[3] Add 12 in. (30cm) of thread to the beadwork, exiting an A at the tip of one of the points. Pick up five As, and sew through the adjacent A on the same tip. Retrace the thread path of the loop, and end the thread.

[4] Open a 4mm jump ring (Basics), and attach the loop of As to an earring finding.

[5] Make another earring. o

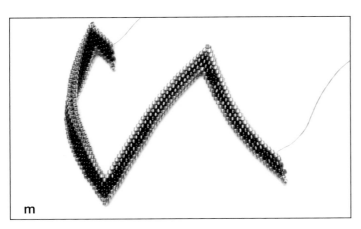

m

n

o

FOUR-DROP PEYOTE STITCH

Abstract
in green
and purple

Rich hues add a dramatic flair to this bracelet.

designed by **Josie Fabre**

This bracelet is done in four-drop peyote stitch, which follows the same technique as two-drop peyote, but uses four beads in each stitch, instead of two.

PATTERN

Bracelet band

1 On a comfortable length of thread, attach a stop bead, leaving a 6-in. (15 cm) tail. Starting in the lower left-hand corner of the **pattern**, pick up 24 11º cylinder beads for rows 1 and 2: one color A, four Bs, one E, one G, one E, one B, one E, four Ds, one E, one B, one E, one G, one E, four Bs, and one A.
2 Following the **pattern**, work in four-drop peyote stitch using the appropriate color beads. End and add thread as needed, and end the working thread and tail when you complete the base.

Toggle tab and beads

1 Add 12 in. (30cm) of thread to one end of the bracelet, and exit the down-bead that is closest to the center of the row, with your needle pointing toward the adjacent down-bead **(figure 1, point a)**. Pick up a D, and sew through the adjacent up-bead **(a-b)**. Pick up a D, and sew back through the D added in the previous stitch **(b-c)**. Working in even-count peyote stitch, use Ds to stitch a tab that is two beads wide and 12 beads long **(c-d)**.
2 Pick up an 8 mm crystal and a D. Sew back through the crystal and the two end beads in the tab **(figure 2, a-b)**. Repeat to add an 8 mm crystal to the end bead, exiting the next bead in the same column **(b-c)**. Repeat once more to attach a third crystal **(c-d)**.
3 Retrace the thread path through the tab, and end the thread in the band.

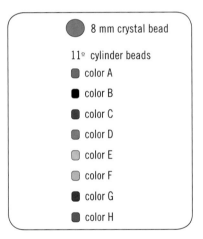

- ● 8 mm crystal bead

11º cylinder beads
- ▢ color A
- ▪ color B
- ▪ color C
- ▪ color D
- ▢ color E
- ▢ color F
- ▪ color G
- ▪ color H

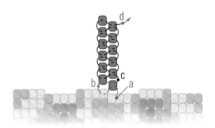

FIGURE 1

Toggle loop

1 Locate the last row at the other end of the base and notice that one side of the row begins with four up-beads. Position your beadwork so these beads are on the left. Add 20 in. (51 cm) of thread to the bracelet base, and exit the ninth bead from the left, with your needle pointing toward the other edge of the band **(figure 3, point a)**.

2 Pick up 37 color D cylinders, and sew through the next set of down-beads with your needle pointing toward the beads your thread exited at the start of this step **(a–b)**.

3 Sew through the beadwork to exit the first cylinder added in step 2 **(b–c)**. Work in peyote stitch around the loop, using one cylinder per stitch **(c–d)**. Sew into the bracelet, and end the thread.

Edging

1 Add 1 yd (.9 m) of thread to the bracelet band, and exit an end cylinder along one edge.

2 Pick up a 15º seed bead, a 3 mm fire-polished bead, and a 15º. Skip one edge cylinder, sew down through the next edge cylinder, and sew up through the following edge cylinder. Repeat this stitch along the entire edge of the band. Sew through the end of the band, and repeat to add edging along the other side. End the threads. ●

FIGURE 2

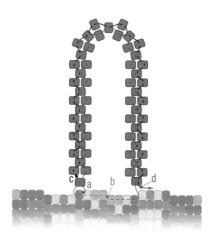

FIGURE 3

Difficulty rating

  ◇ ◇ ◇

Materials
bracelet 7⅜ in. (18.7 cm)

- **3** 8 mm faceted round crystals (Swarovski 5000, palace green opal)
- **62** 3 mm fire-polished beads (black)
- 11º Miyuki Delica cylinder beads
  - **1 g** color A (DB0776, matte transparent kelly green)
  - **4 g** color B (DB0310, jet black matte)
  - **1 g** color C (DB0458, metallic dark green)
  - **2 g** color D (DB0906, sparkling purple-lined crystal)
  - **1 g** color E (DB0249, purple Ceylon)
  - **1 g** color F (DB0691, semi-matte silver-lined mint green)
  - **2 g** color G (DB0609, silver-lined dark purple)
  - **1 g** color H (DB0005, medium blue AB)
- **1 g** 15º seed beads (Miyuki 401, black)
- Fireline, 6 lb. test
- beading needles, #11 or #12

BEAD WEAVING

Bouvardia
necklace

Using a bounty of shaped beads and
seed beads, create star-like bouvardia
blossoms, and connect them with
a net of beads and pearls.

designed by **Akiko Nomura**

Star motifs

1 Work in rounds as follows:
Round 1: On 1 yd. (.9 m) of thread, pick up a repeating pattern of a color B 15º seed bead and a 2.5 x 5mm SuperDuo bead four times. Sew through all the beads again to form a ring, leaving a 6-in. (15cm) tail. Tie a square knot with the working thread and tail, and sew through the first B 15º. With the tail, pick up a B 15º, sew through the outer hole of the nearest SuperDuo, and leave it for now **(figure 1)**.
Round 2: With the working thread, pick up a B 15º, sew through the B 15º your thread just exited, and continue through the inner hole of the next SuperDuo and 15º in the ring. Repeat this stitch to add a B 15º above each existing B 15º. Exit the first B 15º added in this round **(figure 2)**.
Round 3: Pick up a B 15º, three 11º seed beads, and a B 15º, and sew through the B your thread exited at the start of this step to form a loop. Sew through the inner hole of the next SuperDuo, and continue through the following B 15º added in round 2. Repeat these stitches to complete the round, and exit the first B 15º added in the first loop of seed beads **(figure 3)**.
2 Pick up a 6mm two-hole triangle bead (LH), another triangle (RH), two 11ºs, and a third triangle (RH). Sew through the open hole of the first triangle from back to front **(figure 4, a–b)**, causing this to become the middle, front-most triangle of the trio. Continue through the corresponding three B 15ºs in the adjacent loop of seed beads **(b–c)**, pick up a B 15º, and sew through the open hole of the next SuperDuo **(c–d)**. Snug up the beads so the three triangles sit behind the loop of 11ºs, with the two new 11ºs on what will become the underside of the star motif.
3 Pick up a B 15º, and sew through the three B 15ºs in the next loop of seed beads **(figure 5, a–b)**. Pick up two triangles (LH and RH) and two 11ºs, and sew through the open hole of the adjacent triangle from the previous trio from back to front **(b–c)**. Continue through the open hole of the first triangle added in this step, from back to front **(c–d)**. Make sure all the triangles are behind the loop of 11ºs. Sew through the three B 15ºs in the loop **(d–e)**, pick up a B 15º, and sew through the open hole of the next SuperDuo **(e–f)**.
4 Repeat step 3 to add a third trio of triangles.

Difficulty rating

Materials

necklace 26½ in. (67.3cm)
- **96** 6mm CzechMates two-hole triangle beads (21413, brown iris)
- **87** 6mm CzechMates two-hole lentil beads (K0171, matte metallic flax)
- **10** 3 x 6mm CzechMates two-hole brick beads (13720, chocolate brown)
- **19** 6mm baroque pearls (white)
- **19** 4mm snail or round pearls (white)
- **11** 4mm fire-polished beads (magic wine)
- **48** 2.5 x 5mm SuperDuo beads (00030/13130, crystal lava red)
- **8 g** 11º seed beads (Toho 221, bronze)
- **2 g** 15º seed beads in each of **2** colors: A (Toho 221, bronze), B (Toho 84, metallic iris green-brown)
- toggle clasp (JBB, antique brass)
- **2** 6mm jump rings (antique brass)
- Fireline 6 lb. test
- beading needles, #12 or #13
- **2** pairs of chainnose, flatnose, and/or bentnose pliers

6 mm two-hole triangle bead

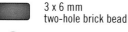
6 mm two-hole lentil bead

3 x 6 mm two-hole brick bead

2.5 x 5 mm SuperDuo bead

6 mm baroque pearl

4 mm pearl

4 mm fire-polished bead

11º seed bead

15º seed bead, color A

15º seed bead, color B

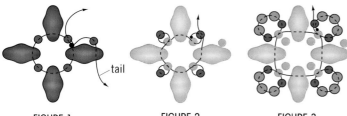

FIGURE 1   FIGURE 2   FIGURE 3

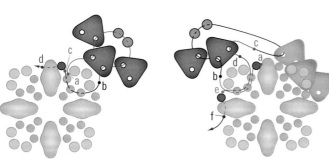

FIGURE 4   FIGURE 5

tips
- Check all two-hole beads to be sure that both holes are clear.
- When you end a thread, leave it untrimmed; you may want to use it later to reinforce the beadwork.
- Pick up the triangle beads as follows: With the point of the triangle facing away from you, pick up the bead through the left hole (LH) or right hole (RH) per the instructions.

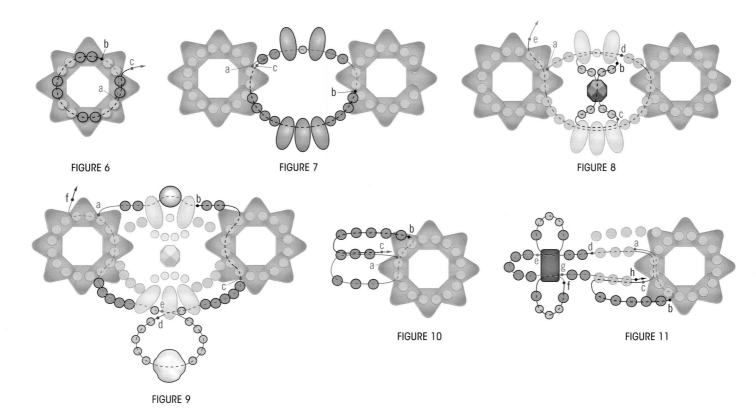

FIGURE 6

FIGURE 7

FIGURE 8

FIGURE 9

FIGURE 10

FIGURE 11

5 Pick up a B 15º, and sew through the three B 15ºs in the next loop of seed beads. To add the last trio, pick up a triangle (LH), and sew through the open hole of the adjacent triangle from the first trio. Pick up two 11ºs, and sew through the open hole of the adjacent triangle from the third trio. Continue through the open hole of the single triangle added in this step. Sew through the three B 15ºs in the loop of seed beads, and pick up a B 15º. Tie the working thread and tail with a square knot, but do not end the tail.

6 Sew through the outer hole of the next SuperDuo, the B 15º added with the tail, and the following two triangles to exit the reverse side of the star. Sew through the adjacent pair of 11ºs.

7 Pick up two 11ºs, and sew through the next two 11ºs **(figure 6, a–b)**. Repeat this stitch to make a ring **(b–c)**. Retrace the thread path to

tighten the ring, sew through the beadwork to exit next to the tail, tie another knot, and end the threads.

8 Make 12 star motifs.

Connections

You'll connect the motifs by the ring of 11ºs on the back of each motif.

1 Add 30 in. (76 cm) of thread to a motif, exiting a pair of 11ºs aligned with a front-layer triangle **(figure 7, point a)**. Pick up two 11ºs, a 6mm two-hole lentil bead, a color A 15º seed bead, a lentil, and two 11ºs. Sew through the two corresponding 11ºs in a second motif **(a–b)**. Pick up four 11ºs, three lentils, and four 11ºs, and sew through the two 11ºs in the first motif **(b–c)**.

2 Sew through the first two 11ºs, lentil, A 15º, and lentil just added **(figure 8, a–b)**. Pick up two A 15ºs, a 4mm fire-polished bead, and two A 15ºs, and sew through the three lentils along the other

edge of the connection **(b–c)**. Pick up two A 15ºs, sew back through the fire-polished bead, pick up two A 15ºs, and sew through the opposite lentil, A 15º, and lentil **(c–d)**. Continue through the entire connection to exit the two 11ºs in the first motif, and sew through two more 11ºs in the ring **(d–e)**.

3 Pick up two 11ºs, sew through the open hole of the adjacent lentil, pick up a 4mm pearl, and sew through the open hole of the next lentil **(figure 9, a–b)**. Pick up two 11ºs, and sew through six 11ºs in the second motif **(b–c)**.

4 Pick up five 11ºs, and sew through the open hole of the next lentil. Pick up an A 15º, and sew through the open hole of the middle lentil **(c–d)**. Pick up five A 15ºs, a 6 mm pearl, and five A 15ºs, and sew through the middle lentil again **(d–e)** forming a loop dangle with the pearl. Pick up an A 15º, and sew

through the next lentil. Pick up five 11ºs, and sew through the corresponding eight 11ºs in the first motif **(e–f)**. End the threads.

5 Connect all 12 motifs.

Neck straps
First brick unit

Continue to work with the necklace face down, connecting each neck strap to the ring of 11ºs on the back of an end motif.

1 Add 1 yd. (.9 m) of thread to an end motif, exiting opposite the previous connection **(figure 10, point a)**. Pick up six 11ºs, and sew through the end pair of 11ºs in the ring plus the following pair of 11ºs **(a–b)**. Pick up five 11ºs, and sew through the column of three 11ºs next to them **(b–c)**. Sew through four 11ºs in the ring **(figure 11, a–b)**, pick up five 11ºs, and sew through the column of three 11ºs next to them **(b–c)**. Sew through the beadwork to exit a column of three 11ºs **(c–d)**.

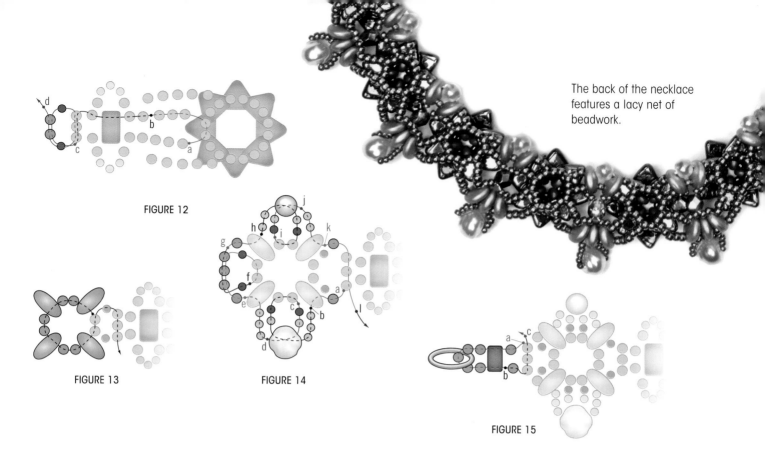

FIGURE 12

FIGURE 13

FIGURE 14

The back of the necklace features a lacy net of beadwork.

FIGURE 15

2 Pick up two 11ºs, a 3 x 6 mm two-hole brick bead, an 11º, three A 15ºs, and an 11º. Sew through same hole of the brick, making a loop atop the brick **(d–e)**. Pick up five 11ºs, and sew through the open hole of the brick **(e–f)**. Pick up an 11º, three A 15ºs, and an 11º, and sew through the same hole of the brick, making another loop **(f–g)**. Pick up two 11ºs, and sew through the next column of three 11ºs **(g–h)**. Continue through two 11ºs in the ring, and the other column of three 11ºs **(figure 12, a–b)**. Sew through the next two 11ºs, the brick, and four 11ºs **(b–c)**.

Lentil unit
1 Pick up a B 15º, two 11ºs, and a B 15º, and sew through the previous three 11ºs and the first B 15º and two 11ºs just added **(c–d)**.
2 Pick up a repeating pattern of a lentil and two 11ºs three times, and then pick up a

lentil. Sew through the two 11ºs and the next B 15º added in the previous step and the adjacent three 11ºs **(figure 13)**.
3 Pick up an 11º, and sew through the open hole of the nearest lentil **(figure 14, a–b)**. Pick up three A 15ºs, a 6mm pearl, an A 15º, and a B 15º, and sew through the next two 11ºs in the inner ring of beads **(b–c)**. Pick up a B 15º and an A 15º, and sew through the pearl **(c–d)**. Pick up three A 15ºs, and sew through the open hole of the next lentil **(d–e)**.
4 Pick up four 11ºs and a B 15º, and sew through the next two 11ºs in the inner ring of beads **(e–f)**. Pick up a B 15º, and sew through the last three 11ºs just added **(f–g)**. Pick up an 11º, and sew through the open hole of the next lentil **(g–h)**.
5 Pick up two A 15ºs, a 4mm pearl, an A 15º, and a B 15º. Sew through the

next two 11ºs in the inner ring of beads **(h–i)**. Pick up a B 15º and an A 15º, and sew through the pearl **(i–j)**. Pick up two A 15ºs, and sew through the open hole of the next lentil **(j–k)**. Pick up an 11º, and sew through the three 11ºs from the previous connection **(k–l)**.
6 Sew through the outer ring of beads to exit the three 11ºs at the other end of the unit.

Subsequent brick units
This brick bead unit is worked similar to the first one except it begins and ends with a single 11º next to the brick; refer to **figure 11, d–h**.
1 Pick up an 11º, a brick, an 11º, three A 15ºs, and an 11º. Sew through the same hole of the brick, making a loop atop the brick. Pick up five 11ºs, and sew through the other hole of the brick. Pick up an 11º, three A 15ºs, and an 11º, and sew through the same hole of the brick, making another loop. Pick

up an 11º, and sew through the three 11ºs in the previous unit. Sew through the next 11º, brick, and four 11ºs.

Keep going!
1 Work as in "Lentil unit" and "Subsequent brick units" until you have a total of four brick units and four lentil units. End and add thread as needed.
2 Exit the three 11ºs at the end of the last lentil unit. Pick up an 11º, a brick, and five 11ºs. Sew through the other hole of the brick **(figure 15, a–b)**, pick up an 11º, and sew through the end three 11ºs in the lentil unit **(b–c)**. Retrace the thread path through the clasp connection, and end the thread.
3 Open a 6mm jump ring, and attach half of the clasp to the end loop of 11ºs.
4 Add the neck strap and clasp to the other side of the necklace. ●

BEAD WEAVING

Chexx it out!
bracelet

This fun bracelet features one of the newest two-hole beads and a pretty palette.

designed by **Aurelio Castaño**

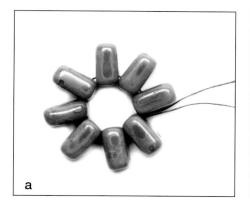

a

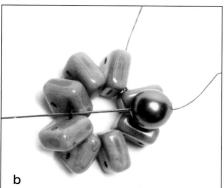

b

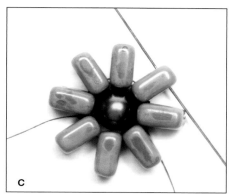

c

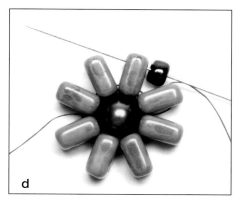

d

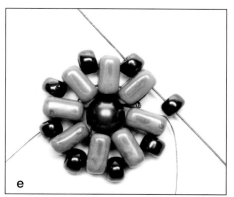

e

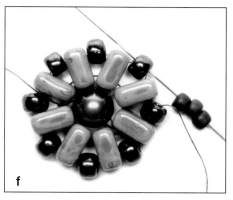

f

Difficulty rating

Materials
gold bracelet 8½ in. (21.6 cm)
- **56** 6 x 6 mm Chexx two-hole beads (**16** crystal, **16** turquoise, **16** purple luminous, **8** chalk bronze lumi)
- **7** 6 mm glass pearls (dark brown)
- **4 g** 6º seed beads (Miyuki 4205, Duracoat galvanized zest)
- **4 g** 8º seed beads (Miyuki 4205, Duracoat galvanized zest)
- **12** 15º seed beads (Miyuki 4205, Duracoat galvanized zest)
- 10 mm magnetic clasp
- Fireline 6 lb. test
- beading needles, #10

bronze bracelet colors:
- 6 x 6 mm Chexx two-hole beads (black, silver, turquoise)
- 6º seed beads (Miyuki 457, metallic dark bronze)
- 8º seed beads (Miyuki 462, metallic gold iris)
- 15º seed beads (Miyuki 462, metallic gold iris)

NOTE:
To adjust the length of the bracelet, just add or omit flowers. Each flower measures 1 in. (2.5 cm) wide.

Flowers

[1] On 1 yd. (.9 m) of thread, pick up eight 6 x 6 mm Chexx two-hole beads. Sew through all the beads twice to form a ring, leaving a 6-in. (15 cm) tail (**photo a**). Tie a square knot with the working thread and tail (Basics).

[2] Pick up a 6 mm pearl, center the pearl in the middle, skip four Chexx beads, and sew under the thread bridge between the fourth and fifth beads (**photo b**). Sew back through the pearl, and pull the working thread tight to center the pearl in the ring.

[3] Sew around the thread bridge where your tail is exiting and back through the pearl. Sew through the open hole of the next Chexx bead (**photo c**).

[4] Keeping a consistent tension, pick up a 6º seed bead, and sew through the open hole of the next Chexx bead (**photo d**). Repeat this stitch to complete the round. End with your thread exiting the first Chexx bead and 6º (**photo e**).

[5] Pick up three 8º seed beads, and sew through the next 6º to form a picot (**photo f**). Repeat this stitch to complete the round. End the working thread and tail (Basics).

[6] Repeat steps 1–5 to make six additional flowers. Do not end the working thread on the final flower.

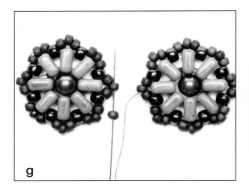

g

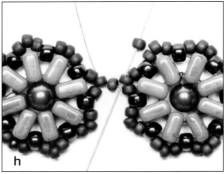

h

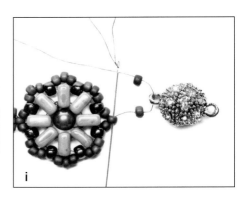

i

j

k

Bracelet assembly

[1] With the working thread from the final flower, sew through the next two 8⁰s.

[2] Pick up an 8⁰, and sew through the center 8⁰ in a picot on another flower **(photo g)**. Pick up an 8⁰, and sew back through the 8⁰ your thread exited at the start of this step **(photo h)**. Retrace the thread path to reinforce the join. Sew through the outer edge of the first flower, and exit the center 8⁰ in a picot on the opposite side.

[3] Work as in step 2 to attach all of the flowers. On the final flower, continue to sew through the outer edge to reach the center 8⁰ in the picot on the opposite side.

[4] Pick up an 8⁰, half of the clasp, and an 8⁰, and sew through the same 8⁰ your thread exited at the start of this step **(photo i)**.

[5] Pick up a 15⁰ seed bead, and sew through the next 8⁰ in the loop. Pick up two 15⁰s, and sew through the clasp **(photo j)**. Pick up two 15⁰s, and sew through the next 8⁰. Pick up a 15⁰, and sew through the same 8⁰ your thread exited at the start of this step **(photo k)**. Retrace the thread path, and end the working thread.

[6] Add 10 in. (25 cm) of thread (Basics) to the opposite end of the bracelet, and repeat steps 4 and 5 to attach the other half of the clasp. ●

This bracelet features a side view of the Chexx beads. A closer look at the loose beads reveals the configuration of the holes.

Silky diamonds bracelet

Embellish two-hole Silky beads with seed beads for a casual everyday look.

designed by **Connie Whittaker**

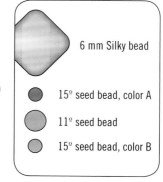

Base

In this project, the front of the Silky bead is the side with the bump, which should be facing up. With the holes of the Silky bead running vertically, we will refer to the right hole (RH) or the left hole (LH).

1 On a comfortable length of thread, pick up a Silky (RH), leaving an 8-in. (20cm) tail.

2 Pick up three color A 15º seed beads, an 11º seed bead, and three As, and sew through the Silky (LH) **(figure 1, a–b)**. Pick up three As, an 11º, and three As, and sew through the Silky (RH) **(b–c)**.

3 Retrace the thread path skipping the 11ºs **(c–d)** and pull tight to make the 11ºs pop out.

4 Pick up four color B 15º seed beads, and sew through the Silky (LH) **(figure 2, a–b)**. Pick up four Bs, and sew through the Silky (RH) **(b–c)**.

5 Pick up three As, a Silky (LH, from top to bottom), and three As, and sew through the Silky your thread exited at the start of this step **(figure 3)**. Retrace the thread path, skipping the center As, and pull tight to make the center As pop out **(figure 4, a–b)**. Continue through the beadwork to exit the RH of the Silky just added **(b–c)**. The exposed edge thread will be hidden by B 15ºs later on.

6 Repeat steps 2–5 for the desired bracelet length, less approximately 1 in. (2.5 cm) for the clasp. Repeat steps 2–4 once more to embellish the final Silky bead.

Clasp

1 Attach the 4 mm jump rings to the toggle ring and the bar.

2 With the thread exiting the RH of the last Silky, pick up six As and a 4 mm jump ring with the toggle ring attached. Sew through the Silky again to form a loop. Retrace the thread path, and end the working thread.

3 With the tail, sew through the beadwork to exit the end hole of the Silky. Repeat step 2 to attach the toggle bar. ❍

Difficulty rating

Materials

bracelet 7½ in. (19.1 cm)

- **20** 6 mm Silky beads (alabaster lilac gold luster)
- **1 g** 11º seed beads (Miyuki 457, metallic dark bronze)
- **2 g** 15º seed beads
  - color A (Toho 703, matte mauve mocha)
  - color B (Miyuki 457, metallic dark bronze)
- Fireline, 6 lb. test
- beading needles, #11 or #12
- 1 toggle clasp
- **2** 4 mm jump rings
- **2** pairs of chainnose, flatnose, and/or bentnose pliers

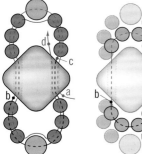

FIGURE 1

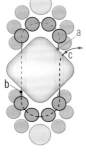

FIGURE 2

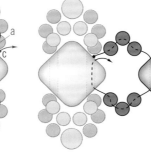

FIGURE 3

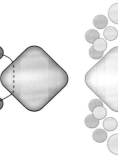

FIGURE 4

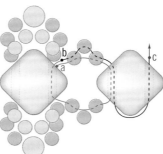

6 mm Silky bead

15º seed bead, color A

11º seed bead

15º seed bead, color B

MODIFIED PEYOTE STITCH

Bold
closure

Magnetic clasps
bring this quick-stitch
project together.

designed by **Dana Rudolph**

Base

1 On a comfortable length of thread, attach a stop bead, leaving a 6-in. (15 cm) tail.

2 Pick up a 5 mm rhinestone rondelle, six 3º seed beads, two rondelles, and a 3º. Working in modified peyote stitch, sew back through the fifth 3º added **(figure 1, a–b)**. The rondelles will sit parallel to each other. Work two more peyote stitches using 3ºs, and sew through the first rondelle added **(b–c)**.

3 Pick up a rondelle and a 3º, and work a peyote stitch **(c–d)**. Work two more peyote stitches using 3ºs, and continue through the next rondelle **(d–e)**.

4 Repeat step 3 until you have 29 rondelles along each edge. End and add thread as needed.

Edge embellishment

1 With your thread exiting the end rondelle, pick up a 4 mm crystal lochrosen and a 15º seed bead, and sew back through the lochrosen and rondelle

(figure 2, a–b). Continue through the next six 3ºs and the rondelle on the opposite edge of the base **(b–c)**.

2 Pick up a lochrosen and a 15º, and sew back through the lochrosen and rondelle **(c–d)**. Sew through the 3ºs to exit the next rondelle on the opposite side of the base **(d–e)**.

3 Repeat step 2 for the length of the bracelet, removing the stop bead before adding the embellishment to the end row. End and add thread as needed.

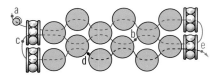

FIGURE 1

FIGURE 2

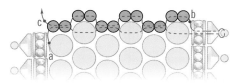

FIGURE 3

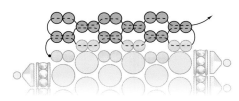

FIGURE 4

Clasp

1 Work in rows as follows using 8º seed beads:

Rows 1 and 2: Continuing with the working thread, work three peyote stitches using two 8ºs in place of a 3º, and sewing through the end rondelle, lochrosen, and 15º. Sew back through the lochrosen and rondelle **(figure 3, a–b)**. Work three more stitches using two 8ºs per stitch **(b–c)**.

Row 3–5: Work three more rows using two 8ºs per stitch **(figure 4)**. End the working thread and tail.

2 The rows of 8ºs will fit into the slot of the 34 x 12 x 7 mm magnetic clasp. Apply E6000 adhesive into the slot of the clasp, and spread it evenly with a toothpick. Insert the 8ºs on the end of the beadwork, wiping away any excess glue. Set aside to dry.

3 When the glue is dry, add 18 in. (46 cm) of thread at the other end of the bracelet, and repeat steps 1 and 2. ●

	5 mm rhinestone rondelle
	4 mm lochrosen crystal bead
	3º seed bead
	8º seed bead
	15º seed bead

a wider variation

Make a wider bracelet by starting the bracelet with eight 3ºs instead of six and using a 37 x 19 x 7 mm magnetic clasp.

Difficulty rating

Materials

blue bracelet 7¼ x 1½ in. (18.4 x 3.8 cm)

- **58** 5 mm rhinestone rondelles (crystal silver plated)
- **58** 4 mm lochrosen crystals (Swarovski, crystal)
- **31 g** 3º seed beads (Toho 288, crystal metallic blue lined)
- **1 g** 8º seed beads (Toho 288, crystal metallic blue lined)
- **1 g** 15º seed beads (Toho 21, crystal silver lined)
- **1** 34 x 12 x 7 mm etched magnetic clasp (silver)
- Fireline 6 lb. test
- beading needles, #11
- E6000 adhesive
- toothpick

grey bracelet 7¼ x 1⅝ in. (18.4 x 4.1 cm)

- **58** 5 mm rhinestone rondelles (crystal with black finish)
- **58** 4 mm lochrosen crystals (Swarovski, crystal)
- **44 g** 3º seed beads (Toho 566, matte metallic antique silver)
- **1 g** 8º seed beads (Toho 566, matte metallic antique silver)
- **1 g** 15º seed beads (Miyuki 401F, matte black)
- **1** 37 x 19 x 7 mm magnetic clasp (silver)

Mums
in bloom

This bracelet of connected mum flowers is easy to make and can be done in a rainbow of colors to complement any look.

designed by **Susan Schwartzenberger**

stepbystep

First flower

[1] On a comfortable length of thread, pick up 10 2.5 x 5 mm SuperDuo beads. Sew through the beads again to form a ring, leaving a 6-in. (15cm) tail. Tie an overhand knot (Basics) with the working thread and tail, and continue through the next SuperDuo.

[2] Pick up a 4 mm pearl, skip four SuperDuos, and sew through the next SuperDuo going in the same direction **(figure 1, a–b)**. Sew through the available hole of this SuperDuo **(b–c)**.

[3] Pick up an 11º seed bead, and sew through the available hole of the next SuperDuo **(c–d)**. Repeat this stitch to complete the round **(d–e)**.

Connector unit

[1] Pick up a SuperDuo, sew through the same hole of the SuperDuo your thread exited at the start of this step, and continue through the SuperDuo just added **(figure 2, a–b)**.

[2] Pick up three 11ºs, and sew through the available hole of the same SuperDuo **(b–c)**. Pick up three 11ºs, and sew through the other hole of the same SuperDuo and the first 11º **(c–d)**.

[3] Sew through the nearest 11º, Super-Duo, and 11º on the edge of the flower **(figure 3, a–b)**. Continue through the next 11º, SuperDuo, three 11ºs, and SuperDuo in the connector unit **(b–c)**.

Additional flowers

[1] Pick up a SuperDuo, sew through the same hole of the SuperDuo your thread exited at the start of this step, and continue through the SuperDuo just added **(c–d)**. Sew through the available hole of this SuperDuo **(d–e)**.

[2] Pick up nine SuperDuos, and sew through the SuperDuo from the start of this step to form a ring **(figure 4)**. Retrace the thread path.

[3] Pick up a pearl, skip four SuperDuos, and sew through the next SuperDuo in the same direction **(figure 5, a–b)**. Sew through the available hole of this SuperDuo **(b–c)**.

[4] Pick up an 11º, and sew through the available hole of the next SuperDuo **(c–d)**. Repeat this stitch to complete the round **(d–e)**.

[5] Sew through the beadwork to exit the 11º, SuperDuo, and 11º attached to the previous connector unit **(figure 6, a–b)**. Continue through the nearest 11º, SuperDuo, and 11º in the connector unit **(b–c)** and the 11º, SuperDuo, and 11º in the flower **(c–d)**. Sew through the next five beads to exit the third Super-Duo from the connector unit **(d–e)**.

[6] Repeat steps 1–3 of "Connector unit" and steps 1–5 of "Additional flowers" to form a zigzag pattern of 11 flowers and 10 connector units. End and add thread (Basics) as needed.

Second row of flowers

[1] After completing the last flower unit, sew through the beadwork to exit the SuperDuo shown in **figure 7, point a**.

[2] Repeat steps 1–3 of "Connector unit," noticing that you will be sewing through one of the same 11ºs you already sewed through when you added the last connector unit. Then repeat

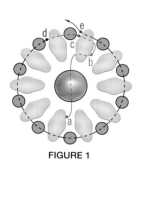

FIGURE 1

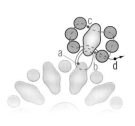

FIGURE 2

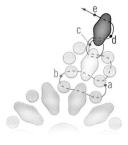

FIGURE 3

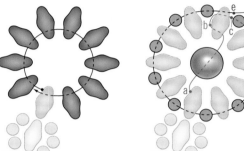

FIGURE 4

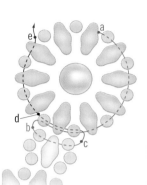

FIGURE 5

FIGURE 6

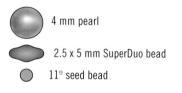

- ⬤ 4 mm pearl
- ⬤ 2.5 x 5 mm SuperDuo bead
- ⬤ 11º seed bead

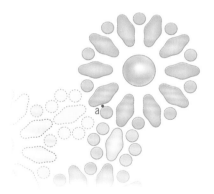

FIGURE 7

Materials

pastel bracelet 7 in. (18 cm)

- 11 g 2.5 x 5 mm SuperDuo beads (burgundy, pastel lilac, pastel light coral, pastel dark coral, pastel light rose, pastel pink, cream)
- **16** 4 mm pearls (Czech, gold)
- 2 g 11º seed beads (Toho 989, bronze-lined crystal)
- **1** 10 mm snap
- OneG thread (gold)
- beading needles, #12

autumn bracelet colors:

- 2.5 x 5 mm SuperDuo beads (dark coral, crystal orange rainbow, Vega on chalk, bronze fire red, bordeaux, crystal violet rainbow, opaque green)
- 4 mm pearls (Czech, antique brass)
- 11º seed beads (Toho 989, bronze-lined crystal)

ADJUSTMENTS

- **Fireline 6 lb. test may be substituted for the OneG thread.**
- **To adjust the length of the bracelet, try attaching the flowers in a different position or use a clasp instead of a snap closure.**

steps 1–5 of "Additional flowers" and steps 1–3 of "Connector unit."

[3] Sew through the corresponding SuperDuo in the next existing flower, the SuperDuo in the connecting unit, and the same SuperDuo in the existing flower. This creates an initial connection. Stabilize that connection as before by sewing through the 11º, SuperDuo, and 11º in the connector unit and the corresponding 11º, SuperDuo, and 11º in the flower. Sew through the existing flower to exit the correct 11º, SuperDuo, and 11º to add the next connector unit.

[4] Continue adding connector units and additional flowers for the length of the bracelet as in steps 2 and 3. End the working thread and tail.

[5] Add 18 in. (46cm) of thread to the end flower from the beginning of

the bracelet, and position the top half of the 10 mm snap to the underside of the flower. Sew through an opening in the snap and through the inner hole of the nearest SuperDuo. Repeat for the remaining holes of the snap. If the holes of the SuperDuos are too tight to sew through, sew around the thread bridges between the SuperDuos instead. End the thread.

[6] Position the bottom half of the snap on the topside of the flower on the other end of the bracelet. Attach the snap as in the previous step, and end the thread. ⬤

BEAD WEAVING

Dream catcher
necklace

Stitch a lavish netted pendant around a rivoli with SuperDuos, pearls, and seed beads. Enhance it with a coordinating bail and shimmering pearl rope.

designed by **Regina Atkins**

stepbystep

Pendant
Back

Work in rounds as follows:

Round 1: On 3½ ft. (1.1 m) of thread, pick up a repeating pattern of a 6 mm pearl and an 11º seed bead eight times. Sew through all the beads again to form a ring (not shown in figure), leaving a 6-in. (15 cm) tail. Tie a square knot with the working thread and tail, and exit the first 11º **(figure 1, a–b)**.

Round 2: Pick up an 8º seed bead, a 2.5 x 5 mm SuperDuo bead, a 15º seed bead, a SuperDuo, and an 8º, and sew through the next 11º in the ring **(b–c)**. Repeat this stitch to complete the round, and step up through the first 8º and the open hole of the first SuperDuo added in this round **(c–d)**.

Round 3: Pick up two SuperDuos, and sew through the open hole of the next SuperDuo. Continue through the following two 8ºs from round 2 and the open hole of the next SuperDuo **(figure 2, a–b)**. Repeat this stitch to complete the round, step up through the first two SuperDuos added in this round, and exit the outer hole of the next SuperDuo from round 2 **(b–c)**.

Round 4: Pick up a color B 4 mm pearl, and sew through the

FIGURE 1

FIGURE 2

FIGURE 3

FIGURE 4

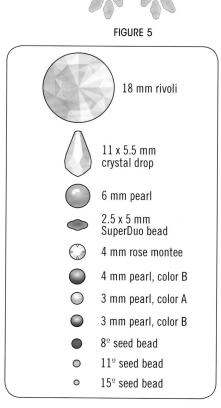

FIGURE 5

outer hole of the next SuperDuo from round 2, the inner holes of the following pair of SuperDuos, and the outer hole of the next SuperDuo **(figure 3, a–b)**. Repeat this stitch to complete the round, sewing through only one SuperDuo in the final stitch **(b–c)**.

Round 5: Pick up three 15ºs, and sew through the open hole of the next SuperDuo from round 3. Pick up a SuperDuo, and sew through the open hole of the following SuperDuo. Pick up three 15ºs, and sew through the outer hole of the next SuperDuo from round 2, the following 4 mm pearl, and the outer hole of the next SuperDuo from round 2 **(figure 4, a–b)**. Repeat these stitches to complete the round **(b–c)**. End the working thread and tail, but try to avoid tying knots in the 15ºs. Set this piece aside.

Front and edging
1 On 5 ft. (1.5 m) of thread, work as in rounds 1–3 of "Pendant: Back."
2 Align the front and back of the pendant. With the working thread from the front, join the components as follows: Sew through a 4 mm pearl of the pendant back **(figure 5, a–b)**, and continue through the outer hole of the next SuperDuo from round 2 of the pendant front **(b–c)**. Pick

Difficulty rating

Materials
green/purple necklace
18½ in. (47cm) with
4¼ in. (10.8cm) pendant

- **1** 18 mm crystal rivoli (Swarovski, vitrail)
- **3** 11 x 5.5 mm crystal drops (Swarovski #6000, crystal AB)
- glass pearls for pendant
  - **24** 6 mm (light olive green)
  - **8** 4mm, color B (wisteria)
  - **9** 3mm, color A (light olive)
- glass pearls for rope
  - **225** 3mm, color A (light olive)
  - **150** 3mm, color B (wisteria)
- **1** 4 mm rose montee (Swarovski, crystal AB)
- **19 g** 2.5 x 5 mm SuperDuo beads (magic violet-green #95000)
- **3 g** 8º seed beads (Miyuki 454, purple iris)
- **9 g** 11º seed beads (Toho 1704, gilded marble lavender)
- **10 g** 15º seed beads (Toho PF557, gold)
- **2** wire guardians (gold)
- clasp
- Fireline 6 lb. test
- beading needles, #13
- thread bobbin or cardboard

18 mm rivoli

11 x 5.5 mm crystal drop

6 mm pearl

2.5 x 5 mm SuperDuo bead

4 mm rose montee

4 mm pearl, color B

3 mm pearl, color A

3 mm pearl, color B

8º seed bead

11º seed bead

15º seed bead

FIGURE 6

up three 15ºs, and sew through the outer hole of the next SuperDuo from round 3 of the pendant front **(c–d)**. Sew through the outer hole of the next point SuperDuo of the pendant back and the outer hole of the next SuperDuo of the pendant front **(d–e)**. Pick up three 15ºs, and sew through the outer hole of the next SuperDuo from round 2 **(e–f)**. Repeat these stitches to complete the round, inserting the rivoli before completing the join.

3 Sew through the beadwork to a shared point SuperDuo, and exit the hole closest to the back of the rivoli. Pick up an 11º, a 15º, a 6 mm pearl, a 15º, and an 11º, and sew through the corresponding hole of the next point SuperDuo. Repeat this stitch to complete the round **(figure 6)**. Sew through all the beads in this round again to tighten, and exit a 6 mm pearl.

note If too much thread shows in this outer round, add two 15ºs instead of one, or use 8ºs instead of 11ºs.

Fringe 1

1 Pick up an 11º, an 8º, a SuperDuo, a 15º, a SuperDuo, an 8º, and an 11º. Sew through the 6 mm your thread is exiting and the first 11º and the 8º just added **(figure 7, a–b)**.

2 Pick up two 15ºs, and sew through the open hole of the next SuperDuo **(b–c)**. Pick up two SuperDuos, and sew through the open hole of the following SuperDuo **(c–d)**. Pick up two 15ºs, and sew through the next 8º, 11º, and 6 mm pearl. Continue through the following 15º, 11º, SuperDuo, and 11º **(d–e)**.

Fringe 2

1 Pick up a 15º, a SuperDuo, a 15º, a SuperDuo, and a 15º. Sew through the 11º, SuperDuo and 11º your thread just

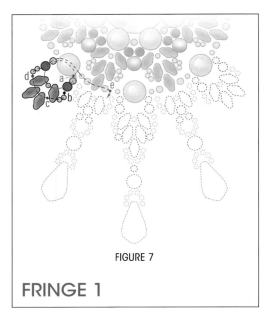

FIGURE 7

FRINGE 1

exited, and continue through the first four beads just added **(figure 8)**.

2 Pick up two 15ºs, and sew through the open hole of the same SuperDuo. Pick up an 8º, sew through the open hole of the next SuperDuo, pick up two 15ºs, and sew through the 15ºs, SuperDuos, and 8º as shown **(figure 9)**.

3 Pick up an 11º, three 15ºs, a color A 3 mm pearl, three 15ºs, an 11 x 5.5 mm drop, and three 15ºs, and sew back through the pearl. Pick up three 15ºs and an 11º, and sew through the bead-work as shown **(figure 10)**. Continue through the next 15º and 6 mm pearl.

Fringe 3

1 Pick up an 11º, an 8º, a 15º, a SuperDuo, a 15º, a SuperDuo, a 15º, an 8º, and an 11º. Sew through the pearl again and the next six beads to exit the second SuperDuo **(figure 11)**.

2 Pick up two 15ºs, and sew through the open hole of the same SuperDuo. Pick up two SuperDuos, and sew through the open hole of the next SuperDuo. Pick up two 15ºs, and sew through the other hole of the same SuperDuo. Continue through the beadwork to exit the second SuperDuo just added **(figure 12)**.

3 Pick up a 15º and an 11º, and sew through the open hole of the same SuperDuo. Pick up a SuperDuo, and sew through the open hole of the next SuperDuo. Pick up an 11º and a 15º,

swapping stash

Make substitutions as desired to suit your stash. For example, in the ivory version, Regina used 8ºs instead of 3mms in the bail and two colors of 15ºs instead of just one. In the turquoise version, we swapped dagger beads for the crystal drops.

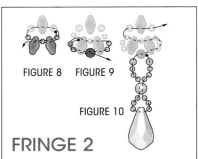

FIGURE 8 FIGURE 9

FIGURE 10

FRINGE 2

and sew through beadwork to exit the SuperDuo just added **(figure 13)**.

4 Pick up an 11º and a 15º, and sew through the open hole of the tip SuperDuo. Pick up a 15º, and an 11º, and sew through the other hole of the same SuperDuo. Sew through the beadwork to exit the last 15º added **(figure 14)**.

5 Pick up two 15ºs, an 8º, a color A 3 mm pearl, three 15ºs, a drop, and three 15ºs. Sew back through the pearl and 8º. Pick up two 15ºs, and sew through the beadwork as shown **(figure 15)**. Continue through the following beads to exit the next 15º and 6 mm pearl.

Remaining fringes

1 Work as in "Fringe 2."
2 Work as in "Fringe 1." End the working thread.

Bail

As you work the bail components, you will often be stepping up through the open hole of a SuperDuo. Note that each time this occurs, you will reverse the direction of your stitching.

Bail back

1 Work in rounds as follows:
Round 1: On 30 in. (76cm) of thread, pick up a repeating pattern of an 11º and a SuperDuo four times. Sew through

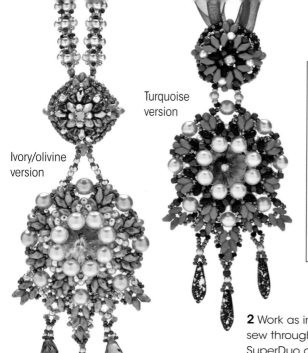

Ivory/olivine version

Turquoise version

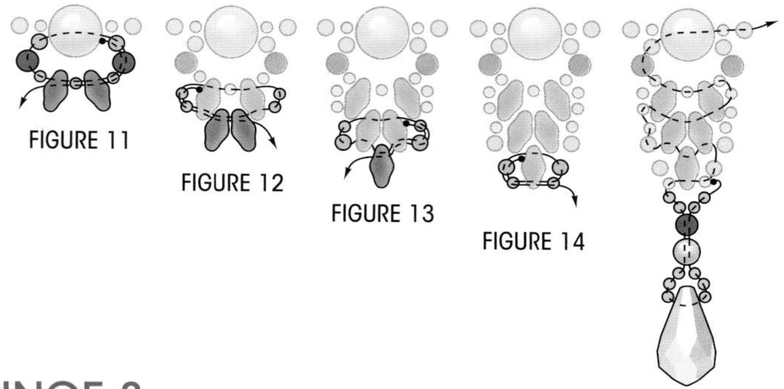

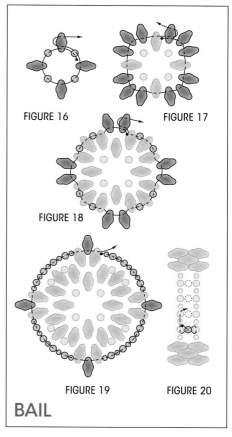

FIGURE 11

FIGURE 12

FIGURE 13

FIGURE 14

FRINGE 3

FIGURE 15

FIGURE 16

FIGURE 17

FIGURE 18

FIGURE 19

FIGURE 20

BAIL

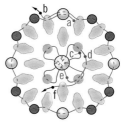

FIGURE 21

all the beads again to form a ring (not shown in figure), leaving a 6-in. (15cm) tail. Tie the working thread and tail with a square knot, and exit the first SuperDuo. Step up through the open hole of the same SuperDuo **(figure 16)**.

Round 2: Pick up three SuperDuos, and sew through the open hole of the next SuperDuo. Repeat this stitch to complete the round, adding a total of 12 SuperDuos. Step up through the open hole of the first SuperDuo added this round **(figure 17)**.

Round 3: Pick up two SuperDuos, and sew through the outer hole of the next SuperDuo in round 2. Pick up an 11°, and sew through the following SuperDuo. Add another 11° in the same way. Repeat these three stitches to complete the round, and step up through the open hole of the first SuperDuo added in this round **(figure 18)**.

Round 4: Pick up a repeating pattern of a 15° and an 11° four times, and then pick up one more 15°. Sew through the next SuperDuo in round 3. Pick up a SuperDuo, and sew through the next SuperDuo, creating a point. Repeat these two stitches to complete the round **(figure 19)**. End the working thread and tail, and set this component aside.

Bail front and join

1 Work as in rounds 1–3 of "Bail back." Match the two pieces together.

2 Work as in round 4 of "Bail back," but sew through the open hole of a point SuperDuo on the back component each time you would otherwise add a new one. Exit the first 15° and 11° after the first shared point SuperDuo.

3 Join the front and back components as follows: Pick up an 11°, and sew through the corresponding 11° in the other component. Sew back through the new 11°, the 11° your thread exited at the start of this step, and the following 15° and 11° **(figure 20)**. Repeat this stitch three times, sew through the corner SuperDuos, and repeat the join for this side. End the working thread and tail.

Top layer

1 On 1 yd. (.9 m) of thread and leaving an 8-in. (20cm) tail, work as in rounds 1 and 2 of "Bail back" using 8°s in place of the 11°s.

note For added interest, you can introduce two more colors of SuperDuos at this point by picking up a color B, a color C, and a color B SuperDuo in each stitch of round 2. This was done in the ivory/olivine necklace, above.

2 Pick up a color A 3 mm pearl, and sew through the next SuperDuo. Pick up an 8°, and sew through the following SuperDuo. Add another 8° in the same way. Repeat these three stitches to complete the round, and exit the first pearl added in this round and the following SuperDuo **(figure 21, a–b)**.

3 With the tail, exit an 8° in the initial ring.

Sew through one channel of a 4 mm rose montee and the 8° on the opposite side of the ring. Sew back through the same channel and the first 8° **(c–d)**. Sew through the ring to exit the next 8° **(d–e)**,

and repeat the connection through the other channel of the montee and the remaining 8°s **(e–f)**. End the tail.
4 Place the new component on top of the bail, matching the trios of SuperDuos in the new component to the trios of SuperDuos in round 2 of the bail.
5 Sew through the SuperDuo directly below in the "Bail front" and the SuperDuo your thread exited at the start of the step. Continue through the next 8° and SuperDuo. Repeat the stitch twice, sewing through the next pearl and SuperDuo for the last stitch **(figure 22)**.
6 Repeat step 5 to complete the round. Do not end the working thread.

Bail attachment

1 Sew through the bail to exit the outer hole of one of the side SuperDuos at the bottom of the bail between the two joined sides. (The rope will pass through the other two open sides.)
2 Pick up an 11°, a 15°, a color A 3 mm pearl, an 8°, a 15°, and an 11°s. Sew through the top 6 mm pearl on the pendant. Pick up an 11°, a 15°, an 8°, a color A 3 mm pearl, a 15°, and an 11°, and sew through the corresponding side SuperDuo at the bottom of the bail **(figure 23)**. Retrace the thread path a few times, and end the working thread.

note You can pick up any assortment of beads for this connection, either to suit your taste or to change the amount of space between the bail and the pendant.

Rope
Side 1

1 Cut 15 ft. (4.6 m) of thread, and wrap half of it onto a thread bobbin or piece of cardboard. With the working thread, pick up a repeating pattern of a color A 3 mm pearl, a 15°, a color B 3 mm pearl, and a 15° twice, and pull the beads down to the bobbin. Sew through all the beads again to form a ring, and tie the working thread and tail with a square knot. Exit an A **(figure 24)**.

FIGURE 22

FIGURE 23

note For a monochromatic rope, use just one color of 3 mm pearl, as in the ivory/olivine necklace, p. 49.

2 Pick up a 15°, an A, and a 15°, and sew through the opposite pearl in the ring, going in the same direction. Pick up a 15°, and sew back through the new pearl. Pick up a 15°, and sew through the A your thread exited at the start of this step **(figure 25)**.
3 Flip over the work, and repeat step 2 on the other side. This completes one unit of the rope.
4 Pick up a 15°, a B, a 15°, an A, a 15°, a B, and a 15°. Sew through the A your thread exited at the start of this stitch to form a new ring, and continue through the next four beads to exit the A just added **(figure 26)**.
5 Repeat steps 2–4 until you have half the desired length of your rope. Add a stop bead to the working thread temporarily.

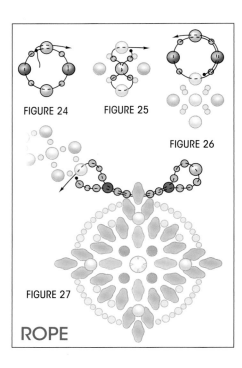

FIGURE 24   FIGURE 25

FIGURE 26

FIGURE 27

ROPE

Center bridge

1 Unroll the other half of the thread from the bobbin. Pick up an 11°, a 15°, an 11°, an 8°, four 11°s, an 8°, an 11°, a 15°, and an 11°. Pass through the top of your bail; the four 11°s will sit within the bail. Pick up an A, an 11°, a 15°, and an 11°, and sew back through the last 8°. Continue through the four 11°s inside the bail and the next 8°. Pick up an 11°, a 15°, and an 11°, and sew through the A from side 1 of the rope **(figure 27)**.
2 Retrace the thread path through the center bridge, and exit the new A where you'll begin the second side of the rope.

Side 2

Repeat step 4 of "Rope: Side 1," and then continue as in steps 2–4 until both sides of the rope are the same length.

Clasp

Exit the end A in the rope. Pick up two 11°s, an 8°, one side of the wire guardian, and the clasp loop. Sew through the other side of the wire guardian and back through the 8°. Pick up two 11°s and sew through the A again. Retrace the thread path, and end the thread. Remove the stop bead from the other thread, and repeat to attach the other half of the clasp to the other end. ◉

Two-hole flower power

Combine new two-hole beads with O-beads to create a fast and fun pair of earrings.

designed by
Connie Whittaker

Difficulty rating

Materials
pair of earrings 1 in. (2.5cm)

- **12** 6 x 6 mm Chexx two-hole beads (bronze)
- **12** 6 x 6 mm two-hole diamond "Silky" beads (alabaster lazure blue)
- **24** 1 x 3.8 mm O-beads (magic blue)
- **1 g** 15º seed beads (Toho 221, bronze)
- pair of earring findings
- Fireline 6 lb. test
- beading needles, #11
- **2** pairs of chainnose, flatnose, and/or bentnose pliers

The two-hole diamond beads have two different sides to them. For the purposes of these instructions, the top side will have the bump on it, and the back will be flat.

stepbystep

[1] On 1 yd. (.9 m) of thread, pick up six 6 x 6 mm Chexx beads. Sew through all the beads twice to form a ring, leaving a 6-in. (15cm) tail. Position the available holes of the Chexx to the outside of the ring.

[2] Pick up a 15º seed bead, and sew through the inside hole of the next Chexx **(figure 1, a–b)**. Repeat this stitch to complete the round, and sew through the outer hole of the Chexx your thread is exiting **(b–c)**.

[3] Pick up a 1 x 3.8 mm O-bead, a 6 x 6 mm two-hole diamond bead (top side facing up), and an O-bead, and sew through the outer hole of the next Chexx **(c–d)**. Repeat this stitch to complete the round **(d–e)**. Retrace the thread path to tighten (not shown in the figure), and exit a diamond **(e–f)**.

[4] Pick up five 15º's, and sew through the outer hole of the same diamond **(figure 2, a–b)**. Pick up four 15º's, and sew through the outer hole of the diamond in the same direction to form a loop at the tip of the diamond **(b–c)**. Pick up five 15º's, and sew through the inner hole of the diamond **(c–d)**. Continue through the next O-bead, the outer hole of the following Chexx, the next O-bead, and the inner hole of the following diamond **(d–e)**.

[5] Repeat step 4 to complete the round.

[6] Sew through the beadwork to exit the two center 15º's in a loop at the tip of a diamond. Pick up six 15º's, and sew through the two 15º's your thread exited at the start of this step. Retrace the thread path of the loop, and end the working thread and tail (Basics).

[7] Open the loop (Basics) of an earring finding, and attach the six-bead loop at the top of the earring.

[8] Make a second earring. ◗

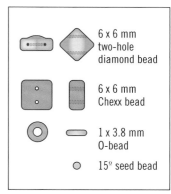

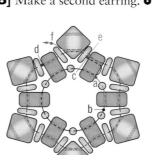

FIGURE 1

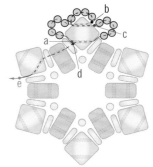

FIGURE 2

6 x 6 mm two-hole diamond bead

6 x 6 mm Chexx bead

1 x 3.8 mm O-bead

15º seed bead

Wrapped in crystals
pendant

Surround a center of pearls with crystal-studded rondelles and bicones, all accented with seed beads.

designed by **Gianna Zimmerman**

stepbystep

[1] On 7 ft. (2.1 m) of thread, pick up a repeating pattern of a 4 mm pearl and a 4 mm rhinestone rondelle six times. Sew through the beads again to form a ring, pulling tight and leaving a 6-in. (15 cm) tail. Tie a square knot (Basics) with the working thread and tail, and

sew through the next pearl.
[2] Pick up a pearl, a 4 mm bicone crystal, and a pearl, and sew through the pearl your thread is exiting in the same direction **(figure 1, a–b)**. Continue through the next rondelle and pearl **(b–c)**. Repeat these stitches to complete the round **(c–d)**, and then sew through the first pearl added in this step **(d–e)**.

[3] Pick up a 15º seed bead, a 3 mm bicone crystal, a 15º, a 3mm, and a 15º. Sew through the opposite pearl with your needle pointing toward the outside of the beadwork **(figure 2, a–b)**.
[4] Pick up a 15º and a 3 mm bicone, and sew through the center 15º added in the previous step. Pick up a 3 mm bicone and a 15º, and sew

through the opposite pearl with your needle pointing toward the outside of the beadwork **(b–c)**.
[5] Sew through the next 4 mm bicone, pearl, rondelle, and pearl **(c–d)**. Pick up a 4 mm bicone, and sew through the previous pearl, rondelle, and pearl **(figure 3)**.
[6] Repeat steps 3–5 to complete the round, and exit

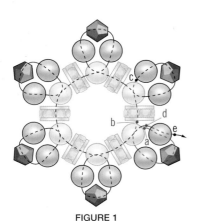

FIGURE 1

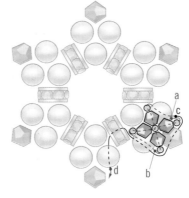

FIGURE 2

FIGURE 3

a

b

c

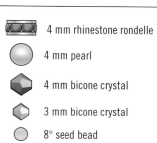
d

a 4 mm bicone.

[7] Pick up an 8º seed bead, and sew through the next 4 mm bicone **(figure 4, a–b)**. Repeat this stitch to complete the round **(b–c)**, but do not pull too tight. There will be a small space between the crystals and the 8ºs. End with your thread exiting a 4 mm bicone.

[8] To add a large picot: Pick up five 11º seed beads, and sew through the 4 mm bicone in the same direction and the next 8º **(figure 5, a–b)**.

[9] To add a small picot: Pick up three 15ºs, and sew through the 8º in the same direction and the next 4 mm bicone **(b–c)**.

[10] Repeat steps 8 and 9 to complete the round, and exit a 4 mm bicone.

[11] Flip the beadwork to the back side. Pick up an 11º, and sew through the first and last 15ºs in the next small picot **(photo a)**. Pick up an 11º, and sew through the next 4 mm bicone **(photo b)**.

Repeat these two stitches to complete the round.

[12] Sew through the next 8º and up through the following 11º added in the previous step, skip the first 11º in the large picot, and sew through the next 11º **(photo c)**. Skip the center 11º, sew through the following 11º in the large picot, and continue through the next 11º added in the previous step **(photo d)**.

[13] Repeat step 12 to complete the round.

[14] Sew through the beadwork to exit the 4 mm bicone behind a 3 mm embellishment, and flip the beadwork to the front side. Sew through the next three 11ºs in the large picot to exit the tip of the picot **(figure 6, point a)**.

[15] Pick up five 11ºs, and sew through the 11º your thread exited at the start of this step. Retrace the thread path twice, and end the working thread and tail (Basics). String the pendant as desired. ●

4 mm rhinestone rondelle	
4 mm pearl	
4 mm bicone crystal	
3 mm bicone crystal	
8º seed bead	
11º seed bead	
15º seed bead	

Difficulty rating

Materials

fuchsia pendant 1¼ in. (3.2 cm)

- 6 4 mm rhinestone rondelles (Swarovski, crystal AB)
- 18 4 mm glass pearls (Czech, silver grey)
- 12 4 mm bicone crystals (Swarovski, crystal AB2X)
- 24 3 mm bicone crystals (Preciosa PC1030, fuchsia)
- 12 8º seed beads (Miyuki 4248, Duracoat silver-lined dark lilac)
- 1 g 11º seed beads (Japanese 589A, gilt-lined antique purple opal))
- 1 g 15º seed beads (Miyuki 551, gilt-lined white opal)
- Fireline 6 lb. test
- beading needles, #11

olivine pendant colors:

- 5 mm rhinestone rondelles (Preciosa, tanzanite/silver)
- 4 mm crystal pearls (Swarovski, cream)
- 4 mm bicone crystals (Preciosa PC1111, deep tanzanite)
- 3 mm bicone crystals (Preciosa PC1038, olivine)
- 8º seed beads (Toho 151, Ceylon grape mist)
- 11º seed beads (Toho PF558, permanent finish aluminum galvanized)
- 15º seed beads (Miyuki 1816, black-lined chartreuse)

FIGURE 4

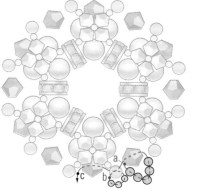

FIGURE 5

FIGURE 6

SUBSTITUTE
You may replace the 4 mm rondelles with 5 mm rondelles, but the beadwork will not be as tight.

Making 3D shapes in peyote stitch

Discover how complex-looking structures begin with the simplest shapes stitched in a basic technique.

designed by **Pamm Horbit**

Like many people, I started beading casually in the '60s, stringing strands of colorful "love beads." I was using bugle beads and seed beads to create the dots and dashes of Morse code, imbuing my jewelry with messages. I didn't realize it at the time, but today I recognize that this was an early indication of the order my brain craved and a precursor to the geometric structures I would come to create some four decades later.

After not beading for 20 years, I hooked up with a circle of friends who beaded together. Most worked in free-form peyote to create incredible jewelry, but I couldn't do it — it hurt my brain! I would sit down with the same tubes of assorted seed beads as the others, but instead of going with the flow, I separated my beads by shape and size and then figured out an orderly design based on those piles.

Around that time, I took a class from NanC Meinhardt, and she changed my world! She said that art is a verb, not a noun, and to truly be an artist, one must figure out their process and then incorporate that process into their art. It clicked immediately — I knew my process! I knew that I needed to start at the end, to see the finished piece, and then work backward, solving design problems as I went. Even today, I won't pick up the first bead until I know what the finished piece is going to look like.

Over time, my passion shifted to 3D forms. I was familiar with Platonic solids from geometry and decided to try making the most basic form — the tetrahedron, which is made up of four identical triangles. After making and connecting the first three triangles, I was skeptical that it would work because the piece was very floppy.

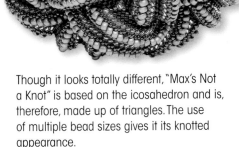

Though it looks totally different, "Max's Not a Knot" is based on the icosahedron and is, therefore, made up of triangles. The use of multiple bead sizes gives it its knotted appearance.

But I went ahead and made one more triangle and zipped it to the previous ones and it worked!

I quickly learned that this approach — creating multiple identical shapes and zipping the edges together — was the key to creating other forms. Four triangles created a tetrahedron. Six squares created a cube (also known as a hexahedron). Eight triangles become an octahedron, 12 pentagons become a dodecahedron, and 20 triangles become an icosahedron. I then

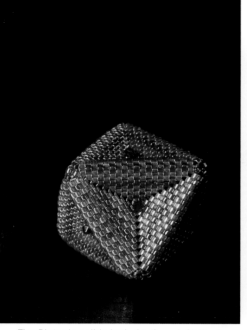

The Platonic solids include (from left) the ico-sahedron, the dodecahedron, the cube, the tetrahedron, and the octahedron.

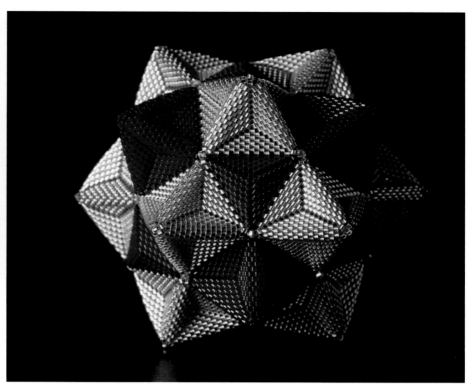

"The San Diego Star" combines pyramids and flat areas with square and triangular bases.

found that I could apply the Cellini technique (working peyote stitch using multiple bead sizes) to the basic triangle shape to create incredible texture. Soon afterward, I began to use different colors within a piece and apply increases to create twists. More mental wanderings led me to add details to mimic blooming plants, as seen in my 2010 BeadDreams entry, "The Nitidus Quasar" (below).

When I discovered a book about Archimedean solids, my beadwork went in new and exciting directions. Whereas Platonic solids are created from surfaces that are all the same shape, Archimedean solids are made up of surfaces that are not all the same. They're still based on triangles and squares, but when combined, create ever more exciting shapes.

Though they look much more complicated, all of my creations can be traced back to my very first experiments with triangles. Launch your own journey into 3D shapes with my "Trillion" pendant, which features a unique method for capturing a rivoli. Connect two triangles back to back for a pendant, or attach four triangles to make an ornament.

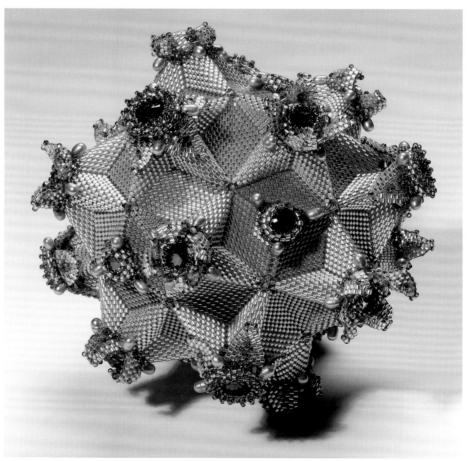

As I experimented with the technique, I discovered how to create blooming flowers.

Making "trillion triangles"

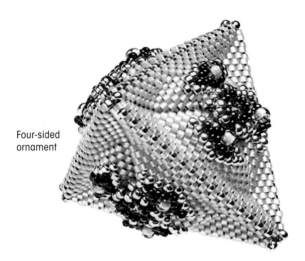

Four-sided
ornament

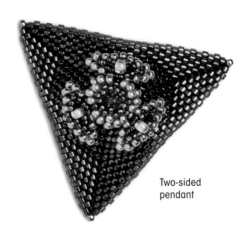

Two-sided
pendant

Basic triangle

To make a triangle with no adornment, use only 11º cylinder beads.

1 Work in rounds, stepping up through the first cylinder added in each round, and ending and adding thread as needed:

Round 1: On a comfortable length of thread, pick up three 11º cylinder beads, and tie them into a ring with a square knot, leaving a 6-in. (15cm) tail. Sew through the first cylinder again **(figure 1, a–b)**.

Round 2: Work a herringbone stitch by picking up two cylinders and sewing through the next cylinder in the previous round. Repeat this stitch to complete the round, and step up through the first bead added in this round **(b–c)**. Throughout the project, the herringbone stitches will be made with two cylinders per stitch and will form the corners.

Round 3: Work a corner stitch **(c–d)**, and then work a peyote stitch by picking up a cylinder and sewing through the next cylinder in the previous round **(d–e)**. Repeat these two stitches to complete the round **(e–f)**.

Round 4: Work a corner stitch **(f–g)** and two peyote stitches with cylinders **(g–h)**. Repeat around **(h–i)**.

Round 5: Work a corner stitch and three stitches in peyote: cylinder, 11º seed bead, cylinder. Repeat these four stitches to complete the round **(i–j)**.

Round 6: Work a corner stitch and four stitches in peyote: cylinder, two 11º seed beads, cylinder. Repeat around **(j–k)**.

Round 7: Work a corner stitch and five stitches in peyote: cylinder, 11º seed bead, a pair of 15º seed beads, 11º seed bead, cylinder. Repeat around **(k–l)**.

Round 8: Work a corner stitch and six stitches in peyote: cylinder, 11º seed bead, two pairs of 15ºs, 11º seed bead, cylinder. Repeat around **(l–m)**.

Round 9: Work a corner stitch and seven stitches in peyote: cylinder, 11º seed bead, a pair of 15ºs, 8º seed bead, a pair of 15ºs, 11º seed bead, cylinder. Repeat around **(m–n)**.

Round 10: Work a corner stitch and eight stitches in peyote: two cylinders, 11º seed bead, two pairs of 15ºs, 11º seed bead, two cylinders. Repeat around **(n–o)**.

Round 11: Work a corner stitch and nine stitches in peyote: three cylinders, 11º seed bead, a pair of 15ºs, 11º seed bead, three cylinders. Repeat around **(o–p)**. Pull tight so the 15ºs fall just below the 8º. Keep a tight tension for the rest of the piece.

Round 12: Work a corner stitch and 10 stitches in peyote: four cylinders, two 11º seed beads, four cylinders. Repeat around **(p–q)**.

Round 13: Work a corner stitch and 11 stitches in peyote: five cylinders, 11º seed bead, five cylinders. Repeat around **(q–r)**.

Rounds 14–17: For each round, use cylinders to work a corner stitch and complete each side in peyote **(r–s)**.

2 To add a joining round, pick up an 11º seed bead at each corner and a

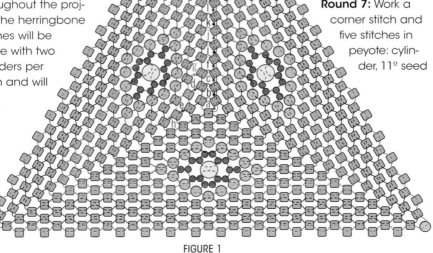

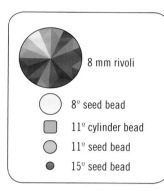

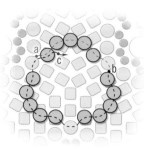

8 mm rivoli

○ 8º seed bead

□ 11º cylinder bead

◐ 11º seed bead

● 15º seed bead

FIGURE 2

FIGURE 3

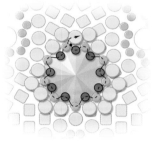

FIGURE 4

FIGURE 5

FIGURE 6

Difficulty rating

   ○ ○

• •

Materials

**two-sided pendant
2 in. (5 cm)**
• **1** 8 mm rivoli (light amethyst)
• **3** 8º seed beads (Toho 777, white cream-lined crystal)
• **5 g** 11º cylinder beads (Toho Aiko 506, teal blue iris higher metallic)
• **1 g** 11º seed beads (Toho 557, permanent finish gold galvanized)
• **1 g** 15º seed beads (Toho 928, purple-lined rosaline AB)
• Fireline 6 lb. test
• beading needles, #12

four-sided ornament
• **4** 8 mm rivoli (golden shadow)
• **12** 8º seed beads (Toho 777, white cream-lined crystal)
• **9 g** 11º cylinder beads (Toho Aiko 2125, cream opal silver lined)
• **1 g** 11º seed beads (Toho 551, permanent finish peach galvanized)
• **1 g** 15º seed beads (Toho 85, metallic iris purple)

cylinder for each peyote stitch **(s–t)**.
3 Sew through the beadwork to exit an 11º seed bead in round 5. Pick up five 11ºs, and sew through the next 11º in round 5 **(figure 2, a–b)**. Repeat this stitch twice, and step up through the first 11º added in this step **(b–c)**.
4 Tuck an 8 mm rivoli into the ring of beads just made. Working along the inner edge, work a round of peyote using 15ºs **(figure 3)**. Repeat to add a second round of 15ºs **(figure 4)**.
5 Add an 11º to the outer edge of the bezel at each corner spine **(figure 5)**. Sew each new 11º to the base as shown **(figure 6)**. End the tail but not the working thread.

Two-sided pendant

1 Make one triangle as in the instructions and another with cylinders only. Also, for the second triangle, omit the joining round. Sew through the beadwork to exit a cylinder along the outer edge.
2 Align the two triangles, and zip up the edges.

Four-sided ornament

1 Make a total of four triangles with the following changes:
• For triangle 2, add joining beads on only two sides.
• For triangle 3, add joining beads on only one side.
• For triangle 4, do not add joining beads at all.
2 Align triangle 1 and triangle 2 so the side without joining beads is adjacent to the first triangle. Zip up this edge.
3 Align triangle 3 with triangle 2 so the joining beads are along the base. Zip up triangle 2 and triangle 3.
4 Zip triangle 3 to triangle 1.
5 Align triangle 4 with the rest of the triangles, and zip up the edges. Add a hanging loop as desired. ●

LADDER STITCH

Playful
Pellet bangle

You'll have fun playing with the new Pellet beads while you create this flexible bangle in a monochromatic or striped palette.

designed by **Kerrie Slade**

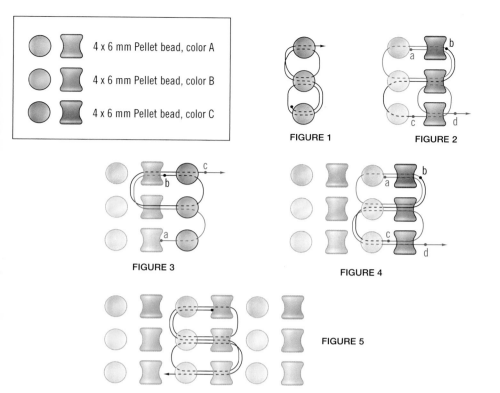

● 4 x 6 mm Pellet bead, color A	
● 4 x 6 mm Pellet bead, color B	
● 4 x 6 mm Pellet bead, color C	

FIGURE 1

FIGURE 2

FIGURE 3

FIGURE 4

FIGURE 5

stepbystep

The following instructions are for the black/silver/topaz bangle, which results in three long stripes around the length of the bangle. You can also work the bangle in all one color, as in the silver version, or modify the pattern for short vertical stripes, as in the blue/green/ivory bangle.

[1] On a comfortable length of thread and leaving a 6-in. (15cm) tail, work in ladder stitch (Basics) to make a three-bead ladder using a color A, a color B, and a color C 4 x 6 mm Pellet bead. The holes in the Pellets should be parallel to each other and oriented horizontally with the flat round ends facing you **(figure 1)**.

[2] Pick up a C and a B, and sew through the B in the previous row. Continue through the C in the previous row and the C just added **(figure 2, a–b)**. The new Pellets should be positioned so that the indented sides are facing you. Sew through the B added in this step, the B in the previous row, and the A in the previous row **(b–c)**. Pick up an A, sew through the B added in this step, and continue through the A just added **(c–d)**. Make sure that the A, like the B and the C, is positioned with the indented side facing you.

[3] Pick up an A and a B, and sew through the B and the C in the previous

row **(figure 3, a–b)**. Position the new Pellets so that the flat round ends are facing you. Pick up a C, and sew through the B added in this step, the B and the C in the previous row, and the C just added **(b–c)**. Make sure that the C, like the B and the A, is positioned with the flat round end facing you.

[4] Pick up a C and a B, sew through the B and the C in the previous row, and continue through the C just added **(figure 4, a–b)**. The new Pellets should be positioned so that the indented sides are facing you. Sew through the B added in this step and the B and the A in the previous row **(b–c)**. Pick up an A, and sew through the B added in this step, the B and the A in the previous row, and the A just added **(c–d)**. Make sure that the A, like the B and the C, is positioned with the indented side facing you.

[5] Repeat steps 3 and 4 for the desired length bangle, ending and adding thread (Basics) as needed and ending with an even number of rows. Our 2¼-in. (5.7cm) diameter bangle has 46 Pellets along each edge. The bangle should just fit around the widest part of your hand.

[6] To join the ends: Work a ladder stitch thread path through the first and last rows **(figure 5)**. Retrace the thread path, and end the working thread and tail. ●

Difficulty rating

Materials

all bangles
- Fireline 6 lb. test or .008 Wildfire
- beading needles, #11 or #12

black/silver/topaz bangle 2¼ in. (5.7cm) diameter
- Preciosa traditional Czech beads 8 g 4 x 6 mm Pellet beads in each of **3** colors: A (23980, jet), B (29942, crystal volcano), C (23901, crystal blond flare)

silver bangle colors:
- 24 g 4 x 6 mm Pellet beads (27400, crystal full chrome)

blue/green/ivory bangle colors:
- 6 g Pellet beads in each of **5** colors: A (teal), B (ivory), C (aqua), D (6NB185, opaque turquoise), E (6NB173, opaque blue)

TENSION NOTE

If your tension is a little loose, you can tighten it up after you complete the bangle: Add 1 yd. (.9 m) of thread to the beadwork, exiting an edge bead. Sew through the beads along one edge, sew through to the opposite edge, and repeat.

Golden glory bracelet

Stitch up fun components with two-hole triangles and lentils in soft, glowing colors.

designed by **Nichole Starman**

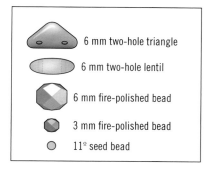

- 6 mm two-hole triangle
- 6 mm two-hole lentil
- 6 mm fire-polished bead
- 3 mm fire-polished bead
- 11° seed bead

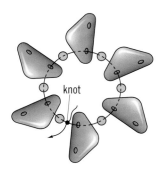

knot

FIGURE 1

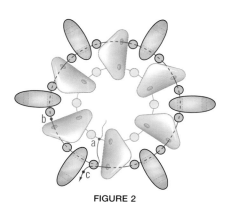

FIGURE 2

FIGURE 3

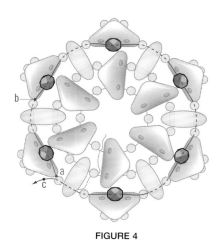

FIGURE 4

stepbystep

Components

[1] On 1 yd. (.9 m) of thread, pick up a repeating pattern of an 11° seed bead and a 6 mm two-hole triangle bead six times, making sure all the triangles are oriented the same way. Tie the beads into a ring with a square knot (Basics), leaving a 6-in. (15cm) tail **(figure 1)**. Adjust the triangles so the available hole of each sits to the outside of the ring.

[2] Pick up an 11°, a 6 mm two-hole lentil bead, and an 11°, and sew through the available hole of the next triangle **(figure 2, a–b)**. Repeat this stitch to complete the round, and sew through the first 11° added in this round **(b–c)**.

[3] Sew through the available hole of the adjacent lentil **(figure 3, a–b)**. Pick up an 11°, a triangle, and three 11°s, and sew through the available hole of the new triangle **(b–c)**. Pick up an 11°, and sew through the available hole of the next lentil **(c–d)**. Repeat these two stitches to complete the round, and sew through the first 11° added in this round **(d–e)**. As you stitch, make sure that each new triangle is pointing in the same direction as the previous triangle. If not, remove the stitch and re-do it with the triangle facing the correct way.

[4] Pick up a 3 mm fire-polished bead, and sew through the next 11°, lentil, and 11° set **(figure 4, a–b)**. Repeat this stitch to complete the round **(b–c)**.

[5] Sew through the next 3 mm and 11° **(figure 5, a–b)**. Pick up three 11°s, and sew through the next 11°, 3mm, and 11° **(b–c)**. Repeat this stitch to complete the round, sewing through just

Difficulty rating

Materials

purple/bronze bracelet 7 in. (18 cm)
- **72** 6 mm CzechMates two-hole triangle beads (regal, halo finish)
- **36** 6 mm CzechMates two-hole lentil beads (matte metallic flax)
- **6** 6 mm fire-polished beads (regal, halo finish)
- **36** 3 mm fire-polished beads (bronze)
- **5 g** 11° seed beads (Toho 999, gold-lined rainbow black diamond)
- clasp
- beading thread, size D or 6 lb. test
- beading needles, #11 or #12

green/bronze bracelet colors:
- 6 mm CzechMates two-hole triangle beads (heavens, halo finish)
- 6 mm CzechMates two-hole lentil beads (matte metallic flax)
- 6 mm fire-polished beads (heavens, halo finish)
- 3 mm fire-polished beads (bronze)
- 11° seed beads (Toho 999, gold-lined rainbow black diamond)

an 11° in the final stitch **(c–d)**. Set the working thread aside.

[6] With the tail exiting the front of the component, pick up a 6 mm fire-polished bead, and sew through the opposite triangle. Sew back through the 6 mm and the first triangle again **(figure 6)**. End the tail (Basics) but not the working thread.

[7] Repeat steps 1–6 to make a total of six components.

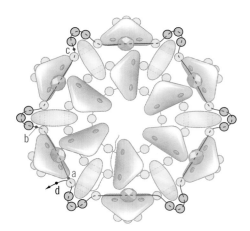

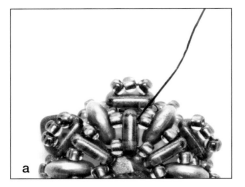

a

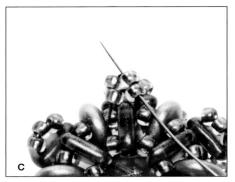

b

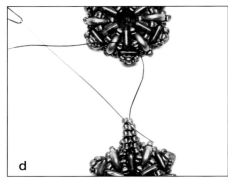

c

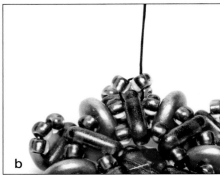

FIGURE 5

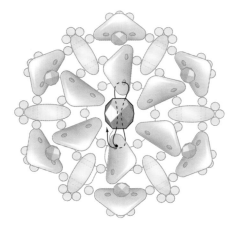

FIGURE 6

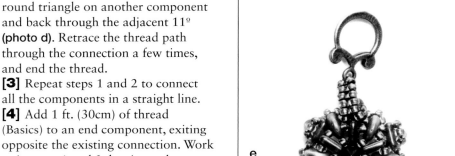

d

e

Assembly

[1] With the working thread from a component, sew through the beadwork to exit the outer hole of a triangle in the inner round **(photo a)**. You'll find it easiest to access this triangle from the back of the component. Pick up two 11º s, and sew through the triangle and the first 11º just added **(photo b)**.

[2] Pick up two 11º s, sew down through the adjacent 11º, sew up through the 11º your thread exited at the start of this step, and continue through the first 11º just added **(photo c)**. Repeat this stitch four times, and then sew through the outer hole of an inner-

round triangle on another component and back through the adjacent 11º **(photo d)**. Retrace the thread path through the connection a few times, and end the thread.

[3] Repeat steps 1 and 2 to connect all the components in a straight line.

[4] Add 1 ft. (30cm) of thread (Basics) to an end component, exiting opposite the existing connection. Work as in steps 1 and 2, but instead of sewing through a triangle on a new component, pick up half of the clasp. Retrace the thread path through the clasp connection several times, and end the thread **(photo e)**.

[5] Repeat step 4 at the other end of the bracelet. **o**

BEAD WEAVING

Button bridges bracelet

Peanut beads surround a SuperDuo base with Crystaletts buttons adding a hint of sparkle down the center.

designed by **Connie Whittaker**

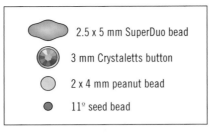

- 2.5 x 5 mm SuperDuo bead
- 3 mm Crystaletts button
- 2 x 4 mm peanut bead
- 11º seed bead

Difficulty rating

Materials

purple bracelet 7½ in. (19.1 cm)
- 6 g 2.5 x 5 mm SuperDuo beads (P15695, opaque gold/smoky topaz)
- 5 g 2 x 4 mm peanut beads (908, gold luster lavender)
- **22** 3 mm Crystaletts buttons (deep tanzanite in black rhodium bezel)
- 2 g 11º seed beads (Toho 85, metallic iris purple)
- toggle clasp
- Fireline 6 lb. test
- beading needles, #11 or #12

green bracelet colors:
- 2.5 x 5 mm SuperDuo beads (P65455, green travertine luster)
- 2 x 4 mm farfalle beads (453, green iris)
- 3 mm Crystaletts buttons (deep tanzanite in black rhodium bezel)
- 11º seed beads (Toho 85, metallic iris purple)

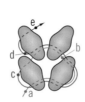   

FIGURE 1   FIGURE 2   FIGURE 3   FIGURE 4

stepbystep

Base

[1] On 2 yd. (1.8m) of thread, pick up two 2.5 x 5 mm SuperDuo beads, and sew through the available hole of the second SuperDuo (**figure 1, a–b**), leaving an 8-in. (20cm) tail. Pick up two Super-Duos, and sew through the available hole of the first SuperDuo from this step (**b–c**). Sew through all four SuperDuos as shown (**c–d**), and continue through the available hole of the last SuperDuo added (**d–e**).
[2] Pick up two SuperDuos, and sew through the available hole of the next SuperDuo (**figure 2, a–b**). Sew through the previous two SuperDuos and the two new SuperDuos as shown (**b–c**),

and continue through the available hole of the last SuperDuo added (**c–d**).
[3] Repeat step 2 for the desired length of the base, ending with an even number of SuperDuos along each edge and allowing ¾ in. (1.9cm) for the clasp. Do not end the working thread or tail.

Clasp

[1] With the tail, pick up two 11º seed beads, the toggle ring, and two 11ºs, and sew through the bottom hole of the next SuperDuo (**figure 3**). Retrace the thread path of the clasp connection, and end the tail (Basics).
[2] With the working thread, pick up three 11ºs, the toggle bar, and three 11ºs, and sew through the available hole of the next SuperDuo (**figure 4**). Adjust the number of 11ºs if needed to allow

FIGURE 5

FIGURE 6

FIGURE 7

the toggle bar to slide easily through the toggle ring. Retrace the thread path of the clasp connection, and end the working thread.

Embellishments

[1] Add a comfortable length of thread (Basics) to the end of the base with the toggle ring, and exit the top hole of the end SuperDuo with your needle pointing away from the bead-work **(figure 5, point a)**.

[2] Pick up three 2 x 4 mm peanut beads, and sew through the top hole of the next SuperDuo, the bottom hole of the following SuperDuo, and the top hole of the same SuperDuo **(a–b)**. Repeat this stitch for the length of the base, ending and adding thread as needed.

[3] Pick up an 11º, and sew through the top hole of the corresponding SuperDuo on the other side of the base. Pick up three peanuts, and sew through the top hole of the next SuperDuo. Continue through the bottom hole of the same SuperDuo and the top hole of the following SuperDuo, creating a mirror image of the first side **(figure 6)**. Repeat this stitch for the length of the base.

[4] Sew through the beadwork to exit the first three peanuts added on the first side of the base.

[5] Pick up three 11ºs, a 3 mm Crystaletts button, and three 11ºs. Sew through the corresponding peanut on the other side of the base **(figure 7, a–b)**.

[6] Pick up three peanuts, and sew through the nearest peanut in the next set of three **(b–c)**. Pick up three 11ºs, sew through the button, pick up three 11ºs, and sew through the corresponding peanut on the first side of the base **(c–d)**.

[7] Pick up three peanuts, and sew through the nearest peanut in the previous set of three **(d–e)**. Cross the band diagonally by sewing through the next three 11ºs, the button, the following three 11ºs, and the next three peanuts **(e–f)**.

[8] Repeat steps 5–7 for the length of the base, and end the thread. ●

RIGHT-ANGLE WEAVE

Bicone bangle

If sparkle is your thing, then these blingy bicone-studded bangles will feed your need to bead!

designed by **Samantha Mitchell**

This bangle requires an internal core support. We suggest using a core with a 2½–3-in. (6.4–7.6 cm) inside diameter, or any other diameter that's large enough to fit over the widest part of your hand. You can use a plain purchased metal bangle as well. Also, see "DIY vinyl tubing core" on p. 136 to learn how to make your own core from supplies available at local hardware and aquarium stores.

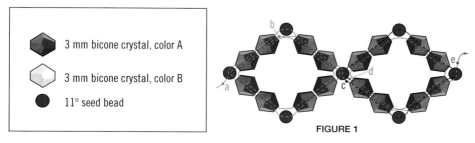

3 mm bicone crystal, color A

3 mm bicone crystal, color B

11º seed bead

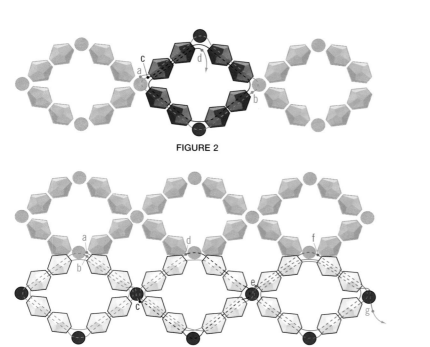

FIGURE 1

FIGURE 2

FIGURE 3

Materials
both bangles
- 2½–3-in. (6.4–7.6cm) inside diameter metal bangle or macramé ring *or* materials to make your own core (see "DIY vinyl tubing core," p. 136)
- Fireline 6 lb. test
- beading needles, #12

blue bangle
3-in. (7.6cm) inside diameter
- **400** 3 mm bicone crystals in each of **2** colors: A (Swarovski, Indian sapphire), B (Swarovski, light Azore)
- 2 g 11º seed beads (Toho 21, silver-lined crystal)

pink/ruby bangle
2½-in. (6.4cm) inside diameter
- **352** 3 mm bicone crystals in each of **2** colors: A (Thunder Polish, mid-Siam AB), B (Thunder Polish, rose jade)
- 2 g 11º seed beads (Miyuki 1436, raspberry transparent silver lined)

AFFORDABLE ADJUSTMENTS
No doubt about it, it is costly to purchase the 800 Swarovski crystals required for this project. As an alternative, you can use Thunder Polish crystals, as in the pink/ruby bracelet. However, Swarovski crystals are slightly smaller, fit together more snugly, and have a smoother finished look. Also, Thunder Polish crystals are very sharp and can shred your thread after multiple passes. To compensate for this, condition your thread and use shorter lengths.

stepbystep

[1] The beadwork for the bangle is worked in four rounds of modified right-angle weave. To work the first stitch of **round 1**: On 2 yd. (1.8 m) of thread, pick up a repeating pattern of an 11º seed bead and two color A 3 mm bicone crystals four times, leaving a 6-in. (15cm) tail. Sew through the first 11º and two As to form a ring **(figure 1, a–b)**. Retrace the thread path of the ring, skipping the 11ºs, and snug up the beads to form a diamond shape. Exit the end 11º opposite the tail **(b–c)**.

[2] To work the next stitch of **round 1**: Pick up a repeating pattern of two As and an 11º three times, and then pick up two As. Sew through the 11º your thread exited at the start of this step **(c–d)**. Retrace the thread path of the stitch, skipping the 11ºs, and exit the end 11º **(d–e)**.

[3] Work as in step 2 until you have a strip that is one stitch short of fitting around the outer edge of your bangle core.

[4] To join the ends of the strip: Pick up two As, an 11º, and two As, and sew through the first 11º picked up in step 1 **(figure 2, a–b)**. Pick up two As, an 11º, and two As, and sew through the 11º your thread exited at the start of this step **(b–c)**. Retrace the thread path of the stitch, skipping the 11ºs **(c–d)**, and end the working thread and tail (Basics).

[5] To work the first stitch of **round 2**: Add 2 yd. (1.8 m) of thread (Basics) to a stitch in round 1, and exit a side 11º. Pick up a repeating pattern of two color B 3 mm bicone crystals and an 11º three times, and then pick up two Bs. Sew through the 11º your thread exited at the start of this step **(figure 3, a–b)**. Retrace the thread path of the stitch, skipping the 11ºs, and exit an end 11º

DIY vinyl tubing core

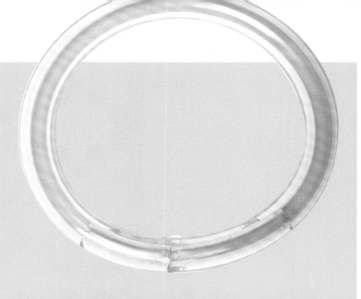

Materials needed:

- clear vinyl tubing with an outside diameter of ⅜ in. (1cm) and an inside diameter of ¼ in. (6mm). You can find this tubing at the hardware store; it is typically used for low-pressure water/food purposes. Our tube is 8 in. (20cm) long.
- airline tubing with an outside diameter of ¼ in. (6mm). This tubing can be found wherever aquarium supplies are sold. We used a 2-in. (5cm) piece.
- superglue

[1] Insert half the length of the airline tubing into one end of the vinyl tubing.

[2] Insert the available end of the airline tubing into the other end of the vinyl tubing. Push together the two ends of the vinyl tubing so there is about a 4–6 mm gap.

[3] Apply a small amount of superglue to each end of the vinyl tubing and the exposed airline tubing, and quickly push together the ends of the vinyl tubing so they touch.

[4] Hold together the ends of the tubing for a few minutes to allow the glue to dry completely.

(b–c).

[6] To work the next stitch of **round 2:** Pick up a repeating pattern of two Bs and an 11º twice, and then pick up two Bs. Sew through the side 11º in the next stitch of round 1 (**c–d**). Pick up two Bs, and sew through the 11º your thread exited at the start of this step. Retrace the thread path of the stitch, skipping the 11ºs, and exit the end 11º (**d–e**).

[7] To work the next stitch of **round 2:** Pick up two Bs, and sew through the side 11º in the next stitch of round 1 (**e–f**). Pick up a repeating pattern of two Bs and an 11º twice, and then pick up two Bs. Sew through the 11º your thread exited at the start of this step. Retrace the thread path of the stitch, skipping the 11ºs, and exit the end 11º (**f–g**).

[8] Repeat steps 6 and 7 to complete the round, and join the ends as before. End the thread.

[9] To work **round 3:** Repeat steps 5–8 on the other side of round 1.

[10] To work the first stitch of **round 4:** Add 2 yd. (1.8 m) of thread to a stitch in round 3, and exit a side 11º. Wrap the beadwork around your bangle core with round 1 on the inside of the ring, and rounds 2 and 3 forming the sides. Pick up two As, an 11º, and two As,

FIGURE 4

and sew through the side 11º in a corresponding stitch of round 2 (**figure 4, a–b**). Pick up two As, an 11º, and two As, and sew through the 11º your thread exited at the start of this step (**b–c**). Retrace the thread path of the stitch, skipping the 11ºs, and exit an end 11º (**c–d**).

[11] To work the next stitch of **round 4:** Pick up two As, and sew through the side 11º in the next stitch of round 2. Pick up two As, an 11º, and two As,

and sew through the 11º in the next stitch of round 3. Pick up two As, and sew through the 11º your thread exited at the start of this step. Retrace the thread path, skipping the 11ºs, and exit the end 11º (**d–e**).

[12] Continue working as in steps 10 and 11 to complete the round, and join the ends. End the thread. ●

RIGHT-ANGLE WEAVE

Crystal birthstone bracelet

Substitute crystals for gemstones in a sparkling special-occasion (maybe your birthday!) bracelet.

designed by **Connie Whittaker**

Make this quick-and-easy birthstone bracelet with peanut beads and bicone crystals. It'll come together in time for your birthday bash, plus it makes a great last-minute gift for all the other birthday girls on your calendar!

materials

bracelet 7½–8 in. (19.1–20 cm)

- **76–100** 3 mm bicone crystals in your birthstone color
- 5 g 2 x 4 mm peanut beads
- 1 g 11º seed beads
- clasp with **2** attached 6 mm jump rings
- Fireline 6 lb. test
- beading needles, #12

OCCASIONS TO CELEBRATE!

- **This bracelet would make a great Mother's Day gift. Select the appropriate crystal to represent each child, and work a repeating pattern that includes them all.**
- **Don't want to use birthstone colors? Use your favorite pairing of crystals and peanut beads for an everyday bracelet.**

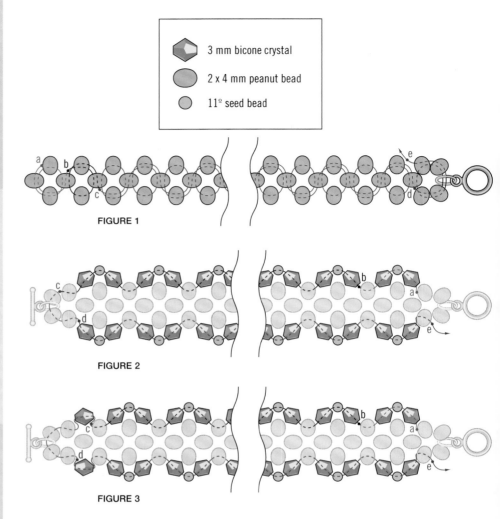

3 mm bicone crystal

2 x 4 mm peanut bead

11º seed bead

FIGURE 1

FIGURE 2

FIGURE 3

step by step

[1] On 2 yd. (1.8 m) of thread, pick up four 2 x 4 mm peanut beads. Tie the beads into a ring with a square knot (Basics), leaving an 8-in. (20cm) tail, and sew through a few more beads (figure 1, a–b).

[2] Work in right-angle weave as follows: Pick up three peanuts, and sew through the bead your thread exited in the previous stitch and the first two beads picked up in this stitch (b–c). Repeat this stitch until the band is the desired length minus the length of your clasp (c–d).

[3] Pick up four peanuts and a jump ring attached to half of the clasp, and sew through the bead your thread exited in the previous stitch. Continue through all the beads picked up in this step (d–e).

[4] With the tail, repeat step 3 to attach the other half of the clasp at the other

end of the band. End the tail (Basics).

[5] With the working thread, pick up a 3 mm bicone crystal, an 11º seed bead, and a 3mm. Skip the next edge peanut, and sew through the following peanut (figure 2, a–b). Repeat this stitch to the end of the band (b–c). Depending on how many right-angle weave stitches are in the band, your last embellishment stitch will end by sewing through the first peanut in the clasp loop (as in **figure 2, point c**) or by sewing through the last right-angle weave stitch (as in **figure 3, point c**). If the latter, pick up a 3mm, and sew through the first peanut in the clasp loop to complete the embellishment.

[6] Sew through the clasp loop (**figures 2 and 3, c–d**), and embellish the other edge as a mirror image of the first edge (**d–e**). End the thread. ●

Birthstone colors crystallized

Many traditional birthstones have direct crystal equivalents, but a few do not.
Find the crystal equivalent of your traditional birthstone below:

Month	Birthstone	Crystal color
January	garnet	garnet or Siam
February	amethyst	amethyst
March	aquamarine	aquamarine
April	diamond	crystal
May	emerald	emerald
June	pearl	light amethyst
July	ruby	ruby
August	peridot	peridot
September	sapphire	sapphire
October	opal	rose
November	topaz/citrine	topaz
December	blue zircon	blue zircon

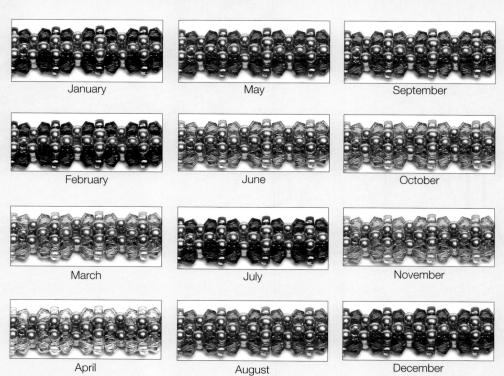

January	May	September
February	June	October
March	July	November
April	August	December

NETTING

FLOWER
Slides

Use striped seed beads to whip up these versatile
components, and then slide them along a ribbon
for a bracelet, or dangle them from earrings.

designed by **Kerrie Slade**

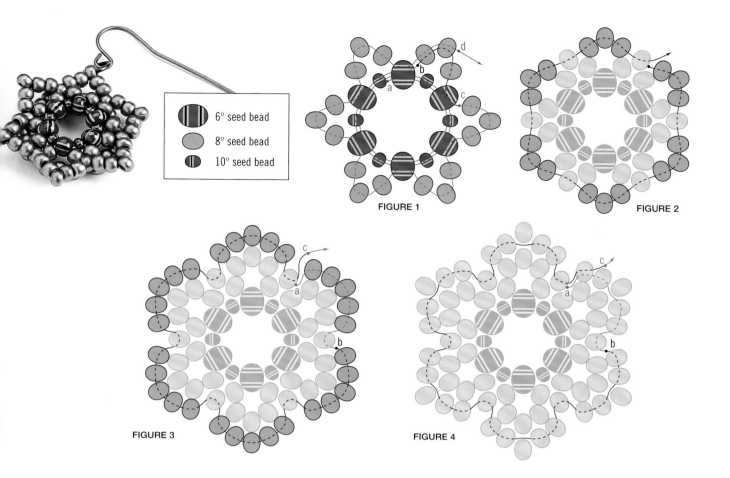

FIGURE 1

FIGURE 2

FIGURE 3

FIGURE 4

6º seed bead

8º seed bead

10º seed bead

stepbystep

Bracelet

[1] On 1 yd. (.9 m) of thread, pick up a repeating pattern of a 6º seed bead and a 10º seed bead until you have a total of 12 beads. Tie the beads into a ring with a square knot (Basics), leaving an 8-in. (20cm) tail, and sew through all the beads again, exiting the first 6º **(figure 1, a–b)**.

[2] Work in rounds of netting as follows:

Round 1: Pick up three 8º seed beads, and sew through the next 6º in the ring **(b–c)**. Repeat this stitch to complete the round, and step up through the first two 8ºs added in this round **(c–d)**.

Round 2: Pick up three 8ºs, and sew through the center 8º in the next stitch of round 1. Repeat this stitch to complete the round, and exit the same 8º your thread exited at the start of this round **(figure 2)**. Pull the thread snug so the beadwork cups slightly. The concave side should face away from you.

Round 3: Pick up five 8ºs, and sew through the center 8º in the next stitch of round 1 **(figure 3, a–b)**. Repeat this stitch to complete the round **(b–c)**. The stitches

will sit on top of the round 2 stitches.

Round 4: Sew through the first two 8ºs in the first stitch of round 3. Skip the center 8º, sew through the following two 8ºs, and continue through the next center 8º in round 1 **(figure 4, a–b)**. Pull the thread snug so the skipped bead pops out to form a point. Repeat this stitch to complete the round **(b–c)**, and end the working thread and tail (Basics).

[3] Repeat steps 1 and 2 to make a total of five flower components.

[4] Cut 24 in. (61cm) of ribbon, and thread it through two opposite loops on the underside of each component. You may find it helpful to pull the ribbon through the loops with the aid of a needle, pin, or chainnose pliers.

Earrings

Work as in steps 1 and 2 to make two flower components. Open a jump ring (Basics), and thread it through the center 8º at one point of a component. Add an earring finding to the jump ring, and close the jump ring. Repeat to assemble the other earring. ●

Difficulty rating

Materials

both projects
- Fireline 6 lb. test, or nylon beading thread, size D
- beading needles, #10–#12

ribbon bracelet with 5 components
- Preciosa traditional Czech beads
  30 6º seed beads (brown striped AB)
  30 10º seed beads (brown striped AB)
  5 g 8º seed beads (copper metallic silk)
- 2 ft. (61cm) ribbon, ¼ in. (6mm) wide

pair of earrings
- Preciosa traditional Czech beads (same colors as the bracelet)
  12 6º seed beads
  12 10º seed beads
  2 g 8º seed beads
- **2** 4 mm inside-diameter (ID) jump rings
- pair of earring findings
- **2** pairs of chainnose pliers

141

Multiple-Stitch Projects

CROSSWEAVE / BEAD WEAVING

Pure elegance bracelet

A base of twisted bugle beads is lavishly embellished with crystals and seed beads to create this captivating bracelet.

designed by **Cary Bruner**

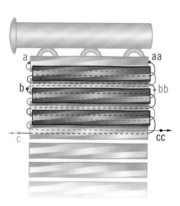

FIGURE 1   FIGURE 2   FIGURE 3

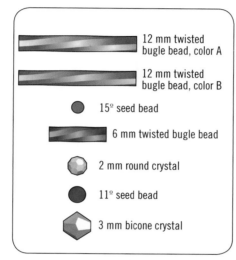

FIGURE 4

12 mm twisted bugle bead, color A

12 mm twisted bugle bead, color B

15º seed bead

6 mm twisted bugle bead

2 mm round crystal

11º seed bead

3 mm bicone crystal

Difficulty rating

Materials
brown bracelet 6¾ in. (17.1 cm)
- 12 mm twisted bugle beads
  - **89** color A (Miyuki 1275, gold antiqued matte black)
  - **54** color B (Miyuki 1285, gold antiqued transparent amethyst)
- **36** 6 mm twisted bugle beads (Miyuki 1265, gold antiqued matte black)
- crystals (Swarovski)
  - **34** 3 mm bicone (bronze shade)
  - **90** 2 mm round (light metallic gold 2X)
- **2 g** 11º seed beads (Toho 378D, metallic wheat-lined transparent root beer)
- **2 g** 15º seed beads (Toho 378D, metallic wheat-lined transparent root beer)
- **1** 3-strand tube clasp
- Fireline, 6 lb. test
- beading needles, #11

green bracelet colors (far left)
- 12 mm twisted bugle beads
  - color A (Miyuki 1265, gold antiqued matte transparent chartreuse)
  - color B (Miyuki 2035, matte metallic khaki iris)
- 6 mm twisted bugle beads (Miyuki 1265, gold antiqued matte transparent chartreuse)
- crystals (Swarovski)
  - 3 mm bicone (crystal AB satin)
  - 2 mm round (black diamond)
- 11º seed beads (Toho 462, metallic gold)
- 15º seed beads (Toho 462, metallic gold)

Base
1 Thread a needle on each end of a comfortable length of thread, and center a color A 12 mm twisted bugle bead.
2 With one needle, pick up an A, cross the other needle through it, and pull the thread tight **(figure 1)**.
3 Repeat step 2 for the desired length of the bracelet, making sure the total number of bugles is divisible by five plus four more. A 6¾ in. (17.1cm) finished bracelet requires 89 bugles. End and add thread as needed.
4 Cross both needles through the previous end A on the base **(figure 2)**. Position half of the clasp with the loops sitting on top of the end A.
5 With each needle, sew through an outer loop of the clasp, and cross both needles back through the A your thread exited at the beginning

of this step **(figure 3, a–b and aa–bb)**. Cross both needles through the end A **(b–c and bb–cc)**.
6 With each needle, sew through the outer loop of the clasp, and cross both needles back through the end A to reinforce the connection. Flip the base over so the clasp loops are on the bottom of the base.

Embellishment
1 Pick up a color B 12 mm twisted bugle bead, and cross the other needle through it. Cross both needles through the following A in the base, and pull the thread tight **(figure 4, a–b and aa–bb)**.
2 Repeat step 1 twice to form a set of three Bs **(b–c and bb–cc)**.
3 Pick up ten 15º seed beads (or enough 15ºs to cover the A your thread is exiting), and cross the

take care
Bugle beads can have sharp edges. To prevent fray, make sure your thread doesn't rub against the edges of the bugles.

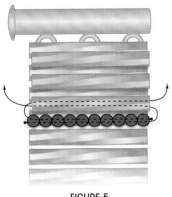

FIGURE 5

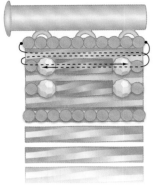

FIGURE 6

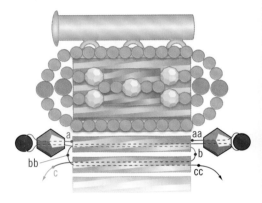

FIGURE 7

FIGURE 8

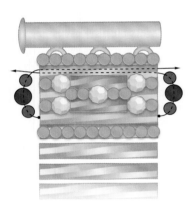

FIGURE 9

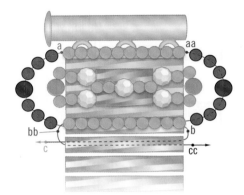

FIGURE 10

FIGURE 11

other needle through them. Cross both needles through the last B added in step 2 **(figure 5)**.

4 Pick up a 15º, a 2 mm crystal, a 6 mm twisted bugle bead, a 2 mm, and a 15º, and cross the other needle through the beads. Working toward the clasp, cross both needles through the following B **(figure 6, a–b and aa–bb)**. Repeat these stitches once **(b–c and bb–cc)**.

5 Pick up ten 15ºs (or enough 15ºs to cover the end A), cross the other needle through them **(c–d and cc–dd)**, and cross both needles through the A directly below the 15ºs.

6 Working away from the clasp, cross both needles through the following B. Continue crossing the needles through the next 15º, 2 mm, and 6 mm bugle **(figure 7)**.

7 Pick up two 15ºs, a 2 mm, and two 15ºs, and cross the other needle through the beads. Working away from the clasp, cross each needle through the following 6 mm bugle, and continue through the next 2 mm and 15º **(figure 8, a–b and aa–bb)**. Cross the needles through the following B **(b–c and bb–cc)**.

8 Working toward the clasp, pick up a 15º, an 11º, and a 15º with each needle, skip the following center B, and cross both needles through the next B **(figure 9)**. Continue crossing both needles through the following A (below the 15ºs) on the base.

9 Working away from the clasp, with each needle pick up three 15ºs, an 11º, and three 15ºs. Skip the following two As, and cross both needles through

the next A in the base **(figure 10, a–b and aa–bb)**. With each needle, cross through the following A (without embellishments) in the base **(b–c and bb–cc)**.

10 With each needle, pick up a 3 mm bicone crystal and a 15º, and sew back through the 3mm. Cross both needles back through the same A your thread exited at the beginning of this step **(figure 11, a–b and aa–bb)** and the following A (away from the clasp) in the base **(b–c and bb–cc)**.

11 Work as in steps 1–10 for the length of the bracelet, but end the final embellishment set at step 9 after crossing each needle through the end A. End and add thread as needed.

12 Flip the base over with the embellishment facing down. Work as in steps 4–6 of "Base" to attach the other half of the clasp. End the threads. ◉

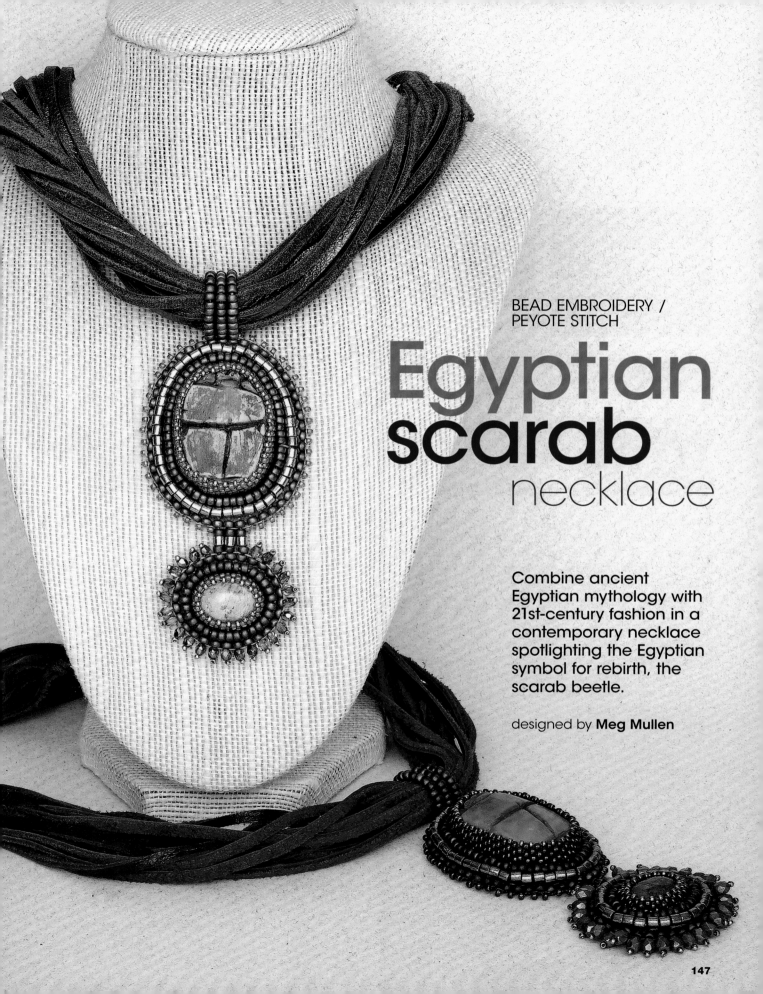

BEAD EMBROIDERY /
PEYOTE STITCH

Egyptian scarab *necklace*

Combine ancient Egyptian mythology with 21st-century fashion in a contemporary necklace spotlighting the Egyptian symbol for rebirth, the scarab beetle.

designed by **Meg Mullen**

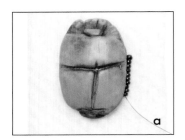

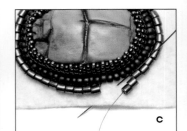

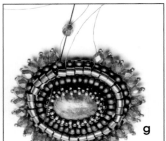

go smaller

Skip the round of 8º cylinder beads in step 5 of the "Pendant" section for a smaller gemstone cabochon pendant, as in the seafoam necklace.

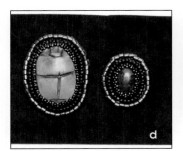

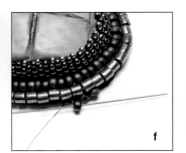

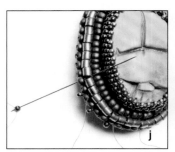

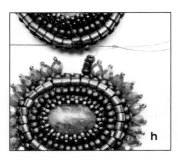

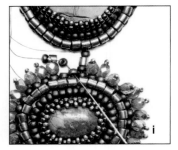

Pendant

1 Cut a 3½ x 2½-in. (8.9 x 6.4 cm) rectangle and a 2½-in. (6.4 cm) square of beading foundation. Apply a thin coat of E6000 to the back of the scarab and gemstone cabochons, and center the scarab cab on the larger piece of foundation and the gemstone cab on the smaller piece, leaving a ¾-in. (1.9 cm) space around each cab. Allow the glue to dry, and set the gemstone cab aside.

2 Tie an overhand knot at the end of 1 yd. (.9 m) of thread. Sew up through the back of the foundation, exiting near the outer edge of the scarab cab. Work in beaded backstitch around the scarab cab **(photo a)**: Pick up two 11º seed beads for each stitch, line them up next to the cab, and sew back through the foundation. Sew up between the two beads and through the second bead just added. End with an even number of beads, and sew through the first 11º in the round, the foundation, and back up through the foundation and next 11º.

3 Using 11ºs, work a round of tubular peyote stitch off the beaded backstitch **(photo b)** and step up. Work four additional rounds. Work a final round using 15º seed beads, and tighten the thread to secure the cab. Exit the beadwork by sewing diagonally down through the beads and the foundation. Make a half-hitch knot, and end the thread.

4 Tie an overhand knot at the end of 1 yd. (.9 m) of thread, and sew up through the foundation next to the round of 11ºs. Picking up two 8º seed beads per stitch, work a round of beaded backstitch. Sew through the first 8º added in the round, and exit through the back of the foundation. Make a half-hitch knot, and end the thread.

5 Using 8º cylinder beads, work as in step 4 to work beaded backstitch along the edge of 8º seed beads **(photo c)**.

inside scoop

If using white beading foundation, color the edge with a marker so it blends with the Ultrasuede.

Carefully trim the foundation close to the beads, being careful not to cut any threads.

6 Repeat steps 1–5 with the gemstone cabochon, except in step 3, work only two rounds of peyote with 11ºs before adding the final round of 15ºs.

7 Apply glue to the back of the beaded cabs, and place each cab on the Ultrasuede **(photo d)**. Allow the glue to dry, and trim the Ultrasuede close to the foundation for each cab.

8 Tie an overhand knot at the end of 1 yd. (.9 m) of thread, and trim the tail. Sew between the scarab cab's foundation and Ultrasuede exiting the front of the foundation about 1 mm from the edge, hiding the knot between the two layers.

9 Work a brick stitch edging: Pick up two 8º seed beads, sew up through both foundation layers one bead's width away from where the thread is exiting, and continue back through the second bead just added **(photo e)**. For each subsequent stitch, pick up an 8º seed bead, sew up through both layers one bead's width away from where the thread is exiting, and continue through the new bead just added **(photo f)**. Repeat this stitch around the perimeter. After adding the final bead, sew down through the first bead in the edging, through the foundation and Ultrasuede, and back through the first bead again. End the working thread in the edging beads.

10 Repeat steps 8–9 with the gemstone cabochon.

Assembly and embellishment

1 To determine where the two cabs will be stitched together, position the scarab cab with the head pointing up and the gemstone cab perpendicular underneath. Locate the three topmost center 8º cylinder beads on the gemstone cab. Temporarily mark these three beads by sewing an unknotted thread through them, and remove the needle. Tuck each end of the thread over the outer edge of the three 8º seed beads directly adjacent to the cylinders to indicate these three 8º seed beads should be reserved and not embellished.

2 Tie an overhand knot at the end of 1 yd. (.9 m) of thread, and sew up between the gemstone cab's layers and through the 8º edge seed bead directly to one side of the reserved 8º seed beads. Pick up a 3 mm or 4 mm fire-polished bead and a 15º seed bead, and sew back through the fire-polished bead and the 8º seed bead your thread exited at the start of this step. Repeat this stitch around the perimeter, stopping

when you reach the other end of the reserved beads **(photo g)**. End the thread.

3 Tie an overhand knot at the end of 20 in. (51cm) of thread, and sew up between the gemstone cab's layers and through the unembellished reserved 8º seed bead on one side. Pick up an 8º seed bead, an 8º cylinder bead, and an 8º seed bead, and sew through the corresponding 8º seed bead on the scarab cab **(photo h)**. Sew though the next 8º seed bead, pick up an 8º seed bead, an 8º cylinder bead, and an 8º seed bead, and sew though the corresponding 8º seed bead on the gemstone cab **(photo i)**. Repeat this stitch on the remaining reserved 8º seed bead. Retrace the thread paths to reinforce the join, and end the thread.

4 To determine where to place the bail on the scarab cab, mark the topmost center three 8º cylinder beads as in step 1. Tie an overhand knot at the end of 1 yd. (.9 m) of thread, and sew up between the scarab cab's layers with the needle exiting the 8º seed bead directly to one side of the reserved 8º seed beads. To embellish the outer edge, pick up an 11º, sew down through the adjacent 8º seed bead, and back up through the next 8º seed bead. Repeat this stitch **(photo j)** around the perimeter twice without adding 11ºs to the three reserved 8º seed beads.

5 To make the bail, tie an overhand knot at the end of 20 in. (51cm) of thread. Sew up between the scarab cab's layers and through the unembellished reserved 8º seed bead on one side of the scarab cab. Lay the leather choker flat, and center it above the scarab cab. Pick up 23 8º seed beads, and wrap them under and over the leather choker, sewing back through the 8º seed bead your thread exited at the start of this step. Repeat this stitch for the remaining two reserved 8º seed beads **(photo k)**, and retrace the thread path through the loops to reinforce the join. ◉

pick your favorite

Polymer clay artist Marian Hertzog also offers these striking scarab cabs in other scrumptious colors.

Difficulty rating

    ⬡ ⬡

Materials

eggplant necklace 17¼ in. (43.8 cm)
- **1** 34 x 23 mm polymer clay scarab cabochon (purple, Marian Hertzog; www.msplace.etsy.com)
- **1** 18 x 13 mm magnesite cabochon (purple)
- **31** 4 mm fire-polished beads (purple AB)
- **3 g** 8º cylinder seed beads (Miyuki DBL1852, Duracoat galvanized pewter)
- **9 g** 8º seed beads (Miyuki 401FR, matte black AB)
- **6 g** 11º seed beads (Miyuki 466, metallic dark raspberry gold luster)
- **2 g** 15º seed beads (Miyuki 4222, Duracoat galvanized pewter)
- shredded leather choker (plum purple; www.thelipstickranch.com)
- nylon beading thread, size D, or Fireline 6 lb. test
- beading needles, #10
- 6 x 2½-in. (15 x 6.4 cm) piece of beading foundation
- 4 x 2½-in. (10 x 6.4 cm) piece of Ultrasuede (coffee bean)
- E6000 adhesive
- scissors

seafoam necklace colors*
- polymer clay scarab cabochon
- **25** 3 mm fire-polished beads (teal AB)
- 8º cylinder seed beads (Miyuki DBL 1846, Duracoat galvanized dark sea foam)
- 8º seed beads (Miyuki 2008, matte metallic patina iris)
- 11º seed beads (Miyuki 351, peach lined aqua luster)
- 15º seed beads (Miyuki 4216, Duracoat galvanized dark sea foam)
- shredded leather choker (olive green)
- Ultrasuede (Montauk)

* A kit for the seafoam color necklace is available at www.beadmylove.com.

PEYOTE STITCH / HERRINGBONE STITCH / BRICK STITCH

HAUTE
Couture cuff

Make a high-fashion
cuff with cylinder
beads and adorable
beaded buttons.

designed by
Eleanna Zegkinoglou

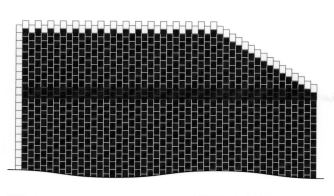

FIGURE 1

FIGURE 2

Cuff base

1 On a comfortable length of thread, pick up 47 color B 11º cylinder beads and one color A 11º cylinder bead, leaving a 6-in. (15cm) tail. These beads are outlined in red in the pattern in **figure 1** and will shift to form the first two rows of beadwork as the next row is added.

2 Working in flat even-count peyote and following the body section of the pattern in **figure 1**, work one row with an A and 23 Bs, and then work a row with 24 Bs. Alternate these two rows until the body of the band is about ½ in. (1.3cm) short of the desired cuff length. End and add thread as needed. The 6¼-in. (15cm) sample bracelet has 185 rows in this section.

3 Taper the end of the band by working decreasing rows:

Taper row 1 (outlined in orange): Work an A and 23 Bs.

Taper row 2: Work an A, 22 Bs, and an A. Make a decrease turn: sew under the nearest thread bridge, and sew back through the last two As.

Taper row 3: Work an A and 22 Bs.

Taper row 4: Work an A, 21 Bs, and an A. Make a decrease turn.

Taper row 5: Work an A and 21 Bs.

Taper row 6: Work an A, 20 Bs, and an A. Make a decrease turn.

Taper row 7: Work an A and 20 Bs.

Taper row 8: Work an A, 19 Bs, and an A. Make a decrease turn.

Taper row 9: Work an A and 19 Bs.

Taper row 10: Work an A, 18 Bs, and an A. Make a decrease turn.

Taper row 11: Work an A and 18 Bs.

Taper row 12: Work an A, 17 Bs, and an A. Make a decrease turn.

Taper row 13: Work an A and 17 Bs.

Taper row 14: Work an A, 16 Bs, and an A. Make a decrease turn.

Taper row 15: Work an A and 16 Bs.

Taper row 16: Work 17 As. Make a decrease turn.

Taper row 17: Work 16 As.

4 Add a new thread at the other end of the body, and repeat step 3 to taper this end. End all threads and tails.

Fold-over flap

1 On a comfortable length of thread, pick up the beads for the first two rows of the flap body (these beads are outlined in red in **figure 2**, reading right to left): an A, 13 Bs, an A, a B, three As, 14 Bs, an A, two Bs, two As, and 10 Bs. Leave a 6-in. (15cm) tail.

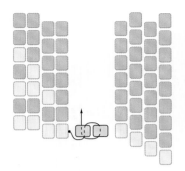

FIGURE 3

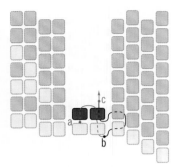

FIGURE 4

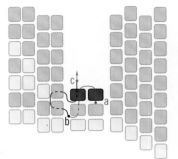

FIGURE 5

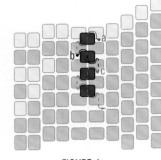

FIGURE 6

2 Working in two-drop peyote, continue to follow **figure 2** to complete the body of the flap. If you prefer to work from a word chart instead of a graphed pattern, go to www.BeadAndButton.com/couture to download the chart.

3 Taper the end as follows:

notations

The flap is worked in two-drop peyote. In the following notation, each stitch is indicated by a "2" followed by an "A" or "B" (meaning to pick up two As or two Bs) or a combination of the letters in the order they should be added. The stitches are separated by commas.

Taper row 1: 2A, 2B, 2B, 2B, 2B, 2B, 2B, 2B, AB, AB, 2B, 2B

Taper row 2: 2B, 2B, 2B, 2A, BA, 2B, 2B, AB, AB, 2B, 2B, 2A, decrease turn

Taper row 3: 2A, 2B, 2B, 2A, 2B, 2B, 2A, 2A, 2B, 2B, 2B

Taper row 4: 2B, 2B, 2A, 2B, AB, 2A, 2B, 2A, 2B, 2B, 2A, decrease turn

Taper row 5: 2A, 2B, 2B, AB, BA, BA, 2B, 2A, AB: 2B

Taper row 6: 2B, 2B, 2B, 2B, 2B, 2B, 2B, 2B, 2A, decrease turn

Taper row 7: 2A, 2B, 2B, AB, AB, 2A, BA, BA, 2B

Taper row 8: 2B, 2B, 2A, BA, 2A, 2A, 2B, 2B, 2A, decrease turn

Taper row 9: 2A, 2B, 2A, 2B, 2B, 2B, 2A, 2B

FIGURE 7   **FIGURE 8**

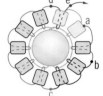

FIGURE 9

FIGURE 10

Taper row 10: 2B, BA, 2B, AB, AB, 2B, AB, 2A, decrease turn

Taper row 11: 2A, 2B, 2B, 2A, 2B, 2B, 2B

Taper row 12: 2B, 2B, AB, 2A, 2B, 2B, 2A, decrease turn

Taper row 13: 2A, 2B, 2B, AB, 2A, 2B

Taper row 14: 2B, 2A, 2B, 2B, 2B, 2A, decrease turn

Taper row 15: 2A, 2B, 2B, AB, AB

Taper row 16: 2B, 2B, 2B, 2B, 2A, decrease turn

Taper row 17: 2A, 2B, BA, BA

Taper row 18: 2B, 2A, 2B, 2A, decrease turn

Taper row 19: 2A, 2B, 2A

Taper row 20: BA, 2B, 2A, decrease turn

Taper row 21: 2A, 2B

Taper row 22: 2B, 2A, decrease turn

Taper row 23: 2A

Taper row 24: 2A

4 Add a new thread at the other end of the band, and taper the other end as in step 3. End all the threads.

Join

1 Add a new thread to the flap, and exit an end A on the wide side. Align this edge of the flap with the narrow edge of the base.

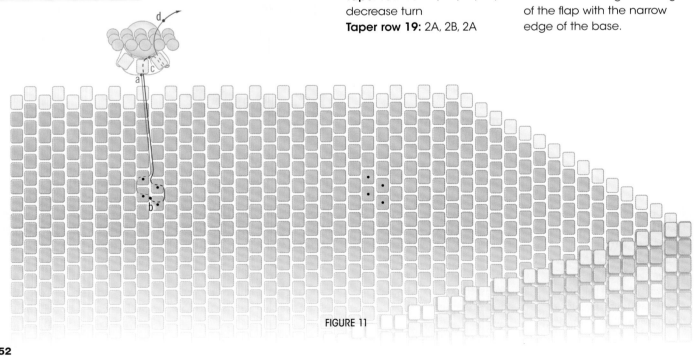

FIGURE 11

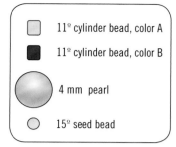

- ☐ 11º cylinder bead, color A
- ■ 11º cylinder bead, color B
- ⬤ 4 mm pearl
- ○ 15º seed bead

2 Pick up two As, and sew through them again to make a two-bead ladder **(figure 3)**. Snug them up to the flap.

3 Pick up two Bs, and sew down through the adjacent A **(figure 4, a–b)**. Sew through the corresponding edge A on the base, and then sew through the next edge B and back through the last B added **(b–c)**.

4 Working in herringbone stitch, pick up two Bs, sew down through the adjacent B **(figure 5, a–b)**, and then sew through the next two edge Bs in the flap and back through the last B added **(b–c)**. Repeat this stitch for the length of the edges. When you reach the other end, you'll be exiting an end join bead. Sew down through the adjacent join bead so your needle is heading back toward the spine of the join beads just added.

5 For additional reinforcement and to make the spine of the join stand out from the edges a bit, work one more row of beads: Pick up a B, and sew through the adjacent join bead in the next row **(figure 6, a–b)**. Repeat this stitch **(b–c)** for the entire length of the join. End the thread. Fold the flap so the last row of beads added are hidden within the fold.

Decorative buttons

1 On 1 yd. (.9 m) of thread, pick up a 4 mm pearl, leaving a 6-in. (15 cm) tail. Sew through the pearl

again to make a thread bridge around one side of the pearl **(figure 7)**. Sew through the pearl twice more for a total of three thread bridges, and arrange them so two of the thread bridges are opposite each other and the remaining bridge is between the other two.

2 Pick up two As, sew under one of the side thread bridges (not the one in the middle), and back through the second A **(figure 8)**. Pick up an A, and sew under the thread bridge and back through the A just added **(figure 9, a–b)**. Repeat this stitch around the pearl until you've added a total of five As **(b–c)**. Continue around, attaching As to the opposite thread bridge, until you have 10 As surrounding the pearl **(c–d)**. Complete the ring by sewing down through the first A, under the thread bridge, and back up through the first A **(d–e)**.

3 Pick up three 15ºs, and sew up through the next A in the ring **(figure 10)**. Make sure the center thread bridge is not facing up at this point. Repeat this stitch nine times around the ring. After adding the loops of 15ºs, there will be a distinct front and back to the button, and the center thread bridge should be on the back.

4 Sew down through the previous A and under the center thread bridge. Working as in step 2, add three As to the center thread bridge. You will attach the button to the bracelet using the middle A on this center thread bridge.

5 Sew down through the center A on the back of the button, sew under the thread bridge, and sew back through the center A. End the tail but not the working thread, and set this button aside.

6 Repeat steps 1–5 to make a second button.

7 Identify the eight beads on the cuff base marked with dots in **figure 11**. This is where you will attach the two buttons.

8 With the thread exiting the center A on the back of a button, sew through two adjacent base beads **(figure 11, a–b)** and the other two adjacent base beads, and then sew back through the center A on the button **(b–c)**. Make sure you are attaching the button to the outer surface of the base. Sew through an adjacent A on the back of the button, under the corresponding thread bridge, and back through the same A **(c–d)**. Sew down through the center A, and retrace the thread path of the connection. Do not end the thread.

9 Repeat step 8 to attach the other button to the other set of four marked base beads.

Snap closure

1 With a working thread remaining from a button, sew through to the inner surface of the base, and work as in step 8 of "Decorative buttons" to attach half of each snap closure to the marked beads in **figure 11**.

2 Add a new thread to the other end of the cuff base, and attach the other half of the snap closures to the outer surface of this end of the base, attaching them to the corresponding sets of beads as those marked in **figure 11**. End the threads. ●

Difficulty rating

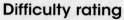

Materials

cuff 6¼ x 2½ in. (15 x 6.4 cm)
- **2** 4 mm glass pearls (white)
- 11º Miyuki Delica cylinder beads
  - **3 g** color A (DB0035, galvanized silver)
  - **42 g** color B (DBC0005, hex-cut blue iris)
- **1 g** 15º seed beads (Miyuki 181, galvanized silver)
- **2** snaps, size 1/0
- Fireline, 6 lb. test (crystal for buttons and smoke for remainder)
- beading needles, #12

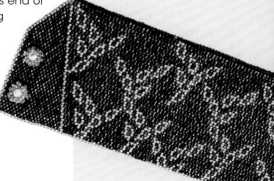

All about the braids

bracelet

Combine braided tubular herringbone strands with right-angle weave slider beads for a bracelet that shouts "look at me!"

designed by **Judy Henegar**

Strands

1 On a comfortable length of thread and leaving an 8-in. (20 cm) tail, work a four-bead ladder using color A 11º seed beads **(figure 1)**. Form the ladder into a ring.

2 Pick up two As, sew down through the next A in the ladder **(figure 2, a–b)**, and continue up through the following A. Work a second herringbone stitch,

and step up through the first A added in this round **(b–c)**.

3 Continue working in herringbone stitch until the beadwork measures 9 in. (23cm), or until you reach the desired length. Once braided, the final length of each strand will be reduced by approximately 1½ in. (3.8 cm). Do not end the working thread or tail.

4 Work as in steps 1–3 to make a

second strand using color B 11º seed beads, and a third strand using a color A and a color B seed bead for each herringbone stitch, alternating the color pattern for each round.

Slider beads

1 On a comfortable length of thread, pick up four 3 mm bicone crystals leaving a 6-in. (15cm) tail. Sew through the first three beads again to form a ring **(figure 3, a–b)**. Picking up three crystals per stitch, work a total of five right-angle weave stitches **(b–c)**.

2 Form the strip into a ring with your thread exiting an edge crystal.

3 Pick up an 11º (color A or B), and sew through the following crystal on the outer edge. Repeat this stitch five times using the same color 11º **(photo a)**.

4 Sew through the beadwork to exit a crystal on the other edge, and work as in step 3 to add six 11ºs on this edge of the slider bead. End the threads.

5 Make a total of nine slider beads.

Clasp

1 With the tail of the two-color strand, pick up a 4 mm pearl, and sew through the first loop of the clasp. Sew back through the pearl and the two adjacent 11ºs in the column opposite where the thread exited at the beginning of this step **(figure 4, a–b)**.

2 Sew up through the two 11ºs in the adjacent column, and continue through the pearl and the first loop of the clasp. Sew back through the pearl **(b–c)**, and continue through the two 11ºs that are not yet attached to the pearl. Retrace the thread path through the clasp loop, pearl, and four end seed beads. End the tail.

3 Repeat steps 1 and 2 for the second and third loop of the clasp with the remaining two strands.

4 Center five slider beads on the two-color strand. Center four slider beads on the other outer strand **(photo b)**.

5 Braid the strands, positioning the sliders in alternating sequence on the outer edges **(photo c)**.

6 To secure the braids, tape the three strand ends together **(photo d)**. If needed, use the working thread to add or remove rounds on each strand to make them all an even length.

7 Work as in steps 1–3 to attach the other half of the clasp. Remove the tape, and end the working thread. ●

a

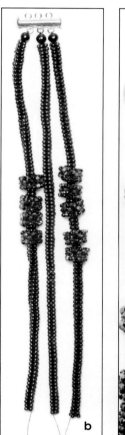

b

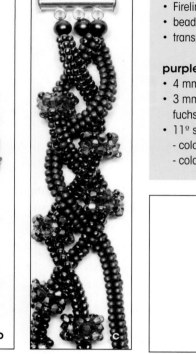

c

d

Difficulty rating

Materials

turquoise bracelet 7¾ in. (19.7 cm)
- **6** 4 mm crystal pearls (Swarovski, jade)
- **162** 3 mm bicone crystals (Swarovski, Pacific opal AB2X)
- **8 g** 11º seed beads
  - color A (Miyuki F470, frosted metallic silver)
  - color B (Miyuki PF484, winter green matte galvanized)
- **1** 3-strand tube clasp
- Fireline, 6 lb. test
- beading needles, #11
- transparent tape

purple bracelet colors
- 4 mm pearls (Preciosa, dark blue)
- 3 mm bicone crystals (Swarovski, fuchsia AB2X)
- 11º seed beads
  - color A (Toho 221, metallic bronze)
  - color B (Toho 515F, matte plum iris tea)

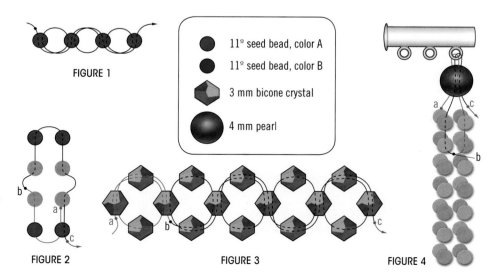

○ ○ ○

FIGURE 1

● 11º seed bead, color A

● 11º seed bead, color B

⬡ 3 mm bicone crystal

● 4 mm pearl

FIGURE 2

FIGURE 3

FIGURE 4

RIGHT-ANGLE WEAVE / PEYOTE / BEAD WEAVING

RADIANT

RIVOLI
NECKLACE

Create this stunning bezeled
necklace that is full of elegant sparkles.

designed by **Abigail Engelking**

FIGURE 1

FIGURE 2

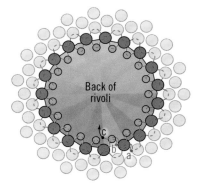

FIGURE 4

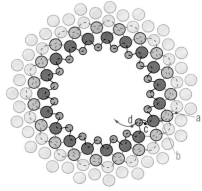

FIGURE 3

Large bezel

1 On 2 yd. (1.8 m) of thread, pick up four color A 11º metal seed beads, and sew through all the beads again. Continue through the next three As to form a ring, leaving a 10-in. (25cm) tail **(figure 1, a–b)**.

2 Working in right-angle weave (RAW), pick up three As, sew through the A your thread exited at the start of this step, and continue through the first two As picked up in this step **(b–c)**. Repeat this stitch for a total of 18 stitches.

3 To join the strip into a ring: Pick up an A, and sew through the first A added in step 1 **(figure 2, a–b)**. Pick up an A, and sew through the A your thread exited at the start of this step **(b–c)**. Sew through the next three As **(c–d)**.

4 Work tubular peyote stitch off the RAW base as follows, stepping up at the end of each round:

Round 1: Work a round using As **(figure 3, a–b)**.

Round 2: Work a round using color B 11º seed beads **(b–c)**.

Round 3: Work a round using color C 15º metal seed beads **(c–d)**.

5 Sew through the beadwork to exit an A on the opposite edge. Place the 18 mm rivoli face down into the bezel setting.

6 To make the bezel back, work in

tubular peyote as follows, stepping up at the end of each round:

Round 1: Work a round using Bs **(figure 4, a–b)**.

Round 2: Work a round using Cs **(b–c)**.

○ 11º metal seed bead, color A

● 11º seed bead, color B

○ 15º metal seed bead, color C

18 mm rivoli

● 2 mm pearl

14 mm rivoli

12 mm rivoli

● 6 mm pearl

○ 8º metal seed bead

● 3 mm pearl

Difficulty rating

Materials

gold/cream necklace 17¼ in. (43.8cm)
- rivolis (Swarovski, golden shadow)
  - **1** 18 mm
  - **2** 14 mm
  - **2** 12 mm
- **23** 6 mm pearls (Swarovski, light gold)
- **238** 3 mm pearls (Swarovski, light gold)
- **75** 2 mm glass pearls (Czech, light cream)
- **2** 8º metal seed beads (24k gold plated)
- **2 g** 11º metal seed beads, color A (24k gold plated)
- **1 g** 11º seed beads, color B (Toho 409, opaque light cream rainbow)
- **1 g** 15º metal beads, color C (24k gold plated)
- **1** toggle clasp
- **2** 4 mm 20 gauge jump rings
- Fireline 6 lb. test
- beading needles, #12 or #13
- **2** pairs of chainnose, flatnose, and/or bentnose pliers

purple/gold necklace (p. 159)
- 18 mm, 14 mm, and 12 mm rivolis (Swarovski, crystal vitrail)
- 6 mm pearls (Swarovski, mauve)
- 3 mm pearls (Swarovski, vintage gold)
- 2 mm glass pearls (Czech, sand)
- 1 g 11º seed beads (Toho 361, lilac color-lined blue)
- 11º seed beads (Miyuki 193, 24k gold light plated)
- 15º seed beads (Miyuki 193, 24k gold light plated)

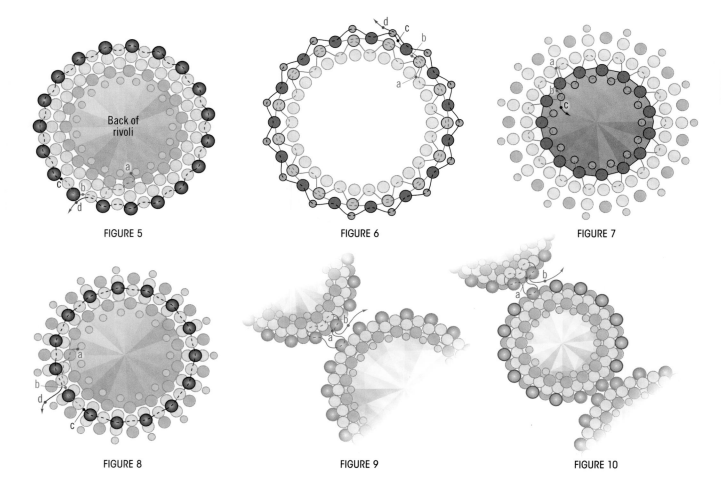

FIGURE 5

FIGURE 6

FIGURE 7

FIGURE 8

FIGURE 9

FIGURE 10

7 Sew through the beadwork, and exit the front-most round of As in the RAW base **(figure 5, a–b)**.

8 Pick up a 2 mm pearl, and sew through the following A **(b–c)**. Repeat this stitch 18 more times to complete the round **(c–d)**. Do not end the working thread or tail.

Medium bezels

1 On 1 yd. (.9 m) of thread, pick up 30 As, and sew through the beads again. Continue through the next two As to form a ring, leaving a 10-in. (25 cm) tail. These beads will shift to form rounds 1 and 2 as the next round is added.

2 Work rounds of tubular peyote stitch

as follows, stepping up at the end of each round:

Round 3: Work a round using As **(figure 6, a–b)**.

Round 4: Work a round using Bs **(b–c)**.

Round 5: Work a round using Cs **(c–d)**.

3 Sew through the beadwork, and exit an A in round 1. Place the 14 mm rivoli in the bezel face down.

4 Work a round of tubular peyote using Bs, and step up **(figure 7, a–b)**.

5 Work a round of tubular peyote using Cs, and step up **(b–c)**.

6 Sew through the beadwork to exit an A in the center round of As **(figure 8, a–b)**.

7 Pick up a 2 mm pearl, and sew through the following A **(b–c)**.

8 Repeat this stitch to complete the round **(c–d)**. Do not end the working thread or tail.

9 Repeat steps 1–8 to make a second medium bezel.

Small bezels

Repeat steps 1–9 of "Medium bezels" except pick up 26 As in step 1, and use 12 mm rivolis. Make two small bezels.

Connections

1 Arrange the bezels in a V with the large bezel in the middle, the two medium bezels on opposite sides of the large bezel, and the small bezels on opposite sides of the medium bezels.

2 Using the working thread or tail, sew through the beadwork of a medium bezel, and exit a 2 mm pearl **(figure 9, point a)**.

3 Attach the medium bezel to the large bezel as follows:

Sew through a 2 mm pearl on the large bezel, and continue through the adjacent 2 mm pearl on the medium bezel. Sew through the next three As and through the 2 mm pearl your thread exited at the beginning of this step **(a–b)**. Retrace the thread path to reinforce the join, and end the thread.

4 Using the working thread, sew through the beadwork of a small bezel, and exit a 2 mm pearl. Position the small bezel to interlock with the medium bezel so that there are six unconnected 2 mm pearls along each outer edge of the medium bezel **(figure 10, outlined in red)**.

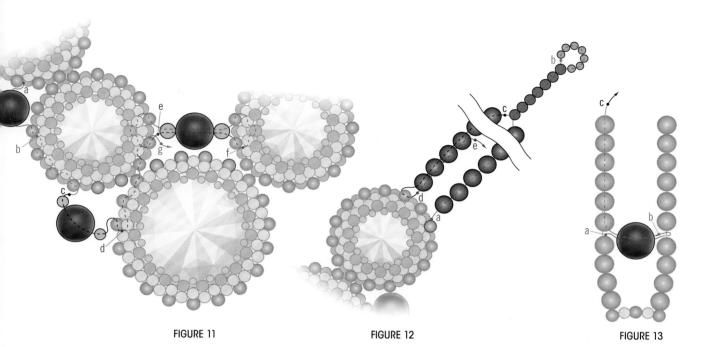

FIGURE 11

FIGURE 12

FIGURE 13

5 Work as in step 3 to attach the small bezel to the medium bezel **(figure 10, a–b)**.

6 Repeat steps 2–5 for the other half of the necklace. When attaching the medium bezel to the large bezel, position the medium bezel so that there are four unconnected pearls between the two medium bezels **(figure 11, outlined in red)**. End all working threads and tails.

Pearl embellishment

1 On 1 yd. (.9 m) of thread, exit a 2 mm pearl on a small bezel adjacent to the pearls used for the connection, with the needle exiting toward the connection **(figure 11, point a)**.

2 Pick up a 6 mm pearl, skip the 2 mm pearl next to the connection on the medium bezel, and sew through the next 2 mm pearl **(a–b)**.

3 Sew through the next six beads along the edge of the medium bezel to exit a 2 mm pearl **(b–c)**.

4 Pick up an A, a 6 mm pearl, and an A, skip the 2 mm pearl next to the connection on the large bezel, and sew through the next 2 mm pearl **(c–d)**.

5 Sew through the beadwork as shown to exit the 2 mm pearl adjacent to the connection, on the inside edge of the medium bezel **(d–e)**.

6 Pick up an 8º metal seed bead, a 6 mm pearl, and an 8º, and sew through the corresponding 2 mm pearl on the opposite medium bezel **(e–f)**. Sew through the beadwork as shown,

and exit the 2 mm pearl your thread exited from at the beginning of this stitch **(f–g)**. End the thread.

7 Repeat steps 1–4 on the opposite side of the necklace, and end the working thread and tails.

Neck straps

1 Add 1 yd. (.9 m) of thread to a small bezel. Exit the fourth 2 mm pearl from the connector 6 mm pearl **(figure 12, outlined in red)** with the needle exiting toward the inside edge **(figure 12, point a)**.

2 Pick up 60 3 mm pearls, seven Bs, and seven Cs **(a–b)**.

3 Sew back through the seven Bs just added **(b–c)**.

4 Pick up 59 3 mm pearls, skip the adjacent 2 mm pearl on the small bezel, and sew through the next 2 mm pearl **(c–d)**.

5 Continue through the next four 3 mm pearls **(d–e)**.

6 Pick up a 6 mm pearl, and sew around the thread bridge between the two corresponding pearls on the other strand **(figure 13, a–b)**. Sew back through the 6 mm pearl and the following six 3 mm pearls **(b–c)**.

7 Repeat step 6 eight times, but when picking up the fifth

6 mm pearl, skip one more pearl on the outer edge side (seven instead of six) before sewing around the thread bridge. This will give the neck strap a slight curve. End the thread.

8 Repeat steps 1–7 for the second neck strap, and end the threads.

Clasp

Open a 4 mm jump ring, and attach half the clasp to an end loop of Cs. Repeat for the other side of the necklace. ●

ZIP bracelet

Connect two strips of fire-polished beads and embellish with seed beads and tiny pearls for an easy-to-wear look.

designed by **Cary Bruner**

Side strips

1 On 3 yd. (2.7 m) of thread, attach a stop bead, leaving a 12-in. (30 cm) tail. Pick up enough color A 3 mm fire-polished beads to fit around your wrist minus ½-in. (1.3 cm) for the clasp. A 6¾ in. (17.1 cm) bracelet uses 49 beads.
2 Pick up an 11º seed bead, and sew back through the last A added **(figure 1, a–b)**.

3 Pick up a color B 3 mm fire-polished bead, an 11º, and a B, and sew through the A your thread is exiting, going in the same direction, to form a loop on one side of the row of As **(b–c)**.
4 Pick up a color C 3 mm fire-polished bead, an 11º, and a C. Sew through the A your thread is exiting and the following A, to form a loop on the opposite side of the row of As **(c–d)**.

5 Pick up a B and an 11º, sew through the adjacent B, and the last A your thread exited **(figure 2, a–b)**.
6 Pick up a C and an 11º, and sew through the adjacent C, the last A your thread exited, and the next A **(b–c)**.
7 Repeat steps 5 and 6 for the remainder of the row of As, keeping a firm tension. After adding the last C bead, your thread should be exiting the end A.

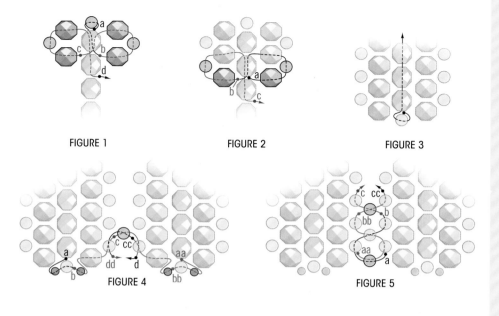

FIGURE 1

FIGURE 2

FIGURE 3

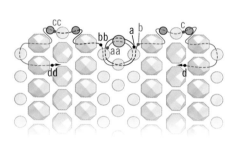

FIGURE 4

FIGURE 5

FIGURE 6

⬡	3 mm fire-polished bead, color A
◯	11º seed bead
⬡	3 mm fire-polished bead, color B
⬡	3 mm fire-polished bead, color C
•	15º seed bead
◉	2 mm pearl

Difficulty rating

   ◯ ⬡

Materials
blue bracelet 6¾ in. (17.1 cm)
- 3 mm fire-polished beads
  - **98** color A (matte denim)
  - **100** color B (denim/copper)
  - **100** color C (light blue/copper)
- **48** 2 mm glass pearls (Tahitian)
- **5 g** 11º seed beads (Japanese 318T, smoked opaque gold luster)
- **2 g** 15º seed beads (Japanese F297, gray matte AB)
- **1** 3-strand tube clasp
- Fireline 6 lb. test
- beading needles, #11

earth-tone bracelet colors
- 3 mm fire-polished beads
  - color A (peridot green)
  - color B (green/brown)
  - color C (cream/brown)
- 2 mm glass pearls (satin taupe)
- 11º seed beads (Toho PF470, permanent galvanized matte silver)
- 15º seed beads (Japanese F451D, gray mist matte metallic)

purple/bronze bracelet colors
- 3 mm fire-polished beads
  - color A (cream/purple)
  - color B (dark purple)
  - color C (light purple)
- 2 mm glass pearl (coffee)
- 11º seed beads (Miyuki 360, aqua-lined amethyst AB)
- 15º seed beads (Japanese 3190, metallic brass)

8 Remove the stop bead, and thread a needle on the tail. Pick up an 11º, and sew through the row of As **(figure 3)**. End the tail but not the working thread.
9 Repeat steps 1–8 to make another strip.

Join
1 Thread a needle on the working thread from each strip, and position them next to each other vertically with the Bs toward the inside.
2 With each needle, pick up a 15º seed bead, and sew through the end 11º going toward the other strip **(figure 4, a–b and aa–bb)**. With each needle, pick up a 15º, and continue through the adjacent B and next edge 11º **(b–c and bb–cc)**.
3 With one needle, pick up an 11º, and cross the other needle through it. With each needle, sew through the adjacent edge 11º **(c–d and cc–dd)**.

4 With one needle, pick up an 11º, and cross the other needle through it. With each needle, sew through the adjacent edge 11º, the center 11º, and the next edge 11º **(figure 5, a–b and aa–bb)**.
5 With one needle, pick up an 11º, and cross the other needle through it. With each needle, sew through the next edge 11º **(b–c and bb–cc)**. Repeat this stitch for the remainder of the base.
6 With one needle, pick up an 11º, and cross the other needle through it. With each needle, sew through the next three 11ºs to exit the 11º your thread exited at the start of the step **(figure 6, a–b and aa–bb)**. With each needle, continue through the end B, pick up a 15º, and sew through the next 11º **(b–c and bb–cc)**. Pick up a 15º and sew through the following C, 11º, and C **(c–d and cc–dd)**.

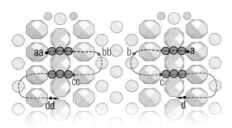

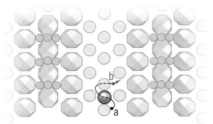

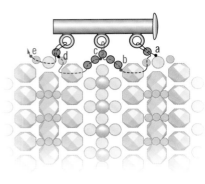

FIGURE 7   FIGURE 8   FIGURE 9

Embellishment

1 With each needle, pick up three 15ºs, skip the row of As, and sew through the corresponding B **(figure 7, a-b and aa-bb)**. Continue through the next 11º and the following B **(b-c and bb-cc)**.
2 With each needle, pick up three 15ºs, skip the row of As, and sew through the corresponding C, 11º, and C **(c-d and cc-dd)**.
3 Repeat steps 1–2 for the remainder of the base.
4 With the longest working thread, sew through the beadwork to exit the end

11º in the center join **(figure 8, point a)**. Pick up a 2 mm pearl, and sew through the next center 11º going in the same direction **(a-b)**. Repeat this stitch for the remainder of the base.

Clasp

1 Sew through the beadwork to exit the 11º at the end of a row of As, with the needle pointing toward the center of the beadwork **(figure 9, point a)**.
2 Pick up a 15º, and sew through the first loop of the clasp. Sew back through

the 15º just added and sew through the next 15º and B **(a-b)**.
3 Pick up three 15ºs, sew through the second loop of the clasp, and continue back through the last 15º just added **(b-c)**. Pick up two 15ºs and sew through the next B, and 15º **(c-d)**.
4 Pick up a 15º, and sew through the last loop of the clasp. Sew back through the 15º just added and the end 11º and 15º **(d-e)**. End the thread.
5 Repeat steps 1–4 for the other end of the bracelet, and end the thread. **●**

Interchangeable channel bangle

This clever bracelet has no clasp, but still fits snugly on your wrist. The secret is the elastic bands of pearls or crystals which can be swapped out to create a whole new look.

designed by **Gabi Gueck**

Cubic RAW how-to

Each cubic right-angle weave (or CRAW) unit has six surfaces — four sides, a top, and a bottom. Each surface is made up of four beads, but since the beads are shared, 12 beads are used to make the first unit, and only eight beads are used for each subsequent CRAW unit. For clarity, we used two colors of beads in the how-to photos.

Working the first CRAW unit

1 On the specified length of thread, pick up four beads. Tie the beads into a ring with a square knot, leaving the specified length tail, and continue through the first two beads in the ring. This ring of beads will count as the first stitch of the unit.

2 Work two right-angle weave stitches off of the bead your thread is exiting to create a flat strip of right-angle weave.

3 To join the first and last stitches: Pick up a bead, sew through the end bead in the first stitch (CRAW 1, a–b), pick up a bead, and sew through the end bead in the last stitch (b–c). CRAW 2 shows a three-dimensional view of the resulting cube-shaped unit.

4 To make the unit more stable, sew through the four beads at the top of the unit (CRAW 3). Sew through the beadwork to the bottom of the unit, and sew through the four remaining beads. This completes the first CRAW unit.

Working more CRAW units

1 Each new CRAW unit is worked off of the top four beads of the previous unit. These beads are identified in CRAW 4. Sew through the beadwork to exit one of these top beads.

2 For the first stitch of the new unit: Pick up three beads, and sew through the top bead your thread exited at the start of this step. Continue through the three beads just picked up (CRAW 5). Sew through the next top bead in the previous unit.

3 For the second stitch of the new unit: Pick up two beads, and sew through the side bead in the previous stitch, the top bead your thread exited at the start of this stitch (CRAW 6), and the next top bead in the previous unit.

4 For the third stitch of the new unit: Repeat step 3 (CRAW 7), and continue through the side bead in the first stitch of the new unit.

5 For the fourth stitch of the new unit: Pick up a bead, and sew through the side bead in the previous stitch and the top bead in the previous unit (CRAW 8).

6 To make the unit more stable, sew through the beadwork to exit a top bead in the new unit, and sew through all four top beads (CRAW 9). This completes the new CRAW unit.

7 Repeat steps 2–6 for the desired number of CRAW units.

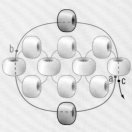

CRAW 1

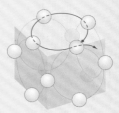

CRAW 2

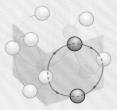

CRAW 3

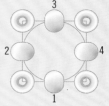

CRAW 4

CRAW 5

CRAW 6

CRAW 7

CRAW 8

CRAW 9

full strength

Use a strong elastic like Elasticity by Beadalon. The .8 mm may be used for the crystals but doesn't pass easily through the pearls.

CRAW tubes

1 On a comfortable length of thread, work the first CRAW unit (see "Cubic RAW how-to" above) using 8º seed beads and leaving a 6-in. (15cm) tail.

2 Using 8ºs, work CRAW units for the desired length off the first one, to form a tube long enough to fit around your wrist without overlapping. Use a tight tension, and end and add thread as needed. End the working thread and tail. Repeat to make a total of three tubes.

Joining tubes

1 Add a comfortable length of thread to the beadwork, exiting a bottom edge 8º in the last CRAW unit of a tube (photo a). Using 8ºs, work a row of flat right-angle weave off of the bottom edge 8ºs (photo b) for the length of the tube, retracing each unit as you go, and using a tight tension. End and add thread as needed.

2 Sew through the beadwork to exit an outside edge 8º in the last flat right-angle weave unit added (photo c). Pick up an 8º, and sew through the corresponding edge 8º

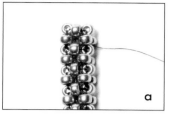

a

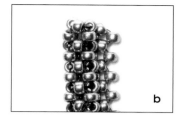

b

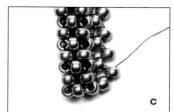

c

d

e

f

g

h

Difficulty rating

◆ ◆ ◆ ◇ ◇

Materials
bangle 6³/₈ in. (16 cm)
- **56–58** 6 mm pearls or bicone crystals (Swarovski, brass or black diamond AB)
- **117** 3 mm bicone crystal (Swarovski, black diamond AB)
- **32 g** 8º seed beads (Miyuki 4221, Duracoat galvanized light pewter)
- Fireline 6 lb. test
- elastic thread, .5 mm or .8 mm (Elasticity, clear)
- beading needles, #11 or #12
- Super New Glue or craft glue

on another tube. Pick up an 8º, and sew through the 8º your thread exited at the start of the step **(photo d)**. Retrace the thread path, and continue through the next 8º added in this step and the following edge 8º on the second tube **(photo e)**.
3 Continue working in right-angle weave to join the tubes together for the length of the beadwork. If you find it easier, you can flip the beadwork to the backside when joining the tubes, being careful not to twist the tubes as you work. End the working thread.
4 Repeat step 1 to add a row of flat right-angle weave to

the tube just added, working off the adjacent edge bead **(photo f)**.
5 Repeat step 2 to join the last tube to the beadwork **(photo g)**. End and add thread as needed, and end the working thread when complete.

Crystal embellishment
1 Add 2 ft. (61 cm) of thread to the topside of a tube, exiting an end 8º. Pick up a 3 mm bicone crystal, cross the unit diagonally, and sew through the opposite 8º going in the same direction **(photo h)**. Repeat this stitch for the length of the tube and end the thread.
2 Repeat step 1 to add crystals to the other two tubes. Make sure to start each embellishment the same so the crystals are all angled in the same direction.

Interchangeable bands
1 Cut a length of elastic 4 in. (10 cm) longer than the length of the beadwork. String enough 6 mm pearls or crystals to match the length of the beadwork. If it's slightly longer, that's OK. Tie a square knot, and dot the knot with glue. Repeat if needed. Trim the ends when dry.
2 Make a second beaded band.
3 Position the beadwork on your wrist, and slide each band into a channel to hold the bracelet in place. ●

bring the bling
Switch the pearls to crystals for more sparkle.

HERRINGBONE / PEYOTE STITCH

Blooming flower pendant

This textured pendant magically blossoms into
a floral shape as the final rounds are stitched.

designed by **Justyna Szlezak**

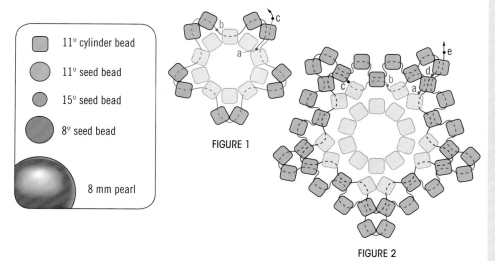

FIGURE 1

FIGURE 2

Materials

gray/green pendant 3 in. (7.6 cm)
- **1** 8 mm pearl (Swarovski, mauve)
- **2 g** 8º seed beads (Toho 512F, higher metallic frosted blue haze)
- **5 g** 11º seed beads (Toho PF558, permanent-finish galvanized aluminum)
- **4 g** 11º cylinder beads (Miyuki DB1851F, Duracoat galvanized matte light pewter)
- **2 g** 15º seed beads (Miyuki 4220, Duracoat eggplant)
- **1** 18 x 6 mm bail (TierraCast, hammertone)
- **1** 6 mm jump ring
- Fireline, 6 lb. test, or size D beading thread
- beading needles, #11 or #12 (Sharps optional)

purple/gold pendant
- 8 mm pearl (Swarovski, antique brass)
- 8º seed beads (Toho 90, metallic amethyst gunmetal)
- 11º seed beads (Toho 221, bronze)
- 11º cylinder beads (Miyuki DB1011, metallic dusty mauve gold iris)
- 15º seed beads (Miyuki P487, silver sage permanent galvanized)

Legend

- 11º cylinder bead
- 11º seed bead
- 15º seed bead
- 8º seed bead
- 8 mm pearl

getting started

Work with 2 yd. (1.8 m) of conditioned thread at a time to prevent fraying. Stitch with a moderate, even tension. Just let the beadwork twist as you go, but don't force it into shape. The floral shape will not start to emerge until the last few steps.

1 On 2 yd. (1.8 m) of thread, pick up 10 11º cylinder beads, and tie them into a ring with a square knot, leaving a 6-in. (15 cm) tail. Sew through the next cylinder. These beads will shift to form rounds 1 and 2 as the next round is added.

Round 3: Pick up two cylinders, skip the next cylinder, and sew through the following cylinder **(figure 1, a-b)**. Repeat this stitch four times to complete the round, and step up through the first cylinder added in the two-bead set **(b-c)**.

Round 4: Work a herringbone stitch by picking up two cylinders, and sewing through the next cylinder in the two-bead set **(figure 2, a-b)**. Work a peyote stitch by picking up a cylinder, and sewing through the first cylinder in the next two-bead set **(b-c)**. Repeat these two stitches four times to complete the round, and step up through the first cylinder added **(c-d)**.

2 Throughout this project, the herringbone stitches will be made with two cylinders per stitch, creating the five points of the flower, and will be referred to as a point stitch. After the point stitch, work the following stitches in peyote unless otherwise directed. Repeat the combination of stitches four more times to complete each round, and step up through the first cylinder in the point stitch after each round.

Round 5: Work a point stitch and two peyote stitches using cylinders **(d-e)**. At this point, the beadwork will start to twist a little. Don't try to flatten it. End the tail thread.

Round 6: Work a point stitch, and three peyote stitches using cylinders.

Round 7: Work a point stitch, and four peyote stitches using cylinders.

Round 8: Work a point stitch, and the following stitches in peyote: two cylinders, 11º seed bead, two cylinders.

Round 9: Work a point stitch, and then: two cylinders, two 11ºs, two cylinders.

two as one

When you start adding 15º seed beads in round 10, pick them up two at a time. When you reach them in the following round, sew through both beads at the same time. Remember, don't try to force the beadwork to look like the finished piece. Let it twist naturally **(photo a)**.

a

167

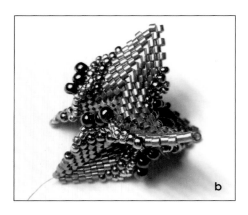

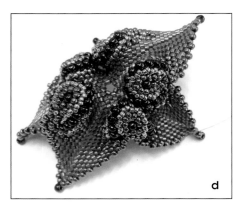

Round 10: Work a point stitch, and then: two cylinders, 11º, a pair of 15º seed beads, 11º, two cylinders.

Round 11: Work a point stitch, and then: two cylinders, 11º, a pair of 15ºs (sew through the next pair of 15ºs in the previous round), a pair of 15ºs, 11º, two cylinders.

Round 12: Work a point stitch, and then: two cylinders, 11º, a pair of 15ºs, an 8º seed bead (sew through the next pair of 15ºs), a pair of 15ºs, 11º, two cylinders.

Round 13: Work a point stitch, and then: two cylinders, 11º, a pair of 15ºs, two 8ºs, a pair of 15ºs, 11º, two cylinders.

forming the arches

At this point your beadwork will be very twisted and you'll see raised arches starting to form. Make sure the arches all face upward on the same side of the base **(photo b)**. Trying to untwist or reshape the base in any other way may cause the thread to break.

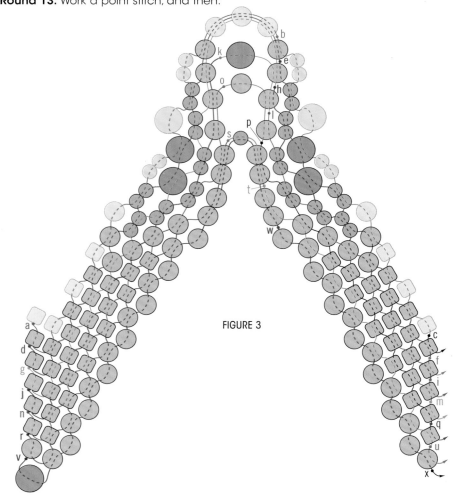

FIGURE 3

Round 14: Work a point stitch, and then: two cylinders, 11º, a pair of 15ºs, 8º, a pair of 15ºs, 8º, a pair of 15ºs, 11º, two cylinders.

Round 15: Work a point stitch, and then: two cylinders, 11º, a pair of 15ºs, 8º, two pairs of 15ºs, 8º, a pair of 15ºs, 11º, two cylinders.

Round 16: Work a point stitch, and then: two cylinders, 11º, a pair of 15ºs, 8º, a pair of 15ºs, 11º, a pair of 15ºs, 8º, a pair of 15ºs, 11º, two cylinders.

Round 17: Work a point stitch, and then: two cylinders, 11º, a pair of 15ºs, 8º, a pair of 15ºs, two 11ºs, a pair of 15ºs, 8º, a pair of 15ºs, 11º, two cylinders.

Round 18: Work a point stitch, and then: two cylinders, 11º, a pair of 15ºs, 8º, a pair of 15ºs, 11º, and then sew through the next two 11ºs **(figure 3 a-b)**, 11º, a pair of 15ºs, 8º, a pair of 15ºs, 11º, two cylinders **(b-c)**.

Round 19: Work a point stitch, and then: two cylinders, 11º, a pair of 15ºs, 8º, a pair of 15ºs, 11º, and then sew through the next four 11ºs **(d-e)**, 11º, a pair of 15ºs, 8º, a pair of 15ºs, 11º, two cylinders **(e-f)**.

changing it up

In the following stitches, the number of peyote stitches using cylinders in the beginning and end will change, and the beadwork will start to get stiffer. Again, do not try to flatten the beadwork **(photo c)**.

Round 20: Work a point stitch, and then: three cylinders, 11º, two pairs of 15ºs, and an 11º, and then sew through the next six 11ºs **(g-h)**, 11º, two pairs of 15ºs, 11º, three cylinders **(h-i)**.

Round 21: Work a point stitch, and then: four cylinders, 11º, a pair of 15ºs, 11º, and then sew through the next 11º **(j–k)**. Pick up an 8º, skip the next five 11ºs previously added, and continue through the corresponding two 11ºs on the opposite side of the raised arch **(k–l)**. Tighten slightly so there is no thread showing. Continue in peyote stitch: 11º, a pair of 15ºs, 11º, four cylinders **(l–m)**.

Round 22: Work a point stitch, and then: five cylinders, 11º, a pair of 11ºs, and then sew through the next 11º **(n–o)**. Pick up an 11º, skip the 8º added in the previous round, and continue through the corresponding two 11ºs on the opposite side of the raised arch **(o–p)**. Tighten slightly so there is no thread showing. Continue in peyote stitch: a pair of 11ºs, 11º, five cylinders **(p–q)**.

Round 23: Work a point stitch using two 11ºs, and then: six 11ºs, a pair of 11ºs, sewing through the next pair of 11ºs **(r–s)**. Pick up a 15º, and sew through the corresponding two 11ºs on the opposite side of the raised arch **(s–t)**. Tighten slightly so there is no thread showing. Continue in peyote: a pair of 11ºs, six 11ºs **(t–u)**.

Round 24: Pick up an 8º, and sew through the adjacent 11º on the point in place of a point stitch. Work the following stitches in peyote: seven 11ºs and sew through the pair of 11ºs for the last stitch. Continue through the next two 11ºs, the 15º added in the previous round, and the next four corresponding 11ºs on the opposite side **(v–w)**. Tighten slightly so there is no thread showing. Work seven stitches in peyote using 11ºs **(w–x)**. End the thread.

almost there

The beadwork will still not look quite like the finished flower **(photo d)**. It will pull together after adding the pearl. To work the next step, it helps to use a short needle (Sharps).

3 Add 1 yd. (.9 m) of thread to the beadwork, exiting the center (eighth) 8º in one of the five raised arches of beadwork. Pick up two 11ºs, and sew through the center 8º in the next arch **(figure 4, a–b)**. Repeat this stitch four more times **(b–c)**, but do not pull the thread tight. Retrace the thread path

once more **(c–d)**, but still do not tighten it. Keep the tension loose.

4 Pick up an 8 mm pearl, skip the next center 8º, and sew through the following center 8º, positioning the pearl in the center of the ring of beads created in the previous step **(figure 5 a–b)**. Continue through the ring of 11ºs and 8ºs, gently pulling the beads tight and forming the beadwork around the pearl as you go **(b–c)**. Retrace the thread path several times.

5 Sew through the beadwork along one of the five raised arches toward the outside edge, exiting the third 11º from the 15º between two of the petals **(figure 6, point a)**. Pick up six 11ºs, and sew through the three corresponding 11ºs on the opposite side of the arch **(a–b)**. Continue through the 15º between the petals and the next three 11ºs on the first side **(b–c)**. Retrace the thread path, and end the thread.

6 Open a 6 mm jump ring and attach the bail to the loop of 11ºs just made. ●

more photos
To see more photos of the pendant in progress, visit www. BeadAndButton.com/flower.

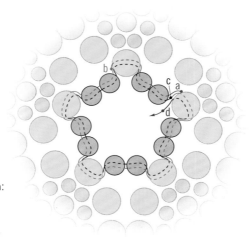

FIGURE 4

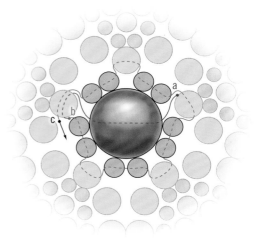

FIGURE 5

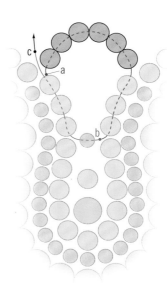

FIGURE 6

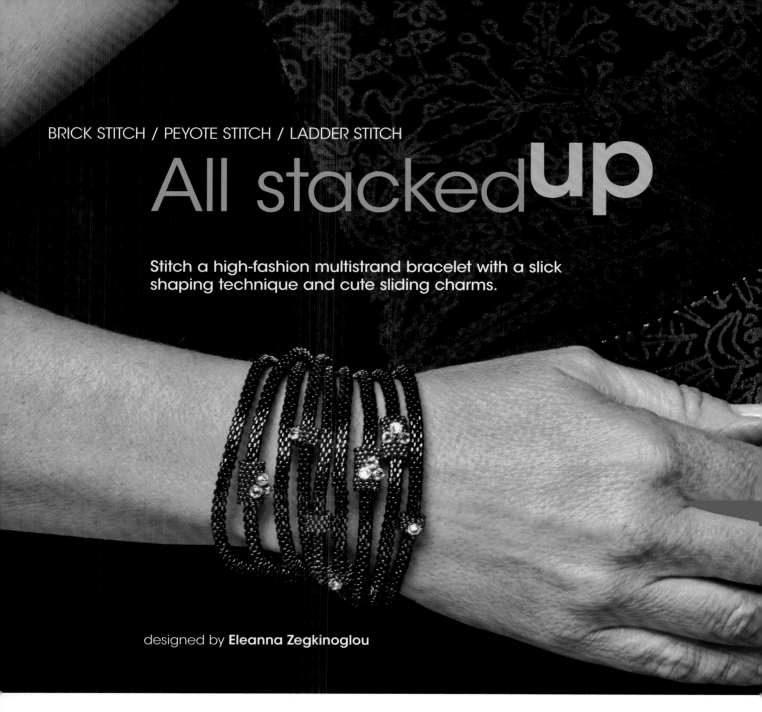

BRICK STITCH / PEYOTE STITCH / LADDER STITCH

All stacked up

Stitch a high-fashion multistrand bracelet with a slick shaping technique and cute sliding charms.

designed by **Eleanna Zegkinoglou**

a matter of time

One factor that helps us determine a difficulty rating is how long the project takes to make. This bracelet relies almost completely on very basic techniques, but takes quite a while to complete, which is why we gave it a four-bead rating. Each rope takes about two hours to stitch, so the entire bracelet took more than 20 hours from start to finish.

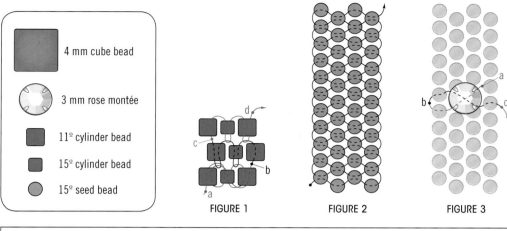

4 mm cube bead

3 mm rose montée

11º cylinder bead

15º cylinder bead

15º seed bead

FIGURE 1

FIGURE 2

FIGURE 3

a

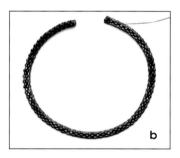

b

c

d

Difficulty rating

Materials
bracelet 7 in. (18 cm)
- Japanese cylinder beads
  - **12 g** 11º (DB-0005, metallic variegated blue iris)
  - **3 g** 15º (DBS-0005, metallic variegated blue iris)
- **4 g** 15º seed beads (Miyuki 457, metallic dark gold)
- **15** 3 mm rose montées (crystal)
- **8 g** 4 mm cube beads (Miyuki 462, metallic gold iris)
- beading needles, #12
- Fireline 6 lb. test

Ropes

1 On a comfortable length of thread and leaving a 6-in. (15 cm) tail, make a three-bead ladder with an 11º cylinder bead, a 15º cylinder bead, and an 11º cylinder **(figure 1, a–b)**.

2 Work rows of brick stitch with an increase at the start of each row: Pick up an 11º cylinder and a 15º cylinder, and sew under the nearest thread bridge at the top of the previous row. Sew back through the new 15º cylinder. Pick up an 11º cylinder, and sew under the next thread bridge in the previous row and back through the new 11º cylinder **(b–c)**. Repeat this row **(c–d)** until the strip is about 6½ in. (16.5 cm). The strip will twist as you work **(photo a)**. End and add thread as needed.

3 To complete the rope, use 11º cylinders to work three rows of peyote stitch along one long edge. The twist will flatten out some as you add the rows. Zip up the edges to form a tube. The tube will be curved **(photo b)**. End the working thread and tail.

4 Repeat steps 1–3 to make a total of nine ropes.

Roller charms
Small charms

1 On 18 in. (46cm) of thread, attach a stop bead, leaving a 6-in. (15cm) tail, and pick up four 15º seed beads. Working in flat, even-count peyote stitch, make a strip that is four beads wide and 22 rows long. There will be 11 beads on each straight edge **(figure 2)**.

2 Sew through the beadwork to exit an edge 15º with the needle facing toward the other edge. Pick up a 3 mm rose montée, and sew through a 15º on the other edge of the strip **(figure 3, a–b)**. Sew through the adjacent 15º, the other channel of the rose montée, and the 15º adjacent to the one your thread exited at the start of this step **(b–c)**. Sew through the beadwork to exit an end bead **(photo c)**.

3 Remove the stop bead, wrap the strip around a rope, and zip up the ends **(photo d)**. End the working thread and tail.

4 Repeat steps 1–3 to make as many small charms as you like. The sample shown has 11. Omit the rose montée on half of them. Arrange the charms as desired on the ropes.

Large charms

On 1 yd. (.9 m) of thread, make a peyote strip that is 10 beads wide and 22 rows long. Work as in step 2 of "Small charms" to attach

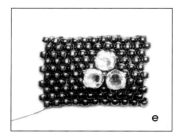

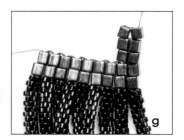

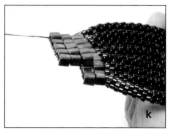

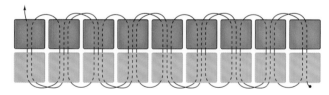

FIGURE 4

three rose montées to the strip in the desired location **(photo e)**. Wrap the strip around a rope, and zip up the ends. Make a total of three large charms.

Clasp and assembly

1 On 2 yd. (1.8 m) of thread, use 4 mm cube beads to make a nine-bead ladder, leaving a 6-in. (15 cm) tail. Work a second row of ladder stitch **(figure 4)**. This is the clasp base.

2 With the thread exiting an end stack of cubes in the clasp base, sew through an end cylinder in a rope, and then sew back through the adjacent cylinder and the stack of cubes **(photo f)**.

Sew under the adjacent thread bridge in the clasp base, and retrace the thread path, sewing through the end cylinders in the rope that has not yet been attached to the clasp base. Sew up through the next stack of cubes.

3 Repeat step 2 to attach all nine ropes to the clasp base.

4 Exiting an end stack of cubes with your needle facing away from the ropes, work three more rows of two beads **(photo g)**.

5 Working off the side of the last row added, work seven more ladder stitches to complete the end row **(photo h)**.

6 Work two more stacks of cubes below the last row

added, and connect this edge to the clasp base **(photo i)**. This completes the clasp opening. End the working thread and tail.

7 Work as in steps 1–3 to make a second clasp base, and attach it to the other end of the ropes.

8 Sew through the second row of cubes to exit the third bead from one edge. Working on the outside edge of the clasp base, ladder stitch five cubes to the five center cubes in the end row **(photo j)**. Work two more five-bead rows **(photo k)**.

9 Working along the inner edge of the last row added, work two more five-bead rows perpendicular to those added in the previous step **(photo l)**.

10 Working down toward the ropes, work two more five-bead rows perpendicular to those added in the previ-

ous step **(photo m)**. This completes the clasp latch. Retrace the thread path through the clasp latch for extra strength, and end the working thread and tail.

11 To cover the exposed holes on the end of the clasp latch, make a small patch of beadwork: On 18 in. (46 cm) of thread and leaving a 6-in. (15 cm) tail, pick up 13 15º seed beads. Working in flat odd-count peyote, make a small strip that is 13 beads wide and 10 rows long. Check to see that it fits over the end of the clasp latch, and adjust if needed. Align it to the end of the clasp latch, and sew under the appropriate thread bridges of the clasp latch and through corresponding beads on the patch to connect them **(photo n)**. End the working thread and tail. •

a different approach

You can use just peyote for these tubes if you wish. Using the brick stitch start may be easier, though, as working a long strip of peyote with cylinder beads can be a bit cumbersome. But if you choose to work in peyote, pick up about 130 11º cylinders to start, and then work a row of peyote with 11º cylinders. Next, work two rows with 15º cylinders and three more rows with 11º cylinders.

EMBROIDERY / BEADWEAVIING / CUBIC RIGHT-ANGLE WEAVE

Shibori
rosette
pendant

Embellish a bezel
with seed beads and
triangles and embroider
it with shibori silk for a
one-of-a-kind look.

designed by **Lisa Kan**

Difficulty rating

Materials

silver pendant 2 x 2¼ in. (5 x 5.7 cm)

- 10 in. (25 cm) shibori silk ribbon (silver)
- **1** 14 mm rivoli (Swarovski, lilac shadow)
- **20** 6 mm CzechMates two-hole triangle beads (linen)
- 11º seed beads
  - **3 g** color A (Miyuki 301, rose gold luster)
  - **1 g** color D (Miyuki 4218, Duracoat dusty orchid)
  - **2 g** color E (Miyuki 4222, Duracoat pewter)
- 15º seed beads
  - **2 g** color B (Miyuki 4222, Duracoat pewter)
  - **1 g** color C (Miyuki 4218, Duracoat dusty orchid)
- 1¼ in. (3.2 cm) Ultrasuede (platinum)
- Fireline 6 lb. test
- beading needles, #11 or #12
- double-sided tape
- thread bobbin or piece of cardboard

khaki pendant colors

- shibori silk ribbon (khaki)
- 14 mm rivoli (Swarovski, vitrail medium)
- 6 mm CzechMates two-hole triangle beads (aquamarine celsian)
- 11º seed beads
  - color A (Toho 221, bronze)
  - color D (Toho RY183, hybrid ultra luster green Picasso)
  - color E (Toho 221F, frosted bronze)
- 15º seed beads
  - color B (Miyuki 313, cranberry gold luster)
  - color C (Toho 509, higher metallic purple green iris)
- Ultrasuede (Aztec)

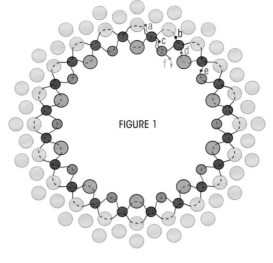

FIGURE 1

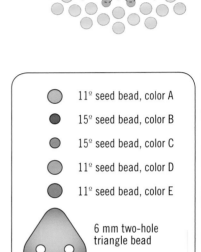

FIGURE 2

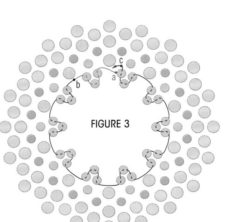

FIGURE 3

- ◯ 11º seed bead, color A
- ● 15º seed bead, color B
- ● 15º seed bead, color C
- ● 11º seed bead, color D
- ● 11º seed bead, color E

△ 6 mm two-hole triangle bead

Bezel

CRAW base

1 On a comfortable length of thread, work the first cubic right-angle weave unit (see "Cubic RAW how-to" p. 177) using color A 11º seed beads, and leaving a 6-in. (15 cm) tail. Continue to work CRAW units to form a tube of 19 units.

2 Using As, connect the ends to form a ring for a total of 20 CRAW units, making sure the tube is not twisted. End the thread.

Peyote capture

1 Center 2 yd. (1.8 m) of thread in a top A on the inside edge of the CRAW base, and wrap half of the thread on a bobbin or piece of cardboard. For clarity, the top layer of As are the only As from the CRAW base shown in figures 1–3.

2 Pick up a color B 15º seed bead, and sew through the next top A on the inside edge of the CRAW base **(figure 1, a–b)**. Repeat this stitch 19 times to complete the round, and step up through the first B added **(b–c)**.

3 Pick up a color C 15º seed bead, and sew through the next B **(c–d)**. Pick up a color D 11º seed bead, and sew through the next B **(d–e)**. Repeat these stitches nine times to complete the round, and step up through the first C added **(e–f)**.

4 Pick up three Cs, and sew through the C your thread is exiting, in the same direction to form a picot **(figure 2, a–b)**.

Continue through the next B, D, B, and C **(b–c)**. Repeat these stitches nine times to complete the round **(c–d)** using a tight tension. Step up by sewing through the three Cs in the first picot **(d–e)**.

5 Skip the adjacent D, and sew through the three Cs in the next picot, pulling the thread tight **(figure 3, a–b)**. Repeat this stitch nine times to complete the round **(b–c)**. End the working thread, unwind the tail, and attach a needle.

6 Sew through the beadwork to exit the corresponding bottom A on the inside edge of the CRAW base. Flip your beadwork over, and place the rivoli in the beadwork face down. Repeat steps 2–5 to work the back of the bezel.

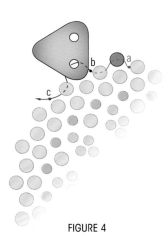

FIGURE 4

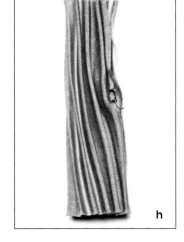

tweaking the loops

If some of the ribbon loops are not positioned just right or have a little gap between them, add a small stitch from the back, making sure it doesn't show.

End the tail, but do not tie any knots in the outer edge beads of the CRAW base.

Edge embellishment

When adding triangles, the point with no hole should face the front of the bezel and an open hole should be positioned to the outside edge. You will work two rounds of triangles—a front round (closest to the face of the rivoli) and a back round.

1 With the front of the bezel facing up, add 2½ yd. (2.2 m) of thread to the beadwork, exiting a top outer edge A in the CRAW base heading in a counterclockwise direc-

tion. For clarity, only the As on the top of the CRAW base are shown in figure 4.

2 Pick up a color E 11º seed bead, and sew through the next top outer edge A **(figure 4, a–b)**. Pick up a two-hole triangle, and sew through the following edge A **(b–c)**. Repeat these stitches nine times to complete the front round.

3 Sew through the beadwork to exit the corresponding A on the outside bottom edge of the CRAW base, with the thread heading in a clockwise direction. Pick up an E, and sew through the next A on the same edge. The

E should be positioned opposite the triangle added in the previous round. Pick up a triangle, and sew through the following A on the same edge. The triangle should be opposite the E added in the previous round **(photo a)**. Repeat these stitches nine times to complete the back round, and sew through the inside hole of the first triangle added.

4 Pick up three Cs, and sew through the open hole of the next triangle in the front round **(photo b)**. Pick up three Cs, and sew through the inside hole of the next triangle in the back round **(photo c)**. Repeat these stitches nine times to complete the round. Sew through the first three Cs added, and the outer hole of the next triangle in the front round.

5 Pick up three Bs, and sew through the open hole of the triangle in the back

round **(photo d)**. Pick up three Bs, and sew through the outer hole of the triangle in the front round **(photo e)**. Repeat these stitches nine times to complete the round, and sew through the first B added.

6 Pick up a B, skip the center B from the stitch in the previous round, and sew through the next B. Continue through the outer hole of the triangle in the back round, and the following B **(photo f)**. Pick up a B, skip the next center B, and sew through the following B. Continue through the outer hole of the triangle in the front round, and the following B. Repeat these stitches nine times to complete the round, and continue through the first B added.

7 Pick up five Bs, and sew through the next B added in the previous round to form a bridge around the adjacent triangle **(photo g)**.

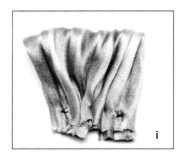

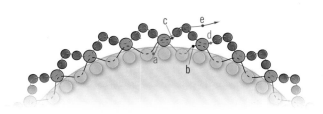

FIGURE 5

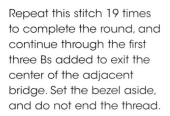

Repeat this stitch 19 times to complete the round, and continue through the first three Bs added to exit the center of the adjacent bridge. Set the bezel aside, and do not end the thread.

Ribbon

1 Cut the shibori ribbon into four 2½ in. (6.4cm) strips. Fold one strip lengthwise so the right (shiny) sides are together. Tie an overhand knot at one end of 12 in. (30cm) of thread, and work three small stitches at the center, sewing through both layers, about ¼ in. (6mm) from the open edge **(photo h)**. End the thread, and tie an overhand knot at the end of the leftover thread.
2 Turn the ribbon right-side out, and position the stitches in the center of the ribbon. Fold the ribbon so the raw edges are together, hiding the stitches in the fold. With the leftover thread, work a couple of small stitches through the layers at one corner, about ¼ in. (6mm) from the edge. Sewing toward the other edge, work several stitches, gently pulling on the thread as you go to create a slight gather. Work a couple of stitches at this corner of the ribbon, and end the thread **(photo i)**.
3 Repeat steps 1–2 for the remaining strips, but use 2 ft. (61 cm) of thread for the last strip, and do not end the thread.

Ribbon attachment

1 Position the last ribbon loop on the left side of the bezel, with the thread on top. Place the remaining loops in a semi-circle with each loop overlapping the next by ⅛ in. (3mm), using the bezel as a guide to create an arc below the bezel. There should be three bridges in the space between loops at the top of the bezel, and the bezel should overlap the ribbon ends to cover the bottom edge stitches **(photo j)**. Remove the bezel, and loosely stitch the ribbon loops together near the bottom edges. End the thread.
2 Place the bezel on the ribbon in the same position as before, with the working thread from the bezel exiting near the edge of the last loop added. Sew through the top layer of the ribbon directly below the B your thread is exiting, pick up a small amount of ribbon, and sew through the same B in the same direction. Sew through the beadwork to exit the center bead of the next bridge. Repeat these stitches to attach all of the bridges to the ribbon except the three in the open space at the top, adjusting the ribbon as needed to maintain the arc and keep the ribbon loops overlapped.

Backing

1 Cut a 1¼-in. (3.2 cm) circle of Ultrasuede. Tie an overhand knot at one end of 5 ft.

(1.5 m) of thread, and sew up through the Ultrasuede near the edge. Using Es, work a round of beaded back-stitch to add a total of 56 Es around the edge.
2 Pick up an E, skip the next E, and sew through the following E **(figure 5, a–b)**. Repeat this stitch 27 times to complete the round, and step up through the first E added **(b–c)**.
3 Pick up three Bs, and sew through the next E added in the previous round **(c–d)**. Repeat this stitch 27 times to complete the round, and continue through the first two Bs added **(d–e)**.
4 Apply double-sided sticky tape to the wrong side of the Ultrasuede. Position it tape-side down on the back of the pendant, lining up three picots with the three bridges in the open space at the top of the bezel, and the working thread near the top right edge of the ribbon.
5 Work as in step 2 of "Ribbon attachment" to attach the tips of the picots to the back of the ribbon, adjusting ribbon if needed.
6 Sew through the beadwork to exit the tip of the next picot in the top open space.

Pick up a B, and sew through the center bead of the corresponding front bridge. Pick up a B, and sew through the B your thread exited at the start of this step **(photo k)**. Continue through the beadwork to exit the center bead of the next picot on the back. Repeat the stitches to connect the following two picots. Continue through the first picot attached to the ribbon on the back and the following E.
7 To make a hanging loop, pick up 11 Es, skip the next E, and sew through the following E as shown **(photo l)**. Retrace the thread path. Sew through the beadwork to the corresponding location on the opposite side of the top opening, and make another hanging loop. End all of the threads.

Cubic RAW how-to

Each cubic right-angle weave (or CRAW) unit has six surfaces — four sides, a top, and a bottom. Each surface is made up of four beads, but since the beads are shared, 12 beads are used to make the first unit, and only eight beads are used for each subsequent CRAW unit. For clarity, we used two colors of beads in the how-to photos.

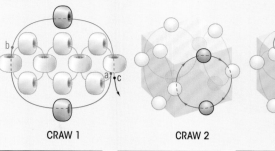

CRAW 1

CRAW 2

CRAW 3

CRAW 4

Working the first CRAW unit

1 On the specified length of thread, pick up four beads. Tie the beads into a ring with a square knot, leaving the specified length tail, and continue through the first two beads in the ring. This ring of beads will count as the first stitch of the unit.

2 Work two right-angle weave stitches off of the bead your thread is exiting to create a flat strip of right-angle weave.

3 To join the first and last stitches: Pick up a bead, sew through the end bead in the first stitch (**CRAW 1, a–b**), pick up a bead, and sew through the end bead in the last stitch (**b–c**). **CRAW 2** shows a three-dimensional view of the resulting cube-shaped unit.

4 To make the unit more stable, sew through the four beads at the top of the unit (**CRAW 3**). Sew through the beadwork to the bottom of the unit, and sew through the four remaining beads. This completes the first CRAW unit.

Working more CRAW units

1 Each new CRAW unit is worked off of the top four beads of the previous unit. These beads are identified in **CRAW 4**. Sew through the beadwork to exit one of these top beads.

2 For the first stitch of the new unit: Pick up three beads, and sew through the top bead your thread exited at the start of this step. Continue through the three beads just picked up (**CRAW 5**). Sew through the next top bead in the previous unit.

3 For the second stitch of the new unit: Pick up two beads, and sew through the side bead in the previous stitch, the top bead your thread exited at the start of this stitch (**CRAW 6**), and the next top bead in the previous unit.

4 For the third stitch of the new unit: Repeat step 3 (**CRAW 7**), and continue through the side bead in the first stitch of the new unit.

5 For the fourth stitch of the new unit: Pick up a bead, and sew through the side bead in the previous stitch and the top bead in the previous unit (**CRAW 8**).

CRAW 5

CRAW 6

CRAW 7

CRAW 8

CRAW 9

CRAW 10

CRAW 11

6 To make the unit more stable, sew through the beadwork to exit a top bead in the new unit, and sew through all four top beads (**CRAW 9**). This completes the new CRAW unit.

7 Repeat steps 2–6 for the desired number of CRAW units.

Working a joining unit

A joining unit is used to connect two completed CRAW units to each other. Units may be joined end to end or perpendicular to one another (as shown here).

1 Sew through the beadwork to exit a top bead in one unit.

2 For the first stitch of the joining unit: Pick up a bead, sew through the corresponding bead in the other unit, pick up a bead, and sew through the bead your thread exited at the start of this step (**CRAW 10**). Sew through the first bead added and the adjacent bead in the next side. If you are joining pieces at an angle, try to do the stitches on the inside of the angle first.

3 For the second stitch of the joining unit: Pick up a bead, and sew through the corresponding bead in the other unit, the previous joining bead, the bead

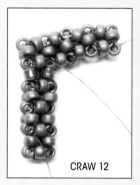

CRAW 12

CRAW 13

your thread exited at the start of this stitch (**CRAW 11**), and the bead just added. Sew through the adjacent bead in the next side.

4 For the third stitch of the joining unit: Pick up a bead, and sew through the corresponding bead in the other unit, the previous joining bead, the bead your thread exited at the start of this stitch (**CRAW 12**), and the bead just added. Sew through the adjacent bead in the next side.

5 For the fourth stitch of the joining unit: All beads are already in place. Simply sew through the four beads that remain unconnected (**CRAW 13**). ○

Magic carpet

This lively loomed piece brings the zing with beads of varying colors and sizes.

designed by **Beth Kraft**

Getting started

The number of beads between each warp thread is determined by the largest bead size. The outer warp threads are doubled for strength and called the selvage edge. The total number of warps is the number of the largest beads in one row from selvage to selvage, plus one.

For this project, 10 6º seed beads, the largest in the pattern, fit across the width, so a total of 11 warp threads are required for proper spacing.

To determine how to space the warps on your loom, put a bead against the spacer bar **(figure 1, point a)**, and count the number of grooves that are covered by the bead.

Warp the loom

1 Tie the end of the thread to a peg on one end of the loom.

2 Position the thread in a groove at this end of the loom, and cross it over the loom to the corresponding groove at the opposite end **(figure 1, b–c)**. Keeping the thread taut, loop the thread around a peg and go back through the same groove. Cross back over to the starting end, and pass the thread through the same groove. This is the first selvage edge.

3 Loop around a peg and guide the thread into the next groove that is one 6º bead space away. Cross over to the opposite end, guiding the thread into the corresponding groove.

taut not tight

If the warps ping when plucked, they are too tight.

4 Continue as in step 3 until there are 11 warp threads. Double the last warp

to create a selvage edge. Make sure the tension is even and the warps are correctly spaced.

5 Tie the thread off around a peg, and trim the thread. Place a piece of masking tape close to the beginning end, under the warps, and fold it over the top of the warps **(figure 1, point d)**. This will keep the end nice and straight.

Weaving

1 Attach a needle to a comfortable length of conditioned Fireline. Tie the end of the thread onto the left most warp close to the masking tape, leaving a 4-in. (10cm) tail. This is the weft thread.

2 Reading the pattern from left to right, and starting from the bottom, pick up 20 color B 11º seed beads for the first row **(figure 2)**. This row of beads will fit inside the tube end finding later.

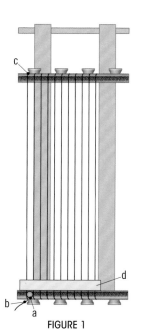

bracelet

Materials
bracelet 6½–7½ in. (16.5–19.1cm)
- **46** 3 mm fire-polished beads (chartreuse)
- **2 g** 6º seed beads (Miyuki 412, opaque turquoise green AB)
- **1 g** 8º seed beads (Miyuki 1477, dyed opaque bright purple)
- 11º seed beads
  - **1 g** color A (Miyuki 1477, dyed opaque bright purple)
  - **3 g** color B (Miyuki F408, matte opaque bright red)
  - **2 g** color C (Toho 55F, matte opaque turquoise)
  - **1 g** color D (Miyuki 416, matte opaque chartreuse)
  - **3 g** color E (Miyuki 2422, matte silver-lined topaz)
- 15º seed beads
  - **1 g** color F (Miyuki 356, purple-lined amethyst AB)
  - **1 g** color G (Miyuki 416, opaque chartreuse)
  - **1 g** color H (Miyuki 332, dark blue-lined green AB)
  - **1 g** color I (Miyuki 1119, luminous lime aid)
- **2** 1¼-in. (3.2 cm) tube end findings
- lobster claw clasp
- toggle clasp
- **4** 6 mm jump rings
- **2–3 in. (5–7.6cm)** of chain, 5–6 mm links
- **1** ¼-in. (6 mm) charm (Thai flower)
- Fireline, 6 lb. test
- beading needles, #12
- Thread Heaven or beeswax
- **2** pairs of chainnose, bentnose, and/or flatnose pliers
- Thread Zapper or clear nail polish
- loom and masking tape

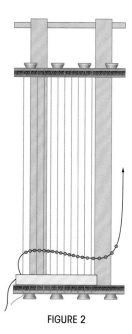

FIGURE 1   **FIGURE 2**

○	6º seed bead
◇	3 mm fire-polished bead
●	8º seed bead
●	11º seed bead, color A
●	11º seed bead, color B
●	11º seed bead, color C
○	11º seed bead, color D
○	11º seed bead, color E
●	15º seed bead, color F
○	15º seed bead, color G
●	15º seed bead, color H
○	15º seed bead, color I

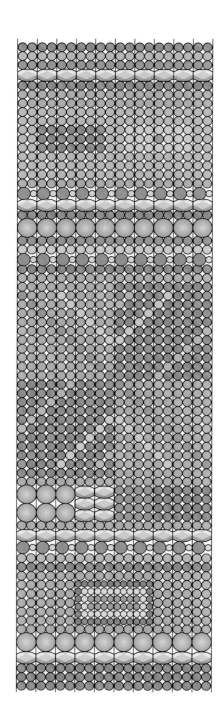

PATTERN

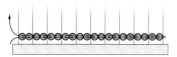

FIGURE 3

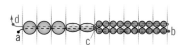

FIGURE 4

3 Pass the beaded weft thread under the warp threads. With the index finger of your other hand, gently push the beads up between the warp threads, two beads per space. Try to get the row as straight as possible.

4 Sew back through the beads, keeping the needle on top of the warps inside the beads **(figure 3)**. This keeps the thread from splitting. Pull the thread snug, and push the beads against the masking tape to align them.

5 Rows 2–6: Work as in steps 2–4 following the **pattern**. Note that you will have only one bead between each pair of warps in rows 4 and 5.

6 Rows 7–11 have both 11ºs and 15ºs. Note that there are actually six rows of 15ºs in this section (an extra row of 15ºs is needed to fill out the space that is taken up by five rows of 11ºs). Work these rows as follows:

Row 7: Work the row with six color E 11ºs, 12 color F 15ºs, and six Es, placing two 11ºs between pairs of warps and three 15ºs between pairs of warps.

Row 8: Work as in row 7 with six Es, an F, 10 color G 15ºs, an F, and six Es.

Row 9: Pick up six Es, an F, a G, eight color H 15ºs, a G, an F, and six Es. Push the beads up between the warps, and sew back through the last six Es and the 12 15ºs. Pass the needle over the warp that is between the left-most 15º and the adjacent E. Pick up an F, a G, eight Hs, a G, and an F. Push the partial row of beads up so they are centered between the center five warps, and sew back through the six Es on the right side of row 8. Pass the thread around the edge warp, and sew back through the six Es, the 12 new 15ºs, and the first 6 Es added in this step. Continue sewing through the remaining six Es in row 9. You will have a partial row of 15ºs extending above the row.

Row 10: Pick up six Es, an F, 10 Gs, an F, and six Es. Push them up between the warps, and sew back through the last six Es and the 15ºs. Sew back through the 12 15ºs in the row below, and continue through the 12 15ºs and last six 11ºs added in row 10.

Row 11: Work as in row 7.

end & add

End your thread when it gets short, and then add thread by sewing into the beadwork and exiting at the left edge of the last completed row.

7 Follow the **pattern** until all rows are completed. Work **rows 15, 45, and 51** with one 8º and one color I 15º between each pair of warps.

FIGURE 5

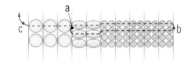

FIGURE 6

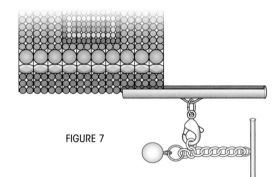

FIGURE 7

To work **row 18**, pick up three 6ºs, two fire-polished beads, four As, and six Bs **(figure 4, a–b)**. Sew back through the 11ºs, and sew over the warp to the left of the 11ºs **(b–c)**. Pick up four As and six Bs, push them up between the warps above the previous set of 11ºs, sew back through the new 11ºs, and continue through the remaining beads in the row **(c–d)**.

To work **row 19**, pick up three 6ºs, two fire-polished beads, four As, and six Bs. Push the beads up between the warps, and sew back through the 11ºs and the fire-polished beads **(figure 5, a–b)**. Sew over the warp to the left of the fire-polished beads, and pick up two

fire-polished beads, four As, and six Bs. Push the new beads up between the warps, and sew back through the beads just added **(b–c)**. Sew back through the 12 beads directly below **(figure 6, a–b)**. Sew through the new beads just added, and continue through the three 6ºs at the beginning of row 19 **(b–c)**.

8 When you finish, cut the beadwork from the loom, leaving the warp threads long enough to tie off. End the working thread and tails, and each warp thread. Zap or apply nail polish to the knots.

Clasp

1 Use a jump ring to attach a lobster claw clasp to one tube end.

2 Use a jump ring to attach the toggle ring to the other tube end.

3 Use a jump ring to attach the toggle bar to one end of the chain. Use another jump ring to attach the charm to the other end of the chain.

4 Slide the end row of beads into the tube end **(figure 7)** and use chainnose pliers to push the tube end closed. Repeat at the other end.

5 To adjust the length of the bracelet, attach the lobster claw on the desired link of the chain. ○

switch it up
- **Experiment with different bead sizes and colors.**
- **Change the width of the bracelet.**
- **Use a colorful thread for the warp.**

Personalized pendant

Use a favorite photo or cabochon as the focal point of this pendant, and embellish it to tell a treasured story.

designed by
Alla Maslennikova

stepbystep

Pendant

Bezeling the focal and stones

[1] Trace the cabochon on the photo, and cut out the photo.

[2] Arrange your embellishments as desired on your work surface **(photo a)**.

[3] Cut a piece of beading foundation or felt large enough to accommodate the embellishments. Draw horizontal and vertical axes, centering them where the focal cab will go. Trace the cab.

[4] Thread a needle with a comfortable length of thread, and tie an overhand knot (Basics) at the other end. Using color A 15º seed beads, work in beaded backstitch (Basics) on the outline for the cab **(photo b)**. Make sure you end up with an even number of beads in the round of backstitch.

[5] Continuing with As, work a round of tubular peyote stitch (Basics) off of the round of backstitch **(photo c)**. Place the photo and the cab inside the beaded outline. Work one round of peyote with color B 15º seed beads, two rounds with color C 15º seed beads, and one round with color D 16º seed beads **(photo d)**. To end the thread: Sew through the beadwork to the back of the foundation, tie a few knots, and trim the thread.

[6] Place the 18 mm round cabochon where you want it to go, and trace it.

a

Work as in steps 4 and 5 to bezel it with five rounds of As, a round of Bs, two rounds of Cs, and a round of Ds.

[7] Position the remaining stones, and trace them **(photo e)**.

[8] Work as in "Bezeling pointed-back stones," p. 185, for each remaining stone **(photo f)**. Save the 14 x 10 mm oval cab to place later.

Embellishments

[1] Place the metal beads or charms in

b

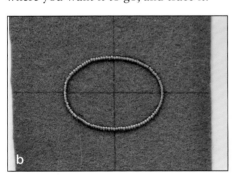

c

d

e

Difficulty rating

Materials

pendant 3 x 5 in. (7.6 x 13cm)

- 3 x 4 cm oval glass cabochon (or other cabochon as desired)
- photo (optional; same size as glass cabochon)
- 23 x 28 mm brass bow finding (www.etsy.com/shop/AnnaChernykh Findings)
- **5** 10–15 mm metal charms or beads (bear, crown, pirate flag, treasure chest, cat; TierraCast, gold plated)
- **1** 8 mm metal bead (gold tone)
- Swarovski stones and cabochons:
  2 18 x 13 mm pear-shaped fancy stones (#4320, light amethyst)
  1 18 mm round cab (Montana)
  1 14 x 10 mm oval cab (Montana)
  1 14 mm rivoli (antique pink)
- **5** 4 mm bicone crystals (Swarovski, light amethyst AB)
- 3 g 15º seed beads in each of **3** colors: A (Toho 999, gold-lined rainbow black diamond), B (Toho 457, green tea), C (Miyuki 1881, silver gray gold luster)
- 1 g 16º Czech seed beads, color D (transparent crystal)
- Fireline 6 lb. test
- beading needles, #12 or smaller
- beading foundation or felt (gray)
- leather or other backing
- craft knife
- E6000 or other adhesive
- permanent marker
- thin cardboard or other stabilizing material

necklace

- **2** 15 mm baroque pearls (gray)
- **1** 10–15 mm metal charm (cherries; TierraCast, gold plated)
- **8** 8 mm metal beads (gold tone)
- **40** 4 mm bicone crystals (Swarovski, light amethyst AB)
- **28** 4 mm round glass beads (alexandrite)
- **60** 3 mm spacers (TierraCast, gold plated)
- lobster claw clasp
- 2 in. (5 cm) 9 mm oval-link chain
- **1** 3 mm jump ring
- **2** pairs of chainnose, flatnose, and/or bentnose pliers

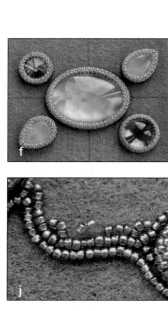

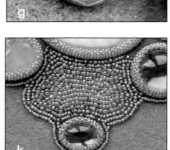

f

g

h

i

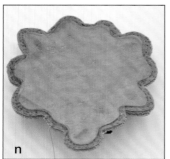

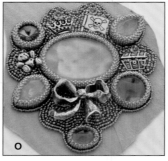

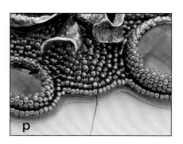

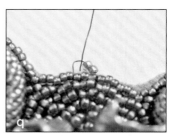

j

k

l

m

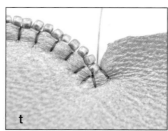

q

n

o

p

r

s

t

v

u

backstitch to outline the entire pendant with As **(photo i)**.

[4] Fill in the large open area below the focal with concentric lines of beaded backstitch, picking up three beads per stitch **(photo j)**. Work a couple of rounds with As, a couple with Bs, and fill in the center with Cs **(photo k)**. End and add thread as needed.

[5] Fill in the remaining background areas in the same manner **(photo l)**.

[6] Sew the bow in place **(photo m)**. End the thread.

Finishing

[1] Carefully cut out the pendant, staying close to the perimeter and being careful not to cut any threads.

[2] Trace the pendant onto a thin piece of cardboard or other stabilizing layer. Cut out the shape, undercutting the outline by about 3 mm

the desired locations, and sew them in place. If you are using a charm, sew up through the foundation and the loop of the charm. Pick up a 4 mm bicone crystal and a 15°, and sew back through the 4mm, charm loop, and foundation **(photo g)**. If using a bead, simply sew up through the foundation, through the bead, and back down

through the foundation several times until the bead is secured **(photo h)**.

[2] Determine the proper position for the final cab, trace it, and attach it as in steps 4 and 5 of "Bezeling the focal and stones," but work only three total rounds of As, and one round each of Bs, Cs, and Ds.

[3] On a comfortable length of thread, work in beaded

so it is smaller than the pendant. Glue the stabilizing layer to the back of the pendant **(photo n)**.

[3] Glue the pendant to a piece of leather or other backing **(photo o)**. Cut around the shape, leaving a 1–1.5 mm perimeter of backing **(photo p)**.

[4] Thread a needle on 2 yd. (1.8 m) of thread, and tie an overhand knot at the other end. Sew up through the top layer so the knot can be hidden between the layers.

[5] Pick up two As, align them so the holes are parallel to the edge, and sew down through both the foundation and the backing. Before pulling the thread tight, sew back up through the loop of thread **(photo q)**. Repeat this stitch around the perimeter of the pendant.

To keep the edging neat at the inner angles:
• Stop stitching approximately 6 mm before the angle. Cut out a small piece of the backing at the angle **(photo r)**, and then continue stitching until you reach the angular point **(photo s)**.
• Make two stitches without a bead, so your second stitch falls next to the last bead added **(photo t – view from back)**.
• Continue working edging stitches with two beads per stitch.

[6] When you reach the bottom center of the pendant, add a charm: Exit the last edge bead added, and pick up an A, a 4mm, an A,

an 8 mm metal bead, an A, a 4mm, nine 15ºs, and the loop of a charm. Skip the charm and the last eight 15ºs, sew back through all the remaining beads added in this step, and continue through the edge bead your thread exited at the start of this step **(photo u)**.

[7] When the edging is complete, end the thread.

Necklace
[1] Determine where you would like the neck straps to be attached. Center 1 yd. (.9 m) of thread in the desired edge bead, and thread a needle on both ends to work with doubled thread.

[2] Pick up beads as desired for the neck strap, or follow this pattern: A 15º, 4 mm round, 3 mm spacer, bicone, 3 mm spacer, 8 mm metal bead, spacer, bicone, spacer, round, spacer, bicone, 8mm, bicone, 15 mm pearl, bicone, 8mm, bicone, spacer, round, spacer, bicone, spacer, and an 8mm. Next, string a repeating pattern of a spacer, a bicone, a spacer, and a round 11 times, followed by a spacer, a bicone, eight As, and a clasp. Sew through the last seven As again to create a loop, and then sew back through the first A **(photo v)**. End the thread (Basics).

[3] Repeat steps 1 and 2 for the other neck strap, but substitute a 2-in. (5cm) piece of chain for the clasp.

[4] Open a 3 mm jump ring (Basics), and attach a charm to the end chain link. ●

Bezeling pointed-back stones
To make a neat bezel for crystals with a pointed back, work as follows:

[1] Cut a piece of beading foundation or felt to fit just inside the outline of the stone. Cut two more pieces, each a bit smaller than the previous one, so that when they are stacked they taper slightly.

[2] Glue the pieces into a stack, placing dots of glue around the perimeter of each layer and being careful to avoid the center.

[3] Leaving a 1–2 mm border, draw another line inside the perimeter on the top layer.

[4] Using a craft knife and following the line you just drew, cut out a conical pit from the top three layers of foundation.

[5] Glue the stone into the pit.

[7] Use the same technique for the pear-shaped stone, but create the pit in the base to fit the back of the stone.

[6] Thread a needle on a comfortable length of thread, and tie an overhand knot at the other end. Sew up through the foundation/felt base, exiting next to the stack. Using A 15ºs, work a round of beaded backstitch around the stack. Work three rounds of peyote with As, one round with Bs, two rounds with Cs, and one round with Ds. End the thread.

PEYOTE STITCH / BEAD WEAVING

Disks & drops

Gemstones sparkle between
delicate peyote medallions
in this elegant necklace.

designed by **Janice Chatham**

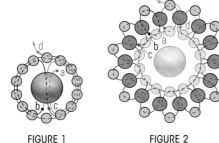

FIGURE 1   FIGURE 2

Medallions

1 Work in rounds as follows:

Round 1: On 1 yd. (.9 m) of thread, pick
up a 4 mm glass pearl and six 15º seed
beads. Sew through the pearl again in
the same direction, leaving a 6-in. (15cm)
tail **(figure 1, a–b)**. This forms a loop of
15ºs around one side of the pearl. Pick
up six 15ºs, and sew through the pearl
again to form a loop on the other side
of the pearl **(b–c)**. Sew through the first
six 15ºs. Pick up a 15º, and sew through
the next six 15ºs. Pick up a 15º, and sew
through the following seven 15ºs to form
a tight ring around the pearl **(c–d)**.

Round 2: Pick up a color A 11º seed
bead, a 15º, and an A 11º. Sew through
the bead your thread just exited and
the next 15º in the ring **(figure 2, a–b)**.
Pick up an A and a 15º, and sew
through the adjacent A in the previous
set, the 15º in the ring, and the next 15º
(b–c). Repeat this stitch 11 times **(c–d)**.
For the last stitch in the round, sew
through the adjacent A in the first stitch,
pick up a 15º, and sew through the last
A added and the 15º in the ring again.
Step up to exit the first 15º added in this
round **(d–e)**.

Round 3: Using 8º seed beads, work

186

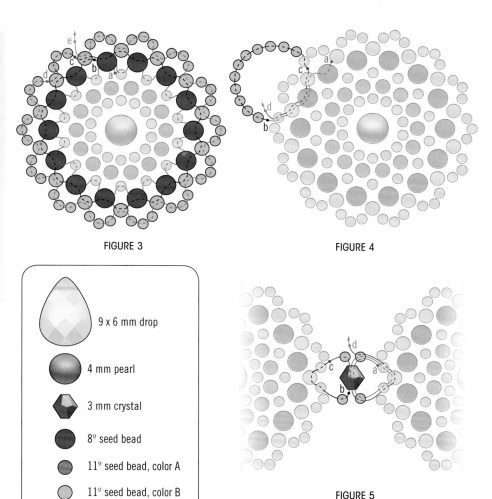

FIGURE 3

FIGURE 4

FIGURE 5

9 x 6 mm drop

4 mm pearl

3 mm crystal

8º seed bead

11º seed bead, color A

11º seed bead, color B

15º seed bead

Difficulty rating

Materials
necklace 15 in. (38cm)
- **7** 9 x 6 mm top-drilled moonstone teardrops
- **8** 4 mm glass pearls (magenta)
- **23** 3 mm bicone crystals (Swarovski, fuchsia AB2x)
- **2 g** 8º seed beads (Miyuki #460, metallic plum)
- 11º seed beads
  - **2 g** color A (Matsuno #399d, matte fuchsia)
  - **2 g** color B (Miyuki #4202, Duracoat galvanized gold)
- **5 g** 15º seed beads (Miyuki #191, 24kt gold plated)
- Fireline, 4 lb. test
- beading needles, #12

a round of circular peyote stitch, sewing through the 15ºs in round 2. Step up through the first 8º in this round **(figure 3, a–b)**.

Round 4: Using color B 11º seed beads, work a round of circular peyote stitch, sewing through the 8ºs in round 3. Step up through the first B 11º in this round **(b–c)**.

Round 5: Pick up three 15ºs, and sew through the next B 11º **(c–d)**. Repeat 13 times to complete the round **(d–e)**. Sew through the following 8º, 11º, 8º, and 11º in round 4 and the adjacent 15º **(figure 4, a–b)**.

2 To make a side loop: Pick up 11 15ºs, skip the previous three 15ºs, and sew through the next 15º **(b–c)**. Sewing back toward the start of the loop, sew through the next 11º, 8º, and 11º, and the following 15º **(c–d)**. Retrace the thread path through the loop, and end the working thread and tail.

3 Repeat rounds 1–5 to make a second medallion, but do not add a side loop or end the threads. Sew through the beadwork to exit at **figure 5, point a**.

4 To connect the new medallion to the previous one, pick up a 15º, a 3 mm bicone crystal, and a 15º, and sew through the adjacent 15º, B 11º, and 15º your thread exited at the start of this step. Continue through the 15º and the crystal just added **(figure 5, a–b)**. Pick up a 15º, and sew through the corresponding 15º, B 11º, and 15º on the other medallion **(b–c)**. There should be four 11ºs along the top edge of the medallion between the side loop and this connection. Pick up a 15º, and sew through the crystal, two 15ºs, a B 11º, and two 15ºs **(c–d)**.

5 Pick up a B 11º, and sew through the next two 15ºs, B 11º, and two 15ºs **(figure 6, a–b)**. Pick up a B 11º, three 15ºs, a teardrop bead, and three 15ºs. Sew through the B 11º in the same direction to form a loop **(b–c)**, and continue through the next two 15ºs, 11º, the following 15º, and the adjacent 15º in the connection **(c–d)**. Retrace the thread path through all the beads in the drop

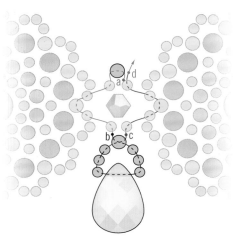

FIGURE 6

attachment again. End the working thread and tail.

6 Repeat steps 3–5 to stitch and connect six more medallions. There should be five 11ºs along the top of each medallion between the connection points. This allows the necklace to sit in a graceful curve when worn.

7 On the last medallion, repeat step 2 to make another beaded end loop.

Chain and clasp

1 Attach a needle to each end of 1 yd. (.9 m) of thread. With one needle, pick up 11 15ºs, and center them on the thread. Pass the beads through an end loop, centering the beads in the loop. With one needle, sew through the 11 beads again. Pick up a B 11º, a 3 mm crystal, and a B 11º **(figure 7, a–b)**. With the other needle, sew through the same B 11º, crystal, and B 11º **(aa–bb)**.

2 With one needle, pick up five 15ºs **(b–c)**. With the other needle, pick up four 15ºs, and cross through the fifth 15º picked up with the first needle **(bb–cc)**. With one needle, pick up four 15ºs, a B 11º, a 3 mm crystal, and a B 11º **(c–d)**. With the other needle, pick up four 15ºs, and sew through the B 11º, crystal, and B 11º in the same direction **(cc–dd)**. Repeat these stitches for a total of six seed bead sections and seven crystals.

3 To make the toggle ring: With one needle, pick up 27 15ºs. Sew back through the fourth 15º **(e–f)**. Pick up three 15ºs, and sew back through the

last B 11º, 3 mm crystal, and B 11º in the chain **(f–g)**. With the other needle, sew through the next four 15ºs, and then work circular peyote around the loop, picking up one 15º per stitch **(ee–ff)**. Sew through the next four 15ºs and the last B 11º, crystal, and B 11º in the chain **(ff–gg)**. Tie the threads together with a square knot, retrace the thread paths through the loop, and end the threads.

4 To make the toggle bar: On 18 in. (46cm) of thread, attach a stop bead, leaving a 6-in. (15cm) tail. Pick up 10 15ºs, and work in flat even-count peyote stitch using 15ºs until you have a total of 10 rows. Zip up the edges to form a tube.

5 Sew through the hollow center of the tube, and pick up a 3 mm crystal and a 15º. Sew back through the crystal and the tube **(figure 8, a–b)**. Add a crystal and 15º at this end of the tube, and sew back through the crystal and tube **(b–c)**. Retrace the thread path through the crystal embellishment, and end the threads. Set the toggle bar aside.

6 To complete the necklace, repeat steps 1–2 at the other end of the necklace. With one needle, pick up seven 15ºs, and sew through two 15ºs in the middle of the toggle bar **(d–e)**. Pick up three 15ºs, and sew back through the fourth 15º picked up **(e–f)**. Pick up three 15ºs, and sew back through the B 11º, crystal, and B 11º at the end of the chain **(f–g)**. Retrace the thread path with the other needle, and end the thread. ●

customize it!

customize it!

Each medallion is about ¾ in. (1.9 cm) in diameter. For a custom fit, stitch more or fewer medallions or vary the length of the chains.

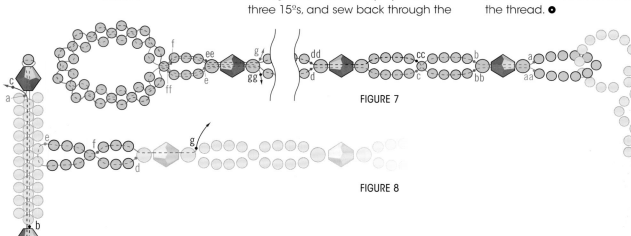

FIGURE 7

FIGURE 8

Surface appeal

Combine seed beads, SuperDuos, and crystals in a beautiful bracelet with texture and dimension.

designed by **Jenny Van**

Difficulty rating

Materials

pink bracelet 7 in. (18 cm)
- **12** 4 mm round crystals (Swarovski 5000, rose water opal)
- **80** 3 mm bicone crystals (Swarovski, fuchsia)
- **10 g** 2.5 x 5 mm SuperDuo beads (14495, crystal red luster)
- **11 g** 8º seed beads (Miyuki 196, 24kt yellow gold-lined opal)
- **2 g** 11º cylinder beads (Miyuki DB031, 24kt gold plated)
- **2 g** 11º seed beads (Toho 22C, silver-lined topaz)
- **2 g** 15º seed beads (Toho 712, 24kt gold plated)
- 6-strand tube clasp
- Fireline 6 lb. test
- beading needles, #11 or #12

green bracelet colors:
- 4 mm round crystals (Swarovski 5000, fern green AB)
- 3 mm bicone crystals (Swarovski, fern green)
- 2.5 x 5 mm SuperDuo beads (aqua sliperit)
- 8º seed beads (Miyuki 196, 24kt yellow gold-lined opal)
- 11º cylinder beads (Miyuki DB031, 24kt gold plated)
- 11º seed beads (Toho 701, 24kt gold-lined crystal)
- 15º seed beads (Toho 712, 24kt gold plated)

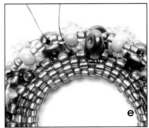

Circle component

1 On 8 ft. (2.4 m) of thread, attach a stop bead, leaving a 4-ft. (1.2 m) tail. Pick up 48 15º seed beads, and sew through the first six beads again to form a ring. These beads will shift to form rounds 1 and 2 as the next round is added.

2 Work rounds of tubular peyote stitch as follows, and step up at the end of each round:

Rounds 3 and 4: Work both rounds using 15ºs.

Rounds 5 and 6: Work both rounds using 11º cylinder beads.

Round 7: Work a round using 11º seed beads. This completes the first side of the circle component. Do not end the working thread.

3 Remove the stop bead, and thread a needle on the tail. Stitching off the 15ºs in round 1, work in rounds on this side as follows:

Round 1: Work a round using 15ºs.

Rounds 2 and 3: Work both rounds using cylinder beads.

Round 4: Work a round using 11ºs.

Edge embellishment

1 Still using the tail, work in right-angle weave as follows: Pick up an 8º seed bead, and sew through the corresponding 11º on the opposite side of the circle component **(photo a)**. Pick up a 2.5 x 5 mm SuperDuo bead, and sew through the 11º your thread exited at the start of this step. Continue through

the 8º, 11º, SuperDuo, and the next 11º in the circle component **(photo b)**.

2 Continue working in right-angle weave, alternating between adding an 8º and a SuperDuo. For the last stitch, sew through the first 8º added, the next 11º, and SuperDuo. Continue through the open hole of the same SuperDuo.

3 Working in modified right-angle weave, pick up a 15º, a 4 mm round crystal, and a 15º, and sew through the open hole of the next SuperDuo **(photo c)**. This will be the front of the circle component. Pick up two 15ºs, an 8º, and two 15ºs, and sew through the SuperDuo your thread exited at the start of this step **(photo d)**. This will be the back of the circle component. Sew through the 15º, 4mm, and 15º just added and the adjacent SuperDuo.

4 Pick up two 15ºs, an 8º, and two 15ºs, and sew through the open hole of the next SuperDuo. Pick up a 15º, a 4 mm round crystal, and a 15º, and sew through the SuperDuo your thread exited at the start of this step. Continue through the two 15ºs, 8º, and two 15ºs just added and the adjacent SuperDuo.

5 Repeat steps 3 and 4 to complete the round, sewing through the first SuperDuo for the last right-angle weave unit. End the thread.

6 With the remaining thread exiting an 11º seed bead on the back of the component, pick up a SuperDuo, and sew through the next 11º on the backside **(photo e)**. Repeat this stitch to

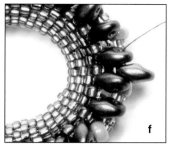

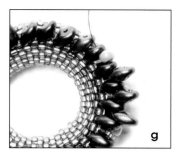

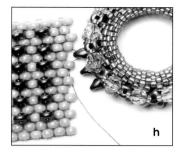

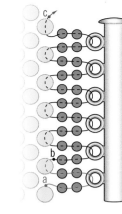

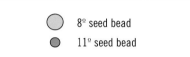

complete the round. Sew through the first SuperDuo added, and continue through the open hole of the same SuperDuo.

7 Pick up a SuperDuo, and sew through the open hole of the next SuperDuo **(photo f)**. Repeat this stitch two more times.

8 Pick up an 8º, and sew through the open hole of the next SuperDuo **(photo g)**. Repeat this stitch eight more times.

9 Repeat steps 7 and 8 once more, and end the thread. Set the component aside.

Bracelet bands

1 On a comfortable length of thread, attach a stop bead, leaving a 12-in. (30 cm) tail. Pick up 14 8ºs. These beads will shift to form rows 1 and 2 as the third row is added.

2 Work in flat even-count peyote for the remaining rows as follows:

Rows 3–9: For each row, work seven stitches using 8ºs.

Row 10: Work one stitch using an 8º and six stitches using SuperDuos.

Rows 11–13: Work three rows using 8ºs.

Rows 14–42: Repeat rows 10–13 seven times, and then work one more row with 8ºs.

Row 43: Work two stitches using 8ºs.

With the front of the circle component facing up, place the open holes of a set of three SuperDuos along the working end of the bracelet band. Sew through the open hole of the first SuperDuo, and continue through the next 8º in the band **(photo h)**. Repeat this stitch for the next two SuperDuos. Work two more stitches using 8ºs.

Row 44: Work two stitches using 8ºs. Pick up an 8º, and sew through the same hole of the SuperDuo as before **(photo i)**. Repeat this stitch twice, and work two more stitches using 8ºs.

3 Retrace the thread path through the last row to exit the other edge.

4 Pick up three 11º seed beads, sew through the next edge 8º, and continue through the following edge 8º **(photo j)**. Repeat this stitch for the length of the band. Sew through the beadwork to the other edge, and repeat this stitch on this side. End the working thread but not the tail.

5 Repeat steps 1–4 on the other side of the circle component.

Band embellishment

1 Add a comfortable length of thread to a bracelet band, exiting the open hole of an end SuperDuo in the row nearest the circle component, with the needle pointing toward the opposite edge.

2 Pick up a 3 mm bicone crystal, and sew through the open hole of the next SuperDuo **(photo k)**. Repeat this stitch

four more times.

3 Pick up a 15º, an 11º seed bead, an 8º, an 11º, and a 15º, and sew through the open hole of the SuperDuo in the next row **(photo l)**.

4 Repeat steps 2 and 3 for the remainder of the SuperDuo rows.

5 Pick up a 15º, an 11º, an 8º, an 11º, and a 15º, and sew through the bicones and SuperDuos in the previous row. Repeat this stitch for the remainder of the rows. End the thread.

6 Repeat steps 1–5 for the other bracelet band.

Clasp

1 With the tail from a bracelet band, exit the end up-bead in the last row, with the needle pointing toward the other edge of the base **(figure, point a)**.

2 Pick up two 11º seed beads, and sew through the first loop of the clasp. Pick up two 11ºs and sew through the next up-bead **(a–b)**. Repeat this stitch to attach the remaining loops of the clasp **(b–c)**. Retrace the thread path of the join, and end the tail.

3 Repeat steps 1 and 2 for the other bracelet band. ●

○ 8º seed bead
● 11º seed bead

BEAD WEAVING / PEYOTE STITCH

Sparkling
snowflake necklace

Stitch lovely beaded
snowflakes for a delightful
winter wonderland motif.

designed by **Shae Wilhite**

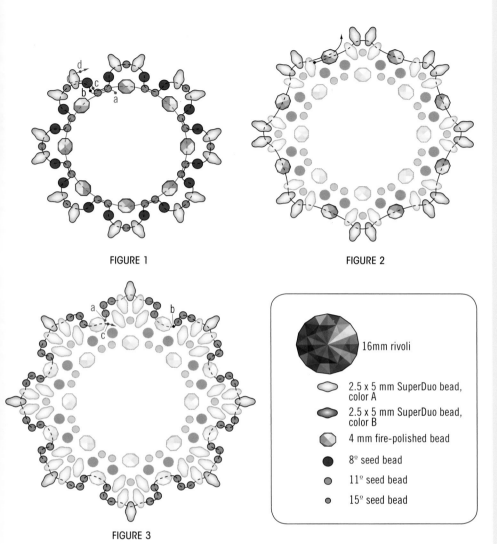

FIGURE 1

FIGURE 2

FIGURE 3

16mm rivoli

2.5 x 5 mm SuperDuo bead, color A

2.5 x 5 mm SuperDuo bead, color B

4 mm fire-polished bead

8º seed bead

11º seed bead

15º seed bead

Difficulty rating

Materials

gold necklace 21 in. (53 cm)
- **1** 16 mm rivoli (Swarovski, crystal golden shadow)
- 2.5 x 5 mm SuperDuo beads
  - **14 g** color A (champagne luster)
  - **8 g** color B (crystal bronze pale gold)
- **16** 4 mm fire-polished beads (smoky topaz AB)
- **16** 8º seed beads (Miyuki 457L, metallic light bronze)
- **4 g** 11º seed beads (Miyuki 577, dyed butter cream silver-lined alabaster)
- **48** 15º seed beads (Miyuki 457L, metallic light bronze)
- hook-and-eye clasp
- Fireline 6 lb. test
- beading needles, #10

silver/white colors
- 16 mm rivoli (Swarovski, crystal AB)
- 2.5 x 5 mm SuperDuo beads
  - color A (white luster)
  - color B (crystal bronze aluminum)
- 4 mm fire-polished beads (white opal)
- 8º seed beads (Miyuki 0271, silver gray-lined crystal)
- 11º seed beads (Miyuki 0271, sparkling silver gray-lined crystal)
- 15º seed beads (Miyuki 1105, sparkling gray-lined crystal)

Center snowflake

1 On a comfortable length of thread, pick up a repeating pattern of two 11º seed beads and a 4 mm fire-polished bead eight times. Sew through the beads again (not shown in figure) to form a ring, leaving a 6-in. (15 cm) tail. Tie a square knot with the working thread and tail, and continue through the next two 11ºs **(figure 1, a–b)**.

2 Pick up an 8º seed bead, a color A SuperDuo bead, an 11º, an A, and an 8º. Skip the fire-polished bead, and sew through the next two 11ºs. Repeat seven times to complete the round **(b–c),** and step up through the first 8º and A added. Sew through the open hole of the same A **(c–d)**.

3 Pick up a fire-polished bead, and sew through the open hole of the next A.

Pick up two As, and continue through the open hole of the following A. Repeat these stitches seven times to complete the round, and continue through the first fire-polished bead added **(figure 2)**.

4 Pick up three 11ºs, and sew through the open hole of the next A in the previous round. Pick up an A, sew through the open hole of the following A, pick up three 11ºs, and sew through the next fire-polished bead **(figure 3, a–b)**. Repeat these stitches seven times to complete the round **(b–c)**.

5 To make the setting for the rivoli, sew diagonally down through the beadwork to exit a fire-polished bead from step 1. Pick up five 11ºs, and sew through the fire-polished bead again, going in the same direction. Continue through the next two 11ºs and the

193

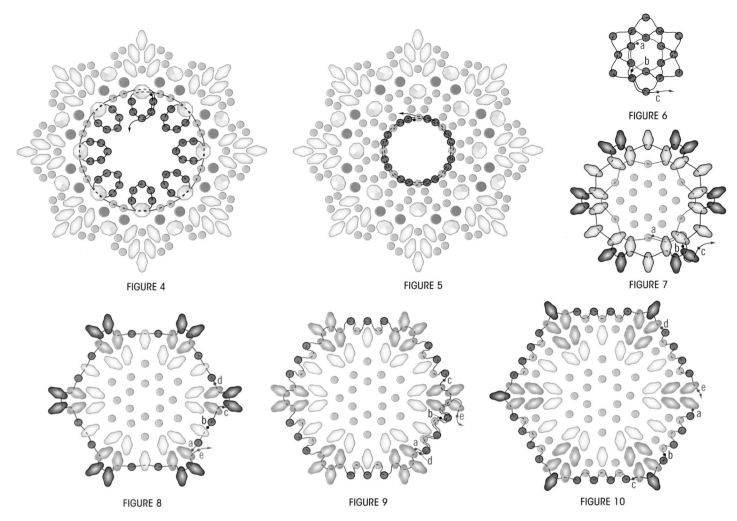

FIGURE 4

FIGURE 5

FIGURE 6

FIGURE 7

FIGURE 8

FIGURE 9

FIGURE 10

following fire-polished bead. Repeat seven times to create eight picots, and continue through the first three 11ºs added **(figure 4)**.

6 Pick up two 11ºs, and sew through the center 11º in the next picot. Repeat seven times to complete the round, and retrace the thread path **(figure 5)**.

7 Sew through to the other side, and exit a fire-polished bead from step 1.

8 Pick up four 15º seed beads, skip the last 15º just added, and sew through the

second to last 15º **(photo a)**. Snug up the beads. Pick up two 15ºs, sew through the opposite side of the fire-polished bead your thread exited in step 8, the next two 11ºs, and the following fire-polished bead **(photo b)**. Repeat these stitches to add a total of eight picots.

9 Sew through the beadwork to exit the point 15º of the next picot. Place the rivoli face-up inside the beadwork, and position the picots to sit on top of the rivoli. Pick up two 11ºs, and sew through the

point bead of the following picot. Repeat seven times to complete the round **(photo c)**. Tighten the thread, retrace the thread path to secure the rivoli, and end the working thread and tail.

Star snowflakes

1 On a comfortable length of thread, pick up six 11ºs, and sew through the beads again (not shown in figure) to form a ring, leaving a 6-in. (15 cm) tail. Tie an overhand knot with the working

a

b

c

FIGURE 11

FIGURE 12

FIGURE 13

FIGURE 14

FIGURE 15

thread and tail, and continue through the next two 11ºs **(figure 6, a–b)**.

2 Work two rounds as follows: For each stitch, pick up an 11º, and sew through the next 11º in the previous round. Step up after each round **(b–c)**.

3 Pick up two As, and sew though the next 11º. Repeat this stitch five times to complete the round, using a firm tension. Sew through the first two As added at the beginning of this step, and continue through the open hole of the A your thread is exiting **(figure 7, a–b)**.

4 Pick up two color B SuperDuos, and sew through the open hole of the next A. Pick up an A, and continue through the open hole of the following A. Repeat these stitches five times to complete the round. Step up through the first B added in this round, and continue through the open hole of the same B **(b–c)**.

5 Pick up an 11º, and sew through the open hole of the next A **(figure 8, a–b)**. Pick up an 11º, and sew through the open hole of the following B **(b–c)**. Pick up two Bs, and sew through the open

hole of the next B **(c–d)**. Repeat five times to complete the round **(d–e)**.

6 Pick up an 11º, sew through the next 11º in the previous round, pick up an 11º, and sew through the following 11º **(figure 9, a–b)**. Pick up an 11º, sew through the outer hole of the next B, the inner hole of the following two Bs, and the outer hole of the next B **(b–c)**. Repeat these stitches five times to complete the round **(c–d)**. Sew through the next seven beads, and then sew through the open hole of the B your thread is exiting **(d–e)**.

7 Pick up an 11º, and sew through the next 11º in the previous round. Repeat twice **(figure 10, a–b)**. Pick up an 11º, sew through the open hole of the next B, pick up a B, and sew through the open hole of the following B **(b–c)**. Repeat these stitches four times **(c–d)**. Repeat once, but don't add the final B **(d–e)**. End the tail, but not the working thread.

8 Make a second star snowflake.

Neck straps

1 On a comfortable length of thread, pick up an A and three 11ºs, and sew through the open hole of the same A, leaving a 10-in. (25cm) tail **(figure 11, a–b)**.

2 Pick up a B, an A, three 11ºs, and an A, and sew through the open hole of the B just added **(b–c)**. Tighten the thread to properly arrange the beads.

3 Pick up an A and three 11ºs, and sew through the open hole of the A just added **(figure 12, a–b)**. Pick up a B, and sew through the open hole of the adjacent A **(b–c)**. Pick up three 11ºs and an A, and sew through the open

hole of the B **(c–d)**.

4 Repeat step 3 27 times, but on the last time, omit the second A. Pick up three 11ºs, and sew through the other hole of the B your thread is exiting **(figure 13, a–b)**. Continue through the next three 11ºs and the other hole of the same B **(b–c)**.

5 Pick up three 11ºs and half of the clasp, and sew back through the last 11º added. Pick up two 11ºs, and sew through the B your thread exited at the beginning of this step, to form a loop. **(figure 14)**. Retrace the thread path several times, and end the working thread but not the tail.

6 Repeat steps 1–5 for the second neck strap.

Assembly

1 Position a star snowflake so the point that doesn't have a B on the tip is adjacent to one of the points on the center snowflake. Using the working thread from the star snowflake, sew through the open hole of the A on the center snowflake and the outer hole of the adjacent B on the star snowflake **(figure 15, a–b)**. Sew through the next two 11ºs along the edge of the same B and through the inner hole of the two adjacent Bs **(b–c)**. Sew through the two 11ºs on this edge of the B and up through the outer hole of the same B **(c–d)**. Retrace the thread path, and end the thread. Using the tail from the neck strap, retrace the join as in step 1. End the tail.

2 Repeat step 1 on the other side of the necklace. ◗

PEYOTE / HERRINGBONE STITCH

Winding
wonder
bracelet

Connect layered components in
an alternating pattern, and add an
optional edge embellishment to create
a bracelet with structure and style.

designed by **Melissa van Dijk**

Components

1 On 28 in. (71 cm) of thread, pick up six color A 11º cylinder beads, leaving a 6-in. (15 cm) tail. Tie them into a ring with a square knot, and continue through the next A **(figure 1, a–b)**.

2 Pick up two As, and sew through the next A **(b–c)**. Repeat this stitch five times to complete the round, and step up through the first A added in the first two-bead set **(c–d)**. End the tail.

Round 2: Work a herringbone stitch by picking up two As, and sewing through the next A **(d–e)**. Work a peyote stitch by picking up a color B 11º cylinder bead, and sewing through the first A in the next two-bead set **(e–f)**. Repeat these two stitches five times to complete the round, and step up through the first A added **(f–g)**. Begin to fold the beadwork in half. The shape will start to take form as the next round is added.

Round 3: Work a herringbone stitch using As, and two peyote stitches using Bs. Repeat these stitches five times to complete the round, and step up through the first A added **(figure 2, a–b)**. Fold the beadwork to form it into shape (figure 2 shows the beadwork unfolded so you can see the entire thread path).

Round 4: Work a herringbone stitch using As, and three peyote stitches using Bs. Repeat these stitches five times to complete the round, and step up through the first A added **(b–c)**.

Round 5: Work a herringbone stitch using As, and four peyote stitches using Bs. Repeat these stitches five times to complete the round, and step up through the first A added **(c–d)**. End the threads, and set the component aside **(photo a)**. The component should look like a triangle with a V-shaped opening between the left and right sides and should have two layers — a top layer and a bottom layer.

3 Repeat steps 1–2 15 more times to make a 7¼ in. (18.4cm) bracelet (measurement includes ½ in./1.3 cm for the clasp).

Assembly

1 Add a comfortable length of thread to a component, exiting the top A in the end herringbone stitch on the left side of the V opening with the needle pointing toward the adjacent outer edge **(photo b)**.

Materials
teal bracelet 7½ in (18.4 cm)
- 14 4 mm fire-polished beads (polychrome orchid aqua)
- 1 3 or 4 mm miscellaneous bead
- 11 g Miyuki Delica cylinder beads in each of **2** colors:
  - color A (DB0799, opaque semi-matte dark lavender)
  - color B (DB1782, white-lined teal AB)
- Fireline, 6 lb. test
- beading needles, #11 or #12

blue bracelet colors
- 14 5 x 3 mm pinch beads (Czech, sapphire)
- Miyuki Delica cylinder beads
  - color A (DB0278, lined cobalt luster)
  - color B (DB0267, opaque blueberry luster)

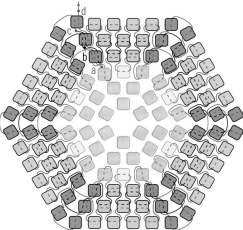

FIGURE 1

FIGURE 2

a

b

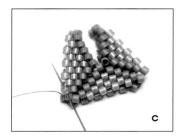

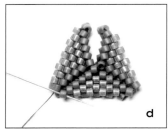

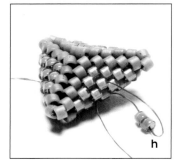

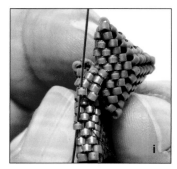

2 Work five peyote stitches using Bs along the top edge, and sew through the corresponding A in the herringbone stitch on the bottom layer of the component. Continue back through the last B added **(photo c)**, and zip up the top and bottom edge layers. Sew through the end two As, and continue back through the beadwork along this edge to exit the second A in the next pair of As on the top layer **(photo d)**.
3 Repeat step 2 for this edge.
4 Sew through the next A and the first up-B along the next top outer edge. Position a new component next to this edge with the V opening of the new component pointing down. Sew through the first up-B in the new component, and the next up-B in the existing component **(photo e)**. Continue zipping up the top-layer edges of the components.

5 With the thread exiting the end A on the top of the previous component, sew through the adjacent end A in the new component. Flip the components over, and sew through the end bottom A in the new component. Continue through the adjacent end bottom A in the previous component. Your needle should be exiting toward the unzipped edges. Zip up this layer of the two components.
6 Sew through the end A on the bottom layer of the new component, and the end A on the bottom layer of the previous component. Flip the component over, and sew through the end A on the top layer of the previous component and the end A on the top layer of the new component. Sew through the beadwork to exit the second A in the next end herringbone stitch.
7 Repeat step 2, and then steps 4–6 to

add a new component but position it with the V opening pointing up **(photo f)**. Repeat these steps for the remainder of the components, alternating the orientation of each component. End and add thread as needed.

Clasp

1 On 24 in. (61 cm) of thread, pick up three As, leaving a 6-in. (15 cm) tail. Tie them into a ring with a square knot, and continue through the next A **(figure 3, a–b)**.
2 Pick up two As, and sew through the next A. Repeat this stitch twice to complete the round, and step up through the first A added in the first two-bead set **(b–c)**.
Round 2: Work a herringbone stitch by picking up two As, and sewing through the next A. Work a peyote stitch by picking up a B, and sewing through the first A in the next two-bead set. Repeat these stitches twice to complete the round, and step up through the first A added **(c–d)**.
Round 3: Work a herringbone stitch using As and two peyote stitches using Bs. Repeat these stitches twice to complete the round, and step up through the first A added **(d–e)**.

double your options

Make this bracelet reversible by using a different color cylinder bead in three adjacent peyote sections in each component, being sure to fold each component appropriately. You can also omit the the side embellishment allowing the bracelet to be more flexible.

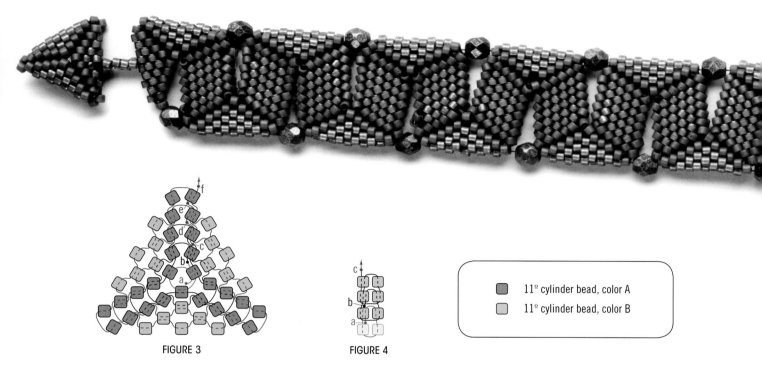

FIGURE 3

FIGURE 4

■	11° cylinder bead, color A
▨	11° cylinder bead, color B

Round 4: Work a herringbone stitch using As and three peyote stitches using Bs. Repeat these stitches twice to complete the round, and step up through the first A added **(e–f)**. End the working thread and tail, and set the component aside.

3 Using 1 yd. (.9 m) of thread, repeat steps 1–2 to make another component, but add one more round with herringbone stitches at the corners, and four peyote stitches on each side. End the tail, but not the working thread.

4 Place the small component on top of the large one so that the edges line up with each other. With the working thread on the large component, sew down through the corresponding end A on the small component. Working back toward the edge you just finished, sew through the next up-B on the large component. Continue to zip up this edge. Sew down through the adjacent end A in the large component, and zip up the next edge. Place a 3 or 4 mm bead between the two components **(photo g)**, and zip up the last edge. Do not end the thread.

5 With the working thread from the clasp, sew through the beadwork to exit a B near the center of one edge.

Pick up two Bs, and sew through an adjacent B on the same edge **(photo h)**. Retrace the thread path exiting the first bead added.

6 Pick up two Bs, sew through the previous two Bs, and continue through the first B added **(figure 4, a–b)**. Repeat this stitch twice using two Bs per stitch to make a strip that is four beads long and two beads wide **(b–c)**.

7 Sew through an edge B near the center of the end bracelet component, an adjacent edge B, and the other end B in the strip **(photo i)**. Retrace the connection several times, and end the thread.

8 On the other end of the bracelet, add 24 in. (61cm) of thread to the final edge, exiting a B near the center of the edge. Work as in step 6 to make a strip that is 28 beads long and two beads wide. Sew back through the corresponding B in the first set of Bs in the strip **(photo j)** Test the fit of the clasp, and add or omit rows if necessary. Sew through the surrounding Bs on the edge and through the adjacent B in the first set of the strip. Retrace the thread path of the join several times, and end the thread.

Embellishment

Add a comfortable length of thread to an end component, exiting an edge A near the first V opening. Pick up a 4 mm bead, and sew through the edge A on the other side of the opening. Continue through the beadwork to exit near the next V opening. Repeat this stitch for the remainder of this edge. Sew through the beadwork to the opposite edge, and repeat this stitch to add 4 mms on this edge. End the thread. ●

SPIRAL ROPE / BEAD EMBROIDERY / FRINGE

Autumnal
equinox
necklace

Harvest hues create clusters of colorful fringed leaves.

designed by **LeAnn Baehman**

Difficulty rating

Materials
necklace 18 in. (46 cm) with 4 in. (10 cm) pendant

- 1 44 x 35 mm cabochon (tiger iron)
- 11º seed beads
  - **20 g** color A (Miyuki 135F, matte transparent root beer)
  - **2 g** color B (Miyuki 135, root beer)
  - **5 g** color C (Toho 222, dark copper)
- **10 g** 15º seed beads in each of **7** colors:
  - color D (Toho 222, dark copper)
  - color E (Miyuki 179, dark green)
  - color F (Miyuki 298, dark red)
  - color G (Miyuki 251, light gold)
  - color H (Toho 423F, matte smoky topaz)
  - color I (Miyuki 9, silver-lined orange)
  - color J (Toho 25 silver-lined tangerine)
- 3 in. (7.6 cm) beading foundation (black)
- 3 in. (7.6 cm) Ultrasuede (black)
- Nymo B beading thread (black)
- beading needles, #12, #12 Sharps, #13
- white craft tacky glue
- cocktail straw
- Thread Heaven
- thread bobbin or cardboard

Spiral rope base

1 Attach a stop bead to a comfortable length of conditioned thread on a #12 needle. Leaving a 10-in. (25 cm) tail, pick up seven color A 11º seed beads, and sew through the first four again **(figure 1)**. These four beads begin the core of the rope, and the other three form a loop. Flip this loop to the left.
2 Pick up four As, slide them down to the core beads, and sew up through the top three core beads of the previous stitch and the first bead just picked up **(figure 2)**. Shift the new outer loop to the left to stack on top of the first loop.

3 Repeat step 2 **(figure 3)**, ending and adding new thread as needed, until the rope is the desired length. Leave at least a 10-in. (25cm) tail for attaching the clasp.

Pendant
Bezel
1 Glue the cabochon to a piece of beading foundation.
2 Attach a #12 Sharps needle to a comfortable length of thread, and tie an overhand knot at the end. Sew up through the foundation close to the edge of the cab. Using color B 11º seed beads, work in beaded backstitch to outline the cab: Pick up two beads, align them next to the cab, and sew down through the foundation. Sew back up through the foundation between the two beads, and sew through the last bead again. Repeat as needed to surround the cab, varying the number of beads picked up in each stitch if desired but be sure to end up with an even number of beads in the round. Sew through all the beads again to cinch up the ring of beads **(photo a)**.
3 Sew down through the foundation and then back up, exiting next to the first round of backstitch. Using Bs,

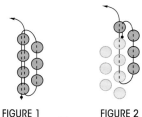

FIGURE 1   FIGURE 2

FIGURE 3

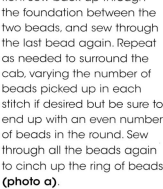
a

⬤	11º seed bead, color A
⬤	11º seed bead, color B
⬤	11º seed bead, color C
⬤	15º seed bead, color D
⬤	15º seed bead, color E
⬤	15º seed bead, color F
⬤	15º seed bead, color G
⬤	15º seed bead, color H
⬤	15º seed bead, color I
⬤	15º seed bead, color J

b

c

d

e

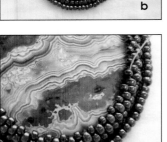

f

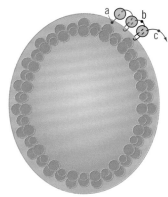

g

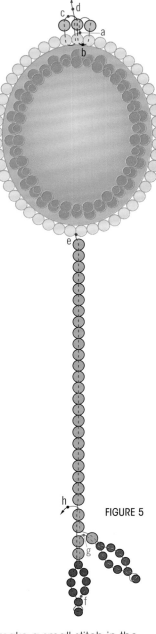

FIGURE 4

FIGURE 5

work a second (outer) round of backstitch **(photo b)**. Sew through the beadwork to exit a bead in the inner round of backstitch.

4 Working off of the inner round of backstitch, pick up a B, skip the next B in the round and sew through the following B **(photo c)**. Repeat this stitch to complete a round of tubular peyote **(photo d)**, and then work another round **(photo e)**. Work a final round of peyote using color D 15º seed beads **(photo f)**, snugging up the beads to curve over the edge of the stone. (*Note:* due to variations in cabochons, you may need to work more or fewer rounds or use different bead sizes to produce a secure, neat bezel). End the thread.

5 Trim the foundation close to the beadwork, being careful not to cut any threads. Glue the wrong side of the Ultrasuede to the back of the foundation, leaving an ⅛-in. (3mm) border free of glue. Trim the backing close to the beadwork.

6 Tie an overhand knot at the end of 1 yd. (.9 m) of thread. Sew up between

the Ultrasuede and foundation, about ⅛ in. (3mm) from the edge of the beadwork. Pick up two color C 11º seed beads, sew from back to front up through the backing and foundation, and up through the second bead just added **(figure 4, a–b)**. The beads should sit next to each other on the edge of the foundation/backing.

7 Pick up a C, and sew up through both layers from back to front and the bead just added **(b–c)**. Repeat this stitch to complete the round. After adding the final bead, pass down through the first edge bead added, through the foundation and backing, and back up through the first edge bead. End the thread in the beadwork.

Bail

1 On 1 yd. (.9 m) of thread, attach a stop bead, leaving a 10-in. (25cm) tail. Sew up through the center edge C at the top of the cabochon.

2 Pick up two Cs, and sew down through an adjacent bead **(figure 5, a–b)**. Sew back up through the center bead and the first bead added in this step **(b–c)**.

3 Pick up a C, sew down through the other adjacent edge bead, and sew up through the center edge bead and the bead on top of it **(c–d)**.

4 Working off the three beads added in the previous step, work as in steps 2–3 until the bail is long enough to fit around the (unembellished) spiral rope. End with your thread exiting the center column.

5 With the working thread, sew down through the center edge bead of the pendant, up through the left edge bead and the beads in the left column **(photo g)**, and down through the left edge bead. Sew back up through the center edge bead, and into the center column. End the thread.

6 Remove the stop bead from the tail, and thread a needle on the tail. Sew up through the edge bead on the right side, and through all the beads in the right column of the bail. Sew down through the right edge bead,

make a small stitch in the backing of the beadwork to anchor the thread and reverse direction, and sew back up through the right edge bead and into the right column. End the tail.

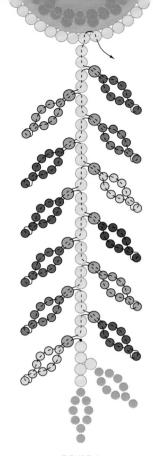

FIGURE 6

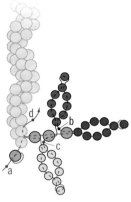

FIGURE 7

FIGURE 8

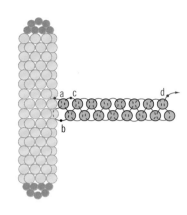

FIGURE 9

Fringe

1 Center a stop bead on 10 ft. (3 m) of thread, and wind half the thread onto a bobbin or a piece of cardboard. This thread will be used to complete the second half of the fringe. Thread a needle on the other end of the thread. Locate the center edge bead at the bottom of the cabochon, and sew down through it with the needle pointing away from the cabochon.

2 Pick up 28 As. These will form the base, or stem, of the fringe strand. Pick up six color E 15º seed beads, skip the last E, and sew back through the fifth E **(figure 5, e–f)**. Pick up three Es, and sew back through the first E picked up in this step and the last two As in the stem **(f–g)**. This creates the first leaf.

3 Pick up an A, create a leaf with color F 15º seed beads (as in step 2), and sew back through the A added in this

step and the next two As in the stem **(g–h)**.

4 Repeat step 3 up the fringe strand, using colors D–J as desired, and then sew up through the edge bead this fringe started from, and back down through the next edge bead **(figure 6)**.

5 Continue to add fringe strands, decreasing the number of As in each stem by two beads. Work a total of seven strands. End the thread.

6 Remove the stop bead from the other end, and add six rows of fringe on the other side of the cabochon, mirroring the completed side. End the thread.

Spiral rope embellishment

1 Using a #13 needle, attach a stop bead to a comfortable length of thread, leaving a 6-in. (15cm) tail. Sew through the end core bead at one end of the spiral rope, exiting between the first and second core beads.

2 Pick up three As to make a branch and six 15ºs in the desired color (D–J). Make a leaf, as in the pendant fringe, sewing back through the third branch A after completing the leaf **(figure 7, a–b)**. Work another leaf in a different

color, and sew through the middle branch A **(b–c)**. Work one more leaf in a third color, but this time sew through the first branch A and the next core A **(c–d)**. This is one embellishment unit.

3 Repeat step 2, working one embellishment unit between each pair of core beads, until half of the rope base minus the width of the pendant bail is embellished. Sew through the core of the rope to leave a section unembellished that equals the width of the pendant bail. Slide the bail of the finished pendant onto the unembellished half of the rope, and snug it up against the embellished half of the rope. Continue embellishing the second half of the rope. Leave a 10-in. (25cm) tail for attaching the clasp.

Toggle bar

1 On 1 yd. (.9 m) of thread, attach a stop bead, leaving a 6-in. (15cm) tail. Pick up 16 Cs. These beads will become the first two rows of the toggle bar as the next row is added.

2 Using Cs, work in flat, even-count peyote until you have a total of 12 rows. Zip rows 1 and 12 together to form a tube.

3 With the thread exiting an end C, pick up three D 15ºs. Sew down through the adjacent end C and up through the next C to form a picot **(figure 8)**. Repeat twice to create a total of three picots. Sew up through the first end C of this step and the first two Ds of the picot. Sew through the center Ds of the picots to close the end of the tube. Retrace the thread path through the center Ds again. Sew through the beadwork to exit the other end of the toggle bar.

4 Trim a cocktail straw to the length of the peyote tube. Slit the straw lengthwise, roll to compress, and insert into the peyote tube. Repeat step 3 to add picots to this end, and close the tube.

5 Sew through the beadwork to exit the seventh C from the end. Pick up a C, and sew through the next C in the row **(figure 9, a–b)**. Pick up a C, and sew back through the C just added **(b–c)**. Continue in flat even-count peyote to create a strip 16 rows long **(c–d)**. Zip the last row to the first row to create a loop. End the threads.

h

i

Toggle ring

1 On 5 ft. (1.5 m) of thread, attach a stop bead, leaving a 6-in. (15cm) tail. Pick up 40 D 15ºs, and sew through the first D again to create a ring. Work a round in even-count tubular peyote with one D per stitch. Step up through the first D added in this round **(figure 10, a–b)**.

2 Using Ds, work another round, picking up two Ds in the first stitch and one in each of the remaining stitches **(b–c)**. Repeat this round **(c–d)**.

3 Work two rounds using C 11ºs, picking up two Cs in the first stitch and one C in each remaining stitch **(d–e)**. Work one more round using Cs, but add a single bead over the two-bead stitch of the previous round to form a point **(e–f)**. Remove the stop bead, and end the tail.

4 With the working thread, sew through the beadwork to exit a D in round 1 (an "up" bead).

5 Work two rounds with Ds, working two-bead stitches in the corresponding places as in the first half of the toggle ring. The beadwork will begin to cup **(photo h)**.

6 Work two rounds using Cs, working two-bead stitches as before. Zip the outer edges together, sewing through the single 11º above the column of two-bead stitches to form a point.

7 Sew through the outer round to exit a C about half-way down the side. Work as in step 5 of "Toggle bar" to create a loop **(photo i)**. End the thread.

Attaching the clasp

Check to make sure the pendant is centered; add more spiral rope and fringe to one side of rope if necessary. Using the tail (it should be exiting the core of the spiral rope base), pick up 15 As and one half of the finished clasp. Sew through the end three-bead outer loop of the spiral rope base and back through the end four core beads. Retrace the thread path through the loop a couple of times, and end the thread. Repeat on other end of rope with other half of the clasp. ●

make it a set Add a pair of earrings with two more toggle rings. Wear them plain or add leaf fringe to complete the look.

FIGURE 10

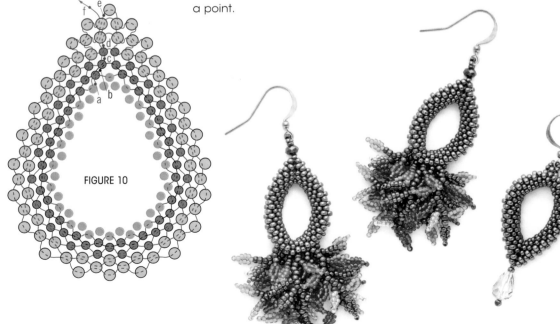

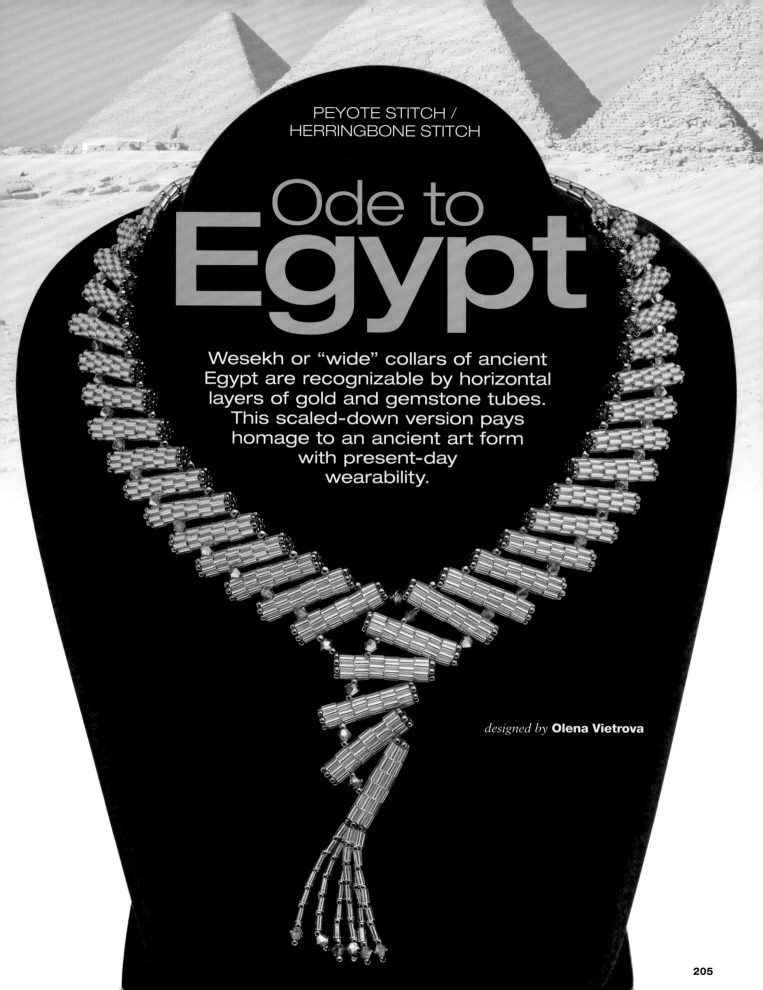

PEYOTE STITCH /
HERRINGBONE STITCH

Ode to Egypt

Wesekh or "wide" collars of ancient
Egypt are recognizable by horizontal
layers of gold and gemstone tubes.
This scaled-down version pays
homage to an ancient art form
with present-day
wearability.

designed by **Olena Vietrova**

Difficulty rating

Materials

necklace 24 in. (61cm)

- **44** 3 mm bicone crystals (Preciosa, vitrail light)
- 15 g 3 mm bugle beads, #1 (Toho 22, silver-lined topaz)
- 1–2 g 11º seed beads (Toho 81, hematite)
- 3 g 15º seed beads (Toho 81, hematite)
- toggle clasp
- Fireline 6 lb. test
- beading needles, #11

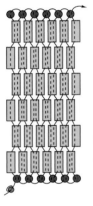

FIGURE 1

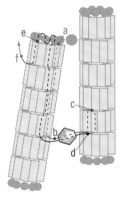

FIGURE 2

3 mm bugle bead

3 mm bicone crystal

11º seed bead

15º seed bead

Each half of this necklace is made continuously, beginning at the center of the necklace, while ending and adding thread (Basics) as needed. For the purposes of these instructions, each peyote tube will have a top (near the connecting 11º seed bead) and a bottom (near the connecting 3 mm bicone crystal). In addition, there are six tiers of bugle beads in each tube, starting with tier 1 at the top of the tube (see the **photo**, below).

stepbystep

Left band

First tube

[1] On 2 yd. (1.8 m) of thread, attach a stop bead (Basics), leaving a 6-in. (15cm) tail.

[2] Pick up a 15º seed bead, six 3 mm bugle beads, and a 15º. These beads will shift to form rows 1 and 2 as the third row is added.

[3] Work a total of 12 rows in flat even-count peyote stitch (Basics), working one stitch with a 15º and three stitches with bugles (**figure 1**). Each straight edge should have six 15ºs.

[4] Roll the strip into a tube, and zip up (Basics) the edges.

[5] Sew down through the nearest 15º with the needle pointing toward the other end of the tube, and continue through the nearest tier 1 bugle.

Subsequent tubes

[1] Pick up an 11º seed bead. This is the connection point at the top of this tube and the next. Work as in steps 2–4 of "First tube."

[2] Sew down through the beadwork of the new tube to exit the bugle in tier 4 that is aligned with the 11º connection (**figure 2, a–b**). Pick up a 3 mm bicone crystal, and sew up through the corresponding tier 5 bugle in the previous tube (**b–c**). This is the connection point at the bottom of the tubes. Sew down through the adjacent bugle (**c–d**), and sew back through the 3mm.

[3] Sew through the beadwork of the new tube to exit the third 15º from the 11º at the top of the tube with the needle pointing toward the other end of the tube (**d–e**). Sew down through the nearest tier 1 bugle (**e–f**).

[4] Work as in steps 1–3 for a total of 15 connected tubes. End the working thread and tail.

Right band

Work as in "Left band" to make a mirror image.

Centerpiece

Work as in "Left band" with the following changes:

- In step 1 of "Subsequent tubes," do not add an 11º at the connection points between the tubes.
- In step 2 of "Subsequent tubes," pick up a 15º, 3mm, and 15º for the 3 mm connection point.
- Make a total of five tubes.
- To add fringe to the last tube: With the thread exiting a 15º at the bottom of the tube, pick up a repeating pattern of a bugle and a 15º six times, and then pick up a 3 mm and a 15º. Skip the 15º, and sew through the remaining beads just picked up and the 15º in the tube. Sew down through the adjacent 15º in the tube, and repeat these stitches to add fringe to each 15º at this end of the tube. End the working thread and tail.

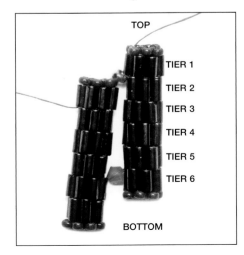

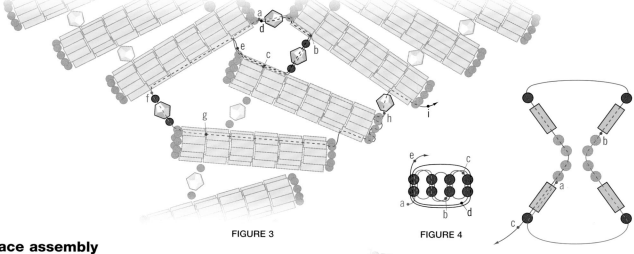

FIGURE 3

FIGURE 4

FIGURE 5

FIGURE 6

Necklace assembly

[1] Position the left and right bands so the tubes stair-step up from the center. Add 24 in. (61cm) of thread to the first tube of the left band, exiting a top 15º opposite the 11º connection point **(figure 3, point a)**. Pick up a 3mm, sew through the corresponding 15º in the first tube of the right band, and continue through the nearest tier 1 bugle in this tube **(a–b)**.

[2] Position the centerpiece between the left and right bands so the 3 mm connection points are closest to the left band, as shown in **figure 3**. Pick up a 15º, a 3mm, and a 15º. Sew through the tier 5 bugle in the first tube of the centerpiece **(b–c)**, and continue through the adjacent tier 6 bugle and the nearest 15º. Sew through the nearest tier 1 bugle and 15º in the first tube of the left band **(c–d)**. Retrace the thread path through the connection **(d–e)**.

[3] Sew through the beadwork of the first tube of the left band to exit a bugle in tier 5 **(e–f)**. Pick up a 15º, a 3mm, and a 15º, and sew through the corresponding 15º and tier 6 bugle in the second tube of the centerpiece **(f–g)**. Sew through the beadwork of this tube and the connection to the first tube, and exit the top 15º in the first tube that is closest to the right band **(g–h)**.

[4] Pick up a 3mm, and sew through the tier 6 bugle in the first tube of the right band **(h–i)**. End the thread.

Ropes

[1] On a comfortable length of thread, work in modified ladder stitch (Basics) as follows: Pick up four 15ºs, and sew through all the beads again to create two stacks of two beads each **(figure 4, a–b)**, leaving an 8-in. (20cm) tail. Pick up two 15ºs, and sew through the last two 15ºs and the two 15ºs just picked up **(b–c)**. Pick up two 15ºs, and sew through the previous stack of 15ºs and the two 15ºs just picked up **(c–d)**. To form a ring: Sew up through the first stack of 15ºs, down through the last stack, and up through the first stack again so your thread is exiting opposite the tail **(d–e)**.

[2] Work in modified tubular herringbone stitch (Basics) as follows: Pick up a bugle, two 15ºs, and a bugle, sew down through the next stack, and continue up through the following stack **(figure 5, a–b)**. Repeat this stitch once, and step up through the first bugle and 15º added in this step **(b–c)**.

[3] Continue in modified tubular herringbone as follows: Pick up a bugle, two 15ºs, and a bugle. Sew down through the top 15º in the next stack, and sew up through the top 15º in the following stack. Repeat this stitch once, and step up through the first bugle and 15º added in this step.

[4] Work as in step 3 until your rope measures 4¼ in. (10.8cm) long, ending and adding thread as needed. Do not end the working thread and tail when you have completed the rope.

[5] With the tail, pick up three 15ºs, half of the clasp, and three 15ºs. Skip the next 15º in the end of the rope, and sew down through the following 15º. Sew through the beadwork to exit the 15º your thread exited at the start of this step, and retrace the thread path through the loop several times to secure. End the tail but not the working thread.

[6] Make a second rope, and attach the other half of the clasp.

Attaching the ropes

[1] With the working thread from a rope, pick up an 11º, and sew through the tier 1 bugle in the last tube of the left band opposite the last 11º connection **(figure 6, a–b)**. Sew through the adjacent bugle in the opposite direction, and retrace the thread path through the connection **(b–c)**.

[2] Sew through the rope to exit the fourth-to-last 15º in the same stack your thread exited at the start of step 1 **(c–d)**. Pick up a 15º and a 3mm, and sew through the corresponding tier 5 bugle in the last tube of the band **(d–e)**. Sew through the adjacent bugle in the opposite direction, and retrace the thread path through the connection **(e–f)**. End the thread.

[3] Work as in steps 1 and 2 to attach the remaining rope to the right band. ◉

MODIFIED PEYOTE STITCH / BRICK STITCH

Tropical Twins bracelet

Create a floral explosion
by linking Twin bead flowers
with lush seed bead leaves.

designed by **Kerrie Slade**

stepbystep

Flowers

[1] On 1½ yd. (1.4 m) of thread, pick up six color A 2.5 x 5 mm Twin beads. Sew through all the beads and the first bead again to form a ring, leaving a 24-in. (61cm) tail. Sew through the available hole of the A your thread is exiting **(figure 1, a–b)**.

[2] Pick up an A, and sew through the available hole of the next A in the ring. Repeat this stitch to complete the round, and step up through the first A added in this round. Sew through the available hole of this A **(b–c)**.

[3] Pick up two As, and sew through the available hole of the next A in the previous round. Repeat this stitch to complete the round, and step up through the first A added in this round. Sew through the available hole of this A **(c–d)**.

[4] Pick up an A, and sew through the first A in the next pair of As. Pick up an A, and sew through the following A **(figure 2, a–b)**. Repeat these two stitches to complete the round, and step up through the first A added in this round. Sew through the available hole of this A **(b–c)**.

[5] Pick up two As, and sew through the next A in the previous round. Pick up an A, and sew through the next A **(c–d)**. Repeat these two stitches to complete the round, and step up through the first A added in this round. Sew through the available hole of this A **(d–e)**.

[6] Pick up an A, and sew through the next A in the previous round. Pick up an A, and sew through the first A in the next pair of As. Pick up two color D 11º

seed beads, and sew through the next A
(e–f). Repeat these three stitches to complete the round, and then sew through the next five beads to exit the first 11º added in this round (f–g).

[7] Pick up a D, and sew through the next D and four As (**figure 3, a–b**). Sew through the available hole of the A your thread is exiting, pick up an A, and sew through the available hole of the previous A (**b–c**). Sew through the next four As and the following D (**c–d**). Repeat these stitches to complete the round (**d–e**).

[8] Sew through the beadwork to exit an A in the original ring, and exit the inside of the flower. Pick up an 8 mm fire-polished bead and a D, sew back through the 8mm, and continue through another A in the original ring. Retrace the thread path through the 8 mm a few times, and end the working thread (Basics).

[9] With the tail, pick up two color E 11º seed beads, sew through the A your thread is exiting, and continue through the first E just added (**figure 4**).

[10] Pick up two Es, sew down through the second E in the previous pair, sew up through the first E in the pair, and continue through the first E just added. Repeat this stitch using two Es per stitch until you have a total of 20

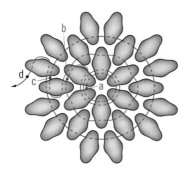

FIGURE 1

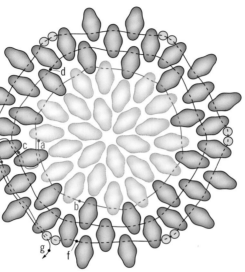

FIGURE 2

Difficulty rating

Materials

bracelet 7 in. (18cm)

- **8** 8 mm fire-polished beads* (**3** gold, **3** purple iris, **2** green iris)
- 25 g 2.5 x 5 mm Twin beads* in each of **3** colors: A (metallic purple), B (transparent purple), C (light transparent purple)
- 11º seed beads*
  10 g color D (metallic gold)
  30 g color E (olivine)
- beading thread, size D or 6 lb. test
- beading needles, #10
- for ribbon closure:
  12–15 in. (30–38cm) ribbon
- for clasp closure:
  clasp
  2 6 mm jump rings
  2 pairs of chainnose or flatnose pliers

* All beads are Preciosa Traditional Czech Beads.

 2.5 x 5 mm Twin bead

 11º seed bead, color D

 11º seed bead, color E

FIGURE 3

FIGURE 4

A loop of seed beads at the base of each component is the secret to constructing this bracelet.

pairs of Es. Create a loop with the strip of Es by sewing through the opposite A in the ring. Retrace the thread path through both of the connections several times, and end the tail.

[11] Make a total of eight flowers, using color A, B, and C Twins and varying the 8 mm fire-polished beads as desired.

Leaves

[1] On 1½ yd. (1.4 m) of thread and leaving a 20-in. (51cm) tail, pick up two Es, and sew through them both again so they sit side by side.

[2] Work in brick stitch with an increase at the start and end of each row (Basics) for a total of eight rows, ending with a row of 10 beads (figure 5, light green beads).

[3] Work in two-drop brick stitch (see the note below) for a total of eight decrease rows, ending with a row that is two beads high and two beads wide (figure 5, dark green beads).

Note: Two-drop brick stitch is done in much the same way as regular brick stitch except that you work stacks of two beads at a time. For the first stitch, pick up four beads, sew under the thread bridge between the second and third beads on this end of the previous row, and sew up through the last two beads just added. The four beads will create two stacks of two beads. For subsequent stitches, pick up two beads at a time and work with them as you would with a single bead in regular brick stitch.

[4] Exiting the two-bead row, pick up an E, and sew through all the edge beads, pulling snug so the leaf cups slightly (figure 6, a–b). End the working thread.

[5] With the tail, pick up two Es, and work as in step 10 of "Flowers" (c–d) until you have a total of 20 pairs of Es. Create a loop by stitching the last pair of Es to the first pair of Es added in this step. Retrace the thread path of the connection several times, and end the tail.

[6] Make a total of 11 leaves.

Buds

[1] On 4 ft. (1.2 m) of thread and leaving a 20-in. (51cm) tail, repeat step 1 of "Flowers" using As.

[2] Continuing with As, work as in step 2 of "Flowers" five times.

[3] Work as in step 5 of "Flowers," adding a total of nine beads in this round.

[4] Work as in steps 6 and 7 of "Flowers." Retrace the thread path through the last round to reinforce, and end the working thread.

[5] Using the tail, work as in steps 9 and 10 of "Flowers."

[6] Make a total of five buds using color A, B, and C Twins as desired.

Fastening ring

On 1 yd. (.9 m) of thread and leaving an 8-in. (20cm) tail, pick up two Es. Sew through both Es again so they sit side by side. Using two Es per stitch, work as in step 10 of "Flowers" to create a strip with 32 rows of Es. Making sure the strip isn't twisted, join the ends into a ring, sewing back and forth between the ends. End the working thread and tail.

Assembly

[1] Pass the loop of a flower through the fastening ring, and then pass the loop of a leaf through the loop of the flower (photo a). Pass the loop of a bud through the loop of the leaf (photo b), and pass the loop of a new flower

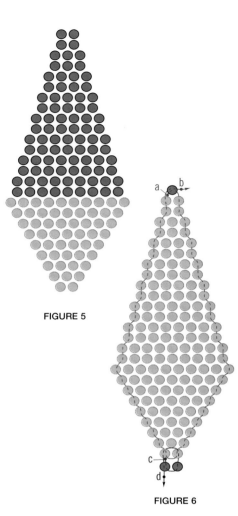

FIGURE 5

FIGURE 6

through the loop of the bud (photo c). Continue connecting components in the desired order, ending with a leaf.

[2] To use ribbon to fasten the bracelet, cut a 12–15-in. (30–38cm) piece of ribbon, pass it through the loop of the final leaf and the fastening ring, and tie a bow.

To use a clasp, open a 6 mm jump ring (Basics), and attach half of the clasp to the loop of the final leaf. Open another 6 mm jump ring, and attach the other half of the clasp to the fastening ring. ○

a

b

c

Coastal flair earrings

Make a bold and playful statement with these colorful soutache earrings.

designed by **Erzsébet Kis Jakab**

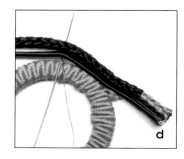

Base

1 Tie a double knot **(Soutache basics, p. 212)** on one end of 24 in. (61 cm) of thread, and trim the tail by the knot. Thread a needle, and set the thread aside.

2 Cut a 24-in. (61 cm) piece of color A soutache braid. Leaving a 1½-in. (3.8 cm) tail, tightly wrap the soutache around the rim of a metal ring **(photo a)** until the ends meet.

3 Position the soutache tails one on top of the other and, using the threaded needle from step 1, sew up through the center of the braids (sew through the V where the fibers intertwine) directly under the base of the ring **(photo b)**. Sew back through the center of the soutache close to where the thread exited **(Soutache basics, Stitch in the ditch)**. Retrace

the thread path to reinforce the join. Lift the working thread out of the way, and trim the soutache tails under the join. Apply a small dot of fabric glue on the ends to prevent them from fraying.

4 Cut a 6½-in. (16.5 cm) piece of color B soutache braid and a 6½-in (16.5 cm) piece of 3 mm bolo cord. Tape both ends of the bolo cord to prevent it from fraying. Create a stack **(Soutache basics)** by laying the bolo cord on top of the color B soutache.

5 Attach the stack to the outer edge of the ring: With the working thread from the ring, sew through both layers of the trimmed tail on the ring, and continue through the center of the stack 1 in. (2.5 cm) from one end **(photo c)**. Sew down through the stack and the

top outer edge of the color A soutache about ¼ in. (6 mm) to the left. Sew up through the color A soutache ¹⁄₁₆ in. (2 mm) to the left of the previous stitch, and continue through the stack **(photo d)**. Sew down ¼ in. (6 mm) to the left of the last stitch going through both the stack and the top outer edge of the color A soutache. Repeat these stitches around the entire ring.

6 When you reach the other side of the tail, join the stack **(photo e)**, and end thread **(Soutache basics)**.

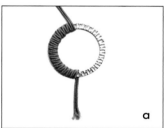

a

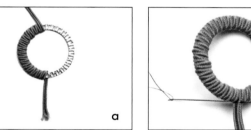

b

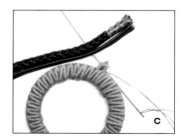

c

d

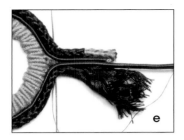

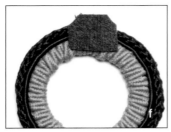

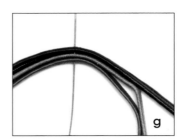

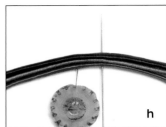

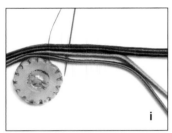

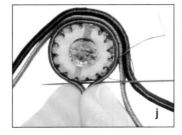

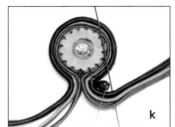

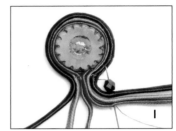

7 Trim the ends close to the knot, and apply a small dot of fabric glue.

8 Cut a piece of Ultrasuede ½ x ⅜-in. (1.3 x 1 cm). Trim the two top corners on a long side. Apply fabric glue to the back, and center it over the tail section **(photo f)**.

Coin bead component

1 Cut an 8-in. (20 cm) piece of soutache braid in each of the three colors, and create

a stack by laying one braid on top of the other, with color B on top, color A in the middle, and color C on the bottom. Make sure the center Vs of all three braids are pointing in the same direction.

2 Begin a new 24-in. (61 cm) thread **(Soutache basics)**, locate the center of the stack, and sew through the center Vs of all three braids from bottom to top **(photo g)**. Sew down through the stack

about ¼ in. (6 mm) to the left.

3 Pick up a 12 mm coin bead, and sew up through the stack near the knot **(photo h)**. Retrace the thread path to secure the bead.

4 Work a shaping stitch: Sew down through the center Vs of the stack ¼ in. (6 mm) to the right **(photo i)**. Sew up ¹/₁₆ in. (2 mm) to the right of the previous stitch, and then down ¼ in. (6 mm)

to the right of the last stitch. Make three additional shaping stitches.

5 Starting with the inner color C braid, join the stack **(Soutache basics)** below the coin bead **(photo j)**.

6 Separate the three rightmost braids, creating a three-braid stack. Pick up a 3 mm fire-polished bead, wrap the three-braid stack snugly half way around the bead, and sew through the stack where

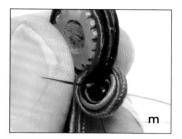

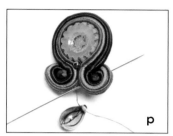

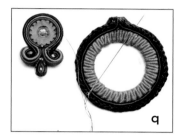

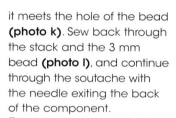

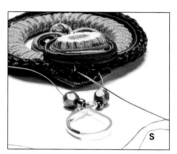

it meets the hole of the bead **(photo k)**. Sew back through the stack and the 3 mm bead **(photo l)**, and continue through the soutache with the needle exiting the back of the component.

7 Pull the tails of the stack behind the coin bead, and end the stack **(Soutache basics)** by making several stitches to secure the stack **(photo m)** and adding whip stitches **(Soutache basics)** **(photo n)** to prevent the soutache from fraying. Trim the soutache tails below the whip stitches.

8 Sew through the back of the work to exit the loose stack on the opposite side, and repeat steps 6 and 7.

9 Sew through the work to exit between the color A and color C braids on one side between the coin bead and the 3 mm bead **(photo o)**. Pick up an 11º seed bead, and sew through the corresponding spot on the stack on the other side of the coin, making sure the seed bead is centered. Retrace the thread path to reinforce the connection.

10 Sew through the work to exit the color C braid about 2 mm from the join.

Pick up a teardrop bead, and sew through the stack on the other side of the join **(photo p)**.

Assembly

1 Sew through the back of the coin bead component, exiting the stack on the right-side toward the top of the coin bead. Sew through the color A soutache and the two-layer stack surrounding the ring with the needle exiting to the right of the trimmed tails **(photo q)**. Pull the thread tight, and position the coin component on top of the tail section of the ring. Sew back through the ring stack close to where the thread exited, and continue from the back to the front of the work **(photo r)**. Sew back through the work close to where the thread exited, and continue through the outer stack on the ring.

Sew through the back of the work, and repeat these tacking stitches on the opposite side.

2 Sew through the ring's stack with the thread exiting the outer edge of the bolo cord above the trimmed tails. Pick up a 4 mm fire-polished bead, an 11º, the loop of an ear wire, an 11º, and a 4 mm, and sew through the bolo cord about 4 mm from where the thread exited **(photo s)**, centering the ear wire above the component. Retrace the thread path to reinforce the join, and end the thread.

3 Cut a ¾ in. (1.9 cm) circle of Ultrasuede, and glue the Ultrasuede to the back of the work with the bottom edge centered above the teardrop bead **(photo t)**.

4 Make a second earring. o

Difficulty rating

Materials
earrings 2 in. (5cm)
- **2** 12 mm coin beads (Czech, green)
- **2** 6 x 9 mm teardrop beads (Czech, blue)
- **4** 4 mm fire-polished beads (matte purple iris)
- **4** 3 mm fire-polished beads (matte purple iris)
- **6** 11º seed beads (Toho 221, bronze)
- ⅛ in. (3 mm) soutache braid
  - 2½ yd. (2.25 m) color A (duck)
  - 29 in. (74 cm) color B (ruby glint)
  - 16 in. (41 cm) color C (poinsettia)
- 6½ in. (16.5 cm) bolo cord, ⅛ in. (3 mm), black
- **2** 1¼ in. (3.2cm) metal rings (TierraCast, rhodium plated)
- **1** x 2-in. (2.5 x 5 cm) piece of Ultrasuede
- 1 pair of earring findings
- Fireline, 6 lb. test
- beading needles, #12
- fabric glue
- scissors
- tape

Flowers
&berries necklace

Use a variety of new and traditional shaped beads to make a blossoming accessory seeded with berries.

designed by **Junko Ando**

stepbystep

Dagger flowers

[1] On 1 yd. (.9 m) of thread, pick up 10 5 x 16 mm two-hole dagger beads, sewing through the end holes of the daggers. Sew through the beads again to form a ring, leaving a 6-in. (15 cm) tail. Tie a square knot (Basics) with the working thread and tail, and continue through the next dagger (**figure 1, a–b**).

Sew through the available hole of the same dagger.
[2] Pick up a 15º seed bead, and sew through the available hole of the next dagger. Repeat this stitch to complete the round (**b–c**), and retrace the thread path, exiting a dagger. Sew through the inside hole of this dagger, and end the tail (Basics) but not the working thread.
[3] Repeat steps 1 and 2 to make two flowers for each color of dagger.

SuperDuo flowers

[1] On 2 ft. (61 cm) of thread, pick up nine 2.5 x 5 mm SuperDuo beads. Sew through the beads again to form a ring, leaving a 6-in. (15 cm) tail. Tie a square knot with the working thread and tail, and continue through the next SuperDuo (**figure 2, a–b**).
[2] Pick up a 4 mm pearl, skip the next four SuperDuos, and sew through the following SuperDuo. Sew back through

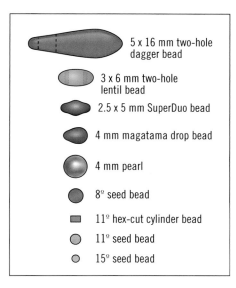

	5 x 16 mm two-hole dagger bead
	3 x 6 mm two-hole lentil bead
	2.5 x 5 mm SuperDuo bead
	4 mm magatama drop bead
	4 mm pearl
	8º seed bead
	11º hex-cut cylinder bead
	11º seed bead
	15º seed bead

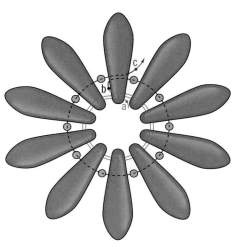

FIGURE 1

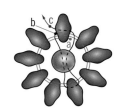

FIGURE 2

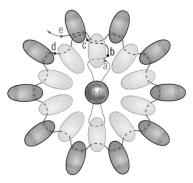

FIGURE 3

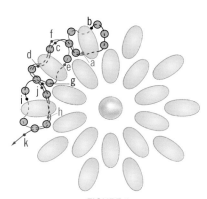

FIGURE 4

the pearl, and continue through the SuperDuo your thread exited at the start of this step **(b–c)**. End the tail but not the working thread.

[3] Repeat steps 1 and 2 to make two more SuperDuo flowers.

Lentil flower

[1] On 1 yd. (.9 m) of thread, pick up 10 3 x 6 mm two-hole lentil beads. Tie the beads into a ring with a square knot, leaving a 6-in. (15 cm) tail. Sew through the first lentil.

[2] Pick up a 4 mm pearl, skip the next four lentils, and sew through the following lentil. Sew back through the pearl, and continue through the lentil your thread exited at the start of this step **(figure 3, a–b)**. Sew through the available hole of the same lentil **(b–c)**.

[3] Pick up a lentil, and sew through the available hole of the next lentil **(c–d)**. Repeat this stitch to complete the round, and continue through the first lentil added in this round **(d–e)**.

[4] Pick up three 15ºs, and sew through the outer hole of the same lentil **(figure 4, a–b)**. Pick up three 15ºs, sew through the inner hole of the same lentil, and continue through the first two 15ºs added in this step **(b–c)**.

[5] Pick up a 15º, and sew through the outer hole of the next lentil **(c–d)**. Pick up three 15ºs, and sew through the inner hole of the same lentil **(d–e)**. Pick up a 15º, and sew through the center 15º around the previous lentil **(e–f)**. Sew through the first 15º added in this step, the lentil, and the next two 15ºs **(f–g)**.

Materials

necklace 17 in. (43 cm)

- **20** 5 x 16 mm CzechMates two-hole dagger beads in each of **2** colors (matte green iris and chocolate brown matte bronze Vega)
- **6** 6 mm faceted disk beads (Czech 72FC244, transparent ruby)
- **16** 6 mm glass bicones (Czech 15056, vintage turquoise)
- **4** 6 mm Czech snail shell pearls (creme)
- **16** 6 x 6 mm CzechMates two-hole tile beads (wild raisin)
- **20** 3 x 6 mm CzechMates two-hole lentil beads (L130, opaque olive peacock)
- **27** 2.5 x 5 mm SuperDuo beads (chalk lazure blue)
- **36** 4 mm magatama drop beads in each of **2** colors (Toho, jet black and opaque red)
- **4** 4 mm glass pearls (matte gold)
- **1** g 8º seed beads (Toho 222, dark bronze)
- **2** g 11º hex-cut cylinder beads (Miyuki 0022, metallic dark bronze)
- **1** g 11º seed beads (Miyuki 457, metallic dark bronze)
- **1** g 15º seed beads (Miyuki 457, metallic dark bronze)
- clasp
- Fireline 6 lb. test
- beading needles, #11 or #12
- thread bobbin or piece of cardboard

FIGURE 5

FIGURE 6

FIGURE 7

FIGURE 8

FIGURE 9

[6] Pick up a 15º, and sew through the inner hole of the next lentil (g–h). Pick up three 15ºs, and sew through the outer hole of the same lentil (h–i). Pick up a 15º, and sew through the center 15º around the previous lentil (i–j). Sew through the first 15º added in this step, the lentil, and the next two 15ºs (j–k).
[7] Repeat steps 5 and 6 to complete the round, and end the tail but not the working thread.

Berries
[1] On 2 ft. (61cm) of thread, pick up three 4 mm magatama drop beads. Tie the beads into a ring with a square knot, leaving a 6-in. (15cm) tail. Sew through the first drop (figure 5, a–b).
[2] Pick up a drop, and sew through the next drop in the ring (b–c). Repeat this stitch to complete the round, and step up through the first drop added in this round (c–d).
[3] Pick up a drop, an 11º seed bead, and a drop, and sew through the next drop in the previous round (figure 6, a–b). Repeat this stitch to complete the round, and step up through the first drop added in this round (b–c). Tighten the beadwork so that it begins to cup.
[4] Pick up a drop, and sew through the next drop in the previous round (c–d). Repeat this stitch to complete the round,

and sew through the first drop added in this round (d–e).
[5] Pick up an 11º, and sew through the next drop in the previous round (figure 7, a–b). Repeat this stitch to complete the round, and step up through the first 11º added in this round (b–c).
[6] Pick up an 11º, and sew through the next 11º in the previous round (c–d). Repeat this stitch to complete the round (d–e), and sew through the first 11º added in this round to tighten. End the tail but not the working thread.
[7] Repeat steps 1–6 to make two berries for each color of drop.

St. Petersburg chain base
Left side
[1] Attach a stop bead (Basics) at the center of 2 yd. (1.8 m) of thread, and wrap half of the thread around a bobbin or piece of cardboard.
[2] Pick up six 11º hex-cut cylinder beads, and sew through the third and fourth beads in the same direction so the fifth and sixth beads form a new column (figure 8, a–b).
[3] Pick up an 11º seed bead, and sew back through the next three hexes in the column (b–c).
[4] Pick up an 8º seed bead, and sew through the two hexes in the newest column (figure 9, a–b).

[5] Pick up four hexes, and sew through the first two beads just picked up so that the last two beads form a new column (b–c). Slide the four beads tight to the existing chain. Pick up an 11º, and sew back through the next three hexes in the column. Pick up an 8º, and sew through the two hexes in the newest column. Repeat this step until you have a total of 16 11ºs along one edge and 16 8ºs along the other. Do not end the working thread.
[6] Remove the stop bead from the starting end of the chain. Pick up six hexes, and sew through the third and fourth hexes again (figure 10), as in step 2.
[7] Pick up an 11º, and sew back through the next three hexes in the column (figure 11, a–b).
[8] Sew through the adjacent 8º in the first side of the chain and the two hexes in the newest column (b–c). Pull the beads snug.
[9] Pick up four hexes, and sew through the first two beads again. Pick up an 11º, and sew back through the next three hexes in the column. Sew through the next 8º in the chain and the two hexes in the newest column. Repeat this step to complete this side of the base, and do not end the thread.

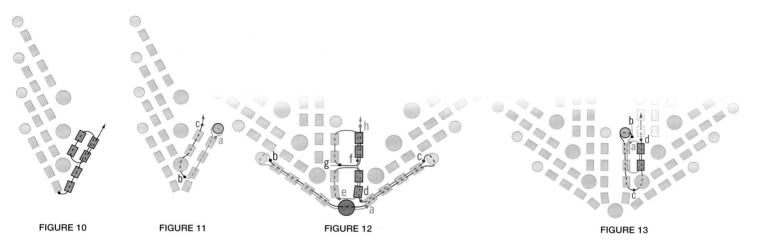

FIGURE 10   FIGURE 11   FIGURE 12   FIGURE 13

Right side

[1] Repeat steps 1–5 of "Left side."

[2] Remove the stop bead from the starting end of the chain. Pick up an 8º, and sew through the next four hexes and 11º in the far column of the left side of the base (**figure 12, a–b**). Sew back through the same four hexes, the 8º just added, and the four hexes and 11º in the far right column of the right side of the base (**b–c**). Continue back through the same four hexes (**c–d**).

[3] Pick up two hexes, sew down through the corresponding two hexes in the left side of the base (**d–e**), and sew up through the two hexes just added (**e–f**).

[4] Pick up two hexes, sew down through the next two hexes in the left side of the base (**f–g**), and sew up through the two hexes just added (**g–h**).

[5] Pick up two hexes, and sew up through the two hexes added in the previous step (**figure 13, a–b**). Pick up an 11º, and sew back through the next three hexes in the column (**b–c**).

[6] Sew through the adjacent 8º in the right side of the base and the two hexes added in the previous step (**c–d**).

[7] Pick up four hexes, and sew through the first two hexes again. Pick up an 11º, and sew back through the next three hexes in the column. Sew through the next 8º in the chain and the two hexes

in the newest column. Repeat this step to complete this side of the base, and do not end the thread.

Neck straps

[1] With one thread from the left side of the base, pick up five 15ºs, a 6 x 6 mm two-hole tile bead, a 15º, a 6 mm bicone, a 15º, a tile, five 15ºs, and a 6 mm disk bead.

[2] With the other thread, pick up five 15ºs, and sew through the available hole of the first tile. Pick up a 15º, a bicone, and a 15º, and sew through the available hole of the next tile. Pick up five 15ºs, and cross through the disk bead.

[3] Repeat steps 1 and 2 two more times.

[4] With one thread, pick up five 15ºs, a tile, a 15º, a bicone, a 15º, a tile, eight 15ºs, four 11ºs, half of the clasp, and three 11ºs. Sew back through the first 11º just added to form a loop, and pull tight. Retrace the thread path through the loop, but do not end the thread.

[5] With the other thread, pick up five 15ºs, and sew through the available hole of the tile. Pick up a 15º, a bicone, and a 15º, and sew through the available hole of the next tile. Pick up eight 15ºs, and sew through the loop of 11ºs connecting the clasp. End the threads.

[6] Repeat steps 1–5 for the other neck strap.

Assembly

[1] Place a dagger flower in the V of the St. Petersburg base. With the working thread, sew through the nearest hex in the base and up through the center of the dagger flower. Pick up a 6 mm snail shell pearl and a 15º, and sew back through the pearl and the hex directly below. Sew through the inner hole of the nearest dagger. Continue to stitch the daggers to the base as needed to secure the flower. End the thread. Attach the remaining dagger flowers in the same manner, positioning them as desired.

[2] Attach the SuperDuo flowers and lentil flower to the base as desired by sewing through a hex directly below, sewing back through a bead in the flower, and repeating at several points around each flower. End each thread when done.

[3] To attach the berries, pick up four 11ºs with the working thread, and sew through a hex in the base in the desired position. Continue back through the four 11ºs just added and the nearest 11º in the berry. Retrace the thread path, and end the thread. Repeat for the remaining berries. ●

Cheops
bangle

Take a design cue from the Great Pyramid of Giza (aka, the Pyramid of Cheops) by stitching a triangular peyote tube with herringbone spines.

designed by **Eleanna Zegkinoglou**

stepbystep

Triangular tube

[1] On a comfortable length of thread, pick up two color A 10º cylinder beads, and sew through both beads again, leaving a 6-in. (15 cm) tail.

[2] Pick up five color B 10º cylinder beads and two As, and sew through the last two As again. Repeat this pattern once. Pick up five Bs, and sew up through the first A added in the previous step to form a ring **(figure 1)**.

[3] Work in rounds as follows:

Round 2: Work a herringbone stitch (Basics) using As **(figure 2, a–b)**, and then work three peyote stitches using Bs (Basics) **(b–c)**. Repeat this pattern twice to complete the round, and step up through the first A added in this round **(c–d)**.

Round 3: Work a herringbone thread path without adding any beads, and continue through the next B picked up in the previous round **(d–e)**. Work two peyote stitches using Bs, and step up through the next A in the previous round **(e–f)**. Repeat this pattern twice to complete the round **(f–g)**.

[4] Repeat rounds 2 and 3 until you have a total of 106 rounds of As along each spine. End and add thread (Basics) as needed. As you work, shape the tube by gently pressing your thumbs against the inside wall of the bangle.

Join

To join the ends of the tube:

[1] Make sure your tube is not twisted. With the thread exiting an A, sew up through the corresponding A on the other end of the tube, and sew

down through the adjacent A **(photo a)**.

[2] Sew down through the corresponding A on the other end of the bangle **(photo b)**.

[3] Sew through the next B up-bead on the other end **(photo c)**, and pull tight on the thread so the two ends meet. Sew through the next B up-bead on the other end. Continue zipping up (Basics) the ends until you sew through the last B up-bead before an A.

[4] Work as in steps 1–3 to continue joining the ends of the tube. Retrace the thread path through the join, and end the working thread and tail. Your bangle will have a top spine and two bottom spines.

Optional embellishments

[1] Add 1 yd. (.9 m) of thread to the bangle, and exit an A in the top spine.

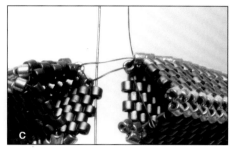

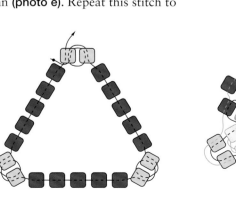

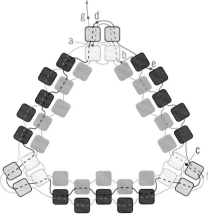

Difficulty rating

Materials
silver/raspberry bangle 2½-in. (6.4 cm) inside diameter
- 53 4 mm bicone crystals (Swarovski, crystal CAL 2X)
- 10º Delica cylinder beads
  8 g color A (Miyuki DBM0012, metallic dark raspberry)
  16 g color B (Miyuki DBM0321, matte nickel plated)
- 11º cylinder beads (Miyuki DB0116, wine gold luster)
- 15º Japanese seed beads (Toho 2113, silver-lined milky pomegranate)
- Fireline 8 lb. test
- beading needles, #10 and #11

gold/bronze bangle colors:
- 10º Delica cylinder beads
  color A (Miyuki DBM0031, 24K gold plated)
  color B (Miyuki DBM0322, matte metallic bronze)

TRICKS OF THE TUBE
- Nylon thread is not suitable for this project.
- Keep your tension consistent and relatively firm, or the walls of your tube will cave in.
- By stretching and molding your tube as you work, you will be able to create smooth outer edges, but the inside will likely be a little puckered.

[2] Pick up a 15º seed bead, an 11º cylinder bead, and a 15º. Skip the next A in the column, and sew through the following A **(photo d)**. Repeat this stitch to complete the round.

[3] Sew through the beadwork to exit the A adjacent to the A your thread exited at the start of this step, and repeat step 2. Continue through the next "skipped" A in the spine.

[4] Pick up a 15º, a 4 mm bicone crystal, and a 15º. Skip a row of As, and sew through the next A in the other column **(photo e)**. Repeat this stitch to

complete the round, and end the thread.

[5] Add 1 yd. (.9 m) of thread to the bangle, and exit an A in a bottom spine. Pick up a 15º, and sew through the next A in the other column **(photo f)**. Repeat this stitch to complete the round.

[6] Sew through the beadwork to exit an A in the remaining bottom spine, and work as in step 5 to embellish this spine. End the thread. ●

FIGURE 1

FIGURE 2

☐	10º cylinder bead, color A
■	10º cylinder bead, color B

LADDER STITCH / BEADWEAVING

Captured cup chain bracelet

SuperDuos and seed beads surround sparkling cup chain for a dramatic look.

designed by **Judy Henegar**

Base

1 Cut a length of cup chain long enough to fit around your wrist, minus the clasp length and ½ in. (1.3 cm).
2 On a comfortable length of thread, pick up eight 11º seed beads, and sew through the beads again, positioning the beads into two rows of four beads each **(figure 1)** and leaving a 12-in. (30 cm) tail.
3 Pick up an 11º, a 3 mm bugle bead, and an 11º, and sew through the row of 11ºs your thread is exiting, positioning the bugle bead set above the row **(figure 2, a–b)**. Working in ladder stitch, use 11ºs to make four more rows **(b–c)** using a tight tension.

4 Place the cup chain on the base so the end cup is next to the bugle bead set. Pick up an 11º, a bugle bead, and an 11º, and sew over the connector between the cups. Continue through the row of 11ºs your thread is exiting **(figure 3)**. Flip the beadwork so the ladder stitch base is on top, and work four more ladder stitch rows using 11ºs **(figure 4)**, and flip it back. Repeat these stitches for the length of the cup chain, ending and adding thread as needed.
5 Add a bugle set to the last row in the base, and then work one more ladder stitch row using 11ºs. Sew through the beadwork to exit the

bugle bead set just added **(figure 5, point a)**.

Edge embellishments

1 Pick up an 8º metal seed bead, a SuperDuo bead, and three 11ºs. Sew through the open hole of the same SuperDuo, pick up an 8º, and sew through the next bugle bead set **(a–b)**.
2 Pick up an 8º, a SuperDuo, and three 11ºs, and sew through the open hole of the same SuperDuo. Pick up an 8º, sew through the previous bugle bead set **(b–c)**, and the row in the base directly below **(c–d)**. Continue through the next four rows, and the next bugle bead set directly above the fourth row.

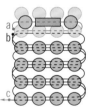

FIGURE 1

FIGURE 2

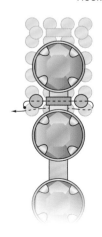

FIGURE 3

3 Repeat steps 1 and 2 for the length of the base using a tight tension, but after adding the last embellishment, sew through the row under the last bugle bead set and the next row instead of sewing through four rows in the base.

4 Flip the beadwork so the ladder stitch base is facing up. Pick up an 11º, an 8º, a SuperDuo, and three 11ºs, and sew through the open hole of the same SuperDuo **(figure 6, a–b)**. Pick up an 8º and an 11º, skip the next row (the row the bugle bead set is attached to), and sew through the following row **(b–c)**.

5 Pick up an 11º, an 8º, a SuperDuo, and three 11ºs, and sew through the open hole of the same SuperDuo **(c–d)**. Pick up an 8º and an 11º, skip the previous row (the row the bugle bead set is attached to), and sew through the row your thread exited at the start of the step **(d–e)**. Continue sewing through the next four rows to exit one row before the row with the attached bugle bead set.

6 Repeat steps 4 and 5 for the length of the base noticing that each SuperDuo added in this row is centered between two SuperDuos in the previous edge

embellishment. End and add thread as needed.

Clasp

1 Sew through the beadwork to exit the end row of the ladder-stitch base. Pick up three 11ºs, and sew through a loop of the clasp **(figure 7, a–b)**. Pick up two 11ºs, and sew back through the end row **(b–c)**. Repeat these stitches to attach the other loop of the clasp **(c–d)**, and retrace the thread path. End the thread.

2 Repeat step 1 using the tail to attach the other half of the clasp, and end the thread. ○

Difficulty rating

   ◇ ◇

Materials
gold bracelet 7¾ in. (19.7 cm)
- 6¾–7 in. (17.1–18 cm) 6 mm cup chain (Swarovski SS29 Tiffany 1088, pacific opal)
- **6 g** 2.5 x 5 mm SuperDuo beads (amber)
- **1 g** 3 mm bugle beads (Miyuki 003, silver-lined gold)
- **8 g** 8º metal seed beads (38148, 24k gold plated)
- **7 g** 11º seed beads (Toho P471, permanent galvanized gold)
- **1** two-strand clasp (gold)
- Fireline 4 or 6 lb. test
- beading needles, #11 or #12

purple bracelet colors
- 6 mm cup chain (Swarovski SS29 Tiffany 1088, white patina)
- 2.5 x 5 mm SuperDuo beads (pastel bordeaux)
- 3 mm bugle beads (Miyuki 460, metallic dark raspberry)
- 8º seed beads (Toho 85, metallic plum iris)
- 11º seed beads (Toho 166C, transparent rainbow amethyst)

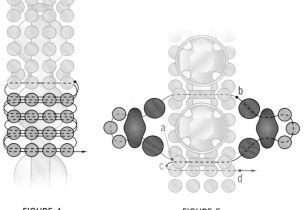

FIGURE 4   FIGURE 5

○ 11º seed bead

▬ 3 mm bugle bead

⬤ 6 mm cup chain

● 8º metal seed bead

◗ 2.5 x 5 mm SuperDuo bead

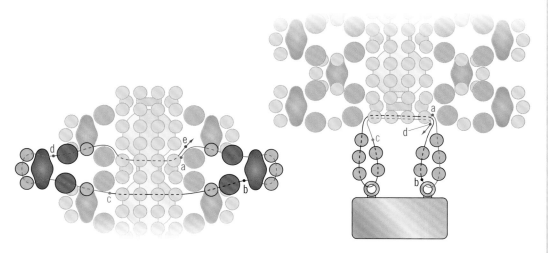

FIGURE 6

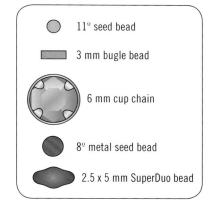

FIGURE 7

Baroque gardens necklace

Stitch a simple three-strand rope necklace to complement a special bead.

designed by **Julia Gerlach**

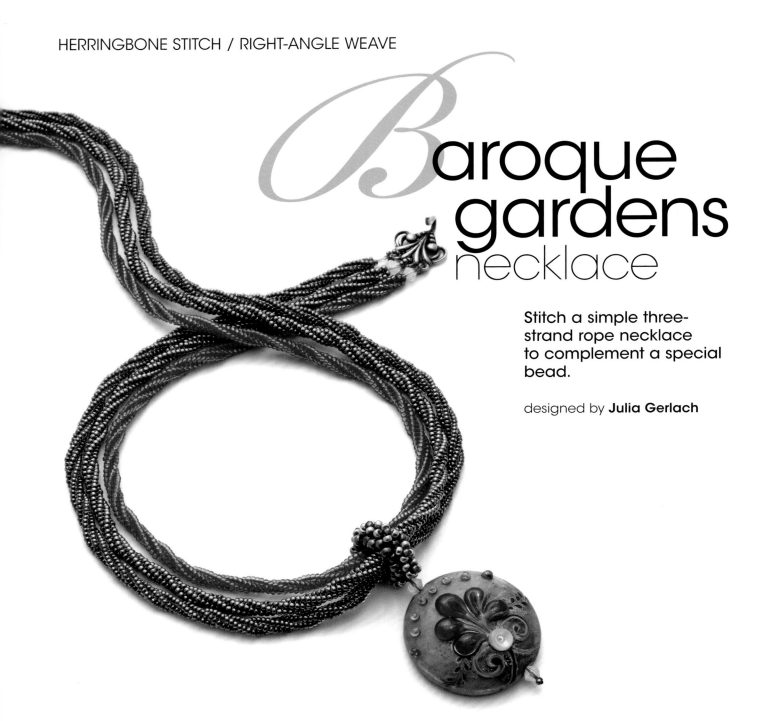

Ropes

1 On a comfortable length of thread and leaving an 8-in. (20 cm) tail, work a four-bead ladder using color A 15º seed beads. Form the ladder into a ring.
2 Pick up two As, sew down through the next A in the ladder, and sew up through the following A. Repeat to work a second herringbone stitch, and step up through the first A added in this round **(photo a)**.
3 Switch to twisted tubular herringbone: Pick up two As, sew down through two As in the next column, and sew up through just one A in the following column **(photo b)**. Pick up two As, sew down through two As in the next column, and sew up through the top two As in the following column **(photo c)**.
4 Repeat step 3 until the rope is 17 in. (43 cm) or the desired length, ending and adding thread as needed. The spiral will be evident after about ½ in. (1.3 cm). Don't end the working thread or tail when the rope is complete.
5 Repeat steps 1–4 with color B 15º seed beads, but make the rope about 1 in. (2.5 cm) shorter than the A rope. Repeat again with color C 15º seed beads, making this rope 1 in. (2.5cm) longer than the A rope.
6 With the working thread from the A rope, pick up a 4 mm bicone crystal, three As, the middle loop of half of the clasp, and three As. Sew

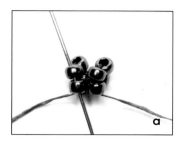

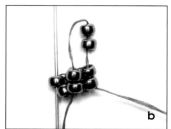

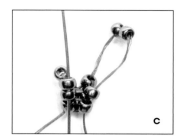

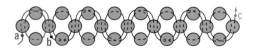

back through the 4 mm and the A in the end of the rope that is opposite the one your thread exited at the start of this step. Sew up through an adjacent A, and retrace the thread path through the connection, making sure the 4 mm is connected to all four end As. End the thread. Using the tail of the A rope, repeat this step, attaching the corresponding loop of the other half of the clasp. End the tail.

7 Repeat step 6 with the B and C ropes, attaching them so the B rope becomes the inner strand and the C rope becomes the outer strand.

Bail

1 On 1 yd. (.9 m) of thread, pick up four 8º seed beads, and tie them into a ring with a square knot, leaving a 6-in. (15cm) tail. Sew through the first few beads again **(figure 1, a–b)**.

2 Using 8ºs, work in right-angle weave (RAW) to create a strip of eight stitches **(b–c)**.

3 Exiting the end 8º, pick up a color D 11º seed bead, a color E 11º seed bead, and a D. Cross diagonally over

the RAW stitch, and sew through the opposite 8º **(figure 2, a–b)**. Pick up a D, sew back through the E, pick up a D, and sew through the 8º your thread exited at the start of this step **(b–c)**. Following the RAW thread path, sew through the next two 8ºs **(c–d)**.

4 Repeat step 3 to embellish each RAW stitch.

5 Wrap the bail around the ropes, and join the ends: Pick up a D, and sew through the opposite end bead **(photo d)**. Pick up a D, and sew through the first end bead. Retrace the thread path several times. This will be the bottom of the bail.

6 Exiting an 8º at the bottom of the bail, pick up a 4 mm and enough 15ºs to span the inside of the focal bead. String the focal bead over

the 15ºs **(photo e)**, and pick up a 4 mm and a 15º. Skip the last 15º, and sew back through all the beads added in this step. Sew through the 8º your thread exited at the start of this step, going in the same direction as before.

7 Sew though the other 8º at the bottom of the bail, and retrace the thread path through the beads added in the previous step so the focal bead is centered below the bail. Exit an 8º along one edge of the bail.

8 Pick up an 8º, and sew through the next 8º along the edge of the bail **(figure 3)**. Repeat this stitch to add 8ºs along the entire edge. Sew through the beadwork to exit an 8º along the opposite edge of the bail, and repeat this step. End the working thread and tail. ❍

Materials

necklace 18 in. (46 cm)

- 1 *Bead&Button* 20th anniversary bead by Lydia Muell (www.BeadAndButton.com/ anniversarybead)
- **8** 4 mm bicone crystals (Swarovski, white opal)
- **1 g** 8º seed beads (Miyuki 462, metallic gold iris)
- 11º seed beads
  - **34** color D (Miyuki 1052, galvanized gold)
  - **8** color E (Toho Takumi large-hole 2223, silver-lined dragonfruit)
- **7 g** 15º seed beads in each of 3 colors:
  - color A (Toho 221, bronze)
  - color B (Miyuki 1606, rose matte transparent)
  - color C (Miyuki 1816, black-lined chartreuse)
- 3-strand clasp
- nylon beading thread, size D
- beading needles, #12

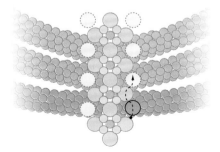

FIGURE 1

FIGURE 2

FIGURE 3

	8º seed bead
	11º seed bead, color D
	11º seed bead, color E

PEYOTE STITCH / BEAD WEAVING

Glamour ring

Metallic bronze cylinder beads add sparkle to this dazzling peyote stitched ring.

designed by **Cassie Donlen**

Base

1 On 1 yd. (.9 m) of thread, attach a stop bead, leaving a 6-in. (15cm) tail.
2 Pick up 10 11º cylinder beads, and work in flat, even-count peyote stitch to make a band long enough for the ends to meet around your finger without overlapping and ending on an odd-numbered row. End and add thread as needed. Work an additional eight rows. Fold over and align the ends to confirm they are a mirror image of each other. If not, remove or work another row. Remove the stop bead, and end the tail.
3 Sew through the beadwork as shown to exit the fourth edge cylinder from the end **(figure 1)**.
4 Align the ends of the band, and create two flaps by pinching the base ¼ in. (6mm) below each end. Sew through the corresponding fourth edge cylinder on the other side with the needle pointing toward the bead-work **(photo a and figure 2, point a)**. Pull the thread tight, and retrace the

connection to reinforce the join.
5 Zip up the flaps: Sew through the fourth cylinder from each end of the band, alternating sides, and pull the thread tight **(figure 3, a–b)**. Sew through the connection cylinders on the last outer column to reinforce the join **(b–c)**.

Embellishment

When adding the pearls, each stitch will be attached to the third cylinder from the end of the flap.
1 Sew through the adjacent edge cylinder sewing toward the end of the flap, with the needle pointing toward the beadwork. Continue through the next cylinder in the following column **(figure 4, a–b)**. Pick up a 15º seed bead, a 5 mm pearl, and a 15º, and sew through the corresponding cylinder on the opposite flap (third column from the outer edge) with the needle pointing toward the beadwork **(b–c)**.
2 Sew through the next two columns **(c–d)**. Pick up a 15º, a pearl, and a 15º, and sew through the following corresponding cylinder on the other flap **(d–e)**.

3 Sew through the next two columns. Pick up a 15º, a pearl, and a 15º, and sew through the following two corresponding columns on the other flap with the thread exiting an edge cylinder **(e–f)**.
4 Pick up four 3 mm fire-polished beads, and place the beads under the flap against the base **(photo b)**. Sew through the fourth edge cylinder on the flap, with the needle pointing toward the beadwork **(photo c)**. Pull the thread tight. Sew through the base to exit the cylinder your thread exited at the beginning of this step. Retrace the thread path through the fire-polished beads to reinforce the connection.
5 Sew through the adjacent connection cylinder with the needle pointing toward the beadwork **(photo d)**, and continue through the adjacent cylinder (third from the end) in the same outer column of the flap without the fire-polished beads, with the needle pointing away from the beadwork.
6 Repeat step 4, and end the working thread and tail. ●

a

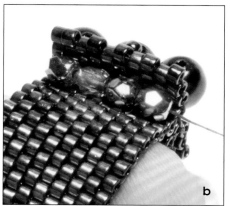

b

c

d

Difficulty rating

  ◇ ◇ ◇

Materials
ring ½ in. (1.3 cm) wide
- **3** 5 mm pearls (Preciosa, blue)
- **8** 3 mm fire-polished beads (crystal marea)
- **5 g** 11º cylinder beads (metallic gold iris)
- **6** 15º seed beads (metallic dark bronze)
- Fireline, 8 lb. test
- beading needles, #12

- ▢ 11º cylinder bead
- ○ 15º seed bead
- ● 5 mm pearl

FIGURE 1

FIGURE 2

Edge   Edge

a

FIGURE 3

E
d
g
e

c b

E
d
g
e

a

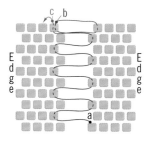

FIGURE 4

a

b

c

d

e

f

Metallic
cuff bracelet

Make a fashion statement with metals and leather by constructing this trendy, contemporary bracelet.

designed by **Marla Salezze**

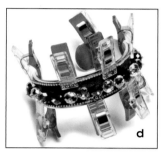

Foundation

1 Using the **template** as a guide, cut a strip of leather ½ x 5¾ in. (1.3 cm x 14.6cm) with rounded corners.

2 Using a pencil and a ruler, draw a centerline down the length of the leather.

3 Tie an overhand knot at the end of 1 yd. (.9 m) of thread. Sew up through the leather ¼ in. (6mm) from one end on the centerline. Working in stop stitch, pick up a rondelle bead and a 15º seed bead, and sew back through the rondelle and the leather **(photo a)**. Tie a half-hitch knot, retrace the thread path to reinforce the connection, and tie another half-hitch knot. Sew up through the leather ¼ in. (6mm) from where your thread exited on the centerline.

4 Work as in step 3, alternating the rondelle colors and positioning the beads to sit next to each other. Continue adding beads until you reach the other end. End the working thread and tail.

Edging and assembly

1 Tie an overhand knot at the end of 1 yd. (.9 m) of thread, and trim the tail. To edge the leather in brick stitch, sew up through the leather about 1 mm from the edge, pick up two 15º seed beads, sew up through the leather about one bead's width from where the thread just exited, and continue up through the second bead just added **(photo b)**.

2 Pick up a 15º, sew up through the leather one bead's width from where the thread just exited, and continue through the new bead **(photo c)**. Repeat this stitch around the perimeter of the foundation. After adding the last bead, sew down through the first bead in the edging, through the leather, and up through the first bead again. End the working thread in the edging beads.

3 Apply adhesive to the back of the leather, and position it inside the channel of the cuff bracelet. Allow it to dry for 24 hours using clips **(photo d)**. ◐

TEMPLATE

Difficulty rating

Materials

copper bracelet 7 in. (18cm)

- 21 5 x 7.5 mm metal faceted rondelle beads (Nunn Design, **7** antique copper, **7** antique silver, **7** antique gold)*
- **2 g** 15º seed beads (Miyuki 331, topaz gold luster)
- channel cuff bracelet (Nunn Design, 7 in. antique copper)*
- ½ x 6 in. (1.3 cm x 15cm) thin leather (brown glove tanned, fish leather, or Ultrasuede)
- nylon beading thread or Fireline 6 lb. test
- beading needles, #10
- clips
- E6000 adhesive
- pencil
- ruler
- scissors

silver bracelet colors

- **19** 5.5 x 8 mm crystal rondelle beads (Swarovski, **7** crystal silver night, **6** jet, **6** crystal silver shade)
- 15º seed beads (Miyuki 551, gilt-lined white opal)
- channel cuff bracelet (Nunn Design, antique silver)*
- ½ x 6 in. (1.3 x 15 cm) thin leather (black glove tanned, fish leather, or Ultrasuede)

Sparkling spikes necklace

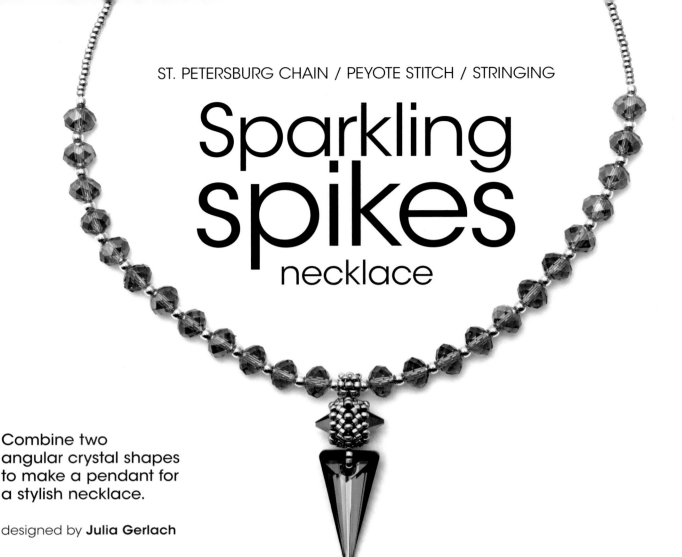

Combine two angular crystal shapes to make a pendant for a stylish necklace.

designed by **Julia Gerlach**

Pendant

1 On 1 yd. (.9 m) of thread, pick up three 11º cylinder beads, leaving a 6-in. (15cm) tail. Sew through the second and third cylinders again, positioning them side by side **(figure 1)**.

2 Pick up an 11º seed bead, and sew back through the cylinder your thread just exited and the one directly below it. Pick up a seed bead, and sew through the adjacent cylinder **(figure 2)**.

3 Pick up two cylinders, and sew through the first cylinder again **(figure 3)**. The second cylinder forms a new column. Pick up a seed bead, and sew back through the previous two cylinders in the column. Pick up a seed bead, and sew through the cylinder in the new column **(figure 4)**.

4 Repeat step 3 until you have 12 11º seed beads on each edge of the strip.

5 With a new thread, work as in steps 1–2, but instead of picking up the second seed bead in step 2, sew through the existing seed bead on the first strip that is nearest the tail, and continue through the remaining cylinder in the new column **(figure 5)**.

6 For the remainder of the strip, work as in step 3, but for the second seed bead, sew through the corresponding 11º seed bead on the first strip instead of adding a new one **(figure 6)**. End the tails but not the working threads.

7 Align the ends of the strip. With either thread, pick up a cylinder, and working as in ladder stitch, sew through the end cylinder at the starting end of the strip. Sew through the new cylinder again, pick up a seed bead, and sew back through the new cylinder and the one below in the same column. Pick up a seed bead, and sew through the three beads in the next column **(figure 7)**.

8 With the other thread, work as in step 7, but sew through the existing center seed bead instead of picking up a new one **(figure 8)**.

9 Slide the strip of beadwork around the double-spike bead, and with each thread, sew through the corresponding edge seed beads to cinch the openings around the spike bead.

10 With one thread, sew through the beadwork to exit a center seed bead that is aligned with the hole in the double-spike bead. Sew through the double spike and the opposite center seed bead. Retrace the thread path through the connection, exiting a center seed bead.

11 To make the bail, pick up a seed bead, and sew through the next center seed bead. Sew through the beadwork to exit the newly added seed bead. Pick up seven 11º seed beads, and sew through the bead your thread just exited to form a loop.

12 Using seed beads, work in tubular peyote around the loop. Using cylinders, work another round of peyote. Sew through to the other edge of the loop,

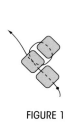

FIGURE 1

FIGURE 2

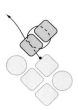

FIGURE 3

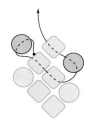

FIGURE 4

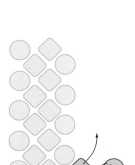

FIGURE 5

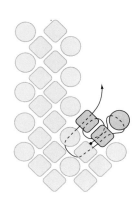

FIGURE 6

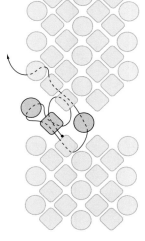

FIGURE 7

Difficulty rating

Materials

necklace 18 in. (46 cm)
- **1** 28 mm spike pendant (Swarovski, Bermuda blue)
- **1** 16 x 8 mm double-spike bead (Swarovski, metallic light gold 2X)
- **24** 5 x 8 mm fire-polished rondelles (black diamond)
- **26** 3 mm round silver-plated beads
- **1 g** 11º cylinder beads (Miyuki DB0035, metallic galvanized silver)
- **2 g** 11º seed beads (Toho 558, permanent-finish galvanized aluminum)
- **1** 12 x 6 mm magnetic clasp
- **2** 2 x 2 mm crimp beads
- **2** 3 mm crimp covers
- flexible beading wire, .014–.015
- Fireline 6 lb. test or nylon beading thread, size D
- beading needles, #12
- crimping pliers
- wire cutters

and work another round of peyote using cylinders. End the thread.

13 With the other thread, sew through the beadwork to exit a center seed bead opposite the bail. Pick up 10 cylinders and the spike pendant, and sew through the seed bead again. Retrace the thread path through the loop, and end the thread.

Necklace

1 On 22 in. (56cm) of beading wire, center three cylinder beads. String the bail over the cylinders.

2 On each side of the pendant, string:
- a repeating pattern of a 3 mm silver bead and a 5 x 8 mm rondelle 12 times
- a 3 mm and 4 in. (10 cm) of seed beads
- a crimp bead and half of the clasp

3 With each wire end, go back through the appropriate crimp bead, and use crimping pliers to compress the crimp bead. Trim the excess wire.

4 Using crimping pliers, close a crimp cover over each crimp bead. ●

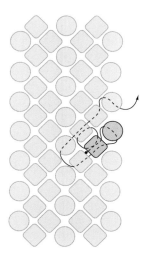

FIGURE 8

11º cylinder bead

11º seed bead

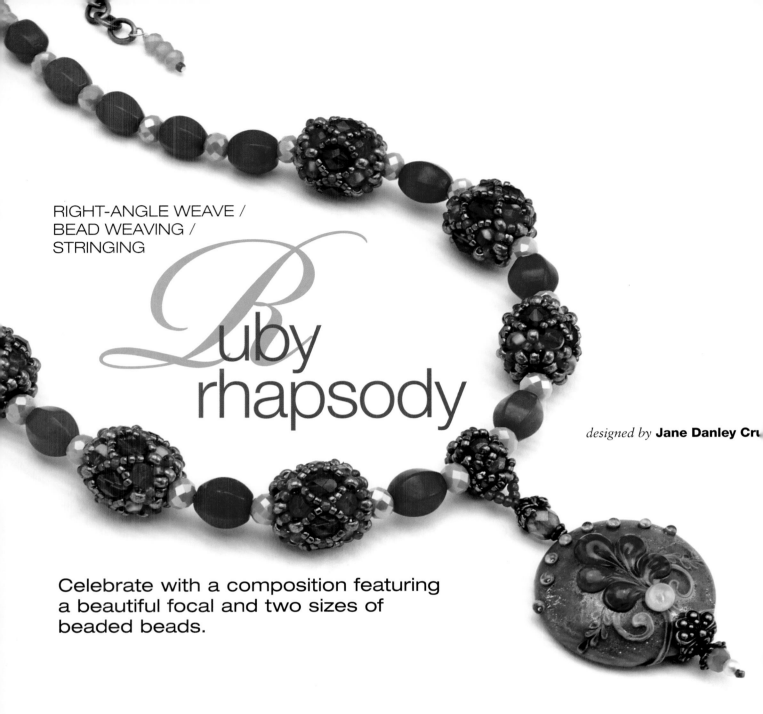

RIGHT-ANGLE WEAVE /
BEAD WEAVING /
STRINGING

Ruby rhapsody

designed by **Jane Danley Cru**

Celebrate with a composition featuring
a beautiful focal and two sizes of
beaded beads.

stepbystep

Large beaded beads

[1] On 1 yd. (.9 m) of thread, pick up
a 6 mm fire-polished bead, a 4 mm
fire-polished bead, a 6 mm, and a 4 mm.
Sew through the first 6 mm again to
form a ring, leaving a 6-in. (15 cm)
tail. Retrace the thread path through all
four beads, and continue through
the next few beads to exit the 6 mm
opposite the tail (**figure 1**).

[2] Work a flat strip of right-angle
weave (Basics) as follows: Pick up a
4mm, a 6mm, and a 4mm, and sew

through the 6 mm your thread exited at
the start of this step. Continue through
the next two beads (**figure 2**). Repeat
this step two times.

[3] Form the strip into a ring (Basics) as
follows: Pick up a 4mm, sew through
the first 6 mm added in step 1, pick up a
4 mm, and sew through the
6 mm your thread exited at the start
of this step. Continue through the
next 4 mm (**figure 3**).

[4] Pick up a color C 8º seed bead, and
sew through the next 4 mm (figure 4).
Repeat this stitch to complete the
round, and step up through the first

C 8º added in this round.

[5] Pick up a color A 11º seed bead,
a C 8º, and an A 11º, and sew through
the next C 8º in the previous round
(**figure 5**). Repeat this stitch to complete
the round, and step up through the
first two beads added in this round.

[6] Pick up a color D 8º seed bead,
and sew through the next C 8º (**figure
6**). Repeat this stitch to complete the
round. Retrace the thread path through
all the beads in this round several times,
pulling tight on the thread to snug up
the beads. Tie a couple of half-hitch
knots (Basics) if necessary to keep

FIGURE 1

FIGURE 2

FIGURE 3

	6 mm fire-polished bead
	4 mm fire-polished bead
	8º seed bead, color C
	8º seed bead, color D
	11º seed bead, color A
	11º seed bead, color B
	15º seed bead

FIGURE 4

FIGURE 5

FIGURE 6

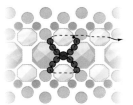

FIGURE 7

Materials

necklace 19 in. (48cm)

- **1** *Bead&Button* 20th anniversary bead by Lydia Muell
- **16** 10 x 8 mm gemstone barrel beads (dyed candy jade or ruby)
- **31** 6 mm round fire-polished beads (cranberry)
- **24** 5.5 x 5 mm crystal rondelles (seafoam AB)
- **10** 4 x 3 mm crystal rondelles (seafoam AB)
- **66** 4 mm round fire-polished beads (fuchsia and pearl)
- **1** 3 mm glass pearl (cream)
- **12** 2 mm glass pearls (fuchsia)
- 8º seed beads
  2 g color C (Miyuki 4219, Duracoat galvanized magenta)
  1 g color D (Toho 1207, marbled opaque turquoise blue)
- 11º seed beads
  67 color A (Toho 2213, milky pomegranate)
  18 color B (Miyuki 2008, matte metallic patina iris)
- 1–2 g 15º seed beads (Toho 459, gold luster dark topaz)
- lobster claw clasp
- TierraCast cap components (antique brass-plated pewter)
  1 7 mm Jasmine bead cap
  1 6 x 8.5 mm Raja pendant cap
  1 3 x 6 mm Jasmine bead cap
  1 2 x 3.5 mm scalloped bead cap
- 3 in. (7.6 cm) chain, 6 mm links
- **1** 2-in. (5 cm) head pin
- **2** crimp beads, #3
- **2** 4 mm crimp covers
- **2** wire guards
- flexible beading wire, .024 in.
- Fireline 6 lb. test
- beading needles, #11
- chainnose pliers
- crimping pliers
- roundnose pliers
- wire cutters

the beads close.

[7] Sew through the beadwork to exit a 4 mm on the other side of the original ring, and then work as in steps 4–6.

[8] With the thread exiting a 4 mm in the original ring, pick up three 15º seed beads, an A 11º, and three 15ºs, and sew through the corresponding 4 mm on the opposite side of the ring, with your needle pointing in the same direction. Pick up three 15ºs, sew back through the A 11º just added, pick up three 15ºs, and sew through the 4 mm your thread exited at the start of this step in the same direction. Continue through the next C 8º and 4 mm (**figure 7**).

[9] Repeat step 8 to complete the round. End the working thread and tail (Basics).

[10] Make a total of six large beaded beads.

Small beaded bead

[1] On 1 yd. (.9 m) of thread, pick up a 4 mm, a 2 mm pearl, a 4 mm, and a 2 mm. Sew through the first 4 mm again to form a ring, leaving a 6-in. (15cm) tail. Retrace the thread path through all four beads, and continue through the next few beads to exit the

4 mm opposite the tail.

[2] Work a flat strip of right-angle weave as follows: Pick up a 2mm, a 4mm, and a 2mm, and sew through the 4 mm your thread exited at the start of this step. Continue through the next two beads. Repeat this step four times.

[3] Form the strip into a ring as follows: Pick up a 2mm, sew through the first 4 mm added in step 1, pick up a 2mm, and sew through the 4 mm your thread exited at the start of this step. Continue through the next 2mm.

[4] Pick up a color B 11º seed bead, and sew through the next 2mm. Repeat this stitch to complete the round, and step up through the first B 11º added in this round.

[5] Pick up a 15º, and sew through the next B 11º. Repeat this stitch to complete the round, and then sew through the beadwork to exit a 2 mm on the other side of the original ring.

[6] Work as in steps 4 and 5 on this side of the ring.

[7] With the thread exiting a 2mm, pick up two 15ºs, a B 11º, and two 15ºs, and sew through the corresponding 2 mm on the opposite side of the ring, with your needle pointing in the same direction. Pick up two 15ºs, sew back through the B 11º just added, pick up two 15ºs, and sew through the 2 mm your thread exited at the start of this step in the same direction. Continue through the next B 11º and 2 mm.

[8] Repeat step 7 to complete the round. End the working thread and tail.

Pendant

[1] Add 2 ft. (61 cm) of thread (Basics) to the small beaded bead, and exit a 4mm. Pick up four A 11ºs, a 7 mm bead cap (narrow end to wide end), a 6mm, a 2 x 3.5 mm bead cap (wide end to narrow), the anniversary bead, a 6 x 8.5 mm pendant cap, a 3 x 6 mm bead cap (narrow end to wide), a 4 x 3 mm rondelle, a 3 mm pearl, and a 15º. Skip the 15º, and sew back through all the beads just added. Continue through the 4 mm your thread exited at the start of this step in the opposite direction.

[2] Pick up three A 11ºs, and sew through the fourth A 11º added in

the previous step. Retrace the thread path through the pendant connection two or three times. End the working thread and tail.

Assembly

[1] Cut 18 in. (46 cm) of beading wire, and center the small beaded bead with the attached pendant.

[2] On each end, string a 5.5 x 5 mm rondelle, a 10 x 8 mm barrel bead, a rondelle, and a large beaded bead. Repeat this pattern on each end until all six large beaded beads have been strung.

[3] On each end, string a repeating pattern of a 5.5 x 5 mm rondelle and a barrel bead five times, and then string a 5.5 x 5 mm rondelle and three 4 x 3 mm rondelles.

[4] On one end, string a crimp bead, half of a wire guard, the end link of the chain, and the other half of the wire guard. Go back through the crimp bead, and crimp it (Basics). Using chainnose or crimping pliers, close a crimp cover over the crimp. Trim the excess wire.

[5] On the other end, work as in step 4, but string a lobster claw clasp in place of the chain.

[6] On a head pin, string an A 11º and three 4 x 3 mm rondelles. Make the first half of a wrapped loop (Basics). Attach the end link of the chain, and complete the wraps. ●

Edgy triangle bangle

Layers of two-hole triangle beads bring an edgy look to this modern-inspired bangle.

designed by **Penny Dixon**

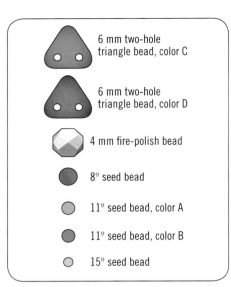

6 mm two-hole triangle bead, color C

6 mm two-hole triangle bead, color D

4 mm fire-polish bead

8º seed bead

11º seed bead, color A

11º seed bead, color B

15º seed bead

Base

1 On 5 ft. (1.5 m) of thread, attach a stop bead, leaving a 24-in. (61cm) tail.

2 Pick up 100 8º seed beads. Test to see if the strand will fit around the widest part of your hand. If it doesn't, increase or decrease the number of beads, but make sure the number is divisible by four. These beads will shift to form the first two rows as the next row is added.

3 Work one row in flat even-count peyote stitch.

4 Remove the stop bead, and make sure the beadwork is not twisted. Form the strip into a ring: Sew through the nearest edge 8º on the other end of the base, the 8º in the center row, and the following edge 8º. Attach a needle to the tail, and sew through the opposite edge 8º, the center 8º, and the following edge 8º as shown **(figure 1)**.

5 With each thread, work one round of tubular peyote stitch using 8ºs on the appropriate edge. The base will have a total of five rounds. End the tail but not the working thread.

6 Sew through the base to exit an 8º in the center round **(figure 2, point a)**. Pick up a color A 11º seed bead, a 4 mm fire-polish bead, and an A. Skip the next 8º in the center round, and sew through the following 8º **(a–b)**. Repeat this stitch 24 times to complete the round, and end the working thread.

7 Center 8 ft. (2.4 m) of thread in a three-bead set (A, 4mm, A) added in step 6 **(figure 3, a–b)**. Wrap one end of the thread on a thread bobbin or piece of cardboard.

8 With the other thread, pick up a color B 11º seed bead, and sew through the next A **(b–c)**. Pick up two 15º seed

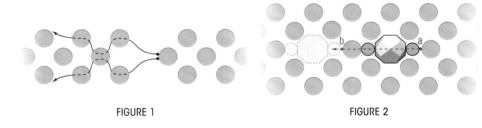

FIGURE 1

FIGURE 2

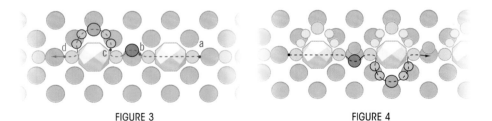

FIGURE 3

FIGURE 4

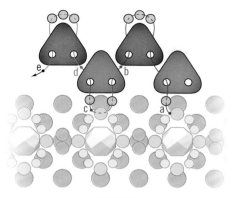

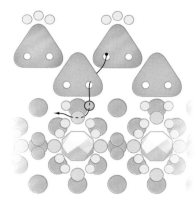

FIGURE 5

FIGURE 6

beads, an A, and two 15ºs, skip the 4mm, and sew through the next A **(c–d)**. Repeat these stitches 24 times to complete the round, positioning the loops to one side of the beadwork. Sew through the beadwork to exit the center A in the first loop.

9 Wrap the working thread on a bobbin, and unwind the tail. Repeat step 8 on the other side of the center round, making sure the Bs sit adjacent to the existing Bs and the loops are opposite the existing loops **(figure 4)**.

Triangle embellishment

How to pick up the triangle beads: With the point of the triangle with no hole facing away from you, pick up the bead through the left hole (LH) or the right hole (RH), per the instructions.

1 With either thread, pick up a 15º, a color C triangle bead (LH), a color D triangle bead (RH), and three 15ºs. Sew through the open hole of the same triangle (LH) from back to front **(figure 5, a–b)**.

2 Pick up a C (RH) from back to front and a 15º, and sew through the center A in the nearest loop **(b–c)**. Tighten the beadwork to snug up the triangles.

3 Pick up a 15º, and sew through the open hole (LH) of the same triangle **(c–d)**. Pick up a D (RH) and three 15ºs, and sew through the open hole (LH) of the same triangle from back to front **(d–e)**.

4 Repeat steps 2–3 23 times to complete the round.

5 Sew through the first C added in the round through the open hole (RH) from back to front, pick up a 15º, and sew through the A in the loop from the start of the round **(figure 6)**. Retrace the thread path of the round, and end the thread.

6 Unwind the bobbin, and repeat steps 1–5 on the other side. ●

Difficulty rating

● ● ● ○ ○

Materials
green bangle 2³⁄₄ in. (7 cm) inside diameter
- **50** 6 mm CzechMates two-hole triangle beads in each of **2** colors:
  - color C: aquamarine celsian
  - color D: metallic brown iris
- **25** 4 mm fire-polished beads (Czech FP0270, transparent gold/smoky topaz luster)
- **6 g** 8º seed beads (Toho 703, matte mauve)
- **11º** seed beads
  - **2 g** color A (Toho 369, sand lined crystal)
  - **1 g** color B (Toho F460R, olivine matte metallic iris)
- **2 g** 15º seed beads (Toho 221, bronze)
- Fireline 6 lb. test
- beading needles, #11 or #12
- thread bobbin or piece of cardboard

purple bangle colors
- 6 mm CzechMates two-hole triangle beads:
  - color C: purple velvet pearl coat
  - color D: polychrome orchid aqua
- 4 mm fire-polished beads (Czech, viridian celsian)
- 8º seed beads (Toho PF557, permanent finish galvanized starlight)
- 11º seed beads:
  - color A (Toho PF557, permanent finish galvanized starlight)
  - color B (Toho 705, matte frosted iris blue)
- 15º seed beads (Toho PF557, permanent finish galvanized starlight)

pink bangle colors
- 6 mm CzechMates two-hole triangle beads:
  - color C: opaque rose/gold luster
  - color D: matte metallic flax
- 4 mm fire-polished beads (Czech, milky pink celsian)
- 8º seed beads (Toho Y181, hybrid opaque luster picasso)
- 11º seed beads:
  - color A (Toho 502, higher metallic amethyst)
  - color B (Toho 246, luster black diamond/opaque yellow lined)
- 15º seed beads (Toho 459, gold lustered dark topaz)

Two-hole
revolution
bangle

New two-hole beads provide
form and function like you've
never seen before.

designed by **Nichole Starman**

stepbystep

Wildfire is strongly recommended for
this project, but other good options
include One-G nylon thread and
Fireline 10 lb. test.

Base

[1] On a comfortable length of thread,
pick up a 3 x 6 mm brick. Leaving a
6-in. (15cm) tail, sew through both
holes of the brick, exiting the second
hole **(figure 1)**.
[2] Pick up an 110 seed bead, a 6 mm
two-hole lentil, and three 11ºs, and sew

through the remaining hole of the lentil
(figure 2, a–b), snugging the new beads
close to the original brick. Pick up an
11º and a brick, and sew through the
remaining hole of the new brick **(b–c)**.
[3] Repeat step 2 **(c–d)** until you have a
strip with a total of 30 bricks. End and
add thread (Basics) as needed. With 30
bricks, the strip will be about 11½ in.
(29.2 cm) at this point but will cinch up
later to become a bangle with a 7½-in.
(19.1 cm) circumference and a 2¼-in.
(5.7 cm) inner diameter. Adjust the
length now if desired. Each additional
brick will add about ⅜ in.

(1cm) to the finished piece.
[4] To form the strip into a ring, align
the ends, making sure the beadwork
isn't twisted. Work as in step 2, but sew
through the first brick instead of adding
a new one **(figure 3, a–b)**.
[5] For the other edge, pick up an 11º, a
lentil, and three 11ºs, and sew through
the remaining hole of the lentil. Pick up
an 11º, and sew through both holes of
the next brick **(b–c)**. Repeat **(c–d)** to
complete the edge. End the working
thread and tail.

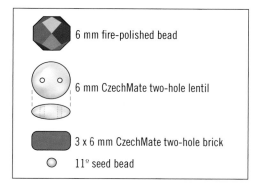

6 mm fire-polished bead

6 mm CzechMate two-hole lentil

3 x 6 mm CzechMate two-hole brick

11º seed bead

FIGURE 1

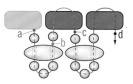

FIGURE 2

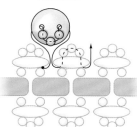

FIGURE 4

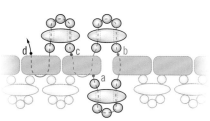

FIGURE 3

materials

bronze bangle 2–2¼-in. (5–5.7 cm) inner diameter

- **30–36** 6 mm fire-polished beads (Czech, metallic gold/topaz)
- **120–144** 6 mm CzechMate two-hole lentils (luster opaque gold smoky topaz)
- **30–36** 3 x 6 mm CzechMate two-hole bricks (iris brown)
- **6 g** 11º seed beads (Toho 176, rainbow black diamond AB)
- beading needles, #11
- Wildfire beading thread

turquoise/rust bangle colors:

- 6 mm fire-polished beads (Czech, umber)
- 6 mm CzechMate two-hole lentils (turquoise and luster opaque gold smoky topaz)
- 3 x 6 mm CzechMate two-hole bricks (Picasso opaque olive)
- 11º seed beads (Miyuki 377J, Capri color-lined metallic teal)

turquoise/topaz bangle colors:

- 6 mm fire-polished beads (Czech, milky topaz)
- 6 mm CzechMate two-hole lentils (turquoise and luster opaque gold smoky topaz)
- 3 x 6 mm CzechMate two-hole bricks (opaque olive)
- 11º seed beads (Japanese SB2168, copper-lined transparent gray)

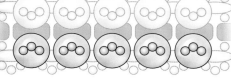

FIGURE 5

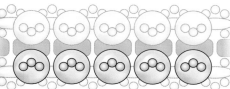

FIGURE 6

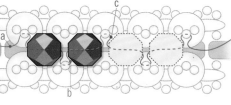

FIGURE 7

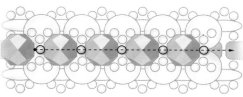

FIGURE 8

Embellishment

[1] Add a comfortable length of thread to the base, exiting a lentil with your needle pointing toward the bricks.

[2] Pick up a lentil and three 11ºs, and sew through the remaining hole of the new lentil, the first hole of the next lentil in the base, the following three 11ºs, and the remaining hole of the base lentil (**figure 4**). Pull snug. Repeat this stitch to complete the round. This round of lentils will sit on top of and perpendicular to the previous round of lentils on this side of the base.

[3] Sew through the beadwork to exit a lentil on the other side of the base, and repeat step 2 to add a round of lentils on this side (**figure 5**). End and add thread as needed.

[4] Sew through the beadwork to exit the middle 11º on top of an embellishment lentil. Pick up a 6 mm fire-polished bead, and sew through the middle 11º on top of the next lentil on the opposite side (**figure 6, a–b**). Repeat this stitch (**b–c**) to complete the round, maintaining an even but moderate tension.

[5] Sew through the first 6 mm, and continue through the middle 11º on top of the next lentil on the other side (**figure 7, a–b**). Zigzag through the 6 mms and the remaining middle 11ºs to complete the round (**b–c**).

[6] Once the 6mms are connected to both rounds of lentils, sew through the first 6 mm again. Pick up an 11º, and sew through the next 6 mm. Repeat this stitch to complete the round (**figure 8**), and end the thread. ●

Other
techniques

Charming WireLace
bracelet

Combine Swarovski big-hole beads with WireLace for a stunning bracelet you can make in a jiffy!

designed by **Linda Hartung**

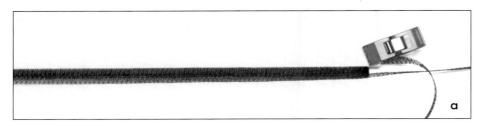

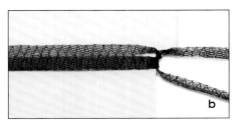

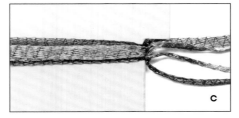

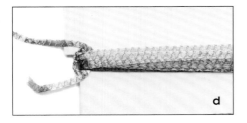

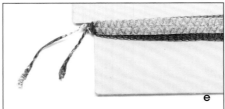

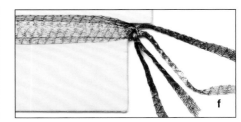

1 Create a jig with two-ply illustration board: Begin by cutting it to 7½ x 3 in. (19.1 x 7.6 cm). Cut a notch on each short side that is ¼-in. (6mm) wide and 1½ in. (3.8 cm) tall (half the height of the board). These notches will allow you to wrap the WireLace easily without it slipping. If you want to adjust the size of your bracelet, be sure to adjust the jig as well by changing the size of the initial board. The WireLace portion of the bracelet is ½ in. (1.3 cm) shorter than the desired bracelet length. The notched portion of the jig should equal that length.

2 Cut 60 in. (1.52 m) of color A WireLace. Leaving a 2-in. (5 cm) tail, clip one end to a short edge of the jig near the notch. Wrap the WireLace four times around the 7-in. (18cm) portion of the jig **(photo a)**. Wrap each layer on top of the previous one, keeping the WireLace smooth and flat. Tie the ends with a square knot, and then slide one tail under all the color A strands **(photo b)**.

3 Using color B WireLace, repeat step 2,

g

h

wrapping color B over the color A strands. Separate the tails, one on each side of the knot **(photo c)**.

4 Starting on the other end of the jig, repeat step 2 with color C WireLace layering it on top of colors A and B. After tying the knot, slide each color C tail under all the strands at this end. Make sure the tails go in opposite directions **(photo d)**, and pull tight to gather all the strands. Tie a square knot on top of all the strands, leaving no gap **(photo e)**.

5 Using the color A tails at the other end, tie another square knot around all the strands. Using the color B tails, tie half of a square knot **(photo f)**.

6 Slide the WireLace off the jig. Squeeze and roll each end between your finger-

tips to taper the ends. Slide a large-hole bead to the center of the WireLace **(photo g)**, and trim the ends flush to the knot.

7 Mix a small amount of two-part epoxy according to the manufacturer's instructions, and fill the well of one half of the clasp about one-quarter full. Let the clasp sit well-side up while you fill the other clasp half. Put a dab of epoxy on the knotted end of the WireLace, and insert it into the clasp. Using a blunt needle or bamboo skewer that's had its sharp tip cut off, push the WireLace into the clasp to make sure it's fully inserted **(photo h)**. Wipe off any excess glue that seeps out. Repeat on the other end, and allow to dry. ●

Difficulty rating

  ◇ ◇

Materials
blueberry bracelet, 7½ in. (19.1cm)

- **60 in.** (1.524 m) 3 mm WireLace in each of **3** colors*:
  - A (navy)
  - B (tanzanite)
  - C (azure)
- **1** Alacarte Simplicity magnetic acrylic clasp (blue)
- **1** Swarovski BeCharmed Medley bead
- rigid 2-ply illustration board, 7½ x 3 in. (19.1 x 7.6 cm)
- scissors
- two-part all-purpose clear-drying epoxy (5-minute dry time)
- bamboo skewer or #13 or larger needlepoint needle
- clip with smooth jaws
- craft knife

More gorgeous color options!

Not feeling blue? Choose one of Linda's other color combinations or come up with your own!

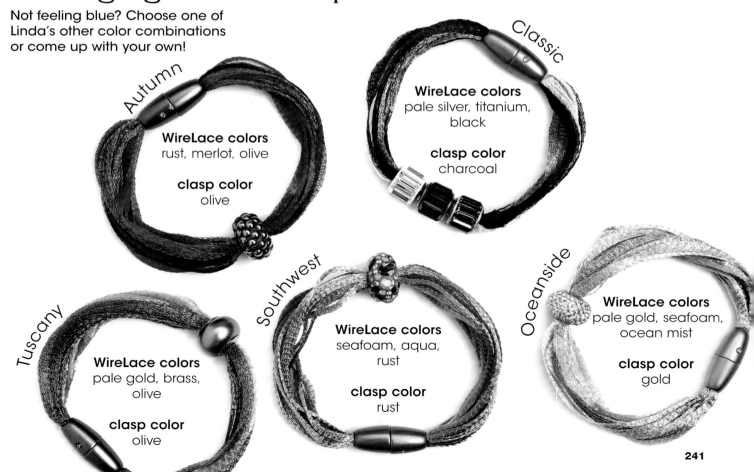

Autumn

WireLace colors
rust, merlot, olive

clasp color
olive

Classic

WireLace colors
pale silver, titanium, black

clasp color
charcoal

Tuscany

WireLace colors
pale gold, brass, olive

clasp color
olive

Southwest

WireLace colors
seafoam, aqua, rust

clasp color
rust

Oceanside

WireLace colors
pale gold, seafoam, ocean mist

clasp color
gold

Use everyday buttons in a fun, swingy necklace.

designed by **Julia Gerlach**

Button fringe
NECKLACE

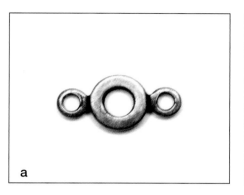

a

b

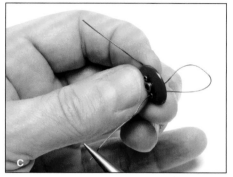

c

d

e

f

Difficulty rating

Materials

necklace with floral buttons
16 in. (41 cm)

- **7** 15 mm two-hole floral buttons (www.etsy.com/shop/berrynicecrafts)
- **8** 6 mm fire-polished beads (Czech, dual-coated tanzanite/fuchsia)
- **7** 3 x 5 mm faceted glass rice beads, in place of 4 mm beads (purple)
- clasp with **2** attached 5–6 mm jump rings or split rings
- 5 ft. (1.5 m) 26-gauge wire
- 3 in. (7.6 cm) 4 mm donut-link chain
- **7** 1½-in. (3.8 cm) head pins
- **2** 5 x 7 mm oval jump rings
- **2** crimp beads
- **2** crimp covers
- 18-in. (46 cm) organza ribbon cord necklace strap
- flexible beading wire, .014-.015
- chainnose pliers
- roundnose pliers
- crimping pliers
- wire cutters

necklace with solid-color buttons
16 in. (41 cm)

- **7** ⅝-in. (1.6 cm) two-hole plastic buttons (**2** red, **2** cranberry, **3** fuchsia; JoAnn fabric and craft stores)
- **8** 6 mm fire-polished beads (Czech, gold-lined crystal)
- **7** 4 mm beads (**2** orange, **2** red, **3** fuchsia)
- clasp
- 28 in. (71 cm) 26-gauge wire
- 3 in. (7.6 cm) 4 mm gear-link chain
- **7** 1½-in. (3.8 cm) head pins
- **2** crimp beads
- **2** crimp covers
- chainnose pliers
- roundnose pliers
- crimping pliers
- wire cutters
- **2** bead stoppers or tape

step by step

Button dangles

[1] Cut a shaped link from the chain (photo a). Repeat to cut a total of seven links.

[2] Cut a 4-in. (10 cm) piece of 26-gauge wire, and make a 180° bend about 1½ in. (3.8 cm) from one end. Slide one loop of a chain link into the bend, and then string both wire ends through a button hole from front to back (photo b).

[3] With the long wire end, go up through the other button hole and loop of the chain link (photo c). Pull tight. Skip the chain link, and go back through the button hole to snug the chain link to the front of the button.

[4] Make a wrapped loop (Basics) with each wire end so each loop extends just past the edge of the button (photo d). The back of the button dangle should look like **photo e**.

[5] On a head pin, string a 4 mm bead, and make the first half of a wrapped loop. Attach it to a loop of the button dangle (photo f), and complete the wraps.

[6] Rotate the top loop of the dangle so it is perpendicular to the face of the button.

[7] Repeat steps 2–6 with the remaining buttons and chain links. Then follow the appropriate steps on the next page to finish the necklace with beading wire or with ribbon and cord.

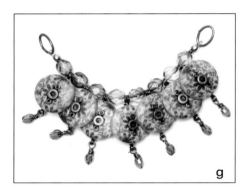

g

h

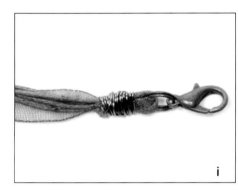

i

Finishing with beading wire

[1] Cut 20 in. (51 cm) of beading wire, and string a repeating pattern of a 6 mm fire-polished bead and the top loop of a button dangle until you have used all the beads and dangles.

[2] On one end, string a crimp bead and half of the clasp. Go back through the crimp bead, and temporarily secure the wire with tape or a Bead Stopper.

[3] Repeat step 2 on the other end, and test the fit. Adjust the length if needed, and then crimp the crimp beads (Basics). Using chainnose or crimping pliers, gently close a crimp cover around each crimp bead.

Finishing with ribbon and cord

[1] Cut 8 in. (20 cm) of beading wire, and string a repeating pattern of a 6 mm fire-polished bead and the top loop of a button dangle until you have used all the beads and dangles.

[2] On one end, string a crimp bead and a 5 x 7 mm oval jump ring. Go back through the crimp bead, and crimp it (Basics).

[3] Repeat step 2 at the other end, leaving no gaps between the beads and dangles. Using chainnose or crimping pliers, gently close a crimp cover around each crimp bead (photo g).

[4] Cut the organza ribbon/cord necklace strap in half, and remove the clasp components. You'll use half of the ribbon/cord bundle on each side of the necklace.

[5] Guide one end of half of a ribbon/cord bundle through a jump ring attached to the button strand. Fold the end ¾ in. (1.9 cm) of the ribbon/cord bundle back on itself.

[6] Cut an 8-in. (20 cm) piece of 26-gauge wire, and tightly wrap it around the doubled ribbon/cord bundle. Trim the excess cord and ribbon (photo h).

[7] Guide the other end of the ribbon/cord bundle through a jump ring attached to the clasp, fold the end ¾ in. (1.9 cm) back on itself, and repeat step 6 (photo i).

[8] Repeat steps 5–7 on the other end of the necklace.

Pearly girl bracelet

Mix casual and sparkly with leather cord and a crystallized pearl or gemstone focal piece.

designed by **Irina Miech**

1 Cut 5–6 in. (13–15 cm) of 2 mm leather cord. Fold it in half, and pass the fold through a 9 mm textured ring. Pass the ends through the fold, and pull tight to make a lark's head knot around the ring **(photo a)**. If needed, grasp the ring with chainnose pliers as you tighten the knot.
2 String a 5 x 9 mm metal slide over both cord ends, and position it near the knot.
3 Cut a 3-in. (7.6cm) piece of 28-gauge wire. Holding the ends of the cord together,

wrap the wire tightly several times around the ends, and trim **(photo b)**. If the cord ends are uneven, trim them so they are flush.
4 If desired, apply glue to the cord ends. Insert the cord ends into a 5 x 9 mm crimp end, and use chainnose pliers to gently squeeze the crimp end closed **(photo c)**.
5 Repeat steps 1–4 to make another bracelet band.
6 Open all the jump rings.
7 The focal component has a loop on each end — one

that sits vertically and one that sits horizontally. Slide the 4 mm jump ring through the vertical loop, and close it.
8 Use two 3 mm jump rings to attach the 4 mm jump ring to a textured ring on one bracelet band **(photo d)**. Use two more 3 mm jump rings to attach the horizontal loop to the other textured ring **(photo e)**.
9 Use two 3 mm jump rings to attach half of the clasp to each crimp end. ●

Difficulty rating

⬡ ⬡ ⬡ ⬡ ⬡

Materials
bracelet 6¾ in. (17.1cm)

- 1 30 mm 2-loop focal component (pearl or gemstone)
- 2 9 mm textured rings
- 2 5 x 9 mm metal slides (TierraCast)
- 2 5 x 9 mm crimp ends
- 10–12 in. (25–30cm) 2 mm leather cord
- 6 in. (15cm) 28-gauge wire
- 1 4 mm inside-diameter (ID) jump ring (18-gauge)
- 8 3 mm ID jump rings (20-gauge)
- toggle clasp
- 2 pairs of chainnose pliers
- wire cutters
- E6000 glue (optional)

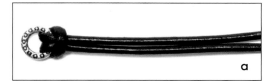

a

b

c

d

e

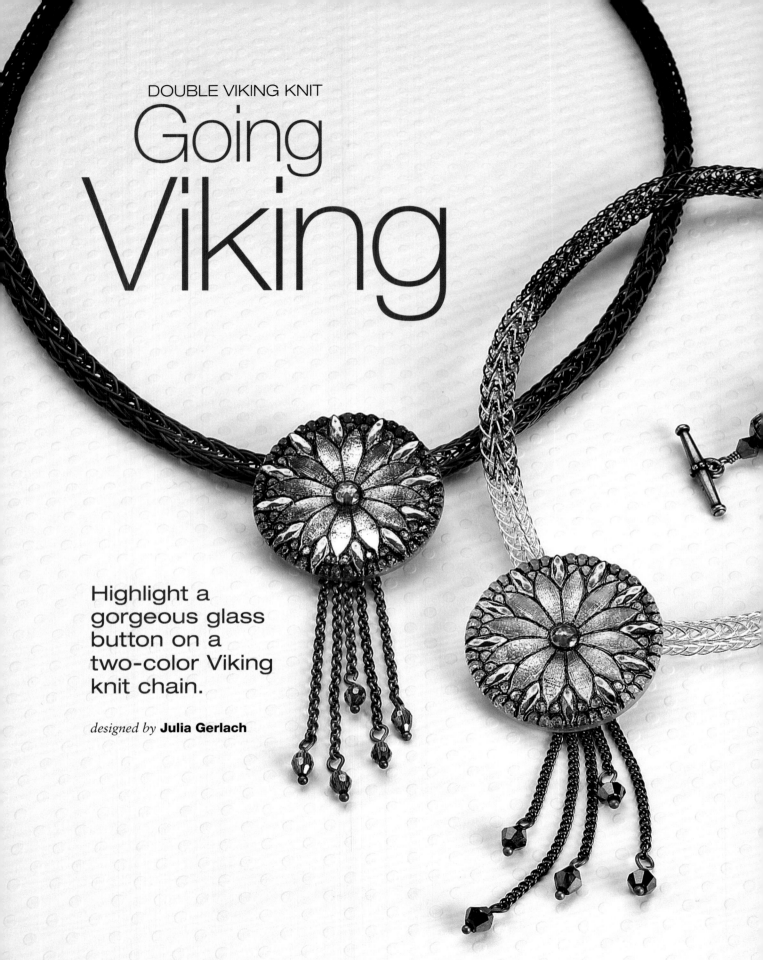

DOUBLE VIKING KNIT

Going Viking

Highlight a
gorgeous glass
button on a
two-color Viking
knit chain.

designed by **Julia Gerlach**

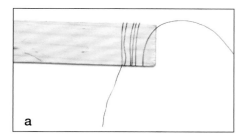

a

b

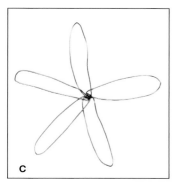

c

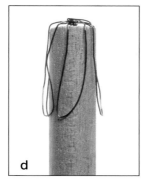

d

e

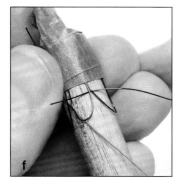

f

g

h

Materials

bronze necklace 18 in. (46 cm)
- **1** 32 mm glass flower button with four-way box shank (sea opal AB; www.spiritbeadsandbuttons.com)
- **7** 4 mm bicone crystals (Chinese, bronze)
- toggle clasp (TierraCast)
- **2** 14 x 12 mm trumpet flower cones
- 6 in. (15 cm) 20–22-gauge wire (bronze)
- 26-gauge wire
  12–15 yd. (11–13.7 m) color A (vintage bronze)
  8–10 yd. (7.3–9.1 m) color B (silver)
- 8 in. (20 cm) 28-gauge wire (silver)
- 6 in. (15 cm) fine-gauge chain
- **5** 1½-in. (3.8 cm) head pins
- chainnose pliers
- roundnose pliers
- wire cutters
- ⅜-in. (1 cm) diameter dowel
- painter's tape
- wooden or plastic draw plate
- wooden ruler

purple necklace colors:
- 32 mm glass flower button with four-way box shank (purple; www.spiritbeadsandbuttons.com)
- 3 x 5 mm faceted glass rice beads (purple/gold)
- toggle clasp (filigree round)
- 8 mm end caps (weaved bullet cone)
- 20–22-gauge wire (brass)
- 26-gauge wire
  color A (Parawire, purple)
  color B (Parawire, matte lavender)
- 28-gauge wire (Parawire, matte lavender)

step by step

Viking knit necklace

Except where an exact measurement is given, work with comfortable lengths of wire (no more than 2 yd./1.8 m) at a time. Add new wire (see "Adding a new wire," p. 248) as needed.

[1] Cut a 12-in. (30 cm) piece of 26-gauge wire, and wrap it around a ruler five times **(photo a)**. Carefully remove the wire from the ruler, and use one end of the wire to wrap through the five loops several times **(photo b)**. Twist the wire ends together, trim the excess wire, and separate the loops **(photo c)**. This will be referred to as the starter bud.

[2] Place the starter bud on one end of the dowel, arranging the loops evenly around the end of the dowel **(photo d)**. Tape the starter bud in place **(photo e)**.

[3] Cut a comfortable length of color A 26-gauge wire, and hold one end near the end of the dowel using the thumb on your nondominant hand. Guide the other end of the wire through two loops on the starter bud from right to left **(photo f)**. (These instructions are for right-handed people. If you are left-handed, work from left to right.) Pull the wire through the loops to make a small loop below and between the two starter bud loops.

[4] Repeat step 3 **(photo g)** until you have five small loops connected by short swags beneath the starter bud.

[5] To begin the next round, guide the wire behind the first loop in the previous round **(photo h)**. Pull snug to make a new small loop. This process

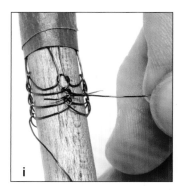

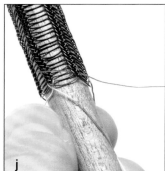

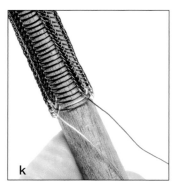

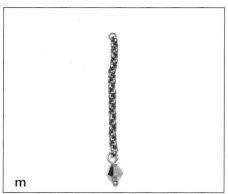

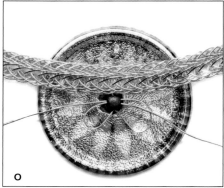

is called a stitch. Repeat this stitch around the dowel, making both the loops and the swags even and equally spaced.

[6] Work one more round as in step 5. You will have three rounds of loops and swags.

[7] Switch to double Viking knit: Work as in step 5, but instead of guiding the wire behind the next loop in the previous round, guide it behind the next loop two rounds up **(photo i)**. Repeat this stitch around, always going behind a loop two rounds prior to the round you are working.

[8] Continue working in double Viking knit until the color A section is 3–4 in. (7.6–10cm) long.

[9] To begin the two-color section, add a comfortable length of color B wire, starting it two loops behind the last color A stitch you worked and two loops up from the bottom.ork another color B stitch **(photo j)**. Switch to the color A wire, and work three stitches. Switch back to the color B wire, and work three stitches. Continue alternating between color A and color B wire **(photo k)** for approximately 1 in. (2.5cm).

[10] When the two-color section is 1 in. (2.5cm) long, continue in double

Viking knit with color B only until the color B section is about 1½ in. (3.8cm). Trim the color A wire after working a round or two of color B only.

[11] Add a new color A wire, and work another 1-in. (2.5cm) two-color section as in step 9.

[12] Complete the knitted piece with a 3–4-in. (7.6–10cm) color A section. Leave the tail for now.

[13] Remove the knitted piece from the dowel, and pull it through several holes of the draw plate **(photo l)** to reduce the piece to ³⁄₁₆ in. (5mm) in diameter.

Adding a new wire

Leave the short tail of your old wire in place for now. Then, hold a comfortable length of new wire below the last stitch made with the old wire. Make sure to leave a short tail on the new wire. Working from right to left, guide the new wire under and around the last stitch made with the old wire, and pull it to the right. Leave both short tails in place as you work another round or two, and then trim the tails close to the work.

Button focal

[1] On a head pin, string a 4–6 mm bead, and make a plain loop (Basics). Repeat to make a total of five bead units.

[2] Cut five pieces of chain to various lengths between 1 and 2 in. (2.5–5cm).

[3] Open the loop of a bead unit (Basics), and attach it to an end link of chain **(photo m)**. Repeat with the remaining chains and bead units.

[4] Cut an 8-in. (20cm) piece of 28-gauge wire, and bend it in half. Guide the cut ends through the middle of the color B section of the knitted piece and the button, making sure the new wire straddles the knit from the inside on the bottom edge **(photo n)**.

[5] Cross the wire ends through the horizontal button hole **(photo o)** to lock the button in place.

[6] String the chains on one wire end in the desired order, and cross the other wire end through them **(photo p)**. Guide one wire end around the button shank, wrap it around the wire stem above the shank **(photo q)**, and trim. Repeat with the other wire end.

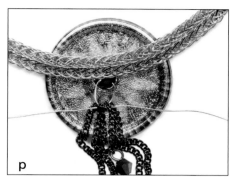

p

q

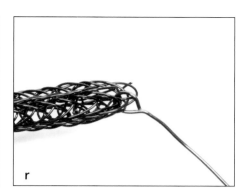

r

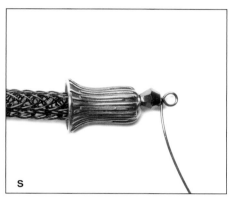

s

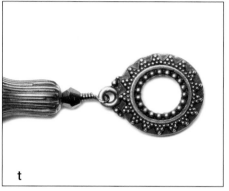

t

Clasp

[1] Cut the starter bud from the end of the knitted piece. Trim the tail from the other end. Inspect your knitted piece to make sure there are no wire ends sticking out. If there are, carefully poke one jaw of your chainnose pliers into the knit, and gently press the wire tail against a spine of loops.

[2] Cut a 3-in. (7.6cm) piece of 20- to 22-gauge wire, and make a plain loop at one end. Open the loop, slide a couple of end stitches into it, and close the loop **(photo r)**.

[3] On the wire, string an end cap or cone and a 4–6 mm bead, and make the first half of a wrapped loop **(photo s)**. Attach half of the clasp, and complete the wraps **(photo t)**.

[4] Repeat steps 2 and 3 at the other end of the necklace.

Jellyfish earrings

These dangly earrings look great whether on land or on sea.

designed by **Lilly Reeve Knackstedt**

stepbystep

[1] Cut an 8-in. (20 cm) piece of 24-gauge wire. Using roundnose pliers, make a loop approximately ¼ in. (6 mm) wide in the center of the wire. Twist the ends together twice at the base of the loop (**photo a**).

[2] With the curved side of the half-moon bead pointing toward the twisted loop, string one wire end through the bead, and cross the other end through to exit the other side. Using chainnose pliers, pull gently to tighten each end, centering the twisted loop slightly above the half-moon bead (**photo b**).

[3] With chainnose pliers, bend one of the wires to the back of the half-moon bead. Trim the wire 2–3 mm from the bead hole, and press the end close to the bead.

[4] Cut 11 2½-in. (6.4 cm) pieces of wire. With roundnose pliers, make a tiny loop on one end of each wire, and use chainnose pliers to pinch each loop closed.

[5] String an 8x1 mm curved tube on one of the wires. Grasp the wire with chainnose pliers or your fingers, and pull the curved tube down to the loop. The wire will curve as you pull the tube down; don't straighten it out. String another curved tube, and slide it down to the first one, twisting the wire so that the new tube curves in the opposite direction. String one more curved tube so that it curves opposite the previous tube (**photo c**).

[6] With your fingers, straighten the remaining end of the wire. Trim the wire to ⅝ in. (1.6cm). Using round-nose pliers, make a double loop at the end of the wire (**photo d**). Set aside.

[7] Repeat steps 5 and 6 for the remaining wires as follows, keeping the completed wires in order:
Wire 2: String five curved tubes.
Wire 3: String three curved tubes.
Wire 4: String four curved tubes.
Wire 5: String six 5 x 1.5 mm

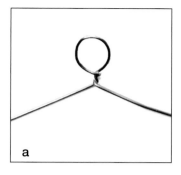

a

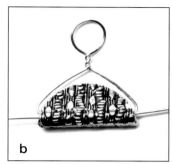

b

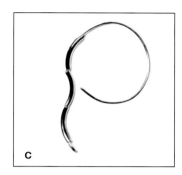

c

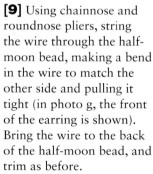

d

e

f

g

Difficulty rating

Materials

pair of earrings ¾ x 2¾ in. (1.9 x 7cm)

- **2** half-moon beads (H3135, silver; www.etsy.com/shop/callie6688)
- **68** 8 x 1 mm curved silver tubes
- **28** 5 x 1.5 mm twisted liquid silver tubes
- **6** ft. (1.8 m) 24-gauge dead soft silver wire or craft wire
- pair of earring findings
- 2 pairs of chainnose pliers
- roundnose pliers
- wire cutters

twisted liquid silver tubes.
Wire 6: String four curved tubes.
Wire 7: String eight twisted tubes.
Wire 8: String four curved tubes.
Wire 9: String three curved tubes.
Wire 10: String five curved tubes.
Wire 11: String three curved tubes.
[8] With the tip of the roundnose pliers, make a bend in the wire exiting the half-moon bead so that the wire is positioned across the bottom edge of the bead (photo e). String the double loop of each beaded wire in order, making sure the loop is pointing toward the back of the earring (in photo f, the back of the earring is shown).

[9] Using chainnose and roundnose pliers, string the wire through the half-moon bead, making a bend in the wire to match the other side and pulling it tight (in photo g, the front of the earring is shown). Bring the wire to the back of the half-moon bead, and trim as before.
[10] Open the loop of an earring finding (Basics), and attach the top loop of the earring.
[11] Repeat steps 1–10 to make another earring, but switch the positions of wires 5 and 7 to make the earrings a mirror image of each other.

251

Contributors

Junko Ando is from Kanagawa Prefecture, Japan, and uses her sense of design to make wearable art works. Email her at undeux_web@yahoo.co.jp.

Regina Atkins has been sharing her passion for beading for the past five years. She currently teaches classes at Beadjoux bead store in Braselton, Ga. Contact Regina via email at thebeadknot@gmail.com, or visit www.thebeadknot.com.

LeAnn Baehman of Springfield, Mo., is a microbiologist. She has been beading for 25 years, and recently gave her young niece her first beading lesson. Contact LeAnn at lbaehman@mchsi.com.

Marcia Balonis started making jewelry as a teenager and her passion has continued in many forms. Often inspired by nature, she focuses on wearable art suitable for the casual lifestyle in rural Fl. Contact her at marcia@baublesbybalonis.net, and see her work at www.baublesbybalonis.etsy.com or www.baublesbybalonis.net.

Cary Bruner works and teaches at Bead Haven in Las Vegas. She finds that patience comes naturally when she remembers her own humble start. Email her at creationsbycary@aol.com or visit www.creationsbycary.etsy.com.

Karen Bruns has been beading for 23 years. She teaches beadweaving and bead embroidery internationally, and at Bead Dreams in Stockton, Calif. Visit Karen at www.etsy.com/shop/KarenBrunsDesigns.

Contact **Aurelio Castano** in care of Kalmbach Books.

Contact **Janice Chatham** at bighjh2@aol.com.

Svetlana Chernitsky has been beading for eight years and loves working with two-hole beads. Email her at lirigal@gmail.com, or visit www.lirigal.com and www.etsy.com/shop/lirigal.

Jane Danley Cruz has been designing jewelry and teaching for more than 15 years. She is a former associate editor for *Bead&Button* magazine and is now working on a book due out in 2016. Email Jane at jmdcruz262@gmail.com.

Katie Dean is from London and has been a full-time beading designer and teacher since 2012. She has published nine books about beadwork and teaches throughout the UK. Contact her at beadflowers@btinternet.com, or visit www.beadflowers.co.uk and www.myworldofbeads.com.

Melissa van Dijk designs seed bead jewelry as a hobby. She can be contacted at van.dijk.m@gmail.com or via her website, www.melissavandijk.com.

Penny Dixon became captivated with beading five years ago. Teaching classes and being a TrendSetters designer for Starman Inc. has only enhanced her love for beading and design. Contact her at pendixon@gmail.com or visit www.pennydixondesigns.com.

Cassie Donlen is an associate editor at *Bead&Button* magazine. Contact her at cdonlen@beadandbutton.com or visit www.cassiedonlen.etsy.com.

Abigail Engelking has been making jewelry for 17 years, having started with wirework and gemstones. Her new venture is silversmithing. Contact her at abigail33@telus.net, or visit www.abigailsbeaddesign.etsy.com and www.facebook.com/abigail.engelking.

Colleen Ewart is a full-time jewelry artist, who owns and teaches at Island Cove Beads & Gallery in Indian Rocks Beach, Fla. She can be contacted at islandcove@rocketmail.com or via her website, island-cove.com.

Josie Fabre, author of *Fast Peyote Stitch Jewelry* (available from Kalmbach Books), has been beading for more than 10 years. As a full-time scientist and mother, she still beads every chance she gets. Her designs are often inspired by photographs she takes. Contact Josie at jpfabre@fabres.net or visit www.josie.etsy.com.

Julia Gerlach is the editor of *Bead&Button* magazine. Contact her at jgerlach@beadandbutton.com.

Contact **Gabi Gueck** in care of Kalmbach Books.

Susan Harle trained as a silversmith and leather worker, and her background led to a passion for bead weaving. She developed the diagonal tubular peyote stitch because of her fascination with geometric shapes. Contact her by email at sueharle@gmail.com, or visit www.sueharle.com.

Linda Hartung is the owner of Alacarte Clasps, WireLace & WireLuxe. Visit www.alacarteclasps.com or www.wirelace.com to see more of her work. Contact her at linda@alacarteclasps.com or call (707) 887-2825.

Olga Haserodt was born in Russia and has been living in Germany for 12 years. She is a self-taught artist who learned how to bead from the Internet when she was expecting her third child. She enjoys the creativity of beading and the joy it brings to others. Contact Olga at perlenharmonyoase.blogspot.de or visit www.PerlenHarmonyOase.etsy.com.

Michelle Heim co-owns a bead shop in Fond du Lac, Wis. and designs at home at night aided by great lighting and two dogs. Contact her at michelle@beadalotta.com or her website www.beadalotta.com.

Judy Henegar teaches her original designs at My Bead Gallery in Englewood, Fla. She is a member of the Florida West Coast Bead Society in Sarasota and a charter member of the Gulf Coast Bead Society of Englewood. Contact Judy at djh2934@aol.com.

Diane Hertzler is an off-loom bead-weaving artist and instructor, who has taught her original designs around the country. She can be contacted at dianehertzler@verizon.net or via her website, www.dianehertzler.com.

Pamm Horbit of Seattle, Wash., worked for many years as a graphic designer. She now teaches beading classes when she's not dreaming up new structures to create. Contact Pamm via email at whitelotusbeading@gmail.com.

Erzsébet Kis Jakab lives in Szolnok, Hungary. She has been making jewelry since 2009 and has experimented with several jewelry-making techniques but has found soutache to be her recent favorite. Follow her blog pankagyongyeblogspot.hu or find her on Facebook under Panka Gyöngye.

Lisa Kan is an author, bead weaver, jewelry designer, and glass artist. She creates elegant, wearable beadwork that is often modular or reversible, and has been published in many beading magazines. Email her at lisakandesigns@yahoo.com or visit www.ariadesignstudio.com.

Contact **Kenji Katsuoka** in care of Kalmbach Books.

Alice Kharon has been beading for 12 years. She specializes in designing contemporary wearable jewelry. She lives in the Chicago suburbs with her husband and their cat. You can reach her at alice.kharon@yahoo.com

Lilly Reeve Knackstedt has been beading since she was 8 when her aunt gave her a box of beads from the attic. She is from Kenai, Alaska, and is married with two college-age daughters. Contact Lilly in care of Kalmbach Books.

Beth Kraft creates colorful art jewelry in several mediums. She can be contacted at web@nordicgypsy.com or via her website, www.nordicgypsy.com.

Isabella Lam is a full-time jewelry artist and instructor who creates original beadwork jewelry with innovative beads. She can be contacted at scarlet@actcom.co.il, or visit her at www.isabellalam.com or www.etsy.com/shop/bead4me.

Annette Mackrel started beading several years ago and instantly fell in love with the vast multitude of colors, textures, and rich history of the medium that spans thousands of years. Her jewelry is playful yet elegant and always very comfortable to wear. Annette sells her jewelry and kits in selected stores and online. She can be contacted at annette@annettemackrel.com or via her website at www.annettemackrel.com.

Alla Maslennikova of Moscow, Russia, likes to incorporate unusual elements in her beadwork. Alla's works have won several awards, including 1st place and Best of Show Runner Up in the Finished Jewelry category in BeadDreams 2015. Contact Alla at beadlady.ru@gmail.com, or visit her website, www.beadlady.ru.

Irina Miech owns Eclectica in Brookfield, Wis., and is the author of several books, including *Beautiful Wire Jewelry for Beaders* (available from Kalmbach Books). Contact her at (262) 641-0910 or info@eclecticabeads.com. You can also visit her store website, www.eclecticabeads.com.

Samantha Mitchell teaches her designs at local bead stores and sells her design instructions online. Contact her at samantha@crystyles.com, or visit her website to view more of her designs at www.crystyles.com.

Meg Mullen fell in love with bead embroidery more than 20 years ago because the design possibilities are endless. Meg owns Bead My Love. Check her website at www.beadmylove.com for beads and embroidery supplies. When she is not traveling, she hosts Beautiful Bead Embroidery Retreats in Rehoboth Beach, Del. Contact Meg at beadmylove@aol.com.

Akiko Nomura lives in Japan with her husband and has three grown daughters. She began designing 18 years ago and loves working with color. Many of her works are inspired by nature, especially flowers. She has worked as a member of TrendSetters to Starman since 2013. Her contact email address is akikonom@aol.com.

Maggie Roschyk is a frequent contributor to *Bead&Button* magazine and the author of *Artistic Seed Bead Jewelry* (available from Kalmbach Books.) Contact Maggie at blueroses@wi.rr.com.

Dana Rudolph is a designer and the owner of My Bead Gallery in Englewood, Fla. Contact her at mybeadgallery@gmail.com, or visit www.mybeadgallery.com to see more of Dana's work.

Marla Salezze has been beading since second grade and loves learning and exploring new media. She is on the 2014 Innovations Team for Nunn Design and is a board member of The Bead Society of Eastern Pennsylvania. Contact her at beadedbymarla@gmail.com, or visit www.beadedbymarla.com.

Susan Schwartzenberger has lived in the bead world for 25 years. She has been teaching bead classes since 2005, and often partners with her daughter Jennifer on projects, many of which have been published. Contact her at sueschw12@gmail.com.

Ora Shai lives in Jerusalem, Israel, and has been an avid beader for the past eight years. She loves to explore all beading techniques but has a fondess for right-angle weave. Email her at orrasha@gmail.com or visit her blog at www.beadtales.blogspot.co.il.

Kerrie Slade is a beadwork designer living in Mansfield, England. She has had her work published in numerous books and magazines around the world. Kerrie now teaches internationally and sells patterns through her website, www.kerrieslade.co.uk and blogs at kerrieslade.blogspot.co.uk.

Wendy Speare started stitching in 2012. Once a software developer, she now has the perfect job at Poppyfield Bead Company, in Albuquerque, N. Mex. She thanks Julia Hecht, Poppyfield's owner, for her encouragement and inspiration. Contact Wendy at beadfingers3@gmail.com.

Nichole Starman has been an integral part of the beading community for 13 years as a wholesaler of Czech glass. Nichole loves the infinite possibilities of using beads to create works of art. Contact her at nichole@starmanbeads.com, or visit www.czechbeads.com.

Justyna Szlezak is from Poland, and after years of making jewelry, she discovered bead weaving, which has become her true passion. She is a self-taught beader who loves designing geometric beadwork. When she is not beading, she enjoys other crafts like knitting and crocheting. Contact her at eridhan@gmail.com or visit eridhan.blogspot.com.

Jenny Van is a senior microbiologist, owner of JJ Bead, and the Creative Director of SenHoa Foundation that fights human trafficking. Contact Jenny in care of Kalmbach Books, and see her work at jjbead.com.

Olena Vietrova lives in Kiev, Ukraine, and works as an editor for the Ukranian beading magazine Modyni (Fashion). She enjoys many crafts besides beading, including knitting, crochet, and hairpin lace making. Contact Olena at avetrova@i.ua.

Connie Whittaker is an associate editor at *Bead&Button* magazine. Contact her at cwhittaker@beadandbutton.com.

Shae Wilhite designs and teaches at Sweet Beads, the Las Vegas bead store she owns with her mother, Stacie. When she isn't beading, Shae is a writer, actress, and baker. Find her kits and patterns at www.sweetbeadslv.com or contact her at sweetbeadslv@gmail.com.

Barbara Zaner retired to Tucson, Ariz., after teaching biology and earth science on Long Island for 33 years. She has spinal stenosis, a condition which restricts the amount of time she can sit. She uses her precious sitting time to string her beads and then does all her crocheting while lying down. See more of Barbara's work at www.tobeadaz.com or email her at tobeadorknottobead@msn.com.

Eleanna Katrivanou lives in Athens, Greece, with her husband and young daughter, and works as a pianist and music educator. She started beading seven years ago and loves the endless possibilities of bead weaving. Contact her at eleannazegkinoglou@yahoo.com.

Gianna Zimmerman is from the Netherlands and has been beading for more than 10 years. She teaches per video on www.youtube.com/user/beading4perfectionists, and will be teaching in person at the Bead&Button show in June 2016.

Index

Learn New Bead Stitches!

Project books from Kalmbach Publishing Co. help you learn while you create stunning jewelry.

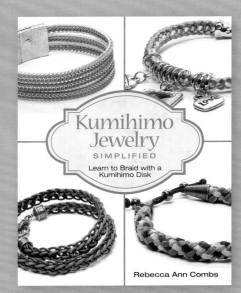

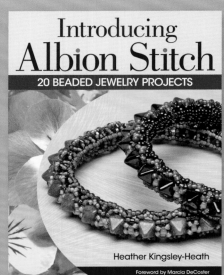

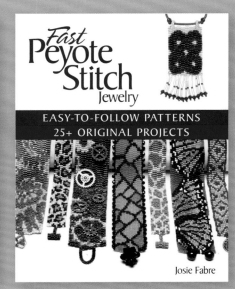

Kumihimo Jewelry Simplified
Make 24 projects with just five kumi-himo braids, plus "creative closures."
#67866 • $22.99

Introducing Albion Stitch
Learn a brand-new stitch in 20 projects you won't find anywhere else.
#67852 • $19.99

Fast Peyote Stitch Jewelry
Discover 25+ peyote projects to make in less time than traditional peyote.
#67871 • $21.99

JewelryandBeadingStore.com
Also available at your favorite craft or bead shop!

Sales tax where applicable.